SPINNING THE SYMBOLIC WEB: HUMAN COMMUNICATION AS SYMBOLIC INTERACTION

The Communication and Information Science Series
Series Editor: Brenda Dervin, The Ohio State University

Subseries:
Communication Pedagogy and Practice, Gerald Phillips, Subseries Editor

Julia T. Wood • Spinning the Symbolic Web: Human Communication as Symbolic
  Interaction

in preparation

Donald Arnstine • The Rhetoric of Educational Reform

Joe Ayers and Tim Hopf • Coping with Speech Anxiety

Alice Horning • The Psycholinguistics of Readable Writing: A Multidisciplinary Exploration

Linda Costigan Lederman • Communication Pedagogy: Approaches to Teaching
  Undergraduate Courses in Communication

Andrew D. Wolvin and Carolyn Gwynn Coakley • Perspectives on Listening

SPINNING THE SYMBOLIC WEB: HUMAN COMMUNICATION AS SYMBOLIC INTERACTION

Julia T. Wood

The University of North Carolina
Chapel Hill, North Carolina

ABLEX PUBLISHING CORPORATION
NORWOOD, NEW JERSEY

Printed in the United States of America.

Library of Congress Cataloging-in-Publication Data

Wood, Julia T.
    Spinning the symbolic web : human communication as symbolic
interaction / Julia T. Wood.
        p.   cm.—(Communication and information science)
    Includes bibliographical references and index.
    ISBN 0-89391-799-0 (cloth); 0-89391-838-5 (ppb)
    1. Communication.   I. Title.   II. Series.
P90.W63   1991
302.2—dc20   91-35890
                                                                        CIP

Ablex Publishing Corporation
355 Chestnut Street
Norwood, New Jersey 07648

This book is dedicated to Robbie—friend, colleague, and life partner. He continually enriches my appreciation of adventure, challenge and—most of all—joy to be created in living.

TABLE OF CONTENTS

Preface

Human communication is a growing field of study. As people increasingly realize how important communication is in their lives, the demand for courses skyrockets. To meet this need, colleges and universities now offer a range of classes that focus on communication in interpersonal, organizational, group, and public settings. The foundation of communication curricula is the basic course, which surveys the discipline and introduces fundamental communication principles and concepts. This book is intended for that basic course.

As interest in learning about communication has mushroomed, so has the number of textbooks in the area. So why is another introductory book needed, you might ask. Perhaps by explaining why I invested time and effort to write another book you'll understand what I see as the purpose and distinction of this text. My primary motivation was that none of the existing books satisfied my goals in teaching my own courses. So, in 1982, I wrote an introductory text titled *Human Communication as Symbolic Interaction*, which was published by Holt, Rinehart and Winston. That book was adopted by instructors who share my views about the nature of human communication and who found that my book met their goals in teaching. Since 1982, however, much has changed in the field of communication, so the book became outdated. Instructors who had used the book requested a new edition of it so that they could continue using the theoretical framework it provided while having a text that reflected contemporary research and communication issues. Rather than simply updating the original text, however, I choose to revise it substantially. The book you are reading, *Spinning the Symbolic Web*, is both similar to the original text in theoretical orientation and different from it in content in that it reflects new knowledge in the discipline and evolutions in my own thinking about communication over the past nine years. I hope this new book retains the strengths of the former one and enriches them with insights and information that have emerged in the past few years.

One of the major changes in the field since 1982 is increased awareness of the centrality of gender to communication. Based on research we now realize that women's and men's attitudes and communication behaviors tend to vary in generalizable and significant ways. This understanding has enlighted us about many of the dynamics in interaction between women and men. We now know, for instance, that women and men typically have distinct orientations toward relationships and that these shape and are reflected in their talk with each other in groups, professional settings, and intimate relationships. We've also learned that while both sexes may grow up in the "same" society, they tend to be socialized in very different ways, ways that affect how they communicate and how they interpret the communication of others. The impressive research on gender over the past eight years is integrated into this book so that we can better understand how gender, along with many other factors, influences our interaction. The consistent attention to gender as one important basis of understanding communication is one of the major distinctions between this book and its predecessor.

Yet, in some respects this book is similar to the first one I wrote. For instance, many of the goals that led me to write the 1982 book are the same as those that motivated me to write this one. For my own teaching purposes, I want a book that gives students a theoretically coherent and substantively rich introduction to the communication field, and I have not found this is other basic texts. Typically they discuss little theory and even that doesn't reflect a single, unified perspective. Also, many introductory texts do not fully reveal the depth of communication principles and practices. It is my intent and hope that *Spinning the Symbolic Web: Human Communication as Symbolic Interaction* avoids these problems. The next few pages introduce this book by explaining how it achieves theoretical unity and substantive depth.

Speech communication is an interdisciplinary field. As such it contributes to and draws from a range of disciplines in the humanities and social sciences. Ideally this intellectual cross-fertilization should enrich speech communication and those disciplines with which it interacts. However, there is a danger inherent in interdisciplinary status. It is all too easy to sacrifice theoretical focus, by pulling from a grab bag of available theories that may not be wholly compatible. Doing so creates an awkward patchwork approach to subject matter. When writers of speech communication texts draw from diverse disciplines with equally diverse theoretical heritages, they too often fall prey to this danger. The result is sometimes they use one theory to explain nonverbal behavior, a second theory to discuss language, a third to examine interpersonal communication, and so forth. Because such books lack theoretical unity, they misrepresent communication as a disjointed field. Readers may be left with the erroneous impression that various kinds of communication are more different than alike.

I hope *Spinning the Symbolic Web* avoids this pitfall. The book reflects my commitment to a perspective that provides an exceptionally rich view of relationships among communication, thought, action, selfhood, and interaction. Symbolic interactionism is a powerful, comprehensive theory of human communication, one that provides insight into communication in the range of forms and contexts in which it occurs. In addition, symbolic interactionism—more than other theories—emphasizes the centrality of communication in human affairs. From this perspective, communication is the heart of human nature and activity, a viewpoint reflected throughout this book.

Part I (Foundations of Human Communication) provides theoretical grounding by elaborating the symbolic interactionist orientation to theory, language, situations, nonverbal behavior, and listening. In Part II (Communication and Individual Development), symbolic interactionist theory is used to explain how selfhood arises in communication with others and how individuals' communicative interactions create and sustain their interpersonal relationships. Part III (Communication and Interpersonal Influence) applies a symbolic interactionist perspective to communication in group, public, and interview settings. Thus, the symbolic interactionist perspective is integrated throughout this book, giving it solid theoretical coherence.

A second goal of this book is to provide a substantively sophisticated understanding of communication. In recent years communication has become a sellword—a hot term. All around us we hear calls for "better communication," a catch-all phrase that is seldom defined helpfully. And we hear communication prescribed as a cure-all remedy for personal and social problems.

As is often the case when important ideas capture popular interest, serious thought is impeded. Sometimes genuine, if not fully informed, enthusiasm leads writers to sacrifice serious consideration of ideas to superficial, jazzy treatments of communication principles. Thus, many textbooks feature games and activities, offer simplistic recipes for effectiveness (three steps to assertive communication, ten rules for effective speaking), and rely on catchy slogans ("meaning is in people, not words"; "the word is not the thing"). Of course, there is often some truth behind slogans, some utility in recipes, and something to be learned from games. Nonetheless, these can only supplement, not replace, serious study of communication and rich understanding of its complexities.

Humanity arises largely out of the uniquely human ability to think and act meaningfully—that is, to use symbols. Consequently, to study speech communication is to study what it means to be human. There can be no more compelling area, no subject matter of more enduring importance in our lives. Because *Spinning the Symbolic Web* recognizes that communication is vital to our humanity, it approaches the subject in a serious, substantive manner. I hasten to add that I think a serious approach to communication doesn't have to be a dull one. I've tried to keep the writing interesting and to use examples that reflect our everyday interactions and concerns.

Spinning the Symbolic Web is appropriate for most introductory courses that adopt a substantive approach to communication. Because this book is broad in scope, it can be used in hybrid and theory oriented courses that cover a range of communication principles, forms, and contexts. It is equally appropriate for performance courses that emphasize application of communication theory. This text also lends itself to basic courses with an interpersonal focus. Because symbolic interactionism emphasizes intrapersonal and interpersonal communication as the foundation of all human interaction, substantial portions of the book focus on individual and interpersonal dimensions of communication.

In summary, *Spinning the Symbolic Web: Human Communication as Symbolic Interaction* presents a substantive and theoretically coherent introduction to human communication. I hope the final product justifies the investments made by me and others who contributed to this project.

No book is an individual effort, and that is certainly true of this one. There are a number of people to whom I owe thanks. I first acknowledge those individuals who reviewed the manuscript and who provided criticism and suggestions that improved both the style and substance of the final work. At the top of that list is Robert Cox (The University of North Carolina at Chapel Hill) who provided ongoing assistance in the development of this book. His critical responses to early drafts led to substantial revisions of many sections. In addition, Robert Cox was inordinately generous in giving me personal encouragement, support, and patience throughout my work on this project. I am also indebted to the very capable editorial staff at Ablex, and most especially to Gerald M. Phillips, who is the editor for the Ablex Series in Communication. Professor Phillips first encouraged me to write this book, provided me with substantial freedom in the tone and content of it, and gave me invaluable editorial assistance. In addition, he remained a good friend, giving support, advice, perspective, and—of no minor importance—humor at important junctures. I am also deeply grateful for the personal support of my family, especially my mother, who has taught me much about communication through the ways she lives her life and nurtures her relationships. Finally, I acknowledge the professional support provided by the faculty and students at the University of North Carolina at Chapel Hill. Lynn Hallstein, in particular, was instrumental in the computational support for preparing this book. My colleagues and students' interest, encouragement and stimulation provided essential provocations and challenges that led me to rethink and refine the ideas reflected in this book.

Julia T. Wood
Chapel Hill, North Carolina
September 1991

Part I

Foundations of Human Communication

CHAPTER 1

INTRODUCTION

Man's freedom is freedom to communicate through symbols of his own creation. This is his glory and his burden.

(Hugh Dalziel Duncan)

The Scope and Value of the Communication Discipline

A Rational for Studying Human Communication

Communication defines humanity
Communication affects the quality of our lives
Interpersonal Life
Professional Life
Societal Life

Overview of the Book

Think about how you spend your time. How much of an average day is spent sleeping, studying, interacting with others, or engaging in recreation? As you reflect on your typical activities, chances are you'll discover that communication is at the heart of much of what you do. In fact, you probably spend more time communicating than doing anything else. Since communication is such a major part of life, it is worthwhile to make it as effective as possible.

Is it necessary to study communication in order to become effective? After all, since infancy you've been communicating. Surely with all that practice you've acquired considerable skill! It is true that most of us have developed our communication through trial and error and through imitation of people we admire. This general experience provides a sound foundation for effective communication, but it alone is not sufficient. To supplement what you've learned from interaction with others, you can benefit from focused study of communication theory and practice.

Theory and practice are interdependent. Attention to communication theory enhances understanding of what is involved in human interaction and why the process proceeds well or poorly in various situations. Theoretical knowledge gives you an overall perspective on the communication process so that you can analyze a range of experiences, break down the complex process into specific parts, diagnose problems, and recognize alternative means of interacting with others. Practical knowledge, on the other hand, involves mastery of specific skills appropriate to various kinds of interaction. The combination of theoretical and practical knowledge is powerful. It provides you with a range of communication behaviors and the understanding required to select and employ those most likely to be effective in a particular situation. Theory and practice are complementary: Each needs the other. Theory alone can be abstract, removed from real, concrete issues. Yet practice without theory may, be uninformed and, consequently, ineffective.

This book, therefore, blends theoretical and practical perspectives. But before getting down to particular issues let us consider two preliminary topics: the scope and value of the communication discipline, and a rationale for studying human communication.

THE SCOPE AND VALUE OF THE COMMUNICATION DISCIPLINE

The discipline of speech communication has a broad scope. Scholars and teachers focus on an extensive range of situations in which communication occurs: small groups, families, friendships, romantic relationships, therapeutic associations, professional life, and public forums. These diverse settings are linked by a central concern with communication as the primary means by which people relate to one another. Humans, by their nature, communicate—they cannot avoid it.

Yet some people communicate more effectively than others, and these people are generally more successful professionally and more satisfied personally. All of us, however, can develop skills and understanding that increase communicative effectiveness. We can learn how to plan and present ideas clearly, how to listen actively, how to participate in discussions, how to adapt communication appropriately to different situations and various people.

Just how important is communication? In most professions it plays a major role. One personnel director for a large insurance firm highlights the need for communication skills: "One of the chief weaknesses of many college graduates is the inability to express themselves well. Even though technically qualified, they will not advance far with such a handicap." One executive explains the relationship between communication and management by noting, "Communication is essential to controlling and directing people."[1] According to a recent survey, professionals in business and industry spend 50 to 80 percent of their working lives communicating, and two-thirds of that time involves oral communication.[2] Many organizations, such as IBM, have established entire communication departments, and other organizations include communication courses in their personnel training programs. Clearly, the professional world places a high premium on effective communication. Yet the value of communication skills goes far beyond the professional world. Effective communication is essential to our interpersonal well-being. In fact, communication—effective communication—may be the single most important process in maintaining good relationships. Edwin J. Thomas, a therapist and professor of psychology, thinks most relationship problems involve poor communication between partners. Dr. Thomas elaborates: "Communication difficulties are probably the most common type of problem encountered in couples who seek assistance to improve their interpersonal relationships. Among frequently heard complaints are that partners argue, quarrel, nag, insult, or put each other down; that they talk past each other, don't say what they mean, mislead, talk out of both sides of their mouths, or lie; that they can't or won't understand what is said, or ignore each other. . . ."[3] Thus, building satisfying relationships requires that we gain communication skills and insights.

A RATIONALE FOR STUDYING HUMAN COMMUNICATION

There are two broad reasons to study human communication. First, because communication defines humanity, studying it helps us understand ourselves. Second, communication affects the quality of our lives, so the better we understand communication the better lives we can create. These two ideas are woven through the entire book, so we will preview them now. In later chapters more detailed discussion will follow.

Communication Defines Humanity

Humans are distinguished from other creatures by their ability to communicate. While other forms of life seem to understand limited signals, only humans are able to create and interact with symbols. Symbols are representations for other things. A symbol may be a word, a diagram, a gesture, an emblem, or anything that represents an act, event, idea, feeling, person, process, or object. We use symbols to represent concrete aspects of our world (furniture, possessions, foods) and abstract dimensions of our existence (ideas, experiences, plans). Humans have the apparently unique capacity to symbolize ideas, experiences, hopes, fears, passions, doubts, dreams, even themselves. Because we think and act symbolically, we can impose order and meaning on our experiences. We can persuade ourselves to new courses of action. We can make sense of our past, adapt to our present, and plan for our future.

When we use symbols to designate our interpretations of events, situations, and people, we construct meanings. The symbols we choose are never descriptive of any "real" events, situations, or people. Instead, they are our personal interpretations of them. For example, I remember well a time when a colleague and I observed interaction between marital partners. I diagnosed the marriage as basically healthy and relatively open. My colleague, however, believed the marriage was filled with unwholesome tensions and resentment. Neither of us described the relationship itself—we described our personal perceptions of it. Each of us was convinced the other was wrong, because our individual descriptions constructed what we saw as the "reality" of that marriage. Throughout our lives we use symbols to define our experiences. In doing so, we construct the reality in which we live. In fact, the only reality we can know is what we designate with our symbols.

Human symbolic ability is a mixed blessing. We not only create and use symbols; we also abuse them. We can and sometimes do use symbols to ridicule others, to perpetuate biases and stereotypes, and to diminish the worth of individuals and groups of people. We too frequently talk ourselves into personal evaluations that limit us, and we may be crippled if we accept negative labels others apply to us. Symbols can be used to persuade people to act in ways that violate their personal values or that infringe on the rights of others. Clearly, we can abuse or misdirect our symbolic abilities. We are both the creators and the prisoners of our symbol usage.

We've seen that humans use and abuse symbols to define their immediate worlds. We should also recognize that we use and abuse symbols to create our futures. If we did not have symbolic power we would, like all other animals, be reduced to an existence based on reactions to the world simply as it is. But this is not the case for us. As humans we not only react to our environment but act upon it. Because we can think with symbols, we can transcend our immediate, physical world and contemplate alternatives to it. We can think about ourselves and our situations in ways other than as they appear in a given moment. We can symbolize possibilities and ideals. When we imagine possibilities other than those presently existing we impel ourselves to action aimed at reaching those visions. Because we can envision alternatives, we are never confined absolutely to the actual, concrete world as presently defined. The uniquely human ability to contemplate the future creatively allows us to imagine and strive for ever-better versions of ourselves and our circumstances.

Symbolic ability is central to humanity. With our unique power as symbol users we may build and realize bold visions of ourselves, our relationships, our professions, our social worlds, and our associations with other groups and nations. We may, just as easily, use our symbols to restrict our individual potentials, to build barren relationships, to diminish the value of our professions and social interactions, and to strain international relations to a point that will destroy us all. The choices are ours. Whatever paths we take, we will be acting in ways uniquely human, because we will employ symbols to reach our ends. Humans have such choices only because we can create, use, and abuse symbols to affect our own lives and worlds. This is why symbolic ability defines humanity. It is also why each of us should learn about our symbolic abilities and how we can use these to enhance ourselves and our worlds.

Communication Affects the Quality of Our Lives

Effective communication is vital to individual growth. Communication influences the quality of our interpersonal, professional, and societal lives. Developing understanding and skills in communication is a foundation for personal and professional growth and for effective participation in society.

Interpersonal life.   Social by nature, humans crave interaction with others. Some social scientists even claim that individuals need physical and psychological contact with others to survive. At the very minimum, interpersonal relations are desirable for stimulation and personal development. To satisfy our interpersonal desires we rely on communication, and the extent to which our relationships meet our goals is directly related to our skills as communicators.

Our first interpersonal relationships were within our nuclear families. Much of that early communication was instruction, teaching us not only language but also values, rules of conduct, and roles for ourselves. Communication during our early years profoundly influenced how we saw ourselves. We learned either to be passive or to exert control over our lives; we learned we were attractive or unattractive, intelligent or unintelligent, lovable or unworthy of love; we learned that only certain behaviors, attitudes, and roles were "acceptable" for us; we even learned what ambitions were appropriate for us. Communication within our families influenced how we viewed the world and ourselves.

As we grew older we interacted with people outside our families. We learned styles of behavior, so that some of us are dominant and others submissive, some of us are extroverted and others introverted. We gained further insights into how others perceived us and we discovered what types of people would be our friends. Through communication with friends and intimates we built "safe" worlds where we were accepted and comfortable. With our friends we could tell secrets, share dreams, confess fears and doubts, form exclusive clubs. We enjoyed the pleasures of a private world with selected others.

As we grow up, many of us seek yet another kind of human relationship: intimate, romantic bonds. We use communication to develop these intimate relationships. Fulfilling intimate relationships are marked by open, supportive climates for communication, by freedom to self-disclose without fear of rejection or shame, by mutual efforts to listen empathically, and by showing interest in each other's feelings and ideas. These and other communication skills are the lifeblood of relationships. Understanding the ways in which communication affects our interpersonal relationships helps us to participate more effectively in interactions with others.

Professional life. More than in previous eras, success in professional life now requires keen communication abilities. Demonstrated competence in communication is essential to gaining a rewarding position, to performing competently, and to advancing. One study of over 3000 managers and supervisors identified the following communication needs as important to success: effective speaking, efficient work with individuals and groups, communication in the organization, listening skills, counseling techniques, management development, and understanding the human aspect of management.[4] These communication skills are not "nice extras"; they are absolutely essential for employment and advancement. Every working day is filled with communication situations. Professionals must know how to interact effectively with subordinates, peers, and superiors. The professional must use communication to establish constructive working climates, to support colleagues, to make decisions, to appraise others, to represent his or her work to others, to solve problems, to diagnose tensions—the list is infinite. Regardless of whether you plan to be an executive or not, to work in a firm or on your own, you will need a variety of communication skills to be professionally successful.

No career can succeed without communication. Even a highly technical position such as computer programmer requires communication skills. An IBM manager who hires computer programmers demonstrated that when he said, "What I look for first in an applicant for a position as computer programmer is the ability to get along well with people and the ability to express himself or herself effectively both orally and in writing. You see, if our applicants lack skills in computer programming, we're prepared to teach them these skills. But we are not prepared to teach them to deal with and to communicate effectively with people if they haven't already learned these skills before they come to us."[5] Learning communication skills directly enhances the quality of every person's professional life.

Societal life. Our entire society depends on effective communication. Our rights to freedom of speech, freedom of the press, and freedom of expression are integral to our country's survival as a democracy. Because we are free to express even unpopular ideas, because the press may investigate and report misconduct even in the White House, and because we are free to disagree publicly with national policies, we have some control over our national life. The exercise of these rights and even their very survival depend on a citizenry skilled in communication.

Each of us needs communication skills to participate in civic and public life. We must be able to listen thoughtfully to varied viewpoints, to evaluate the logic of arguments for and against policies, to guard against our own prejudices so we do not take indefensible positions, to prepare reasoned statements of our own ideas. These are communication skills required of each citizen. They are not reserved for those who choose to run for office. Each of us is responsible for making informed judgments of people and ideas, and to do this we must develop our skills as communicators.

Human communication defines humanity and is profoundly related to the quality of our lives. For these reasons, the thought and effort required for serious study of communication are sound investments in your present and future well being.

OVERVIEW OF THE BOOK

This book presents theoretical and practical material about human communication. Part I, Foundations of Human Communication, consists of this introduction and five chapters that explore theories and concepts basic to understanding and effective practice of communication. To establish an overall perspective for the book, Chapter 2 defines communication, examines several models of communication, and considers some popular misconceptions about communication. Building on this foundation, Chapter 3 considers the situations in which communication occurs. Situations are defined through individuals' interaction with the external world. Thus, situations have both objective and subjective dimensions. Our definitions of situations influence our decisions of what and how to communicate. Chapter 4 probes the nature of verbal language, the elaborate symbolic system at the heart of our communication. Symbols are the primary means through which we know and interact with others and our environment. We examine how symbolic abilities influence our attitudes and actions. In Chapter 5 we look at the nature and function of nonverbal behavior. Finally, Chapter 6 focuses on listening, a critical and often neglected aspect of successful, satisfying interaction.

Part II explores the importance of communication in interpersonal development. Chapter 7 focuses on the dynamic interaction between communication and selfhood.

It is through communication with others that we establish our initial sense of a personal, individual self. In turn, that self serves as the center for how we construct and interpret communication with others and how that affects our ongoing sense of who we are. Chapter 8 extends discussion of selfhood to examine how communication socializes us into the rules and values of a particular culture. We analyze the various kinds of socialization we receive from family, peer groups, work groups, and the overall society. In Chapter 9 we consider the interaction between communication and the evolution of intimate relationships. Here we examine the ways in which individuals use symbols to build, sustain, and sometimes destroy intense relationships.

Part III deals with communication and interpersonal influence. Chapter 10 offers information on how to interact effectively in problem-solving group discussion. Chapters 11 and 12 describe how to plan, develop, research, and present effective individual speeches. Chapter 13 discusses interviewing communication and provides guidelines for both interviewer and interviewee.

As this overview indicates, the book has a broad focus. Its goal is to introduce you to theoretical and practical knowledge about human communication. Your study of this material should lead to three outcomes. First, you should have a solid understanding of the complex process of human communication—what it involves, how it proceeds, and why it is important to your life. Second, you should learn a variety of skills that will enhance your personal effectiveness in interaction with others. Finally, you should catch some enthusiasm for the study and practice of human communication—an outcome that will entice you to learn more about communication through additional reading, course-work, and experiences.

This book is written for students. To make it as useful and readable as possible I've tried to restrict jargon and technical language. Throughout the text, research reports and real-world examples illustrate theoretical material. These reports and examples are ones my own students find helpful in clarifying and extending concepts; in fact, many of the examples came from students. Before I let this book go to press, I asked several students to read it and recommend changes. They were not shy about offering suggestions, most of which I've followed. I hope the final product stimulates you to do more than highlight key passages that you dutifully reread prior to exams. If this is the case, the book not only will inform you, but also will interest and excite you about speech communication and its centrality in your own life. Indeed, you will then understand that there is nothing more vital to the quality of your life than communication.

REFERENCES

[1]Linwood E. Orange, *English: The Pre-Professional Major*, 2nd ed., Rev. New York: Modern Language Association of America, 1973, p. 5.

[2] E. T. Klemmer and F. W. Snyder, "Measurement of Time Spent Communicating," *Journal of Communication, 22*, June 1972, pp. 142-158.

[3]Edwin J. Thomas, *Marital Communication and Decision Making*. New York: Free Press, 1977, p. 1.

[4]Samuel S. Dubin, Everett Alderman, and Leroy Marlow, *Survey Report of Managerial and Supervisory Educational Needs of Business and Industry in Pennsylvania*. University Park, PA: Pennsylvania State University Department of Continuing Education, 1967.

[5]James H. McBath and David T. Burhans, Jr., *Communication Education and Careers*. Falls Church, VA: Speech Communication, 1975.

CHAPTER 2

THEORY AS A FOUNDATION OF HUMAN COMMUNICATION

There is nothing so practical as a good, explicit theory.

(Kurt Lewin)

Defining Communication

    Communication is a dynamic process
    Communication is systemic
      Communication must be understood within its context
      All parts of a system are interrelated
      The whole is greater than the sum of its parts
      Communication systems include constraints that affect meaning

    Communication involves communicators
    Communication is symbolic interaction
    Meaning in communication is personally constructed
    All communication has two levels of meaning

Models of Communication

    Values of models
    Limitations of models
    Models of human communication
    Comparisons among models

A Symbolic Interactionist Model of Communication

Misconceptions about Human Communication

    More communication improves anything and everything
    Speakers are responsible for effectiveness in communication
    Communication breakdowns stop communication
    Communication consists of words
    Meanings are in words
    Effective communicators are born, not made

After your ten o'clock class you ask your professor to clarify the lecture he just presented. When he elaborates the material, you nod in understanding. Then you meet a friend for lunch and discuss a personal problem. Your friend shows a lot of concern and offers her support. On the way back to your place, you stop at a local shop to return a record. You explain to the clerk that the record is defective, and he makes an exchange for you. That night you listen to music with the person you've been dating for four months, and "your song" comes on. The two of you gaze knowingly at each other and, though no words are spoken, you've said a lot to each other.

When you return from you day's classes your roommate complains that you are a "hopeless packrat" and your room is a complete mess *again*. You try to explain how busy you've been, but your roommate storms out, slamming the door. That evening you start on your new job and your co-workers give you odd looks and avoid interacting with you. Although they say nothing, you have the distinct impression they don't like you for some reason. The next week you call home to share your excitement with your parents about deciding to pursue graduate study. Before you even have a chance to discuss your plans, you father interrupts and says "forget that and get a job." The excitement drains out of you.

In the first set of examples, communication took place. It also occurred in the second group of activities, but in these cases it was less satisfying. Words, expressions, movements, and even silence communicated ideas and feelings in both sets, but what distinguishes those that seemed satisfying and effective from those that were less so? To answer that question we need to explore the nature of communication in some detail. We do just that in this chapter, focusing on theoretical understandings that are a foundation for understanding communication. We begin by defining communication. Next we consider a number of models of communication and compare them. Finally, we examine some popular misconceptions about what communication is and does. Studying this chapter should give you a firm conceptual grasp of what human communication is and, just as importantly, what it is not.

DEFINING COMMUNICATION

Over 100 definitions of communication have been proposed by scholars.[1] The fact that so many different views exist should give you some idea of the complexity of communication and the difficulty of pinning it down. Clearly no single definition will ever satisfy everyone. Nonetheless, we need to establish a basic definition for our study. To do this we examine six premises that capture key aspects of communication. Taken together, they provide us with a clear and rich understanding of what human communication is.

Communication is a Dynamic Process

When we describe communication as a dynamic process, we recognize its character as being ever-changing, influx. Because it is a process, it moves constantly; it's never fixed or static. The idea of process also means that there are no clear beginnings and endings of communication. Previous events—even ones we're not consciously aware of—affect current interactions. Communication that you engage in now influences your behavior in the future. So we know that communication is not properly understood as starting when you speak and ending when you stop speaking. A useful metaphor of communication is film: When we observe communication we catch only one frame in an infinite film. We don't know where it began (if, indeed, there is some actual beginning), and we cannot predict where it will end (again, if we can actually define some absolute end).

Because communication is dynamic, all factors in the process (people, settings, events, objects, words, behaviors) constantly interact. Although we have to focus on on just one part of the process at a time to describe communication, this is not reflective of its highly dynamic character. The sequence we use to describe communication is our own arbitrary creation. Frank Dance, a communication scholar, described communication as "something that is in constant flux, motion and process . . . changing while we are in the very act of examining it. . . . Communication while moving forward is at the same moment coming back upon itself and being affected by its past behavior. . . . The communication process, like a helix, is constantly moving forward and yet is always to some degree dependent upon the past, which informs the present and the future."[2] So, in understanding that communication is a dynamic process, you recognize its interactive, changing, evolutionary nature.

Communication is Systemic

Communication does not occur in a vacuum. It occurs within particular contexts. For this reason if we want to describe it accurately, we must recognize the contexts or systems within which it occurs. A system is a group of interrelated elements that interact in ways that influence each other and the system as a whole. All communication takes place within a matrix of systems: the relationship between communicators, the physical setting, the society. Each of these systems influences communication, and each influences the others. To better understand the important concept of system, let's examine four implications of a systemic view of communication.

Communication must be understood within its contexts. We don't communicate in a void. To understand our communication, we must think about the nest of systems within which it is embedded. Consider this example of how systems influence communication:

STUDENT: Dr. Jones, I'm sorry I missed the exam on Wednesday. When may I take the make-up?

DR. JONES: I don't give make-ups. Unless you have a medical excuse, you cannot take one.

STUDENT: But I was too sick to get up on the day of the exam. I couldn't even walk to the infirmary.

DR. JONES: Then you're out of luck. Your exam counts as a zero.

How does this conversation strike you? What are your impressions of the student and Dr. Jones? What do you understand about the communication they engaged in?

Perhaps you think Dr. Jones is unsympathetic to student problems and is rigid about allowing make-up exams. Or maybe you think the student was pretty unimaginative in explaining the failure to show up for the scheduled exam. Perhaps you have some entirely different response to the interaction. Whatever you think, it's based on some assumptions you've made (probably without even recognizing them) about the system in which this communication occurred.

Let's fill in some of the missing information about the system. The interaction took place at five o'clock on a hot, muggy day just as Dr. Jones was leaving her office. This student had been chronically absent from class and had not turned in the two assigned papers in the course. At the beginning of the term Dr. Jones informed students that her policy was to give make-up exams only when students had official medical excuses. Given this information, you might reach the conclusion that Dr. Jones was fair, even if a bit abrupt.

Now let's assume some different things about the system. Let's say we know that Dr. Jones had no announced policy on make-up exams, and she has granted them to several other students in the same class. Further, let's assume that this student has been very consistent in attendance and has turned in all assignments to date. Finally, let's say that just before the student came by Dr. Jones received word that her promotion had been denied so she was feeling angry.

Obviously these two quite distinct understandings of the larger system within which communication occurred influence the meaning we attribute to the interaction. The point is that we need background information to make sense of this exchange and, in fact, of any communication. Communication is systemic—it can be understood only in relation to the systems within which it occurs.

All parts of a system are interrelated.   A systemic view holds that all parts of a system are interrelated. This implies that they are interdependent and interactive, each affecting all others. Communicators influence each other and the messages they exchange; the messages affect future messages as well as the communicators; the physical situation can alter what is said, felt, and done; how communicators behave can affect the physical situation; and so on. For example, think of your speech communication class as a communication system. Parts of that system include you, your classmates, your instructor, this text, the physical classroom, the university and its regulations, and the overall society. Now imagine changing just one of those parts— let's say the textbook. If you had a different book, every aspect of your system would change to some degree. Because you'd be reading different ideas, you'd have a different perception of communication. This would lead to different sorts of lectures from your instructor, different kinds of questions and comments from you and your peers, and changes in tests. This simplified example demonstrates the interrelatedness of parts in a system. Because all elements of a system interact constantly, a change in any single part affects the entire system.

The whole is greater than the sum of its parts.   This statement might distress mathematicians, but it is useful in expressing the point that the whole of a system is something more than just the additive parts. Just as we cannot accurately explain how the human body functions by separately studying the heart, liver, bones, thyroid, spleen, and so on, neither can we understand communication properly by examining individual components such as communicators, symbols, interferences, and setting. To think of communication this way leads to only piecemeal understanding. Instead, we have to recognize not just the individual parts, but also their interactions. For instance, consider a small group discussion. The parts of that system might include members, their task, the physical and social environment, and the messages exchanged. Adding up those parts, however, will not explain new ideas generated by the group, the norms that develop, or the cohesion among members. Ideas, norms, and cohesion arise out of interaction among the initial elements of the group system. In a similar manner, we analyze any communication system by identifying its parts and by studying how they interact to produce new features and modify existing ones.

Communication systems include constraints that affect meaning. All communication systems contain potential constraints. A constraint is something that influences our efforts to communicate and understand each other. They can modify, even distort, the meanings we intend to convey. Systems contain physical constraints such as uncomfortable chairs, smoke-filled air, background noises, and distance between communicators. Sociological factors may also be constraints in some systems: Differences in status, race, gender, and background often interfere with our efforts to communicate. System constraints that potentially influence communication are inevitable—we cannot have a system without constraints. The best that we can do is to recognize constraints and try to adapt to their presence. If we realize that we have an uncomfortable meeting room, for instance, we can plan on frequent breaks for people to move around.

In summary, human communication is systemic. We've seen that this carries four important implications for how we think about communication. First, communication occurs within contexts, which we must take into account when trying to understand it. Second, all parts of a system are interrelated and, thus, interactive. Third, the whole of a system is more than the sum of its parts—it's that plus the interaction among parts and what that produces. Finally, communication systems inevitably include constraints that affect meaning.

Communication involves communicators

At first glance, this premise seems too obvious to need discussion. However, it is useful in limiting our definition of communication. The term "communicators" implies something different than terms like "speaker" and "listener," "sender" and "receiver," or "source" and "destination." Each of these terms suggests that when people communicate they assume only a single role. Further, such terms suggest that communication is a very linear, sequential process in which a speaker speaks (or sender sends) and a listener listens (or receiver receives). Yet we know this is not a realistic depiction of what happens in communication. As we interact, each of us both "speaks" and "listens," and we do so simultaneously. Even as you're listening to someone else speak, you're "speaking" too by the feedback you give—good eye contact, attentive posture, head nodding that indicates agreement; or a bored look, glancing at your watch, and yawning. In communication each person simultaneously occupies both speaking and listening roles, so they're better described as communicators.

Notice how the speaker/listener view ignores the simultaneous sending and receiving of messages by all participants in communication. The speaker/listener view portrays communication as a one-way process—something a speaker does to a listener. The listener is depicted as relatively passive, not an active participant in the process.

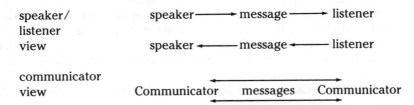

As you can see from this simple diagram of the two views, the speaker/listener conception of communication misrepresents the process. The communicator view is more accurate, because it recognizes the dual and simultaneous behaviors of persons engaged in communication.

Communication is Symbolic Interaction

Chapter 4 examines symbolic interaction theory in detail. For now, you need only understand that human communication is symbolic, which means it is created by us. We can think and act symbolically, an ability not possessed by other forms of life. Thus, in defining communication as *symbolic* interaction, we automatically limit our concerns to communication between humans. As far as we know, animals are not capable of anything more than the most primitive kinds of symbolic activity, and machines operate in purely mechanical ways. So whatever animals and machines do, it is not communication as we define it.

Recognizing human communication as symbolic interaction leads to a distinct perspective on both humanity and the communication process.[3] As we interact with and through symbols, we define and classify our experiences. We use language to represent our understandings of ourselves and our experiences. In this way we imbue our lives with meaning and value. Because we interact with and through symbols, we are distinct from all other species. Unlike other animals, we exercise control over both our interpretations of phenomena and our responses to them. We don't react in simple, automatic ways as do dogs and cats. Instead, we mediate experiences through symbols (usually language) to define what they mean. As we do this, we respond to our interpretations of things, not to the things themselves. This is what sets us apart from other animals. They can only react to what is. In contrast, humans are *proactive*. We act upon our worlds, an ability that elevates us above other kinds of life and that results directly from our capacity to use symbols.[4]

Earlier we discussed the idea of constraints that inhere in systems. Constraints are present in our symbols just as in any other part of systems. The symbols we select and the way in which we organize them affect how others interpret our talk. For some .

people incorrect grammar is so distracting that they cannot attend to the ideas being expressed. For other people particular words interfere with, or constrain, meaning. Your parents, for example, might be offended if you used some of the language accepted on your campus in conversation with them. People who use jargon or technical words sometimes confuse or alienate listeners. Professors sometimes are guilty of doing this when they present material in such abstract ways that it confuses or bores students rather than clarifying their understanding of an area of study. Even word choice can constrain meaning. The title "Ms" for example, means different things to different people, so in using it someone could be misinterpreted by others. Constraints then may inhere in symbols themselves.

To view communication as symbolic interaction is to recognize humans as proactive beings whose control over themselves and their surroundings stems from their ability to interact with and through symbols. Our experiences, knowledge, and relationships are inevitably mediated through our symbols.

Meaning in Communication is Personally Constructed

Each of us interprets communication in our own unique way. No two people will construct the same meaning, even if they see and hear the "same" thing. In fact, two people really cannot experience the same thing—it is different because their interpretations are distinct. Each of us draws on our past experiences and our developed ways of perceiving and valuing to decide what something means, so our meanings are necessarily unique.

You speak to someone else, who interprets your comment and responds. Notice that the response does not directly follow your comment. Instead, the response grows out of the interpretation made of your comment. All communication is like this. We never respond directly to another person, nor even to the symbols she or he uses. Instead, we respond to them and their symbols *as we have interpreted their meanings*. We must perceive and assign meaning to what another says before we can respond, and our interpretations are inextricably bounded by our personal selves—our experiences, thoughts, feelings, needs, expectations, self-concepts, goals, values, and knowledge of those with whom we interact. Because each of us is unique, we interpret in unique ways. Thus, meaning is always personal and it varies among people.

To clarify the personal nature of meaning, consider the word "love." You and I naturally have different interpretations of that word. Perhaps for you the word "love" conjures up images of a particular person you've been dating lately, or perhaps you think of someone you recently broke up with, or maybe you think of a brother or sister for whom you care deeply. Perhaps "love" has a positive feeling for you; or if you've recently had a bad experience, it may feel negative to you. Whatever your meanings, they're different from mine. For me the word "love" has an immediate and well-defined meaning. I think of my partner, with whom I've spent eighteen years—how he looks, acts, and interacts with me. My sense of love and of loving this man is infused with a sense of history we have shared as well as with plans we've made for the future. All of these images and sensations are part of my meaning for "love." They're not part of your meanings, because you and I have different experiences and distinct ways of organizing them. And neither of our meanings for "love" is like that of a child battered by parents, an individual who is separating from a spouse, or a person recently widowed. Differences in meaning may be slight or substantial, but there are always differences. No two people ever have exactly the same meanings for symbols.

Even one individual's meaning varies over time. What something means depends on our experiences, and those change as we grow. Moods and physiological factors can also influence what symbols mean to us. Some days we feel good, optimistic, positive toward ourselves and others. Other days we feel pessimistic, negative toward ourselves and the world. On a "good day" we might respond well or at least neutrally to constructive criticism from a friend. The same criticism might be interpreted as mean-spirited and inviting a fight on one of our "bad days." The idea of a meal means one thing when we're full and something else when we're starving. Meanings vary even within individuals.

All Communication Has Two Levels of Meaning

Researchers who study communication report there are two levels of meaning in all messages.[5] There is a *content level*, which is literal meaning or information in a message. For instance, the content-level meaning of the statement "You were late for our date" is simply that the person speaking thinks you were late. Content-level meaning is straightforward information.

The second kind of meaning is called the *relational level*. This concerns what communication suggests about the individuals and their relationship. In our example, then, the relational level might be that the person speaking is angry about your tardiness. It's also possible that the person speaking is indicating he or she has the right and power to define your behavior as wrong and to reprimand you. There's often a power level in messages. Thus, the relational level of meaning gives us important cues about how to interpret the content level. The statement in our example might be an observation, a criticism, or a warning. It's the relational level of meaning, not the content level, that tells us which it is. Typically, although not always, relational-level meaning is communicated nonverbally. Tone of voice, facial expression, gestures, and so forth, give us cues as to how to interpret what someone is saying about themselves, us, and our relationship.

Content and relationship levels of meaning exist in most, if not all, messages. At work your boss might say "Get this mess cleaned up now" or "This area is looking pretty messy. I'd appreciate your getting it cleaned up a bit when you can." On the content level the two statements are similar. On the relational level, however, they are very different. In the first one, the boss adopts an authoritarian and critical posture, defining his or her role as boss and yours as subordinate. In the second message, the boss implies a much more equal power relationship with you by being less abrupt and critical and by asking, rather than ordering, you to clean up. To understand communication, then, we need to be sensitive to both content and relational levels of meaning.

Meaning is clearly the crux of human communication. It arises as we interact with symbols and with each other through symbols. From this perspective, we are concerned with the mental processes through which humans store and interpret experiences in order to attribute meaning to them. Taken together, the six premises we've discussed lead to a view of communication as a sophisticated, complex activity that is uniquely human. These premises allow us to create a working definition of communication: *Communication is a dynamic, systemic process in which communicators create meanings through interactions with and through symbols.*

Now that we've defined communication, we can move ahead to consider ways to model the communication process.

MODELS OF COMMUNICATION

A model is a description of something else—an object, event, process, or relationship. Models are not explanations of why something exists or *why* it works as it does. Instead, they are descriptions of what something is and/or of how it works. They attempt to represent the important features of what they model.

Models are particularly useful in understanding complex processes like human communication. Over the past 50 years a number of scholars have proposed models of communication. Each is one way of describing what happens when people communicate. We look at five of the best-known models, then compare how they depict communication. After that, we combine the best aspects of these models along with ideas derived from the six premises we've discussed to develop a symbolic interactionist model of communication.

Values of Models

"Why study models?" you might ask. As we'll see, models can advance understanding. Probably at some time in your life you've worked with one or more models. Perhaps you built a model of a car, house, plane, or boat. To build the model you had to scrutinize each individual piece, study it in detail to see what it was, how it was constructed, how it connected to and worked with other pieces; then you had to fit the pieces together, which means you had to figure out the relationships among parts. In working with the model, you gained understanding of what it represented—plane, house, car. Thus, the model aided your comprehension. Similarly models of human communication enhance our understanding of how communication works. Two of the most important values of models are that they organize thinking and they are heuristic.

Models organize. A good model clarifies what it describes. It highlights key features and relationships and omits or de-emphasizes ones the model builder considers less important. Of course, no model can represent all aspects of something as complex as communication. For this reason, any model offers a *selective* representation—one way of portraying what it depicts. A model demonstrates how certain features are related to one another and tries to organize understanding. David Mortensen summarizes the organizing value of models this way:[6]

> Models clarify the structure of complex events. . . . This is particularly important when dealing with an activity comprising a vast and seemingly countless number of influences. . . . With the aid of a high-powered model, the isolated pieces of information can assume meaningful patterns.

Because models identify key features and provide insights into relationships among them, they organize our thinking about communication. Thus, they are a valuable mental tool.

Models are heuristic.   Something is heuristic if it leads us to think in new and innovative ways. A model is heuristic if it stimulates us to think in new ways, to see things and consider possibilities we'd not thought of before. A heuristically strong model, then, prompts us to ask insightful questions and to speculate in new ways about communication. Scholars of communication theory tend to regard heurism as the most sophisticated and potentially valuable quality of models.[7] Thus, a truly heuristic model helps us break out of standard habits of thinking and allows us to make conceptual advances.

Limitations of Models

Along with the values of organizing and heurism, models have limitations. Three important ones are that they are static, partial, and general. These are limitations inherent in models. So these apply to all models, not just the particular ones we'll consider.

Models are static.   A model necessarily freezes or stops the process it represents. This is especially a drawback with something like communication, which we have seen is a highly dynamic, interactive process. No model can really capture the active, changing nature of communication. To represent communication, a model must freeze the process at a particular point and then describe the features and relationships that are present at that point. It cannot represent motion and changes. When we examine models, then, we need to remember that they are more static than what they represent.

Models are partial.   This limitation is the flip side of models' organizing value. Since no model can portray the full complexity of communication, the creator decides which aspects are most important and includes those. As we examine various models in the next section, we'll want to ask whether we agree with the model builders' decisions of which aspects to include and omit.

Models are general.   Models that attempt to represent communication in general cannot identify the features that are most important in each particular context. A single, general model of communication cannot provide a detailed representation of the elements in small group discussion, intimate communication, and public speaking. Instead, a general model attempts to identify features and relationships that are common to all communicative situations. For instance, we know that symbols will be present in any communicative encounter. We also know that communicators will be present in any situation and that they will interact with each other through symbols. These features and relationships exist in all situations, so we would surely include them in a model of communication. Yet we could not describe how these differ among situations. For example, we know that communication between intimates is more personal and informal than public speaking. This difference cannot be fully acknowledged by a model that offers a general representation of communication.

In summary, models are tools of thought. They are valuable because they organize our thinking and stimulate us to think in new ways about communication. Good models combine accuracy of description and innovativeness. Yet models are limited by being static, partial, and general descriptions of a highly dynamic process.

In the next section we evaluate several models of communication. As we consider each one, ask yourself two questions: (a) How accurately and usefully does this model organize features and relationships in the communication process? (b) Does this model provide new insights into communication?

Models of Human Communication

Laswell's model (1948). The most simple kind of model is verbal, and that is what communication scholars first developed. One of the earliest models was advanced by Laswell:[8]

WHO?
SAYS WHAT?
IN WHAT CHANNEL?
TO WHOM?
WITH WHAT EFFECT?

Laswell's model describes communication as a sequence of events that begins with one person and ends with some effect on another person. Laswell limits his model to five key elements of communication: a speaker, message, channel, listener, and message impact. The major weakness of this model is that it represents communication as a linear sequence, rather than as an interactive process.

Shannon and Weaver's model (1949). According to Shannon and Weaver, communication consists of five basic components: an information source, a transmitter, a receiver, a destination, and noise. Designed to describe telephone communication, this model works quite well for its original purpose.[9] The person who places a call is the source of information; the telephone is the transmitter which converts the message into an electronic signal, another telephone is the receiver; and the signal is recovered into a message which is heard by another person (destination). Static and other interferences in the phone wires and transmitters are noises that distort the signal so the message may not be received exactly as sent. Notice what this model adds to Laswell's conception of communication. Shannon and Weaver realized that noise occurs in communication, creating distortion. This is an important heuristic feature of the model (see Figure 2.1).

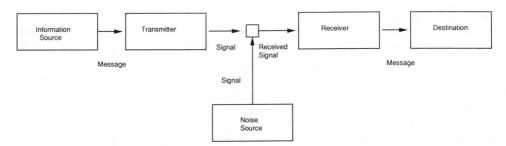

Figure 2.1. Shannon and Weaver's model.

There are three significant weaknesses in Shannon and Weaver's model. First, communication is again represented as a linear sequence rather than as a dynamic process. Second, noise is portrayed as existing only within the message. From our earlier discussion of constraints, it's clear that noise occurs throughout the communication process—not just in messages, but also in people, situations, and relationships. Third, the Shannon and Weaver model is very mechanical. It relies on language (transmitter, receiver) that is inappropriate for describing human interaction. As we'll see, later models avoided some of these problems.

Despite their shortcomings, both of these early models provided starting points for thinking systematically about communication and for building more advanced models.

Schramm's models (1954).   Wilbur Schramm moved beyond verbal and mechanical descriptions to advance four conceptual models of human communication.[10]

Schramm's first model (Figure 2.2, #1) is similar to Laswell's: One person encodes and sends a message to another person. In the second model (Figure 2.2, #2) Schramm emphasizes the importance of communicators' fields of experience, and he indicates that communication occurs only when there is some overlap between communicators' fields. This recognition is one of the highly heuristic qualities of Schramm's work. It stimulated a great deal of thought and research on how our experiences influence our behavior and interpretations of others' communication (see Figure 2.2).

Schramm's third model, Figure 2.2 (3), reminds us that each communicator is both sender (encoder, speaker) and receiver (decoder, listener) and that both encoding and decoding involve personal interpretations. The final model Figure 2.2 (4), is the one Schramm considered his best. It emphasizes the dynamism of human communication by showing it as a cycle of constant interaction between people. Notice that Schramm's fourth model is the first one we've considered that really portrays the processual character of communication.

Schramm's work is more sophisticated than earlier models. His fourth model is particularly strong, because it emphasizes communication as an interactive process. Yet even this most advanced of Schramm's models omits attention to systems and interferences. These omissions are weakness of Schramm's models.

Berlo's model (1960).   David Berlo's model (Figure 2.3) focuses on four primary elements: source, message, channel, and receiver. Because these are the key features, Berlo's model is known as the SMCR model.[11]

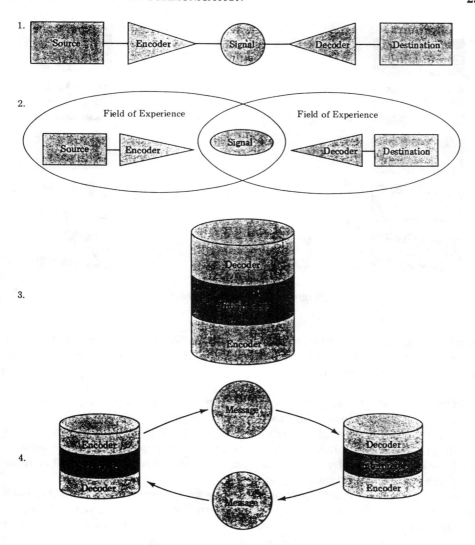

Figure 2.2. Schramm's Models.

According to the SMCR model, source and receiver are influenced by their knowledge, attitudes, and communicative skills. In addition, Berlo recognized the influence of the social and cultural systems in which communicators exist. The message consists of content as well as the communicators' treatment and coding of that content. Channels of communication, the means by which communication is shared, are the five senses.

Berlo's model does not capture the dynamism of communication as fully as Schramm's fourth model does. In this sense, the SMCR model is more static that Schramm's. However, Berlo's model is more advanced than any of the others we've examined in recognizing the complexity of communication. He acknowledges many

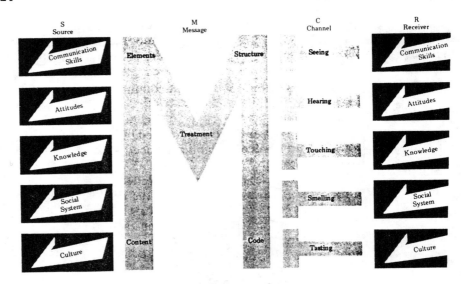

Figure 2.3.   Berlo's model.

factors, including social and cultural systems, that influence communication. In this respect, Berlo's model is quite heuristic in prompting us to think about the ways in which context affect meaning.

Dance's model (1967).   The final model we consider was proposed by Frank E. X. Dance.[12] A quick glance at his model will tell you why it is called the helix. This is one of the most abstract models ever proposed, because it makes no attempt to depict the literal features of communication. Dance doesn't even specify what those features are. Instead, the helix offers a dramatic and metaphorical representation of communication as a cyclical process.

According to this model, communication is progressive, always reflecting back upon itself while at the same time moving forward. The outstanding value of Dance's conception is that it emphasizes the dynamic quality of communication. It shows that communication is an ongoing process—what we say in a given moment is influenced by what has happened previously and influences what will happen next. Thus, the helix depicts communication as having history and future with every communication being part of an ongoing process that has no definite beginning or ending.

Comparisons Among Models

We've now examined five quite distinct models of human communication. Each calls attention to certain features and relationships and each stimulates us to think about communication in particular ways and not in others. To integrate our consideration of these models, we can contrast them in terms of their organizing and heuristic functions.

Figure 2.4.　Dance's model.

	Organizing Value *What features & relationships* *emphasized?*	*Heuristic Value* *What questions & are* *insights are prompted?*
Laswell	Features: speaker, message, channel, effect Relationships: linear & sequential	What are the effects of messages? What is the message? How does channel affect message?
Shannon & Weaver	Features: information source, transmitter, receiver, destination, and noise Relationships: linear & sequential	How do ideas get from source to destination? How does noise distort signals?
Schramm	Features: communicators, messages, fields of experience Relationships: interactive & circular	How is communication affected by overlaps in fields of experience? How do we deal with simultaneous messages?
Berlo	Features: source, message, channel, receiver Relationships: not specified; visual arrangement suggests a linear & sequential view	How do qualities of source & receiver affect messages? How do source variables influence coding? How do channels affect reception?
Dance	Features: time, reflexivity Relationships: cyclical and self-reflexive; temporally situated	How does a message at one time affect later messages? When, if ever, does the impact of a message end?

Clearly, each model stimulates questions, so each has some heuristic value. As the summary chart indicates, each model also highlights particular features and de-emphasizes others. Your evaluation of these models depends on what you consider the important aspects of communication and which of these models best represents those and provokes further thought about them.

A SYMBOLIC INTERACTIONIST MODEL OF COMMUNICATION

Each of the models we've considered offers an interesting perspective on communication. None, however, fully reflects the view of communication developed in this chapter. None of these five really portrays communication as a dynamic, systemic process in which communicators create personal meanings through their interactions with and through symbols.

To represent communication as we've defined it we need a different model. Figure 2.5 captures the perspective on communication that we've discussed. Consistent with that view, dynamism is emphasized throughout the model as a key feature of communication. Notice first that communication is portrayed as symbolic interactions that link communicators. The interactions may be either sequential or simultaneous, since the direction of communication is not specified. Following Dance's helix, our model further stresses dynamism by naming time as an important feature of communication. A given interaction evolves out of previous interactions ($T_1, T_2, T_3 \ldots$) and is

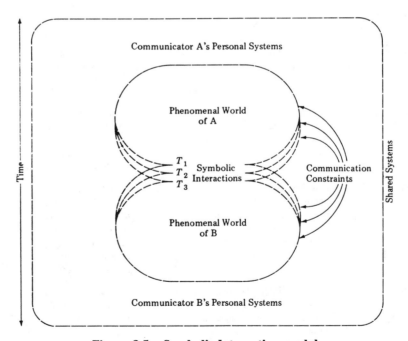

Figure 2.5. Symbolic Interaction model.

influenced by them as well as by what is happening presently. As communication occurs over time, one specific outcome suggested by our model is that communicators' shared world enlarges. As people interact, they learn about each other's values, interests, tendencies for interpreting, and so on. In other words, we increasingly develop a dual perspective as we communicate. Over time people also use symbols to designate ideas, experiences, values, and goals that they share. Couples develop rituals and patterns that define their unique relationship. All of this is part of the shared world that evolves over time as we communicate.

Since a shared phenomenal world is one of the central and distinguishing features of our model, let's consider another example of the process by which it is built. Recently a new person joined my faculty. Our initial interactions were naturally somewhat stilted as we tried to find common areas of interest in our research and teaching as well as our personal lives. After several conversations I came to understand the type of research that interests him and the goals and style of teaching he endorsed. Likewise, he developed a good understanding of my research emphases and my teaching philosophy. In those early interactions we also discovered that we shared a love for dogs, we were both nostalgic about the 1960s, and that he wanted to become vegetarian which I already was. All of that information provided us with a shared world—a set of understandings about each other and the possibilities for a relationship between us. Since then, he and I have served together on a number of committees, collaborated on one research project, and worked together in developing a course. All of these common experiences further enrich the shared world between us. In any relationship—casual, professional, intimate—people use communication to develop and enlarge shared worlds. By emphasizing the temporal dimension of communication, our model calls attention to this.

A second feature highlighted by the symbolic interactionist model is the systemic nature of communication. Several levels of systems are depicted in the model. Both communicators exist within a common social world, which is comprised of all the social systems (political, professional, class, cultural) that make up a given society. Each communicator, however, participates in only some of those systems, and it is those that constitute each person's personal phenomenal world. Notice that each set of systems is represented by dotted lines. This is to remind us that the systems are open to influences outside of them. For instance, professional life is affected by social and political factors (when the government cuts funding for education, resources, facilities and staff of colleges are harmed). The dotted lines remind us of the interrelatedness of systems.

Consistent with our definition of communication, individuals are bounded by their personal phenomenal worlds. This consists of everything that makes up a person—past experiences, self-concept, goals, feelings, thoughts, skills, attitudes, and values. The phenomenal world is additionally affected by transient factors such as passing moods and physical conditions. Our phenomenal worlds are the basis for how we interpret communication. In the model Communicator B interprets A's messages through B's phenomenal world, not through A's. To the extent that these worlds overlap (that there is dual perspective), A and B will have relatively similar understandings and meanings. The model emphasizes the personal construction of meanings by depicting each communicator as situated squarely within her or his personal phenomenal world. Yet, notice that even the personal phenomenal worlds are represented by dotted lines, again indicating that these are open systems. Our world's change as we accumulate experiences and as we are affected by other systems of which we are part.

Finally, our model includes a feature not highlighted by other models: constraints. As indicated by the series of lines, communication constraints are potentially present throughout the communication process. This reminds us of the many factors that influence and can distort communication.

While this model does represent our definition of communication, it is subject to the limitations of all models. It is necessarily static, partial, and general. Clearly, the symbolic interactionist model omits some features of communication, and you may want to discuss these in your class. For instance, channels of communication are not named in this model. At the same time, other features are emphasized more than in the five older models we examined. Communication constraints, shared phenomenal worlds, time, and systems are features this model stresses. Just as you evaluated the first five models according to their organizing and heuristic values, so you should critically consider this one.

So far this chapter has explored premises and models of communication. Now that we've developed a shared basic understanding of what communication is, one task remains. We need to specify what communication *is not*. The final section of this chapter does that by examining some popular misconceptions about communication.

MISCONCEPTIONS ABOUT HUMAN COMMUNICATION

Our assumptions about communication are important. They guide our attitudes and actions as communicators. When we have inaccurate or distorted beliefs, problems are bound to arise. In this section we consider six widely held misconceptions about what communication is and does. By dispelling these, we pave the way for more accurate understanding and, thus, more effective interaction with others.

More Communication Improves Anything and Everything

Contemporary society has become aware of the centrality of communication and the number of ways in which it can be mismanaged. This important insight, however, has led to a dangerous misconception: that communication is The answer to any problem. As communication has become a catch phrase, it is viewed as a cure-all for moral, social, interpersonal, organizational, and political problems. Too often when a problem is described we hear the comment, "What we need is more communication around here." Usually this indicates a desire for more words, more talk.

Many problems, however, cannot be solved by words alone, because they don't arise from inadequate or unclear communication. Problems result from sources that are economic, social, political, technological, and physical. No amount of talk will cure these. Communication—no matter how effective—cannot overcome technological breakdowns, physical diseases, and absolute differences in values. These are not communication problems, so we're misguided if we look to communication for solutions. Many problems, of course, can be addressed through communication. However, there is an important distinction between quality and quantity of communication. The frequently heard call for "more communication" isn't necessarily equivalent to "better communication." *More* communication is seldom a means of improving situations. *Better* communication may facilitate resolution of a great many difficulties. Thus, we need to recognize not only that communication has important strengths, but also that it has definite limitations. It cannot solve all problems, and more communication alone implies no guarantee of quality.

Speakers are Responsible for Effectiveness in Communication

This is a fallacious idea for several reasons. First, as we noted earlier in this chapter, the word "speaker" is not very useful since it suggests a single communication role rather than dual ones carried on simultaneously. Even if we accept the term "speaker," there is a second problem with the idea: It suggests that listening is passive and unimportant to communication. This is patently inaccurate! Effective listening is an active process that requires a great deal of effort. Further, someone who is listening exercises considerable influence over the effectiveness of interaction. When listening a person may give cues (either nonverbal indicators or questions) that an idea is unclear. This helps the person who is speaking realize that further clarification is needed. Listening that is serious, thoughtful, and active contributes substantively to effective communication. By contrast, listening that is careless and inattentive is irresponsible for it hinders effective communication. In Chapter 6 we will discuss listening in detail, and you will appreciate how critical it is to the communication process.

Communication Breakdowns Stop Communication

SKAWILLY.

When you read that word, you didn't know what it meant, right? (I certainly hope you didn't since I invented the word!) Did that nonsense word stop our communication? Of course not. It created confusion, perhaps frustration, but it clearly didn't stop our interaction. This illustrates the misconception in thinking that communication breakdowns stop communication. It's an erroneous idea for two reasons.

First, the idea of breakdown is inappropriate to our view of communication. Something breaks down in a linear sequence. A breakdown occurs in a fixed sequence of events, all of which must take place in the correct order if the process is to operate properly. Communication, as we've seen, is a cyclical, interactive process. It is not linear. Hence, by definition, it cannot break down.[13] Machines break down. Communication does not.

A second problem with the idea that breakdowns stop communication is the implication that communication actually stops. Once we understand that communication is an ongoing process, we realize that we never know where it begins or will end. Words may stop at a particular point, but thought doesn't stop. We may be influenced tomorrow or 10 years from now by a conversation we have today. Further, we may be motivated to keep interacting with someone precisely because their ideas are confusing to us and we need to talk more to understand. Even when we don't understand, even when we're confused (as when you read SKAWILLY), communication is still occurring, though perhaps not with high effectiveness. Communication simply doesn't stop.[14]

Communication Consists of Words

Many people mistakenly think that communication means words. Clearly words are often a very important part of communication. However, the total communication process involves more than just verbal symbols. As we've seen in previous sections of this chapter, symbols become meaningful only as they are interpreted by humans. Thus, the interpretive process is also part of communication. It is, in fact, at least as much a part of communication as words themselves. It is only *as we interact with words* that they become meaningful to us.

There's another way in which communication is more than words. Much of our interaction takes place nonverbally. A tilt of the head may indicate interest, a frown suggests disapproval, a yawn implies boredom. Through tone of voice and vocal inflection we give cues to our mood and attitude toward what we communicate about. Especially on the relational level of meaning, nonverbal behavior is very important. The realm of nonverbal behavior is fascinating and rich, and we'll explore it extensively in Chapter 5. For now, you need only realize that communication is not equivalent to words.

Meanings are in Words

This misconception is related to the previous one. Many people act as if meanings inhere in words. Throughout this chapter we've seen that humans construct meanings and that meanings vary considerably among people. Although most people accept these ideas in theory, they often act as if words do possess intrinsic, absolute meanings. For instance, many people feel strongly about the word "feminist." Some people act as if the word means "man-hating woman." Other people have very positive associations for the word and think it means something like "someone who fights against human oppression." Of course, the word itself is neither good nor bad, and it does not mean either of these things. What it means to you depends on *your interpretation* of the word, not the word *per se*. Humans actively attribute meaning to the symbols with which they interact. The source of meanings, then, is neither in the words nor in the people who use them. It lies in the interaction between humans and their words.

Effective Communicators are Born, Not Made

This is an especially troubling misconception, because it undermines motivation to improve communication. Besides, it's false. A recent study addressed this issue and found that individuals can improve their effectiveness as communicators.[15] Any speech communication instructor can offer further evidence of individuals' ability to improve communication by citing examples of students who have become more effective. My own experiences in teaching and in consulting with businesses firmly convince me that communication skills can be dramatically increased by anyone willing to invest time and effort.

It's true that some people seem to have greater aptitude or acquired skill in communication than others. By the same token, some people have more "natural talent" for sports, music, and mathematics. Yet most of us can become competent athletes even if we'll never be superstars. With discipline we can also learn to play any instrument, although most of us won't ever appear at Carnegie Hall. Similarly, almost any person can enhance communication skills. The understandings, attitudes, and behaviors that comprise effective communication can be learned and refined over time and with practice. So while communication is to some extent an art, it is an art that can be cultivated.

These six misconceptions are dangerous because they lead to misunderstandings of communication and, thus, to inappropriate and ineffective expectations and behaviors. We have seen that communication is not a cure-all, that listening and speaking are equally important parts of communication, that communication neither breaks down nor stops, that communication is not merely words and meaning doesn't inhere in words, and that communication skills can be developed and enhanced through study and practice. Freeing ourselves of misconceptions allows us to study communication in realistic and productive ways.

SUMMARY

This chapter probed the nature of human communication, defined as a dynamic, systemic process in which communicators create personal meanings through their interaction with and through symbols. After developing this definition, we consider five models of communication to see how each organized the process and what kinds of thinking each stimulates. Next we constructed a symbolic interactionist model of communication that reflects the understandings developed in this chapter. More than older models, it represents communicators as acting out of their individual phenomenal worlds as they interact with each other and the symbols they generate.

The final section of this chapter dispelled some misconceptions about communication. Here we showed why six popular beliefs are both fallacious and misleading for us as communicators. The basic theoretical material presented in this chapter provides a broad perspective on human communication. We're now readily to move into more specific analyses of the foundations of communication, beginning with understanding situations, the topic of Chapter 3.

REFERENCES

[1]Frank E. X. Dance, "The Concept of Communication." *Journal of Communication, 20,* June 1970, pp. 201-210.

[2]Frank E. X. Dance, "Toward a Theory of Human Communication." In Frank E. X. Dance (Ed.), *Human Communication Theory: Original Essays.* New York: Holt, Rinehart and Winston, 1967, pp. 293-295.

[3]This discussion is based on pioneer work by Paul Watzlawick, Janet Beavin, and Don Jackson, *The Pragmatics of Human Communication*. New York: W. W. Norton and Co., 1967.

[4]See Kenneth Burke, *Language as Symbolic Interaction*. Berkeley: University of California Press, 1968; and Ernst Cassirer, *An Essay on Man*. New York: Bantam, 1944.

[5]Gerald Phillips and Julia Wood, *Communication and Human Relationships: The Study of Interpersonal Communication*. New York: Macmillan, 1983, pp. 97-98.

[6]C. David Mortensen, *Communication: The Study of Human Interaction*. New York: McGraw-Hill, 1972, p. 31.

[7]Leonard C. Hawes, *Pragmatics of Analoguing: Theory and Model Construction in Communication*. Reading, MA: Addison-Wesley, 1975, pp. 114-115; Mortensen, p. 31.

[8]H. D. Laswell, "The Structure and Function of Communication in Society." In Lyman Bryson (Ed.), *The Communication of Ideas*. New York: Harper and Row, 1948, p. 37.

[9]Claude Shannon and Warren Weaver, *The Mathematical Theory of Communication*. Urbana, IL: University of Illinois Press, 1949, p. 98.

[10]Wilbur Schramm, *The Process and Effects of Mass Communication*. Urbana, IL: University of Illinois Press, 1955, pp. 4-8.

[11]David K. Berlo, *The Process of Communication*. New York: Holt, Rinehart, and Winston, 1960, p. 72.

[12]Dance. "Toward a theory....," p. 296.

[13]C. David Mortensen, "A Frame of Reference." In Thomas M. Steinfatt (Ed.), *Readings in Human Communication: An Interpersonal Introduction*. Indianapolis: Bobbs-Merrill, 1977, p. 11.

[14]D. R. Smith, "The Fallacy of the Communication Breakdown." *The Quarterly Journal of Speech, 34,* 1970, 343-346.

[15]Anthony Mulac, "Effects of Three Feedback Conditions Employing Videotape and Audiotape on Acquired Speech Skill." *Speech Monographs, 41*, 1974, 205-214.

CHAPTER 3

SITUATIONAL AWARENESS AS A FOUNDATION OF HUMAN COMMUNICATION

The limits of my language are the limits of my world.

(Ludwig Wittgenstein)

Situation

Types of Communication Situations

    Intrapersonal communication situations
    Interpersonal & group communication situations
    Public communication situations
    Mass communication situations

Dimensions of Communication Situations

    The dimension of purpose
    The dimension of environment
    The dimension of persons & relationships

Perceiving Situations

    Experiences & perception
    Expectations & perception
    Motivations & perception

Perception, Communication, & Defining Situations

    How communication defines situations
    How symbols influence perceptions
    How defining situations affects communication

Responding to our Labels for Emotions

> For three weeks you've been working as a clerk in a large computer firm. You intend to work another ten weeks until the summer is over, when you'll return to school to live on the salary you've saved. Your immediate supervisor pulls you aside one day and says, "From now on when you sort the mail each day I want you to check for any envelopes with return addresses from competing firms. If you find any from our competitors, hold the mail, and notify me personally at once."

What do the above sentences mean to you? Do they merely recount a series of events and behaviors, or do they describe a situation? What is a situation anyway? And what do situations have to do with understanding human communication? To answer these questions, we need to explore the complex and fascinating relationships among perception, communication, meaning, and situations.

This chapter focuses on how our symbolic behaviors define and create situations in which we communicate. Just as importantly, we'll be discussing the converse—how situations affect our communicative behaviors. Our first task is to clarify the meaning and importance of the term, "situation," so that we understand it to describe human meanings for perceived relationships among selected events, objects, persons, values, and motives. After that, we examine some external ways of defining situations by identifying recognized types of communication situations and the constraints that inhere in them. Next, we consider some of the internal influences on situations—the ways our thoughts and needs and experiences affect our tendencies to perceive and create meanings. The final section of this chapter integrates our discussion of perception, communication, and situational definition to illuminate the complex, dynamic relationships among these activities.

SITUATION

Within symbolic interactionist theory the concept of "situation" is centrally important. Situations are the contexts for all human action, including communication. Thus, to understand more fully the symbolic interactionist view of communication, we must figure out what situation means and what that meaning implies.

There are three prominent ways to define situation. First, we could regard situations as consisting of empirically existing phenomena—people, objects, events, and conditions that we can objectively identify in a particular place and time. This view of situation emphasizes phenomena that are external to individuals; situations consist of things outside of humans. This externally focused definition entails two problems. First, it suggests situations exist independently of our perception. Yet, we know that humans perceive in selective and highly personal ways. We don't perceive, much less respond to, many of the people, objects, events, and conditions around us. Instead, we disregard or only peripherally notice the majority of phenomena surrounding us, and we focus on only a very few aspects of our external environment. So an external definition of situation doesn't adequately recognize the vital role of human perception in selecting and ordering elements of the external world.

Related to the problem of emphasizing what is outside of individuals is a second deficiency of an external definition of situation. It provides no explanation of how situations become meaningful to us. To say that phenomena exist doesn't offer any insight into what those phenomena mean to us, nor why they mean whatever they do.

From our introductory discussions of symbolic interactionism, you'll recall that human meaning is considered the primary basis of our ideas and choices of action. So, without significant attention to how meanings are assigned to external factors, we can have no thorough understanding of why people communicate as they do. In summary, an external definition of situation is inadequate because it neglects the critical issues of perception and meaning, which are the heart of human communication.

A second way situation might be defined is to focus on internal processes through which individuals experience phenomena and assign meanings to them. This view stresses how individuals' needs, goals, experiences, expectations, and so forth influence perceptions. Given our criticisms of the external definition of situation, this second position initially appears inviting. Yet it too has deficiencies. The most serious problem with a purely internal view of situation is that perceptual processes are overemphasized and are regarded in isolation. Obviously without some external conditions to perceive and interpret, there can be no perception of situations (even purely private fantasies and imaginings, after all, include external phenomena we have experienced at some point).

We might follow what some advocates of an internal view have done and modify our viewpoint to include external phenomena as they are perceived by people. Even so, however, there's still a problem. Absolute focus on individuals' needs, goals, and so on restricts awareness of general patterns by which humans experience objects, events, and people. While we know that phenomena themselves do not have any *inherent* meanings, we also know that there are undeniable regularities in how people generally perceive and respond to a great many external phenomena. An internal view of situation is so strictly concerned with individual perceptions that it cannot incorporate what is known about general tendencies in how humans perceive and create meanings.

So, we realize that situation cannot be defined satisfactorily by either external phenomena or individual perceptions. The meaning of a situation is not located in *Just* the self, nor is it found in *Just* the outside world. Both self and the external environment must be included in any reasonable, sound understanding of what a situation is. Now we're ready to turn to a third way of defining situation, one that incorporates and goes beyond the positions of the first two perspectives.

The symbolic interactionist view of situation pays attention to both external phenomena and internal processes in individuals. From this theoretical perspective, *situations are constituted as processes, and factors unique to individuals lead them to select, order, and interpret disparate external circumstances to create patterns that are meaningful to them and that form foundations for their own communication.* Key to this definition is the word "constituted." We literally constitute or create situations in which we act. We define what they mean and act on the basis of the interpretation we have constructed.

From this perspective, we can realize that situations consist of selected aspects of the external world as organized and evaluated by individuals. According to this view, the significance (meaning) we attribute to a situation arises out of our perceptions. In turn, perceptions are influenced by events, objects, and people external to us. Yet, what we believe a situation to be is a matter of what we notice, how we organize and evaluate our impressions of those selected, discrete aspects of the world, and how we interpret their relationship to us as we have defined our own identities.

Consider the example at the beginning of this chapter. A series of statements described certain events and people. Which parts of the description did you particularly notice? If you were the person in that example, and if you really needed the job to earn money for school, you might have zeroed in on the fact that the order came from your supervisor and that you had to stay in good graces with her or him to keep your job for another 10 weeks. On the other hand, if you were working just for the experience and did not really need the money, those parts of the description would probably be less salient to you. If moral principles such as privacy and honesty are important to you, then you might have been most sensitive to the ethical dilemma involved in complying with your supervisor's directive. However, if you are someone who believes in chain-of-command and who thinks that following authority is an important virtue, you might not even think a serious ethical issue is involved here. Lots of other factors influence how you define this situation. For instance, past interactions with your supervisor or others in positions over you may influence how you perceive this particular circumstance.

But perception—selectively tuning into certain aspects of the scenario—is only part of the story. Once you select which aspects of the example to notice, you must still evaluate them. Would following the directive make you a "bad person" because to do so would conflict with your own values? Would you regard the supervisor as a "bad person" or regard the order as "inappropriate and unethical" because it violates your own moral code? Or perhaps you'd feel that you would be blameless if you carried out the instructions because you'd just be "following orders" of a superior. Maybe you'd feel that employees of your company shouldn't be dealing with competing firms, so if they are then they are "bad;" in this case, you might feel it was not only okay, but actually right for you to turn their mail over to your supervisor. Just from these few examples of the many ways you might interpret the example it is clear that there are different ways to define the situation and different meanings it could have for various people. How you select, order, and evaluate the phenomena in relation to yourself (your definition of your identity and your values) is the key to how you define this situation and what it means.

At this point in our discussion, you're probably beginning to appreciate the sophistication of the symbolic interactionist view of situation. Unlike the other two perspectives we examined, this one acknowledges the importance of both external phenomena and the self and seeks to understand how the two are related to create meanings upon which we understand and act. For symbolic interactionists, human interpretation is the vital link between what exists outside of us and what exists inside of us. Both sets of factors influence human interpretation. In turn, our interpretations influence both external and internal phenomena. Thus, our interpretive processes mediate external and internal factors to form our definitions of situations. This relationship can be graphically represented in Figure 3.1.

By focusing on interpretation as the thing that links internal and external phenomena, symbolic interactionism calls attention to the role of symbols in defining situations and directing our action within them. It is through symbols that we indicate to ourselves certain external factors and our own internal, personal responses to those factors. Herbert Blumer, a contemporary symbolic interactionist scholar, explains how we use symbols to define situations.[1]

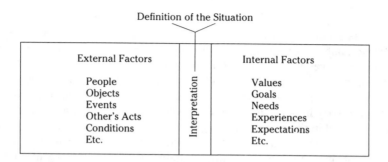

Figure 3.1. **Model of how we define situations.**

The individual human proceeds by pointing out to himself the divergent things which have to be taken into account in the course of his action. He has to note what he wants to do and how he is to do it; he has to point out to himself the various conditions which may be instrumental to his action and those which may obstruct his action; he has to take account of the demands, the expectations, the prohibitions and the threats as they may arise. . . . His action is built up step by step through a process of such self-indication. Self-indication is a moving, communicative process in which the individual notes things, assesses them, gives them meaning, and decides to act on the basis of the meaning.

As Blumer notes, only those phenomena that we indicate to ourselves become part of the situation that we perceive. Further, the labels we use to indicate what we've noticed influence how we feel about those phenomena. For example, when you meet someone for the first time you might define the person as a classmate, a stranger, a potential date, a possible friend, and so forth. Each way of symbolizing the other carries its own meaning and suggests particular courses of action toward that person. You might be somewhat extroverted, perhaps flirtatious with someone you've designated as a potential date; you might seriously discuss academic work with someone you've labeled as a classmate. In essence, each way of defining the other constitutes a different situation within which you act.

When we define situations, we direct our own actions in them. As we interpret external and internal factors and relate them, we indicate what they mean to us and what they imply for our behavior. If you define a situation as "mass lecture," you indicate to yourself your own appropriate role and behaviors—perhaps listening, taking notes, but not asking a lot of questions or trying to initiate discussion in the class. On the other hand, if you define a situation as an "intense seminar," you indicate a different role and range of appropriate behaviors for yourself—probably more vigorous interaction and more efforts to enter into discussion with other classmates. Consider another example. A friend and I have an ongoing disagreement about investing in the stock market. He regards it as foolish gambling and says any profits are pure luck and any losses are just what is deserved by someone frivolous enough to gamble on stocks. Part of his perspective is based on the turmoil his family suffered when his parents lost all of their savings in some bad investments, an event that created severe hardships during his adolescence. In contrast, I regard my small investments as a game of sorts. To me the point is not so much whether I make profits or lose money, but whether I get some fun out of selecting interesting companies that meet my ethical screens and seeing how they do over a period of time. I don't define what I'm doing as gambling and I don't define winning and losing as central to the activity. My view of investing is surely influenced by the fact that my mother was a leading broker early in her career and due to her skill in selecting sound investments, our family did well in the market. I also grew up hearing lively talk between my folks about different stocks and the interest in which ones to select. So, for me, investing in stocks is the intrigue and fun of playing the game. And my friend cannot understand how I could regard anything having to do with money as a game! It's the same external activity, but it means distinct things to the two of us and investing is quite literally a different situation for each of us. Our symbols define what the situation is for each of us and guide how we act in it.

Situation, then, is understood to mean the *interaction* between external and internal phenomena that we symbolically indicate to ourselves in order to organize and evaluate experience and to direct our actions. This view of situation implies that internal and external phenomena assume meaning *only as they are perceived and symbolized by individuals*. The pattern of meaning we create constitutes our definition of a situation.

We now have a good, basic understanding of what "situation" means within symbolic interactionist theory. With this foundation, let's now move to consider how specific elements and processes influence our definitions of situations. The next two portions of the the chapter focus on external aspects of situations. Later we examine internal processes, especially perception and motivation. Although it is necessary to separate internal and external phenomena in order to discuss and analyze them, remember that in reality they are intimately intertwined and they interact dynamically to produce our definitions of situations.

TYPES OF COMMUNICATION SITUATIONS

Communication situations may be classified in various ways. One popular and useful method categorizes them according to the number of people involved and the formality of communication that tends to characterize them. We consider four broad kinds of situation: intrapersonal, interpersonal and group, public, and mass. As we look at each one, we'll see how external aspects of it influence what it generally means to people.

Intrapersonal Communication Situations

Intrapersonal situations are ones that involve a single individual who communicates with herself or himself. Other people and events usually influence how an individual communicates, yet he or she is the only person actually involved in an intrapersonal situation. We engage in intrapersonal communication much of the time: when we muse, reflect on events and ourselves, deliberate about alternative courses of action, remember past experiences, and plan for future adventures. Through internal dialogues we organize our thoughts, consider different ways of looking at an issue, and decide what experiences we've had actually mean. Whether we're alone or surrounded by others, communication with ourselves takes place continuously. Any time we interact with others, we communicate with ourselves as well. As you talk with a friend, you interpret his words, ask yourself what he means by them and what the words mean to you, decide how you want to respond, and figure out the best way of expressing your ideas so that your friend is likely to interpret you as you intend. When you're listening to a class lecture, you attend to what the professor says, try to decide what she considers the most important information, and make notes to yourself highlighting her presentation. So even while you're interacting with someone else—a friend or a professor—you're simultaneously engaged in a complex process of intrapersonal communication.

Intrapersonal communication also occurs when others are not physically present. After a long day, you get home and reflect on what happened, whom you encountered, what significant conversations occurred, whether any important events happened, and how you handled a variety of experiences in your day. Thinking back over your day is a reflective, intrapersonal process through which you sort out experiences and decide which ones are important, what they mean, and what they imply for your future action. Frequently we use intrapersonal communication to plan interactions with others. In our minds we construct different scenarios of what might happen, we try out various ways of presenting and expressing ourselves, we estimate which ways of coming across are most likely to work, and we later use those in the actual situation we've been anticipating. Thus, intrapersonal communication allows us to have "dry runs" that help us plan our communication with others.

Although others are not directly involved in intrapersonal communication, we cannot say they're irrelevant to it. Others are pertinent to intrapersonal communication in two important ways. First, as the foregoing examples indicate, they are often the focus of our communication with ourselves—interpreting them, planning for interaction with them. Second, our history of interactions with others is part of how we think and how we interpret situations and events, so they are "imported" into our self communication. Sometimes when you think about how to handle a situation (intrapersonal communication), you draw on what you've learned from a friend who has dealt with a similar situation and you incorporate your friend's perspective into your own reflection. I remember that when my father was dying in 1986 I was very frightened and unsure of how to comfort and support him. I thought constantly about him and his pain, but I had no personal experience with death, so my own direct knowledge didn't help my intrapersonal communication very much. Fortunately, one of my good friends had more experience with death and dying and even with losing a parent, and much of what she told me of her experiences enriched my own intrapersonal consideration of what was happening and how I could respond most compassionately to my father.

Intrapersonal communication is one of the constant activities of humans. Alone or with others, we engage in self-communication. It is not only a private process through which we deal with our own experiences, but also the foundation of all forms of communication we have with others. In fact, no communication can occur without intrapersonal communication. Chapters 7 and 8 deal in depth with how each of us develops into unique and social beings and how our individual natures affect how we interpret experiences as well as how we communicate with others.

Interpersonal and Group Communication Situations

As the term suggests, interpersonal and group situations involve communication between two or more people. A wide range of situations are classified as interpersonal: casual conversation with friends, highly personal communication with romantic partners, heated conflict with a roommate, job interviews, jury deliberations, task group discussions, bull sessions, family meetings, conferences with doctors, and communication between people from different cultures.

Interpersonal and group situations may be formal (interview, courtroom cross-examination) or informal (rap sessions, gossiping); they may include social topics (who's doing what with whom this weekend) or task topics (deciding policy in a student government meeting or conferring with a professor to get guidance for writing a paper) or both; they may involve only two communicators or many. What is common to all interpersonal and group situations is the directness of interaction among people. Each person is able to address and respond to others in an immediate, personal manner. Because interpersonal and group communication situations involve a number of people engaged in direct interaction, communicators can adjust their style of talking and listening to each other very sensitively. This increases the probability that individual expectations will be met and misunderstandings will be limited. In a four person discussion, for instance, we can see when one person is confused or disturbed by something we said. The ability to see the other directly allows us to pick up feedback cues and to clarify our ideas or to ask the other person to explain the confused look. Immediate response and adaptation are possible because interaction is direct and the number of people involved is limited. So, what distinguishes interpersonal and group communication situations is participants' ability to interact directly with each other. Chapter 9 explores the dynamics of intimate communication while Chapter 10 provides a detailed look at the nature of group communication, and Chapter 13 examines interviewing communication.

Public Communication Situations

A third kind of situation involves a single "speaker" who interacts with an audience. Public discourse allows less direct, less personalized interaction between communicators. William Brooks points out that with a large audience, "it is not possible to know each specifically as an individual person as it is in the case of small group and dyadic situations."[2] Members of an audience cannot be treated as unique individuals, so communication necessarily is less direct and less personal.

Public discourse is additionally distinguished by the way communication is balanced among participants. One person is primarily responsible for preparing and presenting ideas. The other people (audience) are most concerned with listening. As we discovered in Chapter 2, it's not realistic to think of any communicator as only a speaker or listener since we are simultaneously both in all interactions. Nonetheless, the balance of who assumes which role is less even in public communication situations than in intrapersonal and group contexts. Thus, public discourse does not allow the personal, back-and-forth interaction characteristic of communication situations involving fewer people. Instead, in public communication, the "speaker" tries to interpret and adapt to impressions of a collectivity (the audience), rather than to individual listeners. Chapters 11 and 12 cover information on public discourse.

Mass Communication Situations

What is distinctive of mass communication situations is the way in which communicators interact. A speaker or speakers communicate with listeners indirectly through some intermediate means. Communicators do not interact face-to-face. Instead, whoever designs and expresses ideas uses a medium to reach whoever listens. Mass communication situations include television programs, radio broadcasts, films, books, magazines, posters, leaflets, and billboards. We do not directly attend to Connie Chung's news reports on television or to Dennis Quaid in a film. Rather, we see the parts and images of those people and their messages *as they have been edited by program personnel and specific viewing facilities.*

Listeners cannot respond directly to mass communication. Although we may talk back to Chung or to commercials, we are not communicating in any way with the sources of those messages. Thus, listeners' direct influence is fairly limited in mass communication situations. We still do have some power, just not an immediate one. We can, for instance, make a difference in whether a particular show is cancelled or renewed simply by our choices of whether to watch it and our letters to producers supporting renewal or cancellation. This delayed response is possible and important. Currently media specialists are working on devices that will allow viewers to rate programs as they watch, but even this sophisticated system can measure only very broad responses. In mass communication situations it's difficult to make adjustments in process, because communicators cannot interact directly and immediately with each other.

While we've separated these four kinds of communication situations for clarity, it's important to realize there is considerable ambiguity among them. For instance, at some point a large interpersonal situation blends into public communication. Sometimes we know another person so well that we can "talk to" that person in our heads, and sometimes that other person even knows what we're thinking—is this intrapersonal or interpersonal communication? Is a phone conversation an interpersonal situation because of its immediacy or a mass situation because the medium of phone lines, receivers, and transmitters intervenes between the communicators?

Probably it's most useful to think of these four classes of communication situations along general lines. Intrapersonal situations tend to be most personal, informal, and direct. Interpersonal situations tend to be personal, rather informal, direct, and interactive. Public situations tend to be less balanced in communicative roles and less interactive and more formal. And mass communication situations are generally impersonal and typically indirect. Within all of these situations—that is, in all types of communication—interaction may be verbal, nonverbal, or both and may involve people from a single or from several cultures.

Broad distinctions among types of situations provide one way to think about communication. The categories just discussed are descriptive means of classifying situations, and even broad description can be useful to organize our thinking. However, descriptive classification does not explain situations, nor does it assist our decisions of what and how to communicate in particular situations. To understand the complex, mutual influence between situations and communication, we need more information about the dimensions of various situations.

DIMENSIONS OF SITUATIONS

All communication situations have a number of dimensions that characterize them. While these dimensions don't rigidly determine what can occur, they do constrain the kinds of communication that seems appropriate and comfortable within particular circumstances. Effective choices about how to communicate depend on understanding important situational dimensions and what they imply for interaction. We consider three basic dimensions of communication situations: purpose, environment, and people, including relationships among them.

The Dimension of Purpose

Purpose is the situational dimension that most obviously influences communication. Purpose refers to both personal goals of communicators and public, or announced, purposes that are the stated reasons for interaction. Often the two kinds of purpose are consistent or, at least, compatible. For instance, if your goal in an interview is to demonstrate your qualifications to IBM and an IBM representative schedules an interview to screen applicants for an opening in the company, personal and public purposes coincide.

At other times, personal and public purposes may be inconsistent, sometimes even in conflict. Suppose you are interested in dating Person X, so you arrange to join X's Student Environmental Coalition. During meetings of the coalition your personal goal is to impress X favorably, but the public purpose is for the coalition to generate recommendations for enhancing environmental awareness on campus. In this case, your personal goal may well detract from the public one. In fact, you may have to choose between those two goals—should you support X's proposal in order to win X's favor and interest even though you disagree with X's position on an issue, or should you argue what you believe for the good of the committee and the integrity of its recommendations. Realizing that both personal and public goals coexist, sometimes harmoniously and sometimes oppositionally, certainly doesn't lead to any automatic resolution of potential conflicts between them. The understanding does, however, allow you to more clearly reflect on what is happening and to make more informed choices about your own course of action.

Each of us has goals whenever we communicate. We have reasons for talking with others.[3] Always present in any situation is our goal to define who we are and get confirmation of the self we've presented ourselves to be. This is the most pervasive and basic goal in all of our communication.[4] We may want to convince others we are intelligent, witty, attractive as a friend or date, experienced enough to provide assistance, a good person with certain values, and so on. From our discussion in Chapter 2 of two levels of meaning in communication, you've probably realized that the goal of defining self is one that occurs primarily on the relational level of meaning. If you want to be seen as witty, then having others laugh at your jokes counts as confirmation. If you want to be seen as intelligent and experienced in an area, then confirmation may be measured by whether others seek you out for advice and follow it. Being aware of your personal goals in situations is important. It allows you to analyze their fit or lack of fit with public goals, and it allows you to monitor your communication so that it does not interfere with public goals that are present in a setting.

Our personal goals influence how we define a situation and how we direct our own communication within the situation as we have defined it. Think back to the example that opened this chapter. Assume your personal goal in taking the summer job was to earn money *essential* to your continuing school in the fall. Given that objective, you may define the situation as one beyond your control, define your supervisor as "knowing more than I do about what is proper protocol in this company," and define yourself as "low person on the totem pole and not in a position to buck authority." Now consider an alternate scenario. Suppose you have a longstanding friendship with a junior executive in the company and you know she is corresponding with a competing firm. She is, in fact, the person who landed the summer job for you, so you feel some loyalty to her. Your goal may be to maintain the friendship, to repay the favor your friend did for you, to protect your friend from being "discovered" by the supervisor, and to demonstrate that you are a loyal friend. Given this set of objectives, you might define the situation as one you can control (after all, since you sort the mail, who will know if you don't turn in people who correspond with competing firms?), define the supervisor as a busybody who is inappropriately interfering in employees' business and interfering with free enterprise, and define yourself as both loyal to your friend and a defender of the American right to privacy. Both definitions of the situations and the consequent choices of action are tied to your personal goals and the way you define yourself. This makes the point that how we interpret events, persons, and circumstances inevitably is influenced by our own goals, values, and definitions of ourselves.

In addition to personal goals, situations have public purposes. Naturally, our interpretation of public purpose is mediated by our personal goals. Despite this subjective influence, however, we can still recognize public purposes that characterize situations and that imply what kinds of communication are appropriate and out of bounds. While public purposes are not always explicitly announced, they do invariably exist in communication situations. A task group has the purpose of making decisions, considering information, offering recommendations, or crafting policy. A mixer or party has the purpose of passing time pleasantly or getting to know and interact with others. A funeral's purpose is to honor the deceased and to comfort the surviving friends and family. A wedding's purpose is to celebrate a couple's commitment to being together long term and to add to their sene of festivity and joy. An interview's purpose is to let interviewer and interviewee assess each other.

The purpose of a situation suggests what kinds of communication are appropriate and what kinds are off limits. Erving Goffman, who has studied social organization, says "occasions possess a distinctive ethos, a spirit, an emotional structure that must be properly created, sustained and laid to rest, the participant finding that he is obligated to become caught up in the occasion, whatever his personal feelings."[5] Goffman's point is that people get caught up in the public purpose of situations and adapt their ways of communicating to the demands inherent in it. In a sense, we enter already existing, already defined situations and must accommodate ourselves to them. Later, we may choose to communicate in ways that attempt to alter the public purpose of the situation, but initially we need to recognize and fit within the situation in which we find ourselves.

Understanding public purposes helps us to figure out what we are supposed to say, what we are allowed to say, and what we cannot prudently say. In a business conference, for instance, a few social amenities are appropriate, but extensive social conversation is not. The purpose of a celebration calls for good will, lively conversation, friendly interaction; arguments, intense debates, and depressing topics are inconsistent with the situational purpose. In task group discussions a general rule for participation operates, so longwinded monologues are inappropriate and generally unappreciated. An after-dinner speech is expected to be somewhat light and entertaining, so a serious, heavily documented presentation is likely to meet with resistance from listeners. All of these examples illustrate the influence of public purpose on communication in particular settings. Thus, situations may be thought of as "waiting systems" into which we enter.[6] To communicate effectively, we must identify both our personal goals and the operant public purpose and then figure out what these imply for our communicative choices.

The Dimension of Environment

As we saw in Chapter 2, communication is system. This means that it occurs within a system or an environment, and that environment influences the dynamics of interaction. The environmental dimension of situations refers to physical aspects of the system that constrain the communication that takes place. Some homes seem cozy, while others feel cold; some offices exude an air of formality and seriousness while others have a much more casual, light atmosphere. Upper scale restaurants typically provide diners with ample space and privacy as well as low lighting and music, all of which encourage patrons to linger (and to spend more money); fast food eateries, on the other hand, feature cramped seating with little privacy or other inducements to stay. Warmth, formality, and privacy are primary qualities that define a communicative environment.[7] These qualities—our sense of them—are created by physical features in settings. Plants, oil-rubbed furniture arranged in small, intimate groupings, mellow colors, and soft music tend to make a setting seem warm, relaxed, and appropriate for personal conversation. By contrast, steel shelving, straight-backed plastic chairs, walls painted in "institutional beige," and linoleum floors impart a feeling of coldness, formality, and rather impersonal interaction.

The environments in which we communicate can significantly affect our feelings. According to Albert Mehrabian, a noted environmental psychologist, environments can arouse in us feelings such as anger, fear, boredom, pleasure, and interest.[8] Based on his extensive research, Mehrabian believes that we respond, often unconsciously, to the many features in physical environments; in fact, he thinks what we think, feel, and say as well as how we express ourselves can be keenly affected by the setting in which we find ourselves. In his book, *Public Places, Private Spaces,* Mehrabian shows how behavior and communication are influenced by subtle environmental features such as color, space, temperature, light, odor, and noise.

The environmental dimension of situations has clear implications for our communication. Physical features can invite or preclude certain kinds of interaction. A rap session seems inappropriate in a formal conference room. A stiff lecture is out of place in a warm, informal setting. Personal disclosure would be awkward in a crowded social scene. In these examples, what feels appropriate to communicate is constrained by the environments.

In other cases an environment may be deliberately selected or created to advance particular communication goals. A person who invites good friends into a home for a relaxed evening may dim lights and rearrange furniture to invite comfortable, easy interaction. A group leader who wants to encourage balanced participation among members may place chairs in a circle where there is no "head seat." Managers of fast food restaurants create cold, nonprivate environments to encourage rapid turnover of customers, which is important to making a profit. So, the relationship between environment and communication is reciprocal. The physical features of situations influence communication and are influenced by communicators' goals. Understanding how certain environmental features tend to influence communication allows us to make informed choices about the settings we select for communication and to have insight into why we act as we do in particular situations.

The Dimension of Persons and Relationships

Just as purpose and environment influence our definitions of situations, so do our perceptions of others. The third dimension of communication situations concerns the number of people who are present and the relationships among them and between us and them.

The number of people in a situation can dramatically affect the form and content of communication that occurs. Much research in this area shows that the size of a group is an important influence on interaction among members. Groups of five or seven members tend to have the most balanced participation among members and to result in the greatest satisfaction with group process. Fewer than five members tends to make a group too close so that members may feel uneasy expressing views that are not shared by the few other members. Yet, once there are more than seven people in a group, communication tends to become less balanced, so that a few members wind up dominating discussion while others cannot get a word in edgewise. Increasing group size, then, reduces opportunities for members to contribute.[9]

The number of people present also affects interaction in social situations. Generally, as the number of people increases, the depth of conversation decreases. For instance, large mixers, cocktail parties and receptions are known for the superficial conversations that occur. Small dinner parties or get-togethers of just a few people, on the other hand, promote more intensive, sustained conversation. This generalization also applies to what happens in your classes. From personal experience, you know it's virtually impossible to have any personal interaction with an instructor in a 300-person class that proceeds via mass lecture. Yet in a small class of 15 to 25 students you and others are able to bring up issues and ideas that interest you and to have your instructor respond directly to you and your comments. So we know that the number of people in a situation influences the depth, quality, and amount of communication.

Relationships among people in a situation are a second influence on communication. The relationships among communicators can be thought of in terms of similarity, intimacy, and power. Each of these aspects of relationship influences how we feel about ourselves, others, and situations and, thus, how we communicate.

Disraeli is reported to have defined an agreeable person as "one who agrees with me." There's more than a grain of truth to Disraeli's humorous observation that we prefer to communicate with people we perceive as similar to us in basic respects—age, attitudes, race, class, and so on.[10] Similarities provide common ground for communicators, and they increase the chance that interaction will be mutually interesting and rewarding. At professional meetings colleagues discuss shared concerns, projects of common interests, and mutual goals. Neighborhood get-togethers frequently involve conversation about safety, real estate values, protective covenants, taxes, and needs for beautification—topics of common concern to folks living in a community. College mixers invite talk about campus activities, local happenings and places, sports, majors, and other subjects that are part of the daily lives of students. So similarity with others gives us "built-in" communication topics. In addition, shared assumptions and values usually underlie the surface similarities, and these further ease interaction.

Communication tends to be more awkward and less comfortable when people perceive themselves as dissimilar. A 10-year-old starting classes in a new school, for instance, may feel unable to talk with classmates, because he has not yet learned the norms, activities, and basic social rules of his new environment. Factory workers often complain that company executives do not know how to talk with them. The sense of difference between workers and executives breeds discomfort and distrust so that communication is often stiff and guarded. In professional situations women are often perceived as different from their male peers. They are regarded as unlike other professionals and frequently find themselves suffering from exclusion, inattention, and lack of collegial support, all of which isolate them from the crux of organizational communication.[11] Perceived similarity among communicators, then, is an important aspect of communication situations. It influences both amount and type of talk and, in turn, talk between people influences their perceptions of similarities among them.

In addition to similarity, intimacy is a major aspect of the overall relationship among people in communication situations. The warmth, trust, and closeness people feel toward one another profoundly affects the kind of communication that occurs. As we come to feel close to another person and we learn to trust them, our communication becomes increasingly disclosive, informal, smooth, and satisfying.[12] We feel it is safe to be open, honest, and spontaneous with close friends and romantic partners, because we've learned from prior interaction to trust them to accept and not exploit feelings and ideas we' express. As trust grows, so do both pleasure and interest in communicating with another.

A third important aspect of the relationship between communicators is power. Power can be thought of as the ability to influence others and to resist their efforts to influence us. To the extent that you can influence others to do what you want and you feel free not to comply with what they want from you, then you have power.[13] Sometimes communicators have equal power in situations, while at other times power is imbalanced. Research on the relationship between power and communication reveals some interesting connections.[14] We know that powerful individuals talk more than those with less power, and powerful people are talked to more and listened to more closely than people with less power. In business settings top-flight executives tend to state their opinions frequently and freely while employees with less status make fewer comments and usually phrase their ideas more tentatively. We also know that people with less status are likely to support ideas and proposals by high power individuals; the converse is not true. In groups, powerful members can exert a disproportionate amount of influence on collective decisions. Obviously this can create problems, not the least of which is hindering the quality of group decisions. Because power can be used against us, we are often reluctant to be entirely candid with those who have some control over us—our jobs, our grades, or other opportunities we value. One implication of these findings is that if you want to encourage open communication, it is important to minimize power imbalances among people in a situation.

Gender also plays a role in how we perceive and interact with others. It is well established that there are notable differences in how women and men communicate, and these differences can affect both our senses of similarity and power in a situation.[15] One study I conducted, for instance, revealed that men and women perceive and respond to intimate crises in quite different ways. While men tended to define the crisis as a fault in their partners or external circumstances, women were more likely to see a crisis as resulting from problems in the relationship itself—the interaction processes of the couple. These differences in how the sexes perceived crises were compounded by their distinctive ways of responding to relationship problems. Women tended to want to communicate about the problem, to resolve it, and to nourish the relationship. Men, on the other hand, reported preferring to ignore or avoid dealing with problems and/or to rely on various types of laws or normative rules for deciding what to do (for instance, one man said that he couldn't leave his marriage because children were involved and children need both parents).[16] The gender-associated differences in how crises are defined and dealt with can create awkwardness, because men and women may feel they are so dissimilar in what they perceive and in what they feel is appropriate to do about problems.

We also know that in conversations—whether in professional, social, or intimate settings—men tend to dominate. Compared to women, men talk more often, talk for longer periods of time, interrupt more, and are unresponsive to others' communication. These behaviors can create an imbalance in power in which women are dismissed, ignored, or made to feel unvalued in conversation.[17] The distinctive ways in which women and men tend to interpret and respond to communication will be discussed in more detail in Chapters 7, 8, and 9.

So far our discussion has focused on basically "objective" features of situations. We distinguished four broad types of communication situations: intrapersonal, interpersonal, public, and mass. Next, we explored how environment, purpose, and persons and relationships comprise dimensions of situations that affect the amount and kind of communication that is likely to occur. As we saw at the beginning of this chapter, however, the symbolic interactionist view of communication incorporates both objective and subjective features of situations to understand what they mean to individuals. For this reason, we should now turn our attention to the ways in which we as individuals influence the situations in which we communicate. Let's move on to consider how our perceptions and interpretations influence understanding and behavior in various settings.

PERCEIVING SITUATIONS

Objective features such as those we've examined exist, but they have no meaning until people perceive and interpret them. An audience of 20 seems large to one person, yet small to another. A room perceived as elegant by one individual may appear stuffy to another. The actual size of the audience and design of the room are constant and "objective," but they are perceived distinctly by different people. And how we perceive a situation *is* the reality of the situation for us. In other words, the meaning we attribute to a situation depends not so much on what is "outside" of us, but more on what is "inside" of us—our tendencies to interpret and define phenomena around us. There is a constant interaction between us as perceivers and what we perceive, and it is this interaction that defines what we regard as our situation. To put it another way, we cannot understand what a situation is to someone by identifying what features exist in the situation or that person's perceptual tendencies or even both of these. It is the *interaction* between us and the external world that constitutes the situations in which we act.[18]

To better understand how this interaction occurs and how it defines situations, we need to explore the nature of human perception. Perception is a process by which we select, organize, and interpret sensations and phenomena in order to make them meaningful to us. To understand how perception operates and how it pertains to communication, we'll examine three of the most important influences on human perception: experiences, expectations, and motivations.

Experiences and Perception

Our stored experiences are major influences on our perceptions. To interpret any situation, event, person, or communication we draw upon what we have experienced and learned in prior interactions. We make assumptions about a particular phenomenon on the basis of our previous experiences, especially those that we regard as similar to our current circumstances. A gourmet cook can detect the slightest spice in an intricate dish. A physician notes minor variations in skin tone that would go unseen by laypersons. A mechanic hears motor vibrations and has a good idea of what they mean while most of us wouldn't even notice the vibration was there. A seasoned mountain climber is sensitive to minute changes in oxygen level that vary with height above sea level. This acute awareness enhances survival for changes in oxygen can promote hypothermia, and that can be life-threatening. Someone who has followed a particular group's music assiduously will recognizes subtle changes in style, arrangement, and theme that a nonfan simply doesn't hear. In each case, the ability to perceive particular stimuli is based on specialized past experiences that make certain people astute perceivers.

Personal experiences provide a frame of reference which we use to interpret current situations, events, and people. A child whose first encounters with teachers were negative may perceive future teachers as mean or arbitrary and may be turned against education. People who grew up in an environment of traditional male and female roles often speak disdainfully of mothers who work outside of the home and of men who do housework, because both of these activities violate those traditional sex roles. Many people witnessed destructive conflict in their families and so learned to perceive conflict as inherently bad and to avoid it at all costs. We sort through our storehouse of personal experiences (generally without awareness of doing so) to make sense of phenomena and interactions we encounter. Clearly this is helpful in providing us with a framework—a way of organizing and understanding what is happening in our lives. Yet it can also blind us to seeing possibilities beyond those we have experienced in the past. Our discussion of language in Chapter 2 elaborated how our ways of symbolizing things both facilitate and limit our understandings.

Of course, perceptions and even experiences are not entirely individualistic. As symbolic interaction theory maintains, we are unique individuals and simultaneously members of a common culture. Our place in a shared social order—our culture—guarantees that we will have many experiences and perceptual inclinations similar to others in our society. Thus, membership in any culture influences what and how we perceive. Americans brought up with democratic ideas are likely to have negative perceptions of authoritarian leaders. In contrast, people socialized in a dictatorial political system might have more positive perceptions of authoritarian leaders and might, in fact, regard democratic leaders as weak. Most of us would be offended if we were kept waiting an hour by someone with whom we had an appointment. In Latin America, however, a one or two hour delay is considered normal and entirely polite. In Western society kissing is considered appropriate in casual relationships, while in many Eastern cultures it is a statement of intimacy and serious intent. Americans tend to regard as barbaric the Eskimo custom of leaving old people in failing health on ice floats to die, yet the Eskimo think our system of preserving life to the last possible moment, regardless of the pain of the dying person, is cruel and simply extends the pain of dying. Every culture contains numerous rules, definitions, and values, and the bulk of these are internalized by members of a culture. For each of us, then, being part of a particular society predisposes us toward particular assumptions, values, beliefs, and ways of perceiving a broad range of experiences.

Once again we find that gender has to be taken into account in our thinking about how experience in a culture influences perception. Within many societies, including our own, men and women are socialized into cultures that are distinct in important ways. One scholar, Fern Johnson, maintains that in America males and females are socialized in such substantially different ways that we must understand them as growing up in literally different cultures—different systems of thought, values, norms, and codes of behavior.[19] From birth, females are generally taught to attend to others and relationships and to define themselves in ways that emphasize deferring to and caring for others. Males, by contrast, are socialized to be independent, and to define themselves as assertive and powerful in relation to others. One implication of this is that women are more likely than men to perceive relationship issues and to be particularly sensitive to them. It's also the case that because women's socialization emphasizes relatedness, they tend to perceive overlaps and interaction among their experiences. So a woman is likely to perceive connections between what is happening in a family crisis and the issues that come up in her friendships. Men, typically socialized to be independent and to differentiate experiences, are more likely to compartmentalize various things happening in their lives into distinct spheres. Thus, what happens in one part of a man's life may be perceived as entirely unrelated to other aspects of his world. We'll discuss the differences more fully in Chapter 7.[20] For now it is important that you realize only that males' and females' membership in Western society does not necessarily mean they have similar socialization and, thus, it doesn't mean that they will reflect common understanding of American culture.

Experience is a primary influence on how we perceive and interpret communication situations. Each of us has unique personal experiences as well as a set of experiences that are shared by most members of our society. Together these experiences form a filter through which we interpret our worlds and the people and events comprising them. Thus, our perception of phenomena, including ourselves, others, and communication are strongly influenced by years of participation in personal and cultural systems.

Expectations and Perception

Expectations are a second significant influence on what and how we perceive. We tend to perceive what we expect to perceive. Of course, this is related to our previous discussion of experience in that our expectations are based in large part on what we've learned to expect based on our past experiences.

A classic experiment dramatically illustrated the influence of expectations on perception. The researcher, Siipola, told some people they would see a series of words related to animals. Other participants in the experiment were told they would see a series of words pertaining to seafaring. Then both groups were shown the following nonsense terms for just a few seconds:

WHARL   SAEL   DACK

Those participants who had been primed to think they'd see words about animals reported seeing the words whale, seal, and duck, while those who'd been told the words would be about seafaring reported seeing the words as wharf, sail, and deck.[21] In each case, the people perceived what they expected to perceive.

Expectations frequently affect our perceptions. In one study, racially prejudiced and unprejudiced individuals were show pictures of Afro Americans and Caucasians. The prejudiced viewers perceived exaggerated racial characteristics such as broadness of nose and fullness of lips when looking at photographs of Afro-Americans. The unprejudiced viewers did not especially perceive these features in the pictures. The prejudiced viewers' stereotyped expectations distorted what they saw.[22]

All of us have stereotypes and expectations that influence what we perceive and what meaning we assign to it. If you've heard that a professor is interesting and excellent, you're more likely to be impressed by the professor than if what you've heard leads you to expect a dull, boring teacher. If you believe someone dislikes you, it's likely you'll perceive disapproval and hostility in that person's communication with you. If you go to a party expecting to have a good time, you're likely to do that; and if you go expecting to be bored, you're likely to find the party dull and not worth your time. In perceiving the world we tend to confirm our own expectations of what we think is out there. We may fail to notice what we don't expect to find. It's equally likely that we'll perceive some things that aren't really there because we anticipate they will be.

The role of expectations in perceptions highlights once again our own primary role in constructing the reality of our lives.

Motivations and Perception

Motivations are a third major influence on perception. Our desires and needs affect what we perceive. You've probably heard of the mirage phenomenon in which very thirsty people, perhaps ones stranded in a desert, "see" an oasis of water although no water is really there. The need for water is so great that it distorts people's perceptions. The same phenomenon occurs in less dramatic ways in our everyday lives. Neutral pictures shown to hungry people are interpreted as photographs of food.[23] If you need a friend you're more likely to perceive a new acquaintance as friendly and trustworthy than you are if you are not so needy for someone to be close to. In war, combat soldiers need to perceive the enemy as bad, evil, even inhuman in order to engage in killing. The student who receives no bid from The campus fraternity or sorority may thereafter perceive the brothers as snobbish, boring, or otherwise undesirable. When driving most of us don't routinely notice the array of billboards that litter the highway. Yet, if we're hungry we'll see the signs for restaurants, and if we're tired we're likely to see the advertisements for motels. What we need and want influences our perceptions. Since people have differing needs and desires (motives), they have diverse perceptions of situations.

Human perception, then, is not by any means an objective process of taking in situations as they exist. Rather, our perceptions are influenced by our experiences, expectations, and motivations in given situations. The result is that people have different—sometimes dramatically different—perceptions of what a situation is or of what is happening in it. It is pointless to argue about what something *Really* is, since each person's perception constitute what is real to her or him. Generally, it's more constructive to try to understand (understand—not argue or correct) others' perceptions and why they are as they are. We can learn a lot by adopting this stance toward those whose perceptions differ from our own.

The central theme of our discussion is that perceptions are best understood as personal interpretations of situations. Objects, events, people, and situations have no intrinsic or "true" meanings. Instead, their meanings are constructed by us—by the way we perceive them. Yet, from a symbolic interactionist perspective, we understand that perceptions do not reflect only unique, subjective views of individuals. Perceptions arise out of interaction between what is inside us and what is outside of us. We know the world and our experiences through interaction with people and phenomena external to us, and we filter all of that through our storehouse of experiences, expectations, and motivations to define what situations are.

PERCEPTION, COMMUNICATION, AND DEFINING SITUATIONS

Let's now pull together all that we've considered about situations and perception, all that we've discussed about influences inside of us and those outside of us. A primary implication of what we've explored is that the meaning we construct forms our definition of a situation. In turn, how we define a situation is the basis for our choices of how to act and communicate.

Defining a situation is a personal, creative act. John Condon likens the process to that of editing films.[24]

> We, no less than the editor or director, are performing a creative act; we are not merely taking in or presenting 'what is there.' We select, we disregard, we focus. . . we offer a point of view, a tacit judgment of what is to be regarded as important and not important.

Communication and defining situations are parts of a dynamic system in which each influences the other. How we define a situation affects our communication in it and, simultaneously, our communication in a given setting influences our evolving definition of that setting. To conclude our examination of how we define situations, we'll focus on each part of this dynamic system.

How Communication Defines Situations

Words define situations. Whether we actually speak or simply think, we rely on symbols to label, organize, and evaluate the collage of sensations that bombard us. Once we label a situation in a particular way, we limit what we perceive. It becomes difficult for us to see the situation in any alternative way. In effect, then, the symbols we use to define a situation create that situation as we know it. They constitute what it is and what it means to us.

The "reality" of a situation—what it means to us—arises from our communication, from the symbols we use to label our experiences. In essence, we can know reality only through our symbols. Thus, we do not have direct knowledge of situations, and there is no possibility that humans can be objective in what they perceive. Instead, what we know, feel, and experience is indirect knowledge that is mediated by our symbols and the values they reflect.

How Symbols Influence Perceptions[25]

How accurate is eyewitness testimony? A series of studies suggests that what witnesses think they saw depends in part on the language used by attorneys who question witnesses.

Elizabeth Loftus filmed a traffic accident and then asked viewers of the film some questions about what they had just seen. Some viewers were asked, "How fast were the cars going when they *smashed* into each other?" Other viewers were asked, "How fast were the cars going when the *bumped* into each other?" Viewers consistently reported they had seen the cars going at higher speeds when the question contained the word *smashed* than when it contained the word *bumped*. The estimates of speed varied significantly even though all viewers had seen the identical film.

In a separate experiment Loftus again had people view a film of a traffic accident. After watching it, viewers filled out a questionnaire that contained three questions about things that had actually been in the film and three questions about things that were not in the film. For half of the viewers the questions began with the phrase, "Did you see *the*. . . (broken headlight, turn signal, etc)?" For the other half of the viewers, the questions began with the phrase, "Did you see a. . .?" Those viewers asked questions with the key word "the" more frequently reported having seen the item in question than did those viewers asked questions with the key word "a". This happened regardless of whether the item actually appeared in the film. Loftus reasoned that the word "the" suggests definiteness, but the word "a" suggests indefiniteness.

Even such minor variations in word choices as those in Loftus' research demonstrate that the symbols we use to describe experience actually can define the experience for us.

In Loftus' studies viewers "saw" the accident through the symbols used to describe it. Their responses to how fast cars were going and what items were present were not as much a matter of what really existed as of what the symbols they associated with what they saw defined their perception.

The same is true for all of us in everyday life. We perceive our experiences through the symbols we use to describe it. This means that language is extraordinarily powerful. It defines our world, others, experiences, and ourselves—it fundamentally influences our understanding of what they are. That's why politicians, advertisers, and social activists are so careful in what language they use to describe issues. One contemporary controversy in which language is very important is abortion. Those who disapprove of abortion label themselves "pro-life" and, by implication, label those who support abortion as "anti-life," "killers," and so forth. Those who support legalization of abortion consistently argue they are "not anti-life, but pro-choice." The labels we use to describe those on each side of this issue surely influence our perceptions of abortion and those who favor and oppose its legal status.

Academic research and our own experiences, however, are not the only demonstrations of the power of language to influence our perceptions of situations. One of the best examples of how language defines situations comes from the tall tales of Mark Twain. In his chronicle of Tom Sawyer's adventures Twain tells us that on a hot, lazy Saturday afternoon Tom's Aunt Polly "sentenced" him to whitewash a long fence, a task that Tom realized would ruin his entire day. To make matters worse, some of Tom's friends came around and began ridiculing him for having to do such domestic work. Then an inspiration hit Tom. He invented a scheme to escape the chore. When one of his chums happened by and taunted Tom about having to work on a Saturday, Tom asserted "I'm not working at all. Whitewashing a fence is a rare privilege and a responsibility that not just everyone can manage." Afterall, Tom explained, it's not everyday a boy gets to whitewash a whole fence! Tom's ploy worked. He convinced his friend that the chore was fun and an exceptional opportunity that anyone would be lucky to have. By the end of the day the fence had three full coats of pain, not a one of which Tom had put on it. Furthermore, Tom realized a nice profit because he charged them for "the privilege" of whitewashing. Tom redefined the situation. He used language to influence how others' perceived the situation and transformed it from a nasty task to a privilege.

While few of us have Tom's ingenuity or ability to manipulate language so adroitly, we all define situations just by the language we use to describe them to ourselves and others. Each symbol we select implies a particular focus, a distinct view of reality, a way of perceiving a situation. This is inevitable since language is inherently value-laden. Nonetheless, it's important that we realize just how powerful our language is in shaping our perceptions. It's also essential that we not become imprisoned by language that locks us into restrictive perceptions and impairs our ability to see alternate ways of understanding people and situations.[26]

How Defining Situations Affects Communication

Earlier we noted that the relationship between communication and defining situations is systemic and dynamic. So far we've focused on how language defines situations. Now it's time to flip the coin and consider how our definitions of situations influence our communication.

When we define a situation we direct our attitudes and our communication. Our definition establishes the basis for how we act in a situation. Thus, our behaviors, especially our communication, are not so much responses to the "objective" situation as they are responses to the symbols we've employed to define it to ourselves. Elaborating this, a psychologist Carl Rogers explains that individuals react to their worlds as they experience and perceive them and "thus, the perceptual world is, for the individual, 'reality'."[27] The only reality to which we can respond is the one we have defined with our symbols. That *is* our reality.

RESPONDING TO OUR LABELS FOR EMOTIONS[28]

In order for the other's behaviour to become part of self's experience, self must perceive it. The very act of perception entails interpretation. . . .

Let's take, for example, a situation in which a husband begins to cry. The behaviour is crying. This behaviour must now be experienced by his wife. It cannot be experienced without being interpreted. The interpretation will vary greatly from person to person, from culture to culture. For Jill, a man crying is inevitably to be interpreted as a sign of weakness. For Jane, a man crying will be interpreted as a sign of sensitivity. Each will react to a . . . preconceived model which she may or may not be aware of. At its simplest level, Jill may have been taught by her father that a man never cries, that only a sissy does. Jane may have been taught by her father that a man can show emotion and that he is a better man for having done so.

In this example Jill and Jane have label crying differently. Jill defines it as weakness, so she sees the man as weak and responds to him with disdain. Jane defines it is representing sensitivity, so she sees the man as sensitive and responds to him with compassion, acceptance, and respect. The important point is that neither Jane nor Jill can respond to the crying itself. They cannot respond directly to the behavior. They can only respond to their definitions of what is happening—showing weakness or sensitivity.

How we define situations influences our choices of how and what to communicate and how to interpret what others say and do. For instance, a person who defines a job evaluation as threatening may communicate in guarded or hostile ways and may perceive questions from a supervisor as attacks. Couples who define disagreements as "me versus you" virtually ensure they cannot reach some mutually satisfying resolution. In contrast, couples who regard disagreements as "our problem that we have to handle" are likely to communicate in ways that are cooperative and mutually supportive. Similarly research demonstrates that couples whose talk and thought focuses on problems, flaws, and disappointments in their relationship tend to see the relationship more negatively than couples who do not so consistently define problems as salient, and this is true regardless of the extent of problems a couple has.[29] To the old question, "Is the glass half full or half empty?" the answer is clearly "It is both—which way do you choose to define it?" And how you answer that is very important, since the way you define any situation will shape what it is for you.

Communication and situational definition interact dynamically. Communication is the genesis of situational definition—it is our way of labeling what something is. In turn, the definition we choose influences our choices of how to communicate and how we interpret the communication of others. This dynamic, systemic interaction is ongoing—as we define and redefine our experiences, we constantly reshape our universe and our actions within it.

SUMMARY

In this chapter we've explored the complex relationship between how we communicate and how we define situations. While situations do have some "objective" or empirical qualities such as type and dimensions, these features become meaningful to us only as we perceive and interpret them. To do that we rely on our symbols, which reflect our experiences, expectations, and motivations.

Neither the objective situation nor our subjective filters account for how we define situations. Instead, it is the interaction between us and the world "out there" that constitutes our definition of what a situation is and, therefore, of how we will communicate within it. In essence, our communication—intrapersonal and with others—constructs and reflects the situations in which we act. To understand more fully the critical role of symbols in defining situations, we need to explore the peculiarly human condition of living in a symbolic world. That is the focus of the next chapter.

REFERENCES

[1] H. Blumer, *Symbolic Interactionism: Perspective and Method.* Englewood Cliffs, NJ: Prentice-Hall, 1969, p. 81.

[2] W. Brooks, *Speech Communication.* Dubuque, IA: Wm. C. Brown, 1974, p. 11.

[3] G.M. Phillips and J. T. Wood, *Communication and Human Relationships.* New York: Macmillan, 1983, Chapter 3.

[4] G.M. Phillips and J.T. Wood, Chapter 3.

[5] E. Goffman, *Behavior in Public Places.* New York: Free Press, 1963, pp. 4-5.

[6] J.F. Wilson and C C. Arnold, *Public Speaking as a Liberal Art, 3rd ed.* Boston: Allyn and Bacon, 1974, p. 11.

[7] M. L. Knapp, *Social Intercourse: From Greeting to Goodbye.* Boston: Allyn and Bacon, 1978, pp. 72-73.

[8] A. Mehrabian, *Public Places, Private Spaces: The Psychology of Work, Play, and Living Environments.* New York: Basic Books, 1976, p. 8.

[9] J. T. Wood, G. M. Phillips, and D. J. Pedersen, *Group Discussion, 2nd ed.* New York: Harper and Row, 1976, Chapter 2.

[10] S. Brehm, *Intimate Relationships.* New York: Random, 1985, pp. 70-75.

[11] R. M. Kanter, "Numbers: Minorities and Majorities," in *Men and Women of the Corporation.* New York: Harper, 1977, pp. 206-241; J. T. Wood and C. R. Conrad, "Paradox in the Experiences of Professional Women," *Western Journal of Speech Communication, 47*, 1983, 305-322.

[12] Phillips and Wood, Chapters 6-8.

[13] Brehm, pp. 226-257.

[14] Wood, Phillips and Pedersen, pp. 43-45.

[15] Kanter; Wood and Conrad.

[16] J. T. Wood, "Different Voices in Relationship Crises: An Extension of Gilligan's Theory," *American Behavioral Scientist, 29,* 1986, 273-301.

[17] B. Bate, *Communication and the Sexes.* New York: Harper, 1988, Chapter 4.

[18] H. Cantril, "Perception and Interpersonal Relations," *American Journal of Psychiatry, 38,* 1957, 119-126; Blumer.

[19] F. Johnson, "Women's Culture and Communication: An Analytical Perspective." In C. Lont and S. Friedley (Eds.), *Beyond Boundaries: Sex and Gender Diversity in Communication.* Fairfax, VA: George Mason Univ. Press, 1989, pp. 301-316.

[20] C. Gilligan, *In a Different Voice: Psychological Theory and Women's Development.* Cambridge: Harvard University Press, 1982; Brehm; N. Chodorow, *The Reproduction of Mothering.* Berkeley: University of CA, Press, 1978; J.B. Miller, *Toward a New Psychology of Women.* Boston: Beacon, 1976.

[21] E. M. Siipola, "A Study of Some Effects of Preparatory Set," *Psychological Monographs, 46,* 1935, 27-38.

[22] P. F. Secord, W. Bevan, and B. Katz, "The Negro Stereotype and Perceptual Accentuation," *Journal of Abnormal and Social Psychology, 54,* 1956, 78-83.

[23] R. N. Sanford, "The Effects of Abstinence from Food Upon Imaginal Processes: A Further Experiment," *Journal of Psychology, 3,* 1937, 145-159.

[24] J. C. Condon, Jr., *Interpersonal Communication.* New York: Macmillan, 1977.

[25] R. J. Trotter, "The Truth, The Whole Truth and Nothing But. . .," *Science News, 108,* October 25, 1975, 269.

[26] P. Watzlawick, J. Weakland, and R. Fisch, *Change.* New York: W. W. Norton, 1974.

[27] C. Rogers, *Client Centered Therapy.* Boston: Houghton Mifflin, 1951, p. 484.

[28] R. D. Laing, H. Phillipson, and A. R. Lee, *Interpersonal Perception: A Theory and Method of Research.* New York: Harper and Row, 1966, pp. 14-15.

[29] Brehm, Chapter 11.

CHAPTER 4

LANGUAGE AS A FOUNDATION OF HUMAN COMMUNICATION

In this human world the faculty of speech
occupies a central place. We must, therefore,
understand what speech means in order to
understand the "meaning" of the universe.

(Ernst Cassirer)

Signals and Symbols

  Signals
  Symbols
    Symbols are arbitrary
    Symbols are ambiguous
    Symbols are abstract

Human Communication as Symbolic Interaction

Implications of Symbolic Interactionism

  Symbols define
  Symbols organize
  Symbols evaluate
  Symbols construct meanings
  Symbols allow hypothetical thought

    Recognizing alternatives
    Time binding

  Symbols allow self-reflection

    Monitoring of self
    Conceiving the self

What are symbolic abilities?
What does it mean to think and act symbolically?
How do symbolic abilities affect the lives of individuals and
   the conduct of society?

These questions are the focus of this chapter. Our language is an elaborate symbolic system that is the basis of our communication with ourselves and others. To understand communication we must explore its symbolic foundations. To do this we first identify differences between symbols and signals. Next we discuss the implications of symbolic abilities for human thought and action. Our individual lives and the general social order are guided by how we use and abuse symbols. After reading this chapter you should be able to answer the opening questions. In addition, you should have a clear understanding of the verbal foundations of human communication.

.   .   .

.   .   .

.   .   .

Before reading further, try this simple puzzle. Connect the nine dots above with no more than four lines. The lines must be absolutely straight and they must be connected to each other.

SIGNALS AND SYMBOLS

Our lives consist of a collage of experiences that we interpret. Some of these experiences involve direct encounters with furniture, foods, objects, and other physical phenomena. Other experiences involve indirect encounters—we come to know something through something else. We learn about the moon's surface, for instance, through media representations of it. We experience countless adventures and meet a range of people through literature. We know what the Eiffel Tower looks like because we've seen photographs or films of it. Indirect experiences are possible because we have signs that are "elements used to represent other elements."[1] Signs allow us to encounter experiences, objects, people, and situations indirectly. Further, we use signs to identify and assign meaning to our direct experiences with physical phenomena. There are two categories of signs: signals and symbols. We discuss signals briefly and then turn our attention to symbols, which we examine at length.

Signals

A signal is something that refers to some other specific thing. Signals exist in a one-to-one relationship with what they represent. The best known signals are those on the highways:

STOP   YIELD   DO NOT TURN   SCHOOL

Each signal stands for a specific command and calls up a single, predictable response. The stop sign, for instance, gives the order for drivers to halt their cars. The only appropriate response when encountering this sign is to stop the car, unless the car is an ambulance or unless some other unusual factor is present. When we see a stop sign, we stop without even thinking about our action. This is the nature of a signal—it does not require thought, only automatic response.

A few years ago a new signal was invented by companies that manufacture household products containing poison. "Yuckie" signs, usually in bright yellow, appeared on products that could harm or kill children. Yuckies could also be bought in packs and applied by parents to dangerous items around a home. The longstanding signal for poison, the skull and crossbones, no longer worked as a warning. Children were not frightened by the skull and crossbones and they did not associate it with danger, so that signal was replaced with the Yuckie.

All signals announce a particular thing. They refer to some specific idea or phenomenon, and they call for a uniform, predictable response. We stop at stop signs; children exercise caution when they see a Yuckie. Because signals have established meanings that are precise and uniform, little thought is required to respond to them. We do not have to interpret them extensively to decide what they stand for or what they imply for us. Instead, we can assume an established meaning for them and we can react to them in essentially, automatic way.

Symbols

A symbol is quite different from a signal. A symbol is an arbitrary, ambiguous, and abstract designation of something else (object, event, person, relationship, condition, or process). Unlike signals, symbols do not exist in a one-to-one relationship with what they represent. Rather, a symbol is subject to a variety of interpretations by those who use it. To clarify the nature of symbols and how they work, let us consider the three defining features of symbols: arbitrariness, ambiguity, and abstractness.

Symbols are arbitrary. We use symbols to define our world and our experiences in it. Symbols, however, do not provide true or necessary definitions. This is because symbols are arbitrary, which means they are selected randomly or without absolute reason. They do not have a natural correspondence with what they represent. For example, there is no natural reason why what you are reading is called a book, nor is there any natural reason to call its contents pages. These are symbols that were arbitrarily assigned to what you are reading. The labels are useful conventions to increase understanding between people. Without some agreement on what to call things, communication would be impossible. But the labels are arbitrary. We could agree on other labels. We could call this a RAEB instead of a book, and there would be no problem if everybody agreed to use the symbol RAEB to refer to bound reading material. The first quality of symbols is that they are arbitrary; they have no natural or fixed relationship to what they stand for.

Symbols are ambiguous. Something that is ambiguous is open to several interpretations; it does not have a single agreed-upon meaning. Symbols may be interpreted in more than one way. For instance, the term "good course" means different things to different people. Some students define a "good course" as one with an exciting and knowledgeable instructor. For other students a "good course" is one with material that is useful and interesting. For still other students "good course" means a high grade for limited work. Words like "home," "friend," "fun," "trust," and "attractive" are interpreted differently by different people. The different meanings assigned to such words grow out of various individuals' experiences. For a person raised on a farm, "home" may mean open, rolling land, possibly a sprawling ranch house, plenty of animals, and probably fresh or preserved vegetables and meats at meals. A person who grew up in midtown Manhattan, by contrast, may define home as a high-rise apartment in which fish are the only pets, no yard, and food that is commercially frozen or canned. Because each of us has unique experiences, we have different meanings for words.

Meanings of "Love"[2]

Meerloo, a psychiatrist and social psychiatrist, points out the range of meanings for the word "love":

> This is no essay on love and no profound treatise on the variations of feelings of tenderness. I only want to show how much semantic difficulty there is in the expression "I love you"—a statement that can be expressed in so many varied ways. It may be a stage song, repeated daily without any meaning, or a barely audible murmur, full of surrender. Sometimes it means I desire you or I want you sexually. It may mean: I hope you love me or I hope that I will able to love you. Often it means: It may be that a love relationship can develop between us or even I hate you. Often it is a wish for emotional exchange: I want your admiration in exchange for mine or I give my love in exchange for some passion or I want to feel cozy and at home with you or I I admire some of your qualities. A declaration of love is mostly a request: I desire you or I want you to gratify me, or I want your

protection or I want to be intimate with you or I want exploit your loveliness. Sometimes it is the need for security and tenderness, for parental treatment. It may mean: My self-love goes out to you. But it may also express submissiveness: Please take me as I am, or I feel guilty about you, I want, through you, to correct the mistakes I have made in human relations. It may be self-sacrifice and a masochistic wish for dependency. However, it may also be a full affirmation of the other, taking the responsibility for mutual exchange of feelings. It may be a weak feeling of friendliness, it may be the scarcely even whispered expression of ecstasy. "I love you"—wish, desire, submission, conquest; it is never the word itself that tells the real meaning here.

Yet, though the meanings individuals attribute to symbols will vary, interpretations are not entirely random or personal. Within a single society there is a range of associations and meanings that are associated with most symbols. As participants in a common social order, each of us interacts with other members of that order. Through these interactions we encounter ideas and phenomena and we learn how others define these. In turn, the meanings they have become part of the basis for our own meanings. This interaction with other members of a society ensures general agreement on how symbols will be interpreted. Within that broad agreement, each individual develops specialized refinements of meaning. The result is that we have enough general agreement to communicate with each other, but we have enough individual variation to make the meaning of any symbol ambiguous. We can never be sure exactly what someone else means or exactly how they interpret our symbols.

Society as Symbolic Interaction[3]

Usually, most of the situations encountered by people in a given society are defined or "structured" by them in the same way. Through previous interaction they develop and acquire common understandings or definitions of how to act in this or that situation. These common definitions enable people to act alike. The common repetitive behavior of people in such situations should not mislead the student into believing that no process of interpretation is in play; on the contrary, even though fixed, the actions of the participating people are constructed by them through a process of interpretation.

Symbols are abstract. Something abstract is removed from what it represents. It is not concrete or tangible, but it may represent things that are concrete. Symbols are abstract and are used to refer to our world and our perceptions of experiences within it. Words like "liberty," "honor," "faith," and "loyalty" are very abstract. There are concrete actions, events, and objects that these terms stand for, but the terms are broader than, and removed from, any particular one of them. The terms are abstract.

Abstractness is not an all-or-none feature of symbols. Symbols may be more or less abstract. For instance, we can refer to a four-footed, tail-wagging domestic creature as "possession," "animal," "family pet," "dog," "labrador retriever," or "Madhi." All six of these symbols could represent the same concrete thing, but some of the symbols are more abstract than others. "Madhi" is the least abstract, because it refers most clearly to a particular dog. "Possession" is the most abstract of the six symbols, since it can refer to a wide range of things including, but not limited to, the class of things called dogs and, within that class, the particular dog, Shawn. The more abstract a symbol is, the more chance there is that people will have different interpretations for it. So there is a relationship between abstraction and ambiguity. As symbols become more abstract, they also tend to become more ambiguous, more open to varied interpretations.

Symbols—arbitrary, ambiguous, and abstract designations of physical and perceptual phenomena—are learned, not instinctual. They are basic to human thought and experience, and they are the primary foundation of human communication. The next section of this chapter builds on this understanding of symbols to explore the nature of communication as symbolic interaction.

HUMAN COMMUNICATION AS SYMBOLIC INTERACTION

Not all symbols are linguistic. However, all language is symbolic. Languages are among the most extensive symbolic systems devised by humans. In the next few pages we explore how humans interact with each other through language. The perspective presented here is that of symbolic interactionism, based on the thought and writing of scholars such as George Herbert Mead, John Dewey, William Thomas, Hugh Duncan, Herbert Blumer, and Ernst Cassirer. Each of these men was concerned with human interaction, and each recognized the centrality of symbolic communication to meaningful interaction between people.

Most interaction between people is indirect. We interact with others through symbols, often verbal symbols. When you want to tell someone about your home town, for instance, you translate your images of your home town into words, which you then use to express your ideas. The other person assigns meanings to the words to define her or his understanding of your home town. Although the two of you will not have identical meanings for the words, you probably will achieve an adequate level of understanding. You have interacted with each other's ideas through the symbols you used and your interpretations of them. To communicate with others is to interact symbolically.

Symbolic Interaction[4]

The term "symbolic interaction" refers . . . to the peculiar and distinctive character of interaction as it takes place between human beings. This peculiarity consists in the fact that human beings interpret or "define" each other's actions instead of merely reacting to each other's actions. Their "response" is not made directly to the actions of one another but instead is based on the meaning which they attach to such actions. Thus, human interaction is mediated by the use of symbols, by interpretation, or by ascertaining the meaning of one another's actions.

Symbolic interaction refers to a process in which humans interact with symbols to construct meanings. Through symbolic interactions we acquire information and ideas, understand our own experiences and those of others, share feelings, and come to know other people. Without symbols none of this could happen. We would be highly restricted in thought and action. According to Blumer, the core of symbolic interactionism is comprised of three basic ideas, which we will examine.

First, Blumer says, "human beings act toward things on the basis of the meanings that the things have for them."[5] We do not act without reason, and meaning constitutes our reason. We act toward things—people, objects, institutions, and so forth—according to what those things mean to us. This premise seems clear enough not to require discussion. However, the importance of meaning in human life has too often been neglected by the social sciences. Most theories that attempt to understand and explain human behavior have focused either on behavior itself or on the external factors and conditions regarded as producing the behavior. The perspective of symbolic interactionism insists that we cannot understand human action by studying behaviors, the external influences on behaviors, or even both. According to Blumer and other symbolic interactionists, an accurate understanding of human behavior must be centrally concerned with the meanings that humans have for their experiences. External factors surely exist, but until interpreted by a person, those factors have no meaning. It is the individual's interpretation of external elements that creates a meaning for them. This meaning, in turn, is used by the individual to guide his or her behaviors. We cannot understand human action if we look only at external factors or only at behaviors. Instead, we must be primarily concerned with the meanings that individuals attach to external phenomena, because it is those meanings that guide behavior.

The second premise of symbolic interactionism is that the meaning we attach to things "arises out of the social interaction that one has with one's fellows." [6] This premise explains the source of human meanings. They do not inhere in phenomena. They are not intrinsic to things. Neither do meanings reside in just the individual who attributes them to phenomena. According to symbolic interactionism, meanings are social products that are constructed through our interactions with others and the ways in which others act toward phenomena. Blumer explains that "we come to learn through the indications of others that a chair is a chair, that doctors are a certain kind of professional, that the United States Constitution is a given kind of legal document, and so forth."[7] We do not create meanings in a vacuum. Rather, as members of various social groups (family, school, state, region, country) we interact with each other and we participate in each other's creations of meanings. Children learn from their parents that certain things and people are good, others bad; that stoves and knives are dangerous, stuffed toys safe; that snakes are to be avoided, but dogs and cats are to be played with. Our meanings of all objects, people, and experiences are infused with the meanings that we have noted through our interactions with others. Social meanings are an integral part of the individual and they underlie her or his interpretation of all things.

The third major premise of symbolic interactionism is that "meanings are handled in, and modified through, an interpretive process used by the person in dealing with the things he encounters."[8] This complements the second premise's emphasis on social meaning. Meanings arise in the context of social actions, and they incorporate the observed meanings of others. Yet the meaning of a thing to a given individual is not simply an application of another's meanings for the thing. It's not an automatic replay of what has been noted through social interaction. Symbolic interactionism maintains that the person derives meaning from interaction. The person must interpret other people and their actions. Derived meaning will never correspond exactlywith intended meaning, so one person's interpretation of another's actions will not be identical to the interpretation placed by the actor on his or her behavior. The interpretive process is the heart of meaning.

To interpret something, we first communicate with ourselves. We indicate what things are part of our present setting and emotional state, we point out to ourselves which things are significant out of all the possible things to which we could give attention. Second, we must interpret the meanings of those things that we've isolated for our attention. We call upon past experiences with similar things, identify what the things imply for us, and place the things within the context of our own perceptions and reasoning. Only after all of this can we define what the things mean to us. So interpretation is not merely a matter of applying socially established meanings to things. It is not an automatic and rigid process wherein we define a thing by finding where it fits in a preexisting system of meanings. Rather, according to Blumer, interpretation is a formative process in which we use meanings to guide action. Social interaction is the context in which meanings arise, and social interaction gives us a sense of possible interpretations for phenomena. However, it is through the personal process of interpretation that we modify generally established meanings so that we can define particular things that we perceive.

Symbolic interactionism is a distinctive perspective on human nature and human behavior. This perspective, as we have seen, is grounded on three fundamental ideas: (a) Human beings act toward phenomena on the basis of the meanings they attach to the phenomena. (b) These meanings arise in social contexts. (c) Through an interpretive process of self-communication the individual modifies and manages particular meanings. Both social interaction and self-communication, the sources of meaning, occur symbolically. We interact with others and ourselves through symbols, and out of these interactions we construct our meanings. To understand the importance of this perspective, we may now explore the implications of symbolic interactionism for our thoughts and actions.

IMPLICATIONS OF SYMBOLIC INTERACTIONISM

What is the essential nature of humans? This question has intrigued numerous philosophers, ancient and modern. Descartes' was, "I think. Therefore, I am." He believed the definitive quality of human nature was the ability to think. Another philosopher, Cassirer, observed that thinking itself does not define human nature, but the way humans think is distinctive of the species. Cassirer argues that humans alone can think symbolically and that it is this ability that distinguishes humans from all other creatures. For Cassirer, humans are defined as "symbolizing animals."[9] He believes human achievements, motivations, thoughts, and actions are based upon the ability to symbolize. Symbolic abilities and what they imply for human life are major concerns in Cassirer's writings. They are also of major concern to us in this chapter. We have said that communication is symbolic interaction. Now, we can consider the work of Cassirer and others to explore five ways in which human symbolic abilities affect our lives: Symbols enable us to define, organize, and evaluate experiences; and they allow us to think hypothetically and to self-reflect.

Symbols Define

The most obvious symbolic ability is definition. We use symbols to name, to identify, to define experiences, objects, and people. As we've seen in our initial consideration of symbols, we do not use them in an objective, automatic way whereby we simply apply appropriate labels to phenomena. There are no appropriate labels, no correct ways to define our experiences. Instead, the definition of experiences is a selective and individual process in which we shape what our experiences mean by the symbols we use to define them. The names we select emphasize particular aspects of what is being named and neglect other aspects of it. If we label someone an "executive," we emphasize the person's profession instead of other sides of the person. We could just as easily define the person as an "environmentalist" or "active citizen" or "mother" or "Methodist." Each way of naming the person calls attention to one part of her. More importantly, each way of naming the person guides how we act toward her. With a botanist we may discuss plants or seek advice on a sick house plant or the suitability of soil for an herb garden. With a mother, we may discuss children or—if we are deliberating whether to have children ourselves—ask how she manages to balance her career and home life, whether her children have affected her professional advancement, and so forth. We direct our own actions toward persons and things on the basis of how we define them.

The Power of a Name[10]

An unusual name can spoil friendships, success, and your opinion of yourself.

by Mary G. Marcus

> Psychologists have . . . found that names affect the way in which people think of themselves. New Zealanders who like their names are likely to have high self-esteem, and Americans who dislike their names do not feel as good about themselves as people who like theirs.

> A recent study by S. Gray Garwood of Tulane also shows the impact of expectations on behavior. Garwood compared sixth-grade children with desirable names

(Jonathan, James, John, Patrick, Craig, Thomas, Gregory, Richard, and Jeffery) with children with undesirable names (Bernard, Curtis, Darrell, Donald, Gerald, Horace, Maurice, Jerome, Roderick, and Samuel). He found that the children who had names that teachers liked were better adjusted, had higher expectations for academic success, and scored higher on achievement tests than children with names that teachers disliked.

The Ashanti of Ghana name their children in accordance with the day of the week on which the child is born. Monday's child is given the name Kwadwo, and is thought to be quiet, peaceful, and retiring. Wednesday's child, Kwaku, is believed to be quick-tempered and aggressive. In 1954, psychologist Gustav Iahoda read juvenile-court records to verify a rumor that a majority of crimes were committed by children named Kwaku. The records showed that a significantly greater number of crimes against persons were committed by people named Kwaku than those named Kwadwo. It's unlikely that children are born with dramatically different temperaments, so the difference in the crime rate is probably due to different expectations of the parents and different upbringing based on these expectations.

Not only do our definitions guide our actions, but our values, attitudes, goals, and self-concepts influence our definitions. The way in which we define phenomena is not random, but is guided by a variety of factors. Consider the simple example of a shopper browsing through the gourmet section of a market. How will that shopper define a twelve dollar container of escargot? The answer depends on the shopper's attitudes, goals, motives, and previous experiences. Someone who defines herself or himself as a sophisticated person with international tastes may define it as "the perfect thing for an important dinner party." Someone who is wealthy may define it as a "bargain," while a person on the verge of poverty might define it as a "ridiculous extravagance." Who we are and all of our values, motives, and life experiences influence how we define things. In turn, the definitions we give to these things then influence how we see them and ourselves in relation to them.

Humans cannot deal with the full complexity of their experiences. Symbols allow us to label experiences so that we isolate only things of importance to us. Even a simple object such as a chair cannot be completely described—its size, shape, color, texture, density, construction, angles of parts, durability, weight, comfort, and so on. It is even more impossible to describe in full complex phenomena such as friendship, happiness, disappointment, or ambition. To manage our experiences, we simplify them. We notice only some aspects of phenomena and we select names (words) to direct our attention to those aspects we consider important. Most of us, for instance, probably use the label "rock" to describe a class of porous, heavy things. A geologist, however, needs an elaborate, technical vocabulary to distinguish among types of rocks and to call her or his attention to minute differences in rock formations. These features of rocks matter to geologists, so they have invented words to designate the features. Similarly, many people use the term "wine" to refer to a great range of alcoholic beverages. For a wine connoisseur, however, a very precise vocabulary is important to define subtle distinctions among wines: bouquet, aroma, finesse, length, body, tannin, petillance, lilt, and clarity. Each of these words has a specific and important meaning to a seasoned wine drinker. Detailed labels allow the geologist and wine connoisseur to notice—to call attention to—fine features of rocks and wines. Because the majority of us are not familiar with such specialized terms, we are not fully aware of many qualities of rocks and wines.

We create labels to define those things or aspects of things that are important to us. Anthropological research has demonstrated that symbols reflect the values and priorities of the people who use them. Different symbolic systems are used by different cultures because of the particular needs and values of the people within the cultures. Eskimos, for instance, have a series of words to describe what we call "snow." For our purposes in American culture, "snow" is sufficient to refer to the white stuff that falls in winter. Eskimos, however, constantly live with snow, travel in snow, deal with snow, and they must distinguish among its types. They use separate terms for snow that is dry, wet, heavy, light, icy, and powdery. The very specific terms are essential to Eskimos whose activities and survival depend on making keen distinctions among types of snow.[11]

Language defines experiences and phenomena. The definitional capacity of symbols allows us to focus thought and to isolate salient aspects of the world around us. In naming, we define what we will notice, what its meaning is for us, and how we should act toward what we have named.

The definitional capacity of symbols allows us to focus thought and direct actions. These are undeniably useful abilities. However, there are dangers in focusing thought. We can abuse our ability to define phenomena. Sometimes we forget that a symbol is a designation for something else. We act as if the symbol were what it represents. For years Americans would not discuss venereal disease in public, because they thought "decent" people should not use such terms. They acted as if the term "venereal disease" were the actual infections it stood for. The general population remained ignorant of this health problem and some people even died from diseases because the words were taboo. Many people thoroughly enjoy a delicacy until they are told it is rattlesnake meat. Upon hearing this term they often become sick. They are responding to the word, not to the actual sensory experience, which they found pleasing. The labels we use are arbitrary and are not equivalent to what they stand for. We misuse the definitional capacity of language when we act as if the symbol were what it stands for.[12]

When we use language to define things, we necessarily limit our perceptions of them. The label we use guides us to see things in only a particular way. Consequently, we restrict our ability to notice other aspects of the phenomenon. People who define women as "homemakers," for instance, find it difficult to accept women as "career people." Recent reports on eating habits suggest that many chronic overeaters grew up in families where food was defined as "affection" or "love." Cookies and cake were the rewards given for good behavior. When mothers felt particularly loving, they baked something for the children. In adulthood many chronic overeaters still define food as love. The definition they learned in family interaction limits their ability to see food as calories and potentially as health problems. Several diet clinics feature an approach to help such individuals control their eating habits. The key to the program is persuading a person to redefine food so that health problems of overeating are part of the meaning for it.

We've seen that naming limits perception. An extension of this idea is that any name both includes and excludes phenomena. Over the last decade there has been much attention to the power of language to exclude, particularly to exclude women. The best example of this is the controversy over generic language, such as "mankind," and "he" used to refer to all humans. The question is whether a word like "man" really refers to any human or just to a male human. A number of linguistic scholars argue that such generic language excludes women. Research seems to support this position, since it has been shown that when people see a word like "man" or "mankind," they think of males, not all humans. It can also be devaluing to receive letters to "Dear Sir" or "Chairman" if you are a woman. The language seems to exclude women.

A related controversy surrounds use of the word "girl" to refer to adult women. Many women now find this offensive since to them it carries connotations of lack of maturity and responsibility. Yet, we hear executives speak of having "my girl get the file" when that "girl" may be a 45-year-old woman. The term "girl" is one that defines women as less than adult, less than mature. Increasingly, style manuals and general social norms discourage both the use of "girl" to refer to adult women and generic language.

It is necessary for us to define phenomena. However, the danger is that we may freeze our meanings of things so that we cannot recognize changes or new aspects of what we have defined. Parents who define their children as "our little girl/boy" find it difficult to recognize their children as adults. Parents' meanings for their children are based on inappropriate symbols, "little girl" or "little boy," which do not focus parents' attention on the changes in those children, on how they have matured over 20 years. A few years ago I found myself guilty of misusing the definitional capacity of symbols. My sister is eight years younger than I and has always been the "baby" in our family. When she entered the university at which I teach, I began to "look after her." I "helped" her with academic problems, called several times a week to make sure she was all right, gave her advice on nearly everything she did, and in general treated her like a kid sister in need of guidance. After a few months of my "help" she told me in clear terms to "quit mothering me" and to "quit calling me your kid sister." She further informed me that she was "a grown-up adult and wished to be treated as one!" She was no longer the "little sister" I had grown up with, but my labels for her still stressed her vulnerability (kid, baby), so that was how I still acted toward her. My meanings for her were frozen. Until I defined her in new ways I could not see her or act toward her as an adult and peer. Once I considered and revised my ways of defining her, we were able to build an entirely different type of relationship—one between two adults.

In using language we should remember that symbols are arbitrary and ambiguous. They focus our perceptions on certain aspects of phenomena and invite us to overlook other aspects. To avoid abusing our definitional ability, we should leave ourselves room to redefine—to change our designations for people, objects, and experiences. If we recognize that names are not intrinsic to phenomena and that phenomena change over time, we should be able to avoid this misuse of definitional ability.

The Whorf-Sapir Hypothesis about Language

Anthropological study of various cultures suggests that our perceptions are intimately guided by our language. The language of Hopi Indians, for example, does not distinguish between objects that exist and events in motion. In English we use nouns to represent objects and verbs to represent motion. For the Hopis, however, the only distinction between nouns and verbs is one of duration, not quality. The Whorf-Sapir hypothesis is that our ways of thinking and perceiving are dependent upon our language. The ideas of Benjamin Whorf and Edward Sapir are well summarized in Sapir's words: "The fact of the matter is that the 'real world' is to a large extent unconsciously built up on the language habits of the group [society] . . . . We see and hear and otherwise experience what we do because the language habits of our community predispose certain choices of interpretation."[13] There is an interactive relationship between cultural modes of thought and behavior and the language of a culture.

Symbols Organize

The ability of symbols to define allows us to call to our attention particular features of phenomena. The complement to that is our ability to abstract, which allows us to organize and classify experiences. Because we are symbol users, we are able to think in abstract ways. To organize our experiences, we generalize. We create categories to represent groups of similar phenomena and experiences. The general category "houses," for instance, includes houses that are old, new, large, small, brick, wood, ranch style, contemporary, salt-box, well-kept, falling down, and so forth. Any of those terms represents yet a further category. The class "contemporary houses" includes ones with solar energy as well as conventional power sources, ones with several floors as well as those with a single level, ones with numerous windows and skylights, and ones built into a hillside. Most of the time we don't need all of these fine distinctions, so the general term "house" is sufficient for our communication with others. For this reason, abstraction is a useful ability that allows us to organize and group experiences and concepts in convenient ways. Imagine trying to deal with everything you encounter as a specific, unique phenomenon! Life would be completely chaotic if we had no general categories to impose order on experience and perception.

Because we can think in abstract ways, we are able to form general concepts such as "justice," "good life," or "education." These broad concepts elevate us from the biological, practical world and give us access to ideals. In turn, the ideals we define furnish guidance to our lives. Consider the term "responsibility" as a general concept. Each of us has a sense of what responsibility means. Our meanings grow out of a variety of particular interactions with others and the meanings they attribute to the term, as well as our own modified meanings for it. Perhaps you once forgot a chore assigned to you by your father and were scolded about being irresponsible; on another occasion you prepared dinner and were told "that was very responsible of you;" when you saved part of your allowance, your aunt remarked that "you're more responsible than most people your age." Each of these events contributed to your meaning for the general term "responsibility." Yet the word designates a broad concept, one larger than all the specific instances in which you've heard the word. Because we are symbol users, we can think in general about things and ourselves—our values, goals, and actions. If we were not able to use symbols—if we could use only signals—we could not think in general terms. Instead, we could be restricted to thinking of only specific things, particular objects and experiences, with no generalized concepts of them. Because symbols are abstract, they allow us to think in broad terms and to form categories that order our experiences meaningfully.[14] It is the abstract, organizing function of symbols that forms the foundation of sophisticated conceptual thought, a level of thinking unique to human beings.

While abstract thought is a valuable implication of our symbolic natures, it is simultaneously fraught with dangers. We can misuse our ability to generalize. The primary abuse of abstraction is stereotyping. A stereotype is a broad generalization about an entire class of phenomena, based on knowledge of only some members of that class. We stereotype when we use our general categories to define individual members of the class. We think in terms of groups instead of considering individual objects or people. For example, "fratty baggers" and "sorority Sues" are pejorative labels used to generalize about people who belong to Greek organizations. If we use these general labels as a basis for thought, we negatively evaluate anyone who belongs to a fraternity or sorority. The individual will be assigned to a previously defined category without being considered as a unique person. People who think in terms of the stereotype "dumb jocks" will never recognize the intelligent and interesting athletes they meet. Citizens committed to a political party may stereotype all its candidates as "progressive" and vote consistently for them without considering critically each individual candidate's views and merits. When we think only in broad categories, we may fail to distinguish adequately among individual members of that category. Whether our stereotypes are positive or negative, they have a similar potential effect: they encourage rigid, uncritical thought and action. The problem with thinking in generalizations is that we may blind ourselves to legitimate and important differences among the phenomena we place in a single category.

Years ago Johnson described abstract thought as a "process of leaving out details." [15] Clearly, we cannot afford to think in highly detailed ways all of the time. To organize ideas and experiences we must leave out some details much of the time. Categories are useful as a means of organizing experiences and meanings under a single definition. Without the organizational abilities that are possible for symbol users, we could not conceptualize ideals, nor could we deal with general ideas. However, to reap the benefits of our ability to organize meanings and to avoid the dangers, we need to remind ourselves constantly that though generalization is useful, overgeneralization (stereotyping) can result in rigid thought.

Symbols Evaluate

A third symbolic ability is evaluation. Our language is laden with values. Few, if any, of our words are neutral in meaning. Each word has connotative meanings, ones that go beyond the literal definition found in a dictionary. Consider the word "faith," which one dictionary defines as "firm belief in something for which there is no proof . . . something that is believed esp. [sic] with strong conviction." [16] This may be the literal definition of "faith," but for most of us it means other things as well. To some people "faith" means peace, serenity, security, and a personal basis for conduct. Other people who are not committed to religion may define "faith" as a crutch for those too weak to assume responsibility for running their own lives. As a second example, consider a definition of war: "a state of usually open and declared armed hostile conflict between states or nations."[17] This definition, although accurate, hardly suggests the reality of war. Death, destruction, mutilation of people, and devastation of environments are part of my personal meaning for the word "war." All of our symbols have connotative meanings to us. It is these connotative meanings that add the value to our definitions. Because we associate values with our symbols—because, in fact, the symbols are evaluative—our language necessarily suggests attitudes and judgments. This has an important implication for our behavior. We said earlier that our attitudes and actions are directed by our symbolic definitions. Now we see that those definitions imply evaluations. The implication is that the values associated with the symbols we use will influence our thought and behavior toward what our symbols represent. In both subtle and obvious ways, the symbols we select indicate evaluations. Our perceptions of phenomena are influenced by the language we use to define them.

Symbols Influence Meanings
Coke-Pepsi Slugfest[18]

The Day Coca-Cola Beat Coca-Cola blared the strange headline in a recent newspaper ad in Dallas. Starkly pictured beneath the message was the soft drink's familiar hourglass bottle flanked by two glasses, one marked M and the other Q. Thus opened what is becoming one of advertising's most bizarre feuds. It pits the nation's leading soft-drink maker, Coca-Cola, against its closest ranking competitor, Pepsi-Cola, in a taste bud to taste bud donnybrook that for sheer zaniness outdoes anything the ad world has seen in years.

The whole thing began more than 15 months ago, when Pepsi decided to challenge Coke's 3-to-1 sales lead in the Dallas area. (Nationally, Coke is estimated to hold 26.2% of the market, compared with Pepsi's 17.4%.) Pepsi concocted a promotion supposedly showing that more than half the Coke drinkers tested preferred Pepsi's flavor when the two colas were stripped of brand identification. During the test, Coke was served in a glass marked Q and Pepsi in a glass marked M. Within a year Pepsi had whittled Coke's sales lead in Dallas to 2 to 1. Irritated, Coke officials conducted their own consumer-preference test—not of the colas but of the letters. Their conclusion: Pepsi's test was invalid because people like the letter M better than they like Q. Chicago Marketing Consultant Steuart H. Britt theorizes that Q is disliked because of the number of unpleasant words that begin with Q (quack, quitter, quake, qualm, queer . . .).

No Studies. To make its point, Coke put its own cola in both glasses-those marked M and those marked Q. Sure enough, most people tested preferred the drink in the M glass (hence the "Coke beat Coke" headline). Pepsi then revised the letters on its test glasses to S and L and again consumers preferred Pepsi, which was always in the L glass. Again Coke executives cried foul, contending that just as people preferred M to Q, they liked L better than S. Questioned about this, Dr. Ernest Dichter, a motivational research expert, reported that he knew of no studies indicating a bias in favor of the letter L.

Thirsting for bigger sales, Pepsi extended its taste-test campaign to Michigan two months ago. And last week it moved into Los Angeles and New York, the country's richest markets, with the message: NATIONWIDE MORE COCA-COLA DRINKERS PREFER PEPSI THAN COKE Anticipating the move, Coke had already launched a campaign with the theme NEW YORK PREFERS COCA-COLA TO PEPSI 2 TO 1.

The impact that the scrap is having on sales of the two soft-drink giants is so far inconclusive, and many Coke and Pepsi bottlers and some admen are upset about the battle. They worry that the confrontation will feed the public's cynicism about all advertising, attract unwanted attention from Government regulators, and sour consumer attitudes toward both drinks.

The evaluative nature of symbols is recognized by political and social groups who seek to change public perceptions. A symbolic strategy has been used to redefine the meanings associated with sexual preferences. Many people interpret the word "homosexual" negatively, owing to social meanings that have built up over time. In the 1960s people who were "homosexual" and who desired a positive definition of their identity began using the term "gay" to define themselves. This new word had fewer negative associations for most people. "Black power" and "Black is beautiful" are symbolic strategies used to raise blacks' pride in themselves and to alter social meanings of their race.[19] More recently, blacks have begun using the term "Afro American" to define themselves in terms of their African heritage. Each label invites different understandings of identity. The term "Ms" was created to discourage defining women in relation to men. Previously a woman's formal title defined her in terms of her relationship to a man: "Miss" if not married ("poor spinster") and "Mrs." if married ("lucky woman"). Language inevitably shapes our meanings. Whenever we interact with symbols—our own or those used by others—our thought is affected. Attitudes and actions are formed and modified by the linguistic screens through which we interpret our world.

Symbols Construct Meanings[20]

It is no surprise that Americans and Soviet Communists tend to have quite different meanings for concepts like religion and freedom. A clue to why we have such different meanings is provided by the following definitions from Soviet dictionaries:

RELIGION: A fantastic faith in gods, angels and spirits . . . a faith without any scientific foundations. Religion is being supported and maintained by the reactionary circles. It serves for the subjugation of the working people and for building up the power of the exploiting bourgeois classes . . . . The superstition of outlived religion has been surmounted by the Communist education of the working class . . . and by its deep knowledge of the scientifically profound teaching of Marx-Leninism.
INDIVIDUALISM: The-individual-as-a-member-of-the-collective.
FREEDOM: The recognition of necessity.
CHARITY: Help granted hypocritically by representatives of the dominant class

in societies of exploiters to a certain fraction of the disinherited sectors of the population in order to deceive the workers and to divert their attention from the class struggle.

INITIATIVE: Independent search for the best way to fulfill a command.

How might we feel about religion, individualism, freedom or charity had we grown up interacting with others who defined the concepts in the above ways? If you are surprised by the way Russians define these concepts, imagine what a Soviet student would think of your definitions for these terms!

For further thought, consider the Hungarian Communists' version of the Nativity story:

> There was once a poor married couple who had nothing to eat or dress in. They asked the rich people for help but the rich people sent them away. Their baby was born in a stable and covered with rags in a manger. The day after the baby was born, some shepherds who had come from Russia brought the baby some gifts. "We come from a country where poverty and misery are unknown" said the shepherds. "In Russia the babies grow in liberty because there is no unemployment or suffering." Joseph, the unemployed worker, asked the shepherds how they had found the house. The shepherds replied that a red star had guided them.
>
> Then the poor family took to the road. The shepherds covered the little baby with furs, and they all set out for the Soviet paradise.

Symbols are inherently evaluative. In itself this is neither good nor bad. However, the valuations aroused by symbols can be dangerous if we are unaware of them and their power over us. We abuse our symbolic abilities when we fail to recognize that symbols suggest evaluations.

Loaded language is the use of symbols that slant or distort perception and, thus, meaning. On an everyday level, loaded language both shapes and reflects our associations for things. We are more impressed when served "London broil" than when served "a flank cut of beef." We respect people who "stand up for their rights," but are irritated by those who "insist on their point of view." Undergraduates are often more impressed with a teacher whose title is "professor" than with one who is a "graduate teaching assistant." Even if the two are equally competent and interesting they are defined differently—as having more or less status—and, thus, are evaluated differently.

Definition and Impression[21]

Does the way in which a speaker is defined influence that speaker's credibility? This question was addressed by Haiman in a classic study. Haiman divided a group of college students into three sections. All sections heard the identical recorded speech on compulsory health insurance. For section 1 the speaker was identified as the Surgeon General of the United States. In section 2 the speaker was identified as a sophomore speech major. In section 3 the speaker was defined as the Secretary General of the Communist Party in the United States. After students had heard the speech, Haiman measured their attitudes toward compulsory health insurance, which the speech had argued for. Students who thought the speaker was the Surgeon General of the United States were significantly persuaded toward the idea of health insurance. Those who thought the speaker was a sophomore speech major were slightly persuaded toward health insurance. Those who identified the speaker as the Secretary General of the Communist Party were more against compulsory health insurance than they had been prior to hearing the speech.

The content of the speech did not vary, nor did the delivery, since it was recorded. Only the definitions of the speaker were different for the three sections of listeners. Impressions of the arguments in the speech were influenced by how the listeners defined the source.

In extreme form, language can be so loaded that it seriously distorts our interpretations of ourselves and our actions. The book *Sanctions for Evil* analyzes the military's use of loaded language to train newly recruited soldiers to kill other people. It reports that the fundamental training technique is using symbols to alter perceptions of the "enemy." Duster says you must teach the recruits to deny, "the humanity of victims. You call the victims names like gooks, dinks, niggers, pinkos, and Japs . . . yellow dwarfs with daggers."[22] A soldier will be able to kill something that is defined as a nonperson, a subhuman creature. One soldier, reporting on his participation in the My Lai massacre, said the people being killed were "like animals . . . some subhuman species . . . to kill them is no more of a crime than to spray DDT on an annoying insect."[23] Another military observer commented that no one has any feelings for the Vietnamese . . . no one sees the Vietnamese as people. They're not people. Therefore, it doesn't matter what you do to them."[24] Dehumanizing labels for a nation of people perverted soldiers' perceptions to the point where massacres of entire villages were seen as no more horrible than killing insects!

Yet we need not rely on dramatic examples from war to illustrate the prevalence of loaded language. In contemporary society, loaded language distorts our meanings for many groups of people. How often have you heard older citizens described as "over the hill," "has-beens," "old fogies," "spinsters," "geezers," "just a fool who's out of it," "fumbling old men," or "silly ninnies?" Phrases such as these predispose us to think negatively of older people, to view them with contempt, pity, or patronization.

Because symbols are necessarily evaluative, they influence our perceptions of what they describe. When language is loaded, it can distort thought and action. We need to be constantly alert to the power of symbols to influence our attitudes and behaviors.

Symbols Allow Hypothetical Thought

Think about Yourself Ten Years from Now.
Estimate the United States' Energy Needs for the Year 2001.
Imagine Starting Your Career.
Consider the Courses You Might Take Next Term.
Remember Your First Date.
Decide What You Will Do When You Complete This Chapter.

Each of the above statements makes sense to you because you have the ability to think hypothetically. Hypothetical thought is conjecture about possible events and circumstances and conceptualization of things not part of the immediate physical world. You need not be 10 years older to think about yourself in that future time. You can imagine starting your career—scenarios of your first day, your first big achievement on the job. You can consider what the next term will be like—the hours you prefer to have courses, the requirements you need to fulfill. You can remember, often in vivid detail, experiences that are long past and for which you have no concrete record. In each example, you think hypothetically because you think about something other than what exists in the physical world of this moment.

The human capacity for hypothetical thought is possible because we are symbolizing agents. We use symbols to designate various possibilities—hopes, fears, goals, potential future states, alternatives, memories. Once we designate a possibility, we can think about it. We can hold the idea in our mind, turn it around, examine it from various angles, modify it, and consider it again.

To symbolize an idea is to give it existence as something we can evaluate and respond to. With symbols we can create in our minds ideas that have no objective reality, and we can then act to make these ideas real in a concrete sense. At some point, for instance, you imagined yourself as someone with a college degree. Neither the degree nor that version of you is "real" yet; they are only possibilities for the future that you have conceived in your mind. Yet for at least four years you'll attend classes, take tests, read books, and do assignments, and all of this is motivated by the idea that you have of yourself as someone with a college degree. This example demonstrates the power of hypothetical thought. Let's now consider two distinctively human abilities that grow out of our ability to think hypothetically: the ability to recognize alternatives and the ability to bind time.

Recognizing alternatives. Animals accept the world largely as they find it. We train our pets to eat certain kinds of food, to expect a given amount and type of attention, and to follow basic rules of behavior. Our pets then operate in accordance with this training. Animals largely accept their worlds as givens. Human beings do not. We are curious to sample foods different from those we know, to visit places we have read about, to design homes and offices unlike others we have seen. We may want more or less attention than we are currently receiving from our acquaintances. We change the "rules" that guide our behaviors and the goals that direct our lives. Every facet of our existence proves that we can think about alternatives to what we now know and have known. In fact, we cannot avoid recognizing alternatives. This human ability is fundamental to individual and social progress. Consider a few human achievements that began with someone's recognition of an alternative to what presently existed:

- Inventions such as the telephone, heating systems, refrigeration, electricity, movable type, mathematical systems
- Literary achievements, including Shakespeare's works, Wolfe's novels, and Thoreau's passionate portraits of idyllic life in natural settings
- Technological achievements such as pasteurization, mass transportation, space

travel, computerized business operations, in vitro fertilization, media of television, radio, and motion pictures
- Medical advances that led to vaccines for smallpox and polio and sophisticated diagnostic methods with X-rays and lasers.

Without the ability to envision alternatives to what exists in the moment, none of these achievements would have come about.

Human nature requires us to change, to question, to challenge what exists. We do not accept the physical present as all that can be. Instead, we constantly define and redefine our world and our own experiences within it. Because we are symbol-using agents, we create and refine alternatives for ourselves.

It is our ability to conceive of possibilities that enables us to create and organize civilized societies. Cassirer says it is the hypothetical thought unique to symbol users that overcomes human inertia and endows us "with a new ability, the ability to constantly reshape [the] human universe."[25] Cassirer means that the natural tendency of all living organisms is to accept what exists and to make do with that. Because humans think hypothetically, however, we can conceive of new forms of our own existence. Once conceived, the possibilities can be realized through our own actions. Because symbols are definitional and therefore direct our behavior, the conception of a possibility is the first step in making it a reality. The ability to recognize and reach for alternatives elevates humans beyond the physical, concrete world. As Cassirer says, it gives us "access to the ideal."[26]

Time binding. Just as we are not limited to the immediate physical world, neither are we restricted to the immediate temporal world. Rather, because we think hypothetically,we live simultaneously in three dimensions of time: past, present, and future. Each of us has memories of our past. These memories are an edited life history. We highlight important experiences and dismiss ones we define as insignificant, we order volumes of diverse events into an organized whole that we imbue with value and meaning. The product is a self-shaped, carefully edited definition of our past. Memory is not the logical sum of all that has occurred, nor is it objective recollection. Because we are symbolic beings, our memories are symbolically charged. This implies that our remembrances are constructed, not merely given. We reorganize events, assign meanings that may not have been part of the original experiences, redefine what happened and what it meant. Our view of the past is infused with our perspective in the present. A friend of mine for years talked with pleasure of his childhood as a "country boy." He vividly recounted evenings spent in quiet conversation with family on a screened porch with only the sounds of crickets and to interrupt the peace. When I met my friend's brother, I was amazed to learn that according to the brother's memory, my friend has been plagued by childhood allergies to dust, pollen, animal fur, and all the things that make up life in the country. The brother told me my friend had spent a good portion of his childhood in doctor's offices and in bed and had never seemed particularly fond of country life as a child. As an adult who lives in a crowded, noisy, pressured world, this man reconstructed his past to provide a kind of serenity not possible in his current life. We may glorify the past to compensate for a less than ideal present. To do this we reconstruct what happened by resymbolizing the experiences.

Each of us has had embarrassing moments when our parents recalled some of our behaviors as children. Parents seem to have a talent for remembering (and telling with glee) things we have chosen to forget since those things are inconsistent with our current self-definitions. We remember and reshape the past to conform to our current needs and desires. In this sense, the past we live with is a symbolic past, one we constantly reconstruct, using symbols and meanings of the present.

We also live in the future. Each of us has goals, hopes, ambitions, and each of us has fears, doubts, anxieties. We represent these with symbols, which allow us to think about them and to keep editing them and using them to guide ourselves in the present.

Positive Denial: The Case for Not Facing Reality[27]

Richard S. Lazarus interviewed by Daniel Goleman

Clinicians assumed self-deception is pathological, I think, because they saw only people who had trouble facing the truth about the sources of their problems. So the clinical view has become that denial leads to pathology. Paradoxically, poets, playwrights, and novelists have been saying just the opposite: we need our illusions. As Don Quixote puts it in Man Of LaMancha, "Facts are the enemy of truth."

Ibsen's The Wild Duck takes up the theme of necessary illusions. So does O'Neill's The Iceman Commeth. In that play, there are a number of derelicts in a bar who are filled with self-deception. One of their occasional cronies comes by and zealously tells them to stop believing these lies about themselves and face the truth. He succeeds in destroying one man, who commits suicide. Finally, they all give up and go back to their illusions. O'Neill was telling us that life cannot be lived without illusions.

My own research on how people actually deal with life crises has brought me around to the view that illusion and self-deception can have positive value in a person's psychological economy. Indeed, the fabric of our lives is woven in part from illusions and unexamined beliefs. There is, for example, the collective illusion that our society is free, moral, and just, which, of course, isn't always true. Then there are the countless idiosyncratic beliefs people hold about themselves and the world in which they live—for example, that we are better than average, or doomed to fail, or that the world is a benign conspiracy, or that it is rigged against us. Many such beliefs are passed down from parent to child and never challenged.

Despite the fixity with which people hold such beliefs, they have little or no basis in reality. One person's beliefs are another's delusions. In effect, we pilot our lives in part by illusions and by self-deceptions that give meaning and substance to life.

At some point most of us define a professional goal. We use symbols to give form to the vague image we have and, in so doing, we transform it into what seems like a concrete reality to us. It can then guide and motivate us. "I will be a doctor." " I am going to seek political office." "I want a large family." "I intend to become a minister." "I plan to make my first million before I'm thirty." All of these announcements represent symbolized future states, visions of what we may become. Because we can create goals through symbolic designations, we are able to provide direction to our lives. Symbolizing possible futures impels us to action. Without symbols we could not represent to ourselves these possibilities, so they could not be brought to bear on our actions. Language, because it is evaluative, vitalizes ideas.

Through symbolic designations we can represent a future state so vividly that it is "real" enough to motivate our attitudes and actions. Someone whose goal is to be a doctor in eight years must be a disciplined student now, must take sciences courses, must seek experience in hospital settings, and so on. Our present activities are motivated by our visions of the future. Though our lives are enriched and directed by this ability to imagine alternatives, hypothetical thought, like other symbolic capacities, can be abused. Two misuses of hypothetical thought are lack of commitment and evasion of the present.

Because we are symbolizing beings, we present ourselves with series of possibilities, and sometimes we cannot decide among them. We are unable to choose one course of action, to endorse one value, or to take one stand on an issue. We conceive so many possibilities that we hesitate to commit to any one of them. In the mind, a person paints symbolic pictures of what might happen if journalism is pursued as a career: "investigative reporting . . . exclusive stories and contacts with important, exciting people . . . travel . . . shaping public opinion on issues." The same person constructs an equally engaging symbolic portrait of law as a possible career: "courtroom drama . . . eloquent arguments . . . fighting injustice . . . social status and respect." It is difficult to settle on just one possibility when both seem so attractive. Students often run into a similar dilemma when assigned a speech or paper. "What topic shall I research?" Several possibilities come to mind, each is considered, casual discussion is pursued on all of the topics, but no speech or paper is forthcoming. Finally, three days before the assignment is due, the student tosses a coin to decide which topic to develop. If we could not imagine an array of possibilities, we would never be caught in such binds. Since we can see more than one alternative, we constantly run the risks of indecision and lack of commitment. To avoid being caught in this trap, we need to remind ourselves of what is happening—we are constructing the possibilities that make us indecisive. Then we can attempt to reduce the uncertainty associated with our views of the possibilities. The student debating between journalism and law might, for instance, interview practicing journalists and attorneys to get a less abstract idea of each profession and what it involved on a day-today basis. The student trying to decide on a research topic might read a few articles on several possible topics or talk to experts to determine which subjects involved sufficient information to be developed into major presentations and which ones held his or her interest beyond a surface level. Our ability to imagine possibilities can be tempered by supplementing the abstract images with information that refines our ideas.

"He's living in another time." "She's so busy chasing the future she never sees the present." "He's tied to yesterday." "She's out of sync with the times." We have all heard phrases like these to describe people who seem not to live in the present. In *Gone With the Wind* many Southerners were depicted as unable to accept the changes in their lives that followed the Civil War. One of the main characters, Ashley Wilkes, cannot deal with life after the war. He clings to the past, to his memory of other times.

Ashley's life is miserable because he cannot endure the contrast between his memory of what was and his definition of what is.

To conceive of our own past and future is valuable. Yet this human ability may tempt us to live only in the past or the future. We all know people who remember "the good old days" and who constantly downgrade the present by comparison. We also know individuals who live for the future and, therefore, miss living in the present. For these people, symbolic visions of what was or will be are so powerful that the present is overshadowed. Perhaps the saddest cases are those persons who compare all relationships to a previous one and who find none of the current ones can live up to that standard. What is most disturbing about this behavior is that the people seldom realize how much they have exaggerated the previous relationship's virtues, how they have symbolically endowed it with qualities beyond those it had at the time. We may, on the other hand, remember only negative aspects of the past, so that the present seems far better by comparison. Similarly, we may create inviting or fearful images of our futures. For some people the future is symbolized as exciting, challenging, full of new experiences and people to be enjoyed. For others it is symbolized as an ominous cloud, full of personal disasters and social problems. Unrealistic images of the past and future are dangerous because they mar our lives in the present. We can minimize the possibility of being misled by our symbolic visions if we remember that it is we who define past experiences and future ones. We can exercise some choice in how we depict these images to ourselves and, in so doing, control the past and future instead of being controlled by them.

When we symbolize we call up ideas and experiences that need not be parts of the physical, temporal environment. This allows us to consider alternatives and to bind time, two uniquely human abilities. Carried to extremes, however, the ability to think hypothetically can create lack of commitment and evasion of the present. To become trapped within our own hypothetical definitions of yesterday and tomorrow prevents us from productive and satisfying experiences today.

Symbols Allow Self-Reflection

Humans are self-reflective. They are able to reflect on themselves and their own actions. This may be the single most important implication of our symbolic natures. Imagine two cats conversing about how to catch a mouse. Their conversation might go something like this:

Morris: You know, Felix, we should have caught that mouse we chased yesterday.
Felix: Indeed we should have. Thinking back, I think it got away because we both chased after it from behind. Next time, you execute a move to the right and I'll cover the left flank. Then we'll have that little varmint.
Morris: Good plan, Felix. We'll do it that way.

This conversation could never occur between cats or other animals. Only humans engage in the kind of analysis and planning illustrated in the dialogue between Felix and Morris. Self-reflection was described by Mead as the ability of the self to stand outside the self and view it as an object—describe it, evaluate it, respond to it.[28] Because we can reflect on our own nature, we can perceive ourselves, define ourselves, act toward ourselves, and direct ourselves. We are able to reflect on our own behaviors, judge them, and, if we choose, revise them in future situations. We can plan our activities, analyze what courses of attitude and action are necessary to our goals, and organize ourselves to implement the behaviors we've decided upon. Thus, we can think of self reflection as the ability to think about and act toward the self. Even from this introductory discussion, you probably grasp how important this capability is to humans. It is fundamental to who we are and to what we make of ourselves. Self-reflection is the foundation of two symbolic processes; monitoring of self and conceiving of self.

Monitoring of self. Monitoring of self involves observing and regulating our attitudes and behaviors. We monitor ourselves physically to decide when to go on a diet, start an exercise program, or change style of dress. We monitor our interpersonal experiences to judge how others perceive us, whether we are being effective, and how we compare with other people. We monitor ourselves mentally when we note our attitudes toward objects or people, scrutinize the basis of the attitudes, and decide whether we want to modify them. We may observe any aspect of ourselves and our activities in order to better control ourselves. Symbols are essential to monitoring. To monitor yourself, you must stand outside yourself in a way—observe how you act, and indicate to yourself what those actions mean. After noting your activities, you contemplate alternative ways of behaving (hypothetical thought), evaluate the different possibilities (evaluation), decide which one seems most desirable, direct yourself to enact the behavior you've chosen, and then stand back to assess it and its effects. This is how the monitoring process proceeds. It's an internal dialogue within the self. Change in any behavior, whether physical (dancing), interpersonal (conversation), or academic (study habits) is possible because we can symbolize ourselves to ourselves—we can self-reflect. We single out our own actions, use symbols to indicate them to ourselves so that we become aware of them, and then rely on those symbolic designations to remind ourselves of the actions and to regulate the actions. "Don't interrupt." "No second helpings." "Develop discipline." "Be on time." "Take the medicine at noon every day." "Prepare for class." "Don't forget to go by the automatic teller machine to get some cash." These are examples of self-indications, symbolic designations that focus our attention and allow us to control our behaviors.[29] Without symbols we could not designate particular actions or aspects of ourselves, so we could not direct our attention to regulating those parts of us. We can monitor our own attitudes and actions because symbols allow us to reflect on ourselves.

Conceiving the self. Conceiving of self is an ongoing process in which we define and redefine ourselves to ourselves. Our self-definitions are still symbolic descriptions that we modify constantly as we engage in interaction with others. We use labels or images to designate who we are: sister, daughter, student, psychology major, Tri-Delt, future executive. Each self-designation is a way of conceiving and directing the self. When you think of yourself as a student, you define yourself in the context of your campus, your classes, assignments you have, grade averages, and your major. When you label yourself as a son or daughter, you think of yourself as a member of your family; perhaps you also think of your home, the town or city where you grew up, and the relationships you have with your parents. Chances are you have quite different thoughts about yourself when you define yourself as a student. For instance, it's likely that you think of yourself in terms of academic matters, goals, and concerns and the social life on your campus. When you conceive of yourself as son or daughter, you probably direct yourself to act in ways consistent with that role—for instance, to show respect to your parents, follow rules that prevail in your home, and listen to your folks' advice (even when it's unsolicited and even unwelcome!). We use symbols to symbolize ourselves. They allow us to designate who we are in any given moment and context and to organize our behaviors accordingly.

Yet conceiving a self is a process, not a static state. Our self-definitions vary over time and according to context. Years ago, for example, you defined yourself quite differently than you do today. Then your primary sense of self was probably as your parents' child. Today your family role is still part of your self-definition, but other relationships (friends, roommates, lovers, mentors) and your future goals are major parts of your self-definition, parts that did not exist 10 years ago. Our self-definitions also vary across situations. Since you are reading now, you have designated yourself as a student for the time being, and you engage in activities consistent with that definition of self: a degree of concentration, perhaps taking notes or highlighting passages of this chapter. An hour from now you may define yourself as a friend or a date and pursue very different activities—ones that conform to that role you've defined for yourself. If you have a job interview tomorrow, you'll define yourself as a candidate for employment or a prospective professional, and that label will suggest yet a third series of behaviors: formal dress, attentive posture, serious conversation, alert answers to questions. In each case you use symbols to tell yourself who you are in the moment and to indicate what activities are appropriate for the self that you've defined. Symbols, then, allow self-reflection. We rely on them to think about ourselves, to monitor our actions, and to guide how we act in diverse situations. The importance of self-reflection is summarized by the sociologist Rosenberg. He says that while all animals have consciousness, only humans have *self*-consciousness. He concludes that the ability to conceive of the self is distinctive of humans.[30] Our ability to self-reflect enables self-definition and control, both of which are potentially valuable. However, we can use self-reflection in ways that are not productive. Just as we can direct our lives in a progressive manner, so can we restrict our lives by labeling ourselves in limiting ways or by accepting restrictive labels that others apply to us.

A Case of Self-Fulfilling Prophecy[31]

Rosenthal and Jacobson, two researchers, decided to see whether labels really did affect perceptions and behaviors. To test the idea, they randomly selected 20 percent of the students in an elementary school and reported to the teachers that these children were highly gifted intellectually. For the next eight months the teachers expected these children to learn more than "normal" children. The teachers' expectations influenced how they treated the children. At the end of the eight months, these children had actually gained significantly in scores on a standard instrument for measuring intelligence. Other children, who had not been labeled "intellectual bloomers" and who had not received the consequent attention from teachers, did not gain substantially in their IQ scores.

The teachers defined the 20 percent as gifted and treated them as gifted, and they, in fact, became gifted. Self-fulfilling prophecy occurred.

When we act according to the symbols we or others apply to us, we engage in self-fulfilling prophecy. We tend to live up to or down to the symbols we accept as defining us. Children described as "troublemakers" tend to become troublemakers, just as children described as "irresponsible" tend to act responsibly. The children believe the labels applied by parents and act to fulfill those labels. Many people fulfill gender stereotypes that others apply to them from birth. For instance, research shows that parents describe boy babies with words such as "strong, active, big, and brave," while they describe girl babies with words like "dainty, quiet, little, and shy. What's particularly interesting about this finding is that the same gender-associated terms were used regardless of babies actual size and level of physical activity. Active girls were still described as dainty and quiet; small boys were still described as big and strong. Gender socialization continues throughout the early years. Little boys are told "You're so strong," "You should get on the Little League team," You're going to be quite a businessman when you grow up." Little girls are more likely to hear "You're so pretty," "You're becoming quite a little cook," "You'll be a good mother when you grow up." Most children hear these or similar descriptions of themselves, so it is not surprising that many males grow up to be strong, athletic, and successful, and females frequently grow up to be pretty (or constantly concerned with the attempt), kitchen-oriented, and mothers.[32] If we let the labels define us, they become a prophecy that we attempt to fulfill through our behaviors.

We cannot do without labels for ourselves. As noted earlier, they provide direction and a crucial sense of identity. However, we can and should avoid unthinking adherence to labels. To prevent misuse of our ability to self-reflect, we need to question labels we and others have applied to us. In what situation were they originally used? Are they still accurate? How do these labels direct our current attitudes and actions? Are they restricting us? Do we still fit the labels, or have we changed? Do we want to modify these definitions of ourselves and change the behaviors directed by them? When we ask ourselves questions like these (which in itself is a process of self-reflection) we minimize the chance of being trapped in outdated and inaccurate definitions of who we are.

SUMMARY

Symbols are the basis of language and, thus, of human communication. Because symbols are arbitrary, ambiguous, and abstract, they have no standard, "correct" meanings. Rather, they become meaningful as a result of associations built up through human interaction. The meanings we attach to things as a result of our interactions with others are modified through our individual interpretive processes. Those meanings, once constructed, form the basis of our thought and action.

Humans are distinguished from all other life forms by the way in which they think: Humans can think symbolically. It is this essential human capacity that allows us to define, organize, and attach value to our experiences, to conceive alternatives to what exists in a given place and time, and to self-reflect. Symbols are the foundation of selfhood. If we could not think symbolically, we would be confined to a primarily biological existence, accepting the world as given and reacting to it reflexively.

We may use symbols wisely or unwisely. If we abuse our symbolic capacities, we decrease our potential as humans by limiting our perceptions, stereotyping, being taken in by loaded language, being unable to commit ourselves, or living up to symbolic labels applied to us. Humans are fundamentally symbolic beings. Symbols and how we use them may enhance or diminish the quality of our lives. The choice is ours, and—because we are self-reflective and able to see alternatives—we have responsibilities, for the choices we make in using our symbols.

How Symbols Guide Thought

Were you able to solve the nine-dots puzzle presented at the beginning of this chapter?

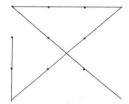

Most people who cannot solve this puzzle are blocked by how they define the problem. If you define the nine dots as a "square," you will attempt to connect the dots while staying within the "square" you have defined. Nothing in the directions for this puzzle, however, indicates that you must stay within the dots. The symbol "square" defines how you see the problem, and it guides your behaviors in attempting to solve it. Only when you redefine the problem with new symbols is it possible to solve the puzzle.

REFERENCES

[1]Don F. Faules and Dennis C. Alexander, *Communication and Social Behavior: A Symbolic Interactionist Perspective.* Reading, MA: Addison Wesley, 1978, p. 27.

[2]Joost A. M. Meerloo, *Conversation and Communication.* New York: International Universities Press, 1952.

[3] Herbert Blumer, *Symbolic Interactionism: Perspective and Method.* Englewood Cliffs, NJ: Prentice-Hall, 1969, p. 86.

[4]Blumer, pp. 78-79

[5]Blumer, p. 2.

[6]Blumer, p. 2.

[7]Blumer, p. 11.

[8]Blumer, p. 2.

[9]Ernst Cassirer, *An Essay on Man*. New Haven, CT: Yale University Press, 1978, Chapter 3.

[10]Mary G. Marcus, "The Power of a Name," *Psychology Today*, October 1986, pp. 75-108.

[11]Franz Boas, *The Mind of Primitive Man*, Rev. ed. New York: Macmillan, 1938; Benjamin L. Whorf, *Language, Thought and Reality*. New York: MIT Press/Wiley, 1956.

[12]Harry L. Weinberg, "Some Limitations of Language." In *Levels of Knowing and Existence*. New York: Harper and Row, 1959, pp. 34-47.

[13]Quoted in B. L. Whorf, p. 134.

[14]The implications of the abilities to classify and categorize are helpfully elaborated in Jerome S. Bruner, Jacqueline J. Goodnow, and George A. Austin, *A Study of Thinking*. New York: John Wiley, 1956.

[15]Wendell Johnson, *People in Quandaries*. New York: Harper and Row, 1946, p. 151.

[16]*Webster's Seventh New Collegiate Dictionary*, p. 300.

[17]*Webster's*, p. 1003.

[18]*Time*, July 26, 1976.

[19]G. A. Maddox and R. S. Ross. "Strong Words," *Childhood Education, 45*, January, 1964, 260-264.

[20]These examples were drawn from three sources: *Time*, January 29, 1951, p. 62; *Newsweek*, September 21, 1953, p. 62; and Hadley Cantril, *Soviet Leaders and Mastery Over Man*. New Brunswick, NJ: Rutgers University Press, 1960, pp. 8, 52, and 58.

[21]Franklyn S. Haiman, "An Experimental Study of the Effects of Ethos in Public Speaking." *Speech Monographs, 16*, 1949, 190-202.

[22]Troy Duster, "Conditions for a Guilt-free Massacre," In Nevitt Sanford, Craig Comstock, and Associates (Eds.), *Sanctions for Evil*. San Francisco: Jossey Bass, 1971, p. 27.

[23]Robert J. Lifton, "Existential Evil." In Sanford and Comstock, p. 41.

[24]Edward M. Opton, Jr., "It Never Happened and Besides They Deserved It." In Sanford and Comstock, p. 55.

[25]Cassirer, p. 62.

[26]Cassirer, p. 41.

[27]Richard S. Lazarus as interviewed by Daniel Goleman, "Positive Denial: The Case For Not Facing Reality," *Psychology Today*, November 1979, p. 47.

[28]George Herbert Mead, *Mind, Self, and Society*. Chicago: University of Chicago Press, 1934.

[29]Mead, pp. 260-328.

[30]Morris Rosenberg, *Conceiving the Self*. New York: Basic Books, 1979, pp. 6-7.

[31]Robert Rosenthal and Lenore Jacobson, *Pygmalian in the Classroom*. New York: Holt, Rinehart and Winston, 1968.

[32]Susan A. Basow, *Sex-Role Stereotypes: Traditions and Alternatives*. Monterey, CA: Brooks-Cole, 1980.

CHAPTER 5

NONVERBAL BEHAVIOR AS A FOUNDATION OF HUMAN COMMUNICATION

My mother was an expert in untalk—she could emit a silence so loud as to drown out the scuffle of feet, the whish of corduroy trousers, and even the grind of my father's power machinery.[1]

Communication is not restricted to words. We communicate with others with silence, facial expressions, body movements, and tone of voice. Sometimes communication without words is more clear and powerful than any words can be.

Words, in fact, account for only a small portion of the meaning in human communication. While researchers agree nonverbal behavior is important to human communication, they do not agree on exactly how important it is. Some scholars estimate that nonverbal cues make up as much as 93 percent of the social meaning in communication (55 percent face and body motion; 38 percent vocal cues; 7 percent verbal).[2] More conservative estimates claim that about 65 percent of human communication is nonverbal.[3] Even if we accept the lower figure, nonverbal behavior must be recognized as a major foundation of human communication.

This chapter focuses on the nonverbal aspects of human communication. We first define nonverbal behavior and compare it with verbal behavior. Second, we examine particular kinds of nonverbal behavior. Then we consider three primary functions of nonverbal behavior that help us understand how nonverbal actions fit into the overall communication process. The last section of this chapter emphasizes the danger of assuming we can "read" nonverbal behavior accurately. Nonverbal cues are interesting and important aspects of communication, but we need to exercise caution in interpreting what they mean.

DEFINITION OF NONVERBAL BEHAVIOR

Nonverbal behavior refers to cues without or in addition to words (verbal behavior). This includes movements of face and body, personal physical features as well as environmental factors, and how words are uttered. The significance of nonverbal cues is based on the meaning attributed to them by others—meanings do not inhere in the cues themselves. Further, our attributions of meaning should take into account the cultural and personal contexts in which nonverbal cues operate, as well as the verbal communication they often accompany.

Distinctions between Verbal and Nonverbal Behaviors

Nonverbal behavior is not equivalent to verbal communication. Nonverbal cues most often qualify a verbal message and sometimes substitute for it, but the two kinds of behavior operate in distinct ways. We can identify three basic differences between nonverbal cues and verbal communication. First, verbal communication is discrete, whereas nonverbal behavior is continuous. Second, verbal communication is digital, while nonverbal behavior is analogical. Finally, verbal communication tends to be more intentional than nonverbal behavior. Let's consider each of these distinctions more closely.

Discrete/continuous. Verbal symbols are discrete. Words are defined units with abrupt beginnings and endings. By contrast, nonverbal cues are continuous. They flow constantly, without clear starts and stops. Ray Birdwhistell, a leading scholar in the field of nonverbal behavior, distinguishes between verbal and nonverbal behavior by noting that verbal communication is "rare and intermittent in occurrence—the other continuous."[4] Consider a conversation between two people. The verbal part of their interaction consists of a series of sentences. We can note the beginning and ending of each sentence and even identify where each word starts and stops. We would have great difficulty, however, in identifying the beginnings and endings of all the nonverbal cues: changes in pitch, eye contact, subtle body movements, intonation. All of these nonverbal cues provide a context for the verbal message. They evolve continuously, one facial expression gradually blending into another, and slightly different expression, one vocal tone slowly changing to another.

Digital/analogical. A second difference between verbal and nonverbal behavior is that the former is digital, while the latter is analogical. In digital expressions there is no natural relationship between form and content. The relationship we assume between the word "tree" and a tall, leafy object is arbitrary. The form of expression (the word "tree" in this example) is not intrinsically related to the actual content (the real tree). By contrast, with analogical expression, form and content resemble each other.[5] For instance, a person says "I'm angry!" The tone of voice and the tension of body (form) resemble the emotions being expressed (content). The nonverbal cues are analogous to the actual content of the message. In his book *Joy*, Schutz refers to the body as the "analogue of the state of mind."[6] Schutz believes that our nonverbal behaviors provide cues to our internal states, feelings, and thoughts. The expressions of our bodies represent or resemble the feelings inside us. They are analogues.

Intentional/unintentional. A third difference is that we have greater control over verbal communication than over nonverbal behavior. We choose to speak or not to speak. We make decisions about the words we will or avoid. We select particular ways of arranging words into phrases and sentences we believe will be effective. We have considerably less control over our nonverbal behavior. We cannot govern such nonverbal cues as basic vocal quality, paleness or flushing of skin, or other physical characteristics, and we can only partially govern other cues such as tension, tone, or eye contact. Because we have less control over nonverbal cues, they are often thought to reveal "true" feelings and emotions more than words do. Notice that we only Think nonverbal behaviors reveal real feelings. This may or may not be true, but we tend to assume it is. This is the basis of the adage that "Actions speak louder than words." Sigmund Freud, a keen observer of human behavior, knew the importance of nonverbal cues. He wrote, "No mortal can keep a secret. If his lips are silent, he chatters with his finger tips; betrayal oozes out of him at every pore."[7]

Nonverbal cues are continuous, primarily analogical and not entirely under our control. In contrast, verbal communication is discrete, digital, and largely governed by its users. These three basic differences as well as more subtle distinctions are summarized in the following list based on research by psychiatrist Jurgen Reusch.[8]

Differences Between Verbal and Nonverbal Behavior*

Verbal

- Verbal communication is based on discontinuous functions; sounds and words have discrete beginnings and endings.
- Verbal communication is governed primarily by arbitrary, human-made principles.
- Verbal communication influences thinking.
- Understanding verbal behavior is based on prior verbal agreement.
- Verbal communication uses younger brain structures, particularly the cortex.
- Verbal communication is learned later in life.
- Words do not exist in their own right. They are arbitrary symbols representing abstractions of events.
- Verbal communication is intellectual to a great extent.

Nonverbal

- Nonverbal behavior is continuous; the hand, for instance, is continually involved in movement.
- Much nonverbal behavior is regulated by biological impulses and urges. Eye blinks, for example, are an instinctual response designed to protect eyes and keep them lubricated.
- Nonverbal behavior influences perception, coordination, and integration.
- Understanding nonverbal cues, when correct, involves participants' empathic knowledge of what behaviors means. No explanation is needed for understanding what pain is.
- Nonverbal behavior uses the old structures of the central and autonomic nervous systems.
- Nonverbal behavior is learned in early life and is a prerequisite for learning verbal behavior.
- Action and objects exist in their own right.
- Nonverbal behavior is largely related to emotions and feelings.

Symbols or Signals?

Probably you've heard people talk about "nonverbal communication" and "nonverbal language." If so, you might wonder why this chapter avoids those in preference for "nonverbal behavior." To talk about nonverbal language or nonverbal communication, we must assume that nonverbal behaviors are symbolic, a point of considerable controversy. A few people believe nonverbal behavior is symbolic. Scott and Powers,

---

*These differences are not absolute, but are verbal and nonverbal tendencies.

for instance, argue that "human communication is symbolic on more than one dimension. In addition to the verbal symbol system, we have a nonverbal symbol system."[9]

Yet, most scholars assume a more qualified position. Faules and Alexander point out that "nonverbal behavior may be signal in one context and symbolic in another, depending on intent and ambiguity."[10] Charles Larson adds another criterion for deciding whether nonverbal behavior is symbolic. He says some nonverbal behaviors such as blushing are signals, while other nonverbal behaviors such as touching are symbols. The dividing line is whether the behaviors are instinctive or learned.[11]

The symbolic interactionist perspective used in this book is compatible with the views of Larson and of Faules and Alexander. Some nonverbal behaviors are symbols in sonic contexts, but the majority of nonverbal behaviors are signals. To be considered symbolic, a nonverbal cue must have the three basic features of symbols that we discussed in Chapter 3: (a) It must be arbitrary, which implies it is learned and mediated rather than being instinctual. (b) It must be ambiguous, which means it has the potential to represent a variety of meanings and must be interpreted rather than calling for a single and automatic response. (c) It must be abstract and therefore it represents something other than itself. Any nonverbal behavior that satisfies these three criteria is symbolic. All others are signals. A wink, for example, would meet the criteria for symbolic activity.

At this point it might also be useful to distinguish nonverbal behavior from interpretation of that behavior. Even if we realize that many, perhaps most, nonverbal behaviors are not symbolic, our interpretations of them are symbolic. As we perceive a behavior, we label it and assign meaning to it. When this happens, the behavior takes on symbolic significance for us. It is symbolized through our interpretation. So while many nonverbal cues are not mediated by those who enact them, they may well be mediated by others and, thereby, gain symbolic character. With this perspective on the nature of nonverbal behavior, let us move on to consider specific kinds of nonverbal cues that influence communication.

TYPES OF NONVERBAL BEHAVIORS

Scholars have devised a number of ways to classify nonverbal behaviors, ranging from three to eighteen categories.[12] Mark Knapp came up with a typology that seems both clear and comprehensive, so we'll rely on his system.[13]

Kinesics

Kinesics are motions of the body and face. Included in this category are posture; gait; movements of hands, arms, and legs; gestures; facial expressions; and angles of interaction between people. A person who does not wish to interact with others may indicate this by folding her arms, crossing her legs, and engaging in minimum eye contact. Cues such as these are generally interpreted by others to mean the person is "closed to conversation." In classes students who do not want to be called upon engage in ostrich behavior by lowering their heads and eyes: "If I don't look at the instructor, maybe she won't look at me." The face alone is capable of over a thousand different expressions, achieved by subtle variations in angle of head, motion of eyes and mouth, and use of brows and forehead.[14] The eyes have been called the "mirror of the soul," and there may be some truth to this idea. Infants can read their mothers' moods by watching the eyes. In fact, babies become terrified when they cannot see their mothers' eyes, although not seeing other parts of mothers' faces does not alarm them.[15] Long after childhood, most people continue to seek eye contact to judge confidence, honesty, and interest. Posture and gait are often good indicators of mood. An erect posture and a brisk gait suggest determination, pride, or confidence. Sagging shoulders and shuffling feet are indicative of depression, fatigue, or reluctance. The human body and face, in fact, are remarkably expressive and versatile, and kinesics provide extensive cues about mood, intent, and openness to interaction. It's interesting to notice differences in men's and women's kinesic behaviors. In comparison to women, men tend to use more open and expansive body postures, to use more and larger gestures, to engage in more and more vigorous leg, foot, and arm movements, and to adopt a standing posture that has a more backward lean.[16] These differences are ones that seem to reflect how women and men are socialized, so they are probably learned behaviors.

Physical Characteristics

A second type of nonverbal behavior is our physical qualities. In our culture physical attractiveness is closely related to self-esteem and the ability to form interpersonal relationships.[17] Initial impressions of others are based largely on stereotypes about physical characteristics. An interesting research project investigated impressions of body types. Round, soft, plump bodies are associated with laziness, weakness, and jolliness. Thin, angular bodies are associated with youth, drive, nervousness, stubbornness, and pessimism. Athletic, muscular body shapes are interpreted as strong, adventurous, natural, and self-reliant.[18] Basic body shape, over which we have limited control, is too often a basis of initial evaluations of personalities.

Not only do others judge us by our bodies, but our own self-esteem is affected by our body image. *Psychology Today* reported that people who have positive body images perceive themselves as above average in other ways. They rate themselves as more popular, assertive, intelligent, and conscientious than most people. People with negative or less positive body images tend to rate themselves as average or below average on the same qualities.[19] Contemporary American society has placed an undue emphasis on bodily attractiveness.

The body, however, is not the only physical characteristic upon which judgments are based. Height, weight, skin color, body odor, and features of face are additional physical qualities that influence interpersonal perceptions. It is doubtful that physical characteristics have much intrinsic validity as bases for judgment. Despite this, most of us do render evaluations, at least initially, on superficial qualities.[20] Our concern with physical attractiveness and our consequent responses to attractive and unattractive people may be responsible for some of the stereotypes. Furthermore, our attitudes about physical features may create self-fulfilling prophesies like those we discussed in Chapter 4. For instance, if we treat plump people as lazy and weak they may become so, and if we treat muscular people as strong and adventurous, they may develop those qualities.

It is unfortunate that some people are prone to such superficial judgments. When we assume people who are not physically attractive are also not intelligent or desirable as friends, we expose our own shallow bases of evaluation. Judgments based on physical qualities reveal more about those who make the judgments than about those being judged. Physical qualities, of course, have no intrinsic meanings or values; whatever meanings we associate with particular physical features derive from our interpretations—a point worth remembering.

Touching Behavior

Another important type of nonverbal behavior is touching. Touch is the first of our five senses to develop, [21] and many researchers think touching and being touched are essential to healthy psychological growth. Birdwhistell studied mother-child touching in a disturbed family and reported a pattern in which the mother subtly, but persistently, pushed her child away, rejecting the child nonverbally.[22] Upset by her six-year-old daughter's withdrawal, another mother sought a counselor's help and was advised, "There is one means you haven't tried yet—touch. Touch her every chance you get . . . . Caress her. Put your hand on her shoulder, your arm around her. Pat her back. Hold her. Every chance you get."[23] The touch therapy proved effective, and the mother reported she learned to let her child "feel" love. While most of us are not so deprived as these children, we all need to be touched. Unfortunately, our culture does not encourage touching behavior except between intimates. Compared to people in other cultures, Americans touch each other relatively seldom. Jourard observed touching between couples sitting in cafes in several countries and reported these findings:[24]

San Juan, Puerto Rico	180 touches per hour
Paris, France	110 touches per hour
Gainsville, Florida	2 touches per hour
London, England	0 touches per hour

Perhaps the British and Americans have earned their reputations for being reserved. Yet, perhaps we should learn to be more expressive in our tactile behavior. Because touch is such a powerful means of expressing acceptance, affection, and reassurance, it is valuable as a primary and important way of relating to others.

Touching can indicate more than positive emotional feelings. It is also related to status. We know, for instance, that people with high status or power touch others more than do people with less status. It's also the case that people with status and power tend to "invade" the space of others (kinesic), while people with lower power tend not to do this. These differences are related to gender. Presumably because men have traditionally held more status and power in our culture, they touch and invade more than women. These differences are interestingly explored by Nancy Henley in her book, *Body Politics: Power, Sex, and Nonverbal Communication.*[25]

Paralanguage

Paralanguage refers to sounds and vocal qualities such as pitch and rate. Paralanguage involves how we say things rather than what we say. How we interpret what others say depends largely on cues of tone, inflection, rhythm, articulation, and resonance.[26] A statement made in a firm, unhesitating voice is more likely to command belief than the same statement uttered in a soft, halting manner. Sarcasm is nearly always conveyed by vocal tone that is at odds with verbal content. Pitch and tone provide cues to the intended meaning of words—they help us decide how to interpret content.

We tend to regard paralanguage as indicating mood. Children display amazing accuracy in deciphering parents' moods by tone of voice. Similarly, intimates can detect the slightest changes in each other's vocal emphases and can judge what that indicates regarding mood. Filler sounds such as "um," "er," "ah," and "uh" are often interpreted as signs of nervousness.

Can a speaker's honesty be determined by his or her paralanguage? Many people believe they can tell whether someone is being truthful by the tone and strength of voice. This long-favored intuitive method of detecting deceit has been turned into a scientific system. An invention called the Psychological Stress Evaluator (PSE) measures minute tremors and quivers of the voice to determine whether a person is speaking truthfully. Dektor Counterintelligence and Security Inc., the firm that invented the PSE, claims the device has a 94.7 percent success record in detecting lies on television shows like "To Tell the Truth." Further, the PSE has been used in several court trials.[27] The voice may indeed provide a wealth of information not found in words alone. In addition to vocal tone and stability, there are other paralinguistic cues. Whispering has long been associated with secretiveness and intimacy. Sighing may reflect boredom, resignation, or empathy, depending on its context. Whining, mumbling, and shouting influence perceptions of verbal content in communication. Accents are an interesting kind of paralanguage. Rightly or wrongly, personal qualities are associated with accents and dialects. A person with a strong Bronx accent may be perceived as brash; an Appalachian dialect may be interpreted as evidence of ignorance or lack of education; broad a's are often cultivated since they were originally associated with "upper class" speech; and someone with a Southern accent (drawl) may be perceived as lazy or very easygoing—a stereotype that became painfully clear to me when I and my Southern accent lived in Pennsylvania for two years! Numerous paralinguistic cues surround verbal communication and add to the total impact of messages.

Proxemics

Proxemics refers to our use and perception of space. From extensive research we know the distance between people varies among cultures. In Latin American countries people generally interact at close distance, while in more reserved cultures like ours a greater distance is usually maintained.[28] Edward Hall studied the interaction spaces used by Americans and reported these findings:[29]

Intimate distance	0–1 1/2 feet
Personal distance	1 1/2–4 feet
Polite, social distance	4–12 feet
Public distance	12 feet and farther

Notice the distance between people as they interact and see whether you can confirm Hall's research about how Americans use space.

In addition to distance, proxemics includes how we use space. We may sit opposite others, beside them, or at an angle to them. These positions respectively are interpreted as indicating hostility, equality, and cooperation. Seating arrangements and architectural features such as those discussed in Chapter 3 are part of proxemics. Did your father sit at the head of the table in your home? Have you noticed that group leaders often assume the head position? People with high status tend to take central places, so the proxemic behavior is analogous to the status of the individual. Not only do dominant people take central positions, but they also command more space by spreading belongings around or by extending their bodies. Further, dominant individuals are much more likely to move into other people's space than vice versa.[30] You can check this by observing interaction between a boss and a secretary or between any professionals with differing status.

How do people use space? The term "territorality" refers to the tendency of animals and humans to stake out personal territories.[31] We tend to feel "This is my space, so don't invade it!" Each of us has a sense of our appropriate personal territory—how much private space we need to be comfortable. People forced to live in crowded spaces—dorm rooms, for instance—usually define certain areas as off-limits to each other—personal territory. Sometimes one roommate will leave the room and study in the library to obtain more privacy than can be had in the room. Some people arrange office space so that they can interact openly with visitors.

Others place a desk between them and chairs for guests—the desk may be a barrier that defines both territory and status. Territorial needs underlie Robert Frost's idea that "Good fences make good neighbors." Human use and perception of space are interesting aspects of nonverbal behavior. Proxemics provide cues to personal and cultural preferences for interaction and privacy.

Artifacts

Artifacts are personal objects that can affect personal image and others impressions of us. Some examples are glasses, jewelry, briefcases, colognes, pipes, clothes, uniforms, and hair adornments. Much of how we interpret others is based on our inferences about what their artifacts mean. Research shows we tend to obey and defer to people whose dress or uniform suggests authority, but we are less likely to respond respectfully to individuals whose clothes are casual or sloopy.[32] The military uses very obvious artifacts of stripes and medals to define a rigid hierarchy among its members. Yet the military has no monopoly on the practice of using clothes to designate status or membership in a particular group. In the 1960s and early 1970s students typically wore the student uniform of jeans. Today students have other ways of symbolizing their roles as students and who is "in." Jeans are still a favorite, and tee-shirts have become another part of the "student dress." Wearing the most up-to-date styles and the "right" name brands are markers of status among students. In the business world, the gray flannel suit was a uniform for businessmen in the 1930s (and there were so few women in business that the term "businessperson" would be misleading!). Contemporary styles for businessmen have considerably more range, but the tie and jacket are virtually required parts of the uniform. It's been interesting to observe the emergence of professional styles for women. In the early 1970s when women were first entering professions in substantial numbers, the most frequent form of dress was a suit that essentially imitated the style of men's suits. In the past decade women have exercised considerably more freedom and personal style in their professional dress.

Jewelry, cosmetics, and cologne are used deliberately to make personal statements. Expensive necklaces and rings announce wealth, although the wearer may, in fact, have incurred debt to project this image. People who wear glasses tend to be judged as more intelligent and industrious than those without them. As women increasingly enter careers, they select artifacts that are different from those that were once nearly universal signals of femininity. Traditionally feminine make-up and clothing are giving way to cosmetics and styles that are meant to convey the impression of professionalism and to be functional for professional activity. For instance, few professional women wear the high and uncomfortable heels that were once worn by most women. Artifacts can also be used to alter images of people. I remember one graduate student who purchased a very expensive briefcase that he could not afford to increase his appearance of professionalism. On the other hand, several male colleagues quit wearing ties and one even began wearing jeans in the hope that students would perceive them as more informal and approachable. We all use artifacts to express something of ourselves or the selves we want others to see in us.

Environmental Factors

The last class of nonverbal cues is environmental factors. These are elements in settings that influence how we perceive, define, and act in situations. Included are furniture, decorations, lighting, colors, smells, temperature, and sounds. Features of environments influence our comfort and the way in which we interact with others. Most of us have been in homes where it seems no one lives or has ever lived—dust free, every item precisely placed, formal chairs, spotless counters and no personal items anywhere to spoil the appearance of absolute order. Relaxed, casual conversation is virtually impossible in these museum-homes. We feel stiff and formal because of the environmental factors. An entirely different atmosphere—one of reverence and solemnity—is exuded by places of worship with their quiet colors and powerful symbols such as altars, stained glass, menorahs, and candles. Libraries are designed to minimize interaction. Fast food restaurants feature uncomfortable chairs and crowded tables to encourage customers to eat quickly and move on. Offices of executives often include massive desks and expensive leather chairs as if to say the occupants are important.

Albert Mehrabian, an environmental psychologist, vividly describes the impact of the environment in mental hospitals on the health of the patients. According to Mehrabian, prior to the 1930s mental hospitals were extremely monotonous and drab: uniformly painted in serviceable colors; lacking decoration; designed without concern for facilitating social interaction. Psychologists intuitively sensed the inhumanity, of these unstimulating

> environments and recommended that they be furnished with colorful carpeting, paintings or posters and reasonably comfortable furniture .... These particular recommendations . . . proved to be effective in improving the behavior and mental health of many patients.[33]

How comfortable we are in interaction with others can be influenced by a range of environmental factors, only some of which we can control. Think of places where you tend to feel comfortable and relaxed. Analyze the environmental factors in each and see whether you can explain why you feel as you do in these settings.

Environment and Interpersonal Judgment[34]

Does the attractiveness of a room influence our perceptions of others? An experiment was conducted to answer this question. Sixteen people were placed in a "beautiful room" with soft chairs, sculptures, a Navaho rug, and warm beige walls. Sixteen others were placed in an "ugly room" with dingy gray walls, a torn lamp shade, jumbled furniture, unemptied ashtrays, and a layer of dust over everything. Ten people were placed in an "average room" that was clean but not particularly luxurious or comfortable. All subjects in the experiment were then asked to describe how energetic and pleased people appeared in a series of negatives. An average rating was 35, with ratings of below 35 indicating judgments of fatigue and displeasure and ratings of above 35 indicating judgments of high energy and pleasure. The results are summarized below:

Ugly Room	31.81
Average Room	34.00
Beautiful Room	37.99

Apparently environments do influence our perceptions of others, an important finding since our interaction is always situated in some physical environment.

So far we've examined seven kinds of nonverbal behavior: kinesics, physical characteristics, touching, paralanguage, proxemics, artifacts, and environmental factors. These nonverbal cues influence our moods, judgments, self-image, and comfort, and they affect the ease and quality of our interaction with others. We now turn to a more detailed consideration of the influence of nonverbal cues as we explore how they function in human interaction.

FUNCTIONS OF NONVERBAL BEHAVIOR

Nonverbal behavior serves three basic functions. First, it frequently qualifies verbal messages. Second, it can express attitudes and emotions more clearly than words can. Third, it defines relationships and regulates interaction between communicators. In the following pages these functions will be elaborated.

Qualification of Verbal Communication

When nonverbal cues accompany verbal messages, they function in relation to the spoken words. As part of a total message, nonverbal cues may emphasize, contradict, or complement verbal communication. Nonverbal behavior that operates in this manner is referred to as qualifying verbal communication.

Emphasizing verbal communication. Written language uses underlining, capitalization, and italics to emphasize key ideas. Spoken language relies on paralanguage and kinesics to achieve the same effects. What does it mean when your roommate says, "Your side of the room looks a little messy"? How you interpret this statement depends in large measure on paralinguistic cues that indicate what parts of the message are most important. "YOUR side of the room looks a little messy" is not equivalent to "Your side of the room looks a LITTLE messy" or to "Your side of the room looks a little MESSY." The nonverbal cues indicate what part of the message to emphasize. Professors emphasize key ideas by changing voice level, by pausing, or by repeating—each signals students that "This is important—take notes."

Kinesics, movements of body or face, are also used to emphasize what we say. The exclamation "I'm furious!" is more powerful when accompanied by clenched fists or forceful gestures. A smile, touch, or use of intimate distance functions to emphasize the verbal message, "Gee, it's good to see you!" When providing directions, we often point or gesture, giving nonverbal cues that essentially repeat the verbal message. Nonverbal cues, particularly paralinguistic and kinesic ones, function to accent verbal messages. In this way they typically increase the overall impact of communication.

Contradicting verbal communication. Nonverbal behavior can also contradict verbal communication. Some people can indicate they are very angry by the tone of voice used to say "I am not upset" or "Nothing is wrong." The way in which the statements are uttered can completely contradict the words themselves. According to veterinarians, many people have trouble training puppies because disciplinary words ("Bad dog:"'No," "Stop that") are spoken in soft, cajoling tones. The puppies understand only the nonverbal message, which indicates no criticism of wrongdoing. Some instructors announce to classes, "I am open to conferences. Please drop by my office." This verbal message, however, may be contradicted nonverbal cues such as tapping fingers, checking the watch, and shuffling papers whenever a student does come by to discuss ideas. It is difficult to believe a person who says "I'm interested in you" while watching television or reading a paper.

When verbal and nonverbal behaviors are contradictory, a mixed message is the result. Interpretation of the total communication requires you to believe one part and disbelieve the other. Which behavior—verbal or nonverbal—should we accept when confronted with mixed messages? Some researchers argue nonverbal cues are more believable, because they are more natural and harder to fake.[35] This makes sense if we assume that all nonverbal behaviors are natural—that they are signals, not symbols. However, as we've seen, much of our nonverbal behavior is learned, and some individuals are adept at nonverbal deception. To the extent that nonverbal behaviors are learned, they can be controlled and are no more or less valid than verbal communication.[36] Mixed messages, however, create confusion by communicating two different and opposing things. Thus, they can create serious constraints in communication.

Complementing verbal communication. A third form of nonverbal qualification is complementation of verbal messages. Nonverbal cues often modify or extend the meaning of verbal communication. Birdwhistell analyzed films of Fiorello La Guardia, a popular New York politician of the 1940s. He noted that La Guardia was a master of nonverbal behavior:[37]

> LaGuardia spoke Italian, Yiddish and American English . . . . The astonishing thing was that even with the sound removed, any observer who knew the three cultures could immediately detect whether he was speaking English, Yiddish or Italian . . . [by La Guardia's nonverbal behaviors].

La Guardia was truly multilingual, because he knew both the verbal and nonverbal behaviors of the three cultures. Nonverbal cues other than paralanguage may complement verbal communication. Touching or holding hands while talking may create a backdrop of affection for conversation. Someone who dresses in the latest fads may have difficulty being taken seriously. We sense authority in people who occupy posh offices and may interpret their words more positively (or more cynically!). A roaring fire—an environmental factor—is effective in creating a cozy setting that complements open, intimate communication. Intentional and unintentional nonverbal behaviors continuously complement verbal messages, providing a context for interpretation and interaction.

Nonverbal behaviors qualify verbal messages when they emphasize, contradict, or complement verbal communication. By qualifying verbal messages, nonverbal cues add to the meaning we interpret in communication with others. Usually qualifying nonverbal behaviors assist our understanding, but sometimes—as with mixed messages—they can confuse our efforts to understand.

Expression of Attitudes and Emotions

A second function of nonverbal behavior is to express attitudes and emotions. Verbal communication is most useful to convey information, while nonverbal cues are more indicative of feelings. William Brooks says, "In courtship, love, or combat, nonverbal communication is the effective mode. One can, of course, verbally profess love or trust, but it is most meaningfully communicated through the nonverbal codes."[38]

Touch, kinesics, paralanguage, and proxemics are primary ways of demonstrating emotions. Anger is expressed through bodily tension, gesture, and vocal tone and volume. Declarations of affection are believed when accompanied by a soft voice, touch, and use of intimate interaction distance. We infer hostility in people who maintain distance from us and who use eye expressions that challenge or avoid contact.[39]

Not only do nonverbal cues influence our interpretation of emotions, but we often regard them as indicating the intensity of those emotions. Muscle tone, rate of speech, and vocal volume may suggest to us how deeply someone feels about what she or he is saying. In intimate relationships partners often learn to read the degree of anger, disappointment, hurt, and other emotions of each other. Subtle nonverbal cues indicate the intensity of these emotions. How we think another feels about what he or she is saying, in fact, depends primarily on nonverbal cues we interpret.

An individual's attitude toward people or information is inferred from nonverbal cues. Posture and facial expression tend to vary according to whether we like others with whom we interact.[40] According to Leathers, expressions of evaluation and interest are suggested largely through nonverbal behavior, particularly facial cues.[41] A verbal message such as "I love the gift" is made more effective when it is accompanied by paralinguistic and facial cues that emphasize approval and pleasure.

Regulating Interaction and Defining Relationships

Nonverbal behavior helps us regulate interaction and define relationships with others. Eckman and Friesen coined the term "regulators" to refer to nonverbal cues listeners use to influence a speaker's behaviors. Through facial expressions and motion, listeners may suggest a speaker is talking too quickly or slowly, is being understood or is confusing, is interesting or dull.[42] Kinesic cues such as head nods or attentive posture indicate understanding and interest, attitudes that encourage a speaker to continue talking. A wrinkled brow, by contrast, may be interpreted by a speaker as a signal to clarify ideas. Either way, nonverbal cues regulate interaction between communicators. The regulative function extends beyond the formal arena of public speaking. Nonverbal cues, especially eye contact, regulate speaking turns in interpersonal interaction. Knapp reports conversants generally use eye contact to signal completion of an idea. When a person begins talking she looks away; she returns eye contact when ready for the other person to take his turn in the conversation.[43] We tend to look at someone who is talking until we want to speak ourselves; then we look away to signal "My turn." Throat clearing is a paralinguistic cue that may suggest a person speaking needs to wind down so another communicator can enter the conversation. Nonverbal behaviors constitute an intricate, although seldom noticed, system of regulating interaction. Nonverbal behavior is also important in defining the relationship between communicators. Our perceptions of relationships and our roles within them seem to arise largely from the nonverbal dimension of interaction. Millar and Rogers say communication "is largely a negotiation process whereby persons reciprocally define their relationships and themselves."[44] To define a relationship and the persons within it participants must settle on both the balance of control and the level of intimacy.

The control dimension of a relationship concerns dominance of partners. How much power does each person have to influence the other? Who directs whom at what specific times or in regard to which particular issues? Who makes the decisions regarding where to go, how money is to be spent, what activities to pursue? Whose preferences take priority and who defers? These are control issues in relationships. Control and power are suggested by a variety of nonverbal cues, but kinesics are especially important here. Posture, body tension, and body angle are primary cues persons use to interpret status and power. Persons with high status or power tend to assume more relaxed positions than do individuals with less power. Furthermore, people who have power command and use greater amounts of personal space (territory) than people who have less power.[45] Check the sizes of offices in any business to verify this observation. Facial position and eye contact are also associated with control. In interaction, the less powerful person tends to be more attentive to the more powerful one. An individual with low power tends to orient his or her body toward a person with greater power and tends to maintain more constant eye contact than the more powerful person. All of these kinesic behaviors signal the balance of power between people in relationships.

There are some intriguing differences in how women and men use nonverbal behaviors to regulate communication and define relationships. Research has shown that women establish more eye contact than men.[46] Given what we just discussed about status and eye contact, this indicates that men may be perceived and may perceive themselves as having more power than women. Similarly, women are more likely than men to avert their eyes, while men are more likely to engaging in staring behavior than women.[47] Again, this seems related to power since powerful individuals have the prerogative to stare and nonpowerful people are more likely to engage in the deferential behavior of averting their gaze. Yet power is only one way of interpreting these differences. Attentive listening, indicated by eye contact, and averting eyes may also reflect interest and responsiveness to others, qualities more associated with women than men. So perhaps both power and interpersonal sensitivity explain differences in the sexes' use of nonverbal behavior to regulate communication and define relationships.

Intimacy is a second aspect of relationships that is largely established by nonverbal behavior. The openness between persons is frequently reflected in their kinesic behaviors. How often do partners touch and how intimate is the touching behavior? Both are positively associated with closeness between people.[48] Paralinguistic cues reflect warmth or aloofness, either of which may be interpreted as indicating level of intimacy between people.

Intimacy may also be reflected in artifacts such as rings, pins, or mementos. Another artifact that seems to reflect intimacy is tee-shirts. For the past several years, female college students have worn the tee-shirts or sweat shirts of their male partners. One of my students even confessed that she had a "collection" of these shirts from past partners! Artifacts and environmental factors may be used to create a scene that reminds partners of their shared past. As they interact amidst posters from movies they've attended and with candles dripping on wine bottles from special occasions they've celebrated, feelings of closeness may be heightened. Proxemic cues are also associated with the degree of intimacy between people. Typically, the more intimate we are with another person, the more we share space and allow that person to enter our private territory. Increasing the amount of shared space and the frequency of occupying common space escalates intimacy; at the same time increased intimacy generally leads to increased assignment and use of common space. Intimacy and space are reciprocally influential in defining a relationship.

The Common Space of Intimates[49]

Living together maximizes the number of occasions intimates can conjoin themselves and thickens the glue that cements their psychological joints together. Intimates who live together have more opportunities to experience common circumstances than do those who live apart: they can be in each other's presence more often; they can decorate their living quarters to suit their common taste; they have a common place in which to entertain and confront their friends as a pair. Intimates who live together can more easily harmonize their physiological rhythms, such as eating, sleeping, and sex. A common household expedites the transformation of individual . . . into mutual.

The converse is also true. We tend to be especially protective of our personal territory around people we define as nonintimates, particularly ones who are ex-intimates. We do not want to share space with them, and we don't want them invading our private zones.

Denial of Common Space by Nonintimates[50]

One occasion in which an individual must take action to keep from integrating his self-components with another's occurs when neither particularly wants the resulting intimacy, but external forces compel them to intersect their selves. Although a limited supply of funds and housing in a college town may force two nonintimates to live together, each of them is likely to take steps to ensure his independence from the other. Each may keep his food in separate parts of their refrigerator, may create private alcoves in their common abode, may keep different hours, and, in general, may attempt to segregate as many of his self-components as he can within their overall state of forced integration.

In the early stages of a relationship, individuals often engage in nonverbal negotiation of an appropriate level of intimacy. Kendall persistently reaches over to touch Chris; Chris just as persistently pulls away or freezes. The two are nonverbally arguing over the level of intimacy that will define their present relationship. The same pattern can be identified in nonintimate relationships. Businessperson X has just met businessperson Y and wants to convince Y to go along with some corporate deal. Interaction proceeds, with X slapping Y's back, moving into Y's personal space, and using a chummy longtime-friends tone of voice to convince Y they are friends. Meanwhile Y is uncomfortable with X's overly friendly kinesics, and so Y moves away from the backslapping, moves behind a desk to regain personal space, and employs formal paralinguistics. Again, we have a nonverbal negotiation over how the relationship is to be defined.

Nonverbal behaviors regulate interaction and define relationships. We use and respond to a variety of nonverbal cues to regulate turntaking in conversation and to suggest ways to modify the content of communication. In relationships nonverbal behaviors define control and intimacy between persons. Through a range of nonverbal cues we negotiate and eventually establish a power balance and an acceptable level of intimacy between us and those with whom we interact. More importantly, it is the nonverbal dimension of interaction that establishes a context appropriate to the kind of relationship we have or desire with another. By arranging our environments and ourselves we create scenes that invite particular ways of relating to others.

To summarize, nonverbal behavior serves three basic functions. First, it qualifies verbal messages by emphasizing, contradicting, or complementing the verbal communication. Second, it is the primary basis for our interpretations of attitudes and emotions as well as the intensity of each. Third, nonverbal behavior regulates interaction and partially defines relationships by establishing control and intimacy and by constituting the scene for interaction.

EXERCISING CAUTION IN INTERPRETING NONVERBAL BEHAVIOR

Efforts to understand communication traditionally have focused on the verbal dimension. Only, in the past few decades have we become aware of the major importance of nonverbal behavior as part of the total communication process. Because attention and study are recent, current knowledge is limited. Many questions have yet to be answered:

How much of our nonverbal behavior is learned rather than instinctual?
Do different people interpret nonverbal cues the same way?
How much do our cognitive and emotional states influence our interpretations of nonverbal cues?
Can we learn to control our nonverbal behaviors in order to manage our images more effectively?

These and other questions are currently under study, but we cannot answer them yet. Because we lack complete understanding of nonverbal cues and their role in communication, we need to exercise caution in our use and interpretation of them. Some people are convinced they can read anyone's nonverbal behavior with accuracy. In addition, they often think they can manipulate their own nonverbal actions precisely in order to project the image they want others to have of them. These assumptions, though faulty, are understandable. They are probably held by people who have been taken in by some of the popular books on nonverbal behavior that promise you can learn to "read" other people, can pick up dates by recognizing nonverbal signals of availability, and so forth. Such promises sell books, but they also mislead many readers. It is naive to believe we can decipher something as complex and individual as nonverbal behavior with real precision. And it is often dangerous to attempt it. You could misread someone and offend them by acting on Your interpretation of their behaviors.

This chapter presented many generalizations about nonverbal behavior. For instance, we noted that folded arms are frequently associated with being closed to interaction, dominant individuals use more space than less powerful persons, and touching generally reflects affection. All such generalizations are broad statements regarding what has been observed about a majority of people in specific contexts. They do not necessarily pertain to any particular person in any given situation. The generalizations presented in this chapter (and most of those you encounter in other places as well) should be qualified by contextual and personal considerations.

Contextual Qualification

Nonverbal cues cannot be understood apart from the context in which they occur. This reflects the nature of communication as systemic, which we first discussed in Chapter 2. Suppose you meet someone who has a "closed" posture and who uses tense, clipped paralanguage. Is that person indicating "I don't like you" or "I'm nervous in this situation" or "I'm working something out privately right now" or "Something entirely apart from this situation is unpleasant to me"? The point is that you can't know from the nonverbal cues which of these interpretations is correct or whether, in fact, any of them is. Most people are more relaxed in their own homes or apartments than in unfamiliar settings, and it is likely their nonverbal behaviors will reflect this. Probably we would sense greater warmth and openness if we met someone at home than in a conference center. We might be tempted to describe the person we met at-home in one way and the same person, met at a conference center, in quite another way based on differences in nonverbal behavior. So the setting is a major consideration we need to take into account when we try to interpret nonverbal cues.

Even more than immediate context, nonverbal behaviors must be considered within their cultural contexts. Americans are (in)famous for misunderstanding the nonverbal behaviors of people from other cultures, and vice versa. Touching, for instance, tends to be more free in France than in the United States. A French person who touches an American frequently during conversation may not be suggesting intimate intentions, but the American may infer them. Arabic people interact at much closer distances than is typically comfortable for Americans, so they are often misinterpreted by Americans as being "pushy." In Japan, maintaining eye contact is often a sign of disrespect. When a Japanese person does not meet an American's eyes, the American is prone to impute motives of dishonesty or evasion. This is a misinterpretation, based on how widely cultural rules for nonverbal behavior vary.

Even within our own country, ethnic and regional differences invite misinterpretations of nonverbal behaviors. A New Yorker who moves to Georgia may be judged as abrupt or cold on the basis of kinesic and paralinguistic cues that are completely appropriate in New York. Conversely, a Georgian who moves to New York may be viewed as inefficient on the basis of slower motion and softer speech. By now you should realize that's it's essential to consider situational and cultural contexts when interpreting nonverbal behavior.

Personal Qualification

We've already noted that what we know about nonverbal behavior consists of generalizations. By definition, a generalization states what is generally the case, and by implication this means that it does not state what is always the case—that, in fact, there are exceptions to the generalization. Thus, what may be true of nonverbal behavior of people in general may not pertain to a given person. Nonverbal behaviors vary among individuals and even vary for a particular person over time. The professor who directed my doctoral studies seldom looked at people when conversing. Instead, he drew elaborate geometric designs on a large tablet he carried with him. It was tempting for others to assume he was disinterested in what they had to say, because his nonverbal behaviors suggested he wasn't paying attention. A number of students did draw this conclusion—much to their dismay when they found out just how carefully he had been listening. This professor's questions and responses invariably made it clear that he had not only listened, but listened intently. He could and generally did respond with the most incisive and difficult questions of any of the faculty. He simply had an unusual way of listening! Generalizations about the relationship between eye contact and interest did not apply in the case of this individual.

When we are tired we tend to move more slowly, sit less attentively, use fewer gestures, engage in less eye contact, and employ less inflection in our speech. Consequently, a person who is fatigued may be interpreted as bored or unfriendly. Crossed arms may in some cases mean a person is closed to interaction. However, they may just as easily mean the person feels cold! Because such ambiguities are present, we need to exercise caution in our interpretations of others' nonverbal behaviors. This is especially true when we try to interpret the behavior of people whom we don't know well—we have no history to go on and no understanding of the range of their individual nonverbal expressions.

A Case for Caution[51]

There are many people whose emotional intentions and self-images are out of harmony with their actual behavior. I shall never forget two examples of this discordance. One girl, who tried like everyone else to appear angry, fearful, seductive, indifferent, happy and sad . . . appeared to her judges as angry in every case. Imagine what a difficult world she must have lived in. No matter where she set the thermostat of her emotional climate, everyone else always felt it as sweltering hot. Another girl in our experiment demonstrated a similar one dimensionality; only in her case, whatever else she thought she was doing, she invariably impressed her judges as seductive. Even when she wanted to be angry, men whistled at her.

We assign meanings to others' behaviors. The behaviors themselves do not contain meanings. Since we interpret others' actions, it is our responsibility to be appropriately careful in the judgments we draw. To communicate effectively we should qualify our interpretations with an awareness of how context and personal style influence each individual's nonverbal behaviors. John Condon makes this point well when he says, "There is a great difference between reading and reading into the expressions of others."[52] Effective communicators recognize this distinction and attempt to avoid reading into others' nonverbal behaviors.

SUMMARY

This chapter explored nonverbal behavior as a foundation of human communication. Nonverbal behavior was defined as cues that exist without or in addition to words. Researchers believe nonverbal cues are responsible for at least 65 percent of the meaning assigned to communication. Compared with verbal communication, nonverbal behavior is more continuous, more analogical, and less controlled. These differences cast doubt on the symbolic nature of nonverbal cues. According to current understandings, the most reasonable position is that some nonverbal behavior in some contexts is symbolic, but other forms of nonverbal behavior, perhaps the majority, are signals. Moreover, as we interpret nonverbal behaviors, they take on symbolic character and, therefore, become communicative. This symbolic quality, however, results from an interpreter's mediation, not from the behaviors themselves.

We considered seven kinds of nonverbal behavior: kinesics, physical characteristics, touching, paralanguage, proxemics, artifacts, and environmental factors. These nonverbal behaviors function in three basic ways: They qualify verbal messages by emphasizing, contradicting, or complementing communication; they are generally superior to verbal communication in conveying attitudes and feelings; and they regulate and define interaction between people. By serving these three functions, nonverbal behaviors supplement and enrich the overall process of human communication.

Finally, we noted that nonverbal behavior is a relatively new area of study. For this reason we have limited knowledge of how people use and interpret it. To avoid "reading into" others' behaviors, communicators should consider nonverbal cues within context and in reference to the particular individuals using them. In addition, communicators may increase their personal effectiveness by becoming more aware of their own nonverbal behaviors and the meanings they may suggest to others. Because nonverbal cues influence our impressions of others and our interactions with them, they form an important foundation of human communication. A solid understanding of the nature and importance of nonverbal behavior requires us to recognize our own involvement in attributing meaning to behaviors. It is crucial to distinguish between nonverbal behavior itself and our interpretation of it. Once this distinction is granted, we should acknowledge the need to be cautious and responsible about our interpretations of others' behaviors and their underlying intentions, feelings, and attitudes.

REFERENCES

[1]Ray L. Birdwhistell, *Kinesics and Context*. New York: Ballantine, 1970, p. 66.
[2]Albert Mehrabian, "Communication Without Words," *Psychology Today*, September 1968, p. 53.

[3]Birdwhistell, as cited in Mark Knapp, *Nonverbal Communication Systems*. New York: Holt, Rinehart, and Winston, 1972, p. 12.

[4]Birdwhistell, p. 96.

[5]John Condon, *Interpersonal Communication*. New York: Macmillan, 1977, p. 86.

[6]William Schutz, *Joy*. New York: Grove Press, 1967.

[7]Cited in William Brooks, *Speech Communication*. Dubuque, IA: Wm. C. Brown, 1974, p. 176.

[8]Jurgen Reusch, "Nonverbal Communication," *Psychiatry, 18*, 1955, 323-330.

[9]Michael D. Scott and William G. Powers, *Interpersonal Communication: A Question of Needs*. Boston: Houghton Mifflin, 1978, p. 35.

[10]Don F. Faules and Dennis C. Alexander, *Communication and Social Behavior: A Symbolic Interactionist Perspective*. Reading, MA: Addison-Wesley, 1978, p. 38.

[11]Charles U. Larson, *Communication: Everyday Encounters*. Belmont, CA: Wadsworth, 1976, p. 50.

[12]Randall P. Harrison, *Beyond Words: An Introduction to Nonverbal Communication*. Englewood Cliffs, NJ: Prentice-Hall, 1974, p. 29.

[13]Mark L. Knapp, *Nonverbal Communication in Human Interaction*. New York: Holt, Rinehart and Winston, 1972, pp. 5-8.

[14]Paul Eckman, W. Friesen, and P. Ellsworth, *Emotion in the Human Face: Guidelines for Research and an Integration of Findings*. Elmsford, NY: Pergamon Press, 1971.

[15]Rene Spitz, *The First Year of Life*. New York: International Universities Press, 1965.

[16]Judy C. Pearson, *Gender and Communication*. Dubuque, IA: Wm. C. Brown, 1985, p. 252.

[17]D. Byrne, S. London, and K. Reeves, "The Effects of Physical Attractiveness, Sex, and Attitude Similarity in Interpersonal Attraction," *Journal of Personality, 36*, 1968, 259-272.

[18]W. Wells and B. Siegel, "Stereotyped Somatypes," *Psychological Reports, 8*, 1961, 77-78.

[19]W. Wells and B. Siegel, *Psychology Today*, November 1973, p. 126.

[20]P.B. Warr and C. Knapper, *The Perception of People and Events*. New York: John Wiley, 1968, pp. 508-516.

[21]Dale G. Leathers, *Nonverbal Communication Systems*. Boston: Allyn and Bacon, 1976, p. 142.

[22]Birdwhistell, pp. 13-28.

[23]Cited in R. Adler and N. Towne, *Looking Out/Looking In*. New York: Holt, Rinehart, and Winston, 1975, pp. 265-267.

[24]Reported in Knapp, p. 109.

[25]N. Henley, *Body Politics: Power, Sex, and Nonverbal Communication*. Englewood Cliffs, NJ: Prentice-Hall, 1977.

[26]G.L. Trager, "Paralanguage: A First Approximation," *Studies in Linguistics, 13*, 1958, 1-12.

[27]G.L. Trager, "Big Brother is Listening," *Time*, Cited in Adler and Towne, p. 260.

[28]E.T. Hall, *The Silent Language*. Greenwich, CT: Fawcett Publications, 1959.

[29]E.T. Hall, *The Hidden Dimension*. New York: Anchor Books/Doubleday, 1966, pp. 111-129.

[30]R. Sommer, "Further Studies of Small Group Ecology," *Sociometry, 28*, 1965, 337-348.

[31]E.T. Hall, *The Hidden Dimension*, p. 13.

[32]L. Bickman, "Social Roles and Uniforms: Clothes Make The Person," *Psychology Today*, April 1974, pp. 49-51.

[33]A. Mehrabian, *Public Places, Private Spaces*. New York: Basic Books, 1976, p. 185.

[34]A.H. Maslow and N. L. Mintz, "Effects of Esthetic Surroundings: Initial Effects of Three Esthetic Conditions upon Perceiving 'Energy' and 'Well-being' in Faces," *Journal of Psychology, 41*, 1956, 247-54.

[35]Brooks, p. 179.

[36]Knapp.

[37]Birdwhistell, pp. 130-131.

[38]Brooks, p. 177.

[39]S. Feldman, *Mannerisms of Speech and Gesture in Everyday Life*. New York: International Universities Press, 1959.

[40]H.M. Rosenfield, "Instrumental Affiliative Functions of Facial and Gestural Expressions," *Journal of Personality and Social Psychology, 4*, 1966, 65-72.

[41]Leathers, pp. 33-34.

[42]Eckman, Friesen, and Ellsworth.

[43]Knapp, p. 131.

[44]F. E. Millar and L. E. Rogers, "A Relational Approach to Interpersonal Communication." In G. R. Miller. *Explorations in Interpersonal Communication*. Beverly Hills, CA: Sage Publications, 1976, p. 88.

[45]Henley.

[46]Henley; Pearson.

[47]Henley; Pearson.

[48]E. G. Beier, "Nonverbal Communication: How We Send Emotional Messages," *Psychology Today*, October 1974, pp. 53-56.

[49]M. Davis, *Intimate Relations*. New York: Free Press, 1973, pp. 192-193.

[50]Davis, p. 199

[51]Beier, p. 55.

[52]Condon, p. 87.

CHAPTER 6

LISTENING AS A FOUNDATION OF HUMAN COMMUNICATION

We have been given two ears and but a single mouth in order that we may hear more and talk less.

(Zeno of Citium)

Commitments to Listening

    Responsible participation in communication

    The value and rights of Individuals
        Value of individuals
        Freedom of expression
        Value of self-determination

    Dual perspective

    Situational Sensitivity

Listening Behaviors

    General listening behaviors
        Preparation
        Controlling biases and expectations
        Determinaton of listening purpose

Behaviors Adapted to Particular Listening Goals

    Listening for infomation

    Listening for understanding

When most people think about communication, they think of talking. Talking is important, yet it is not the whole of communication. Because communication is interaction between people it must involve more than just a person expressing ideas. There must also be someone to listen and respond.

Few people practice effective listening—a fact that is disturbing since roughly 40 percent of the average person's communication activity is listening to others.[1] If we don't listen well, we're being ineffective communicators 40 percent of the time! A primary reason for poor listening in America is our culture's emphasis on individual expression and assertion. Chase, a scholar of listening, explains that "competition in our culture puts a premium on self-expression even if the individual has nothing to express."[2] But as Johnson wryly pointed out years ago, "Communication is a process with four legs."[3] What he meant by this is that communication involves more than one person who talks: It also involves people who listen or there can be no sharing of ideas. In fact, if you think about it, you'll realize that without listeners talking is pointless. As Chase reminds us, "If people stop listening, it is useless to talk."[4]

Because listening is a primary foundation of human communication, this entire chapter focuses on it. As we'll see, to develop personally and to contribute to others and our communities, we need to become sensitive and skilled listeners. But what does it mean to be a sensitive and skilled listener? To begin answering that question let's establish a definition of listening.

> Effective listening consists of commitments and behaviors that promote understanding, growth of self and others, and responses adapted to particular communication situations.

Effective listening grows out of commitments to the process of human communication, to individual rights, to understanding others' perspectives, and to awareness of situations. These commitments underlie the behaviors associated with responsible listening. Furthermore, effective listening behaviors are not always the same. As we saw in previous chapters, communication always occurs within a context. Because it is systemic, effective engagement in communication depends on understanding the situation within which it occurs. The purposes of situations and the goals of communicators vary among contexts. This implies that what is effective listening will also vary among contexts. Critical judgment, for instance, is appropriate when listening to a persuasive message, but the same listening style might be out of place when listening to an intimate's disclosure. There is no universal recipe for listening behaviors—they, like all aspects of communication, must be adapted situationally.

In this chapter we first examine several general commitments and behaviors that promote effective listening, regardless of situation. We then explore how situational constraints influence how we adapt those general commitments and behaviors into specific choices that are appropriate in particular situations.

COMMITMENTS TO LISTENING

Human behavior reflects commitments. Individuals who lobby and protest against strip mining do so because of a commitment to the integrity of the environment. The person who returns a lost wallet reflects a commitment to honesty. The scientist who works overtime in a laboratory is committed to research and its ability to explain phenomena. The vegetarian who does not to eat meat for moral reasons (and perhaps not fish or dairy by-products either) is committed to kindness toward animals and perhaps the nutritional health of citizens in third world countries. Your choice to attend college, even your reading of this chapter right now, suggests you are committed to education, either as something intrinsically valuable or as a means to some other goal you consider worthy. None of the behaviors in these examples takes place without commitment. In fact, most human choices of attitude and action are motivated by our commitments. They are the reasons for what we do.

The centrality of commitment to human behavior pertains to listening. The choices we make about when and how to listen reflect particular commitments on our parts. These are the foundation of the way we listen—or fail to. Some commitments tend to be more useful than others in promoting effective, situationally sensitive listening. So we want to consider four commitments that underlie good, responsive listening. You might think of these as goals toward which you can strive in your overall effort to become a more effective communicator.

Responsible Participation in Communication

Previous chapters stressed the dynamic, active quality of human communication. Participants in communication must also be active, whether talking or listening. Responsibility for the effectiveness of any communication is shared by those who speak and those who listen. As we noted in the opening chapter, the speaker alone cannot ensure effective communication and should not be held solely responsible for doing so. Instead, all participants in an interaction must assume responsibility for the quality of communication. To do this requires a basic commitment to communication itself. "Listening demands work," says Egan. "The effort will not be expended unless the listener has deep respect for the communication process."[5] To respect the communication process is to value both talking and listening as equally important parts of it.

Someone who speaks or writes cannot be successful without the cooperation of someone who listens or reads. No matter how much effort I devote to writing this book, I cannot make it meaningful to you. You must invest thought, time, and effort too. If the ideas you find here assume meaning and value for you, the credit belongs to us both. If the material in this book does not become important to you, the blame lies with us both. We are involved in joint transaction, and we share responsibility for effectiveness. Face-to-face communication is also a joint transaction in which responsibility is shared. According to Weaver, listening "is an active, not a passive process. We cannot just make sure that our ears are alert or open and let the rest come naturally . . . . It does not just happen. We have to make it happen . . . . It takes energy and commitment."[6] Effective listening is possible only when listeners accept their responsibility as active participants in the total process of human communication.

Communication occurs when humans interact with symbols. But, as we have seen, our symbols do not have fixed, uniform meanings. Each person attributes meaning to particular symbols. An important implication of this point is that listeners must interact with speakers' symbols. Merely using words and nonverbal behaviors is not meaningful, except as intrapersonal communication. Only when one person interacts with the symbols used by another person can communication between people take place. Without a listener's involvement, a message has meaning only to the person who speaks. The potential of communication to link people depends on their mutually investing in creating meanings.

Symbols, in turn, can become meaningful only through participation in communication. For Kelly, listening is a central concern. He emphasizes the necessity of active participation by listeners in communication situations. Kelly says, "It is easy to sit back in your chair and complain to yourself that the discussion is boring or unimportant . . . . Obviously there are times when a person may be just as well off not listening, but the poor listener tends to make this a crutch for the easy way out."[7] Kelly's point is that a message becomes interesting or important to listeners only if they participate actively in communication. To be a good listener, then, we must first commit to active participation in communication, realizing that effectiveness and meaning are achieved jointly by those involved.

The Value and Rights of Individuals

A second foundation of effective listening is an ethical commitment to the value and rights of individuals. Initially, this idea may appear out of place in a discussion of listening, but a little reflection will demonstrate the close connection between respect for individuals and listening. To listen to another person we must first believe there is some potential value in that person and her or his thoughts. Further, we must believe in that individual's right to express ideas, even ones that we dislike. Finally, we must believe in each individual's freedom to determine and act upon personal convictions without coercion or interference. Commitment to the worth of individuals entails all three of these beliefs.

Value of Individuals. Sensitive communicators—whether speaking or listening—act from the assumption that others are important. Attention and response convey the crucial message "I am aware of your existence and I think you are important and unique." This is an attitude of rhetorical sensitivity that is based on respect for both self and others and for the interaction between communicators.[8] Respect for others does not necessarily mean agreement with their ideas. You may disagree, even disagree strongly, with an individual's stands on particular issues. Yet it is still possible to value the individual as a person. In so doing, you invite continued communication that may allow eventual agreement between you and the other person. By accepting others as persons you increase opportunities for presenting your own ideas and perhaps influencing those of others. Rogers believes people are most likely to change their ideas when they feel accepted as persons, because their self-esteem is not at stake if they consider anothers position.[9] Building on Rogers' point, Brown and Keller say, "If there is a chance of persuading a person, it is because the person is permitted to retain his or self-esteem."[10] When we listen reflectively to someone else's point of view, we earn the right to state our own. Out of the exchange of ideas both communicators have a chance to grow and to refine the positions they originally held.

To demonstrate that they value other persons and are open to ideas, good listeners refrain from coercive responses such as interruptions, frowns, and exaggerated head-shaking. Later, listeners may present different points of view, debate issues with the original speaker, and engage in a lively exchange of opinion. In fact, listeners who ask questions and bring out differing ideas actually complement speakers. These responses demonstrate interest and attention which confirm listeners' respect for the personhood of the speaker.

Freedom of expression. A commitment to the worth of individuals implies a firm belief in freedom of expression. In addition to respecting others as persons, good listeners also respect others' rights to express ideas. This means each person deserves as a full hearing without interference. In theory, most people support freedom of expression, yet far fewer act in ways consistent with the principle. A common excuse for not hearing someone out is "Some ideas simply don't deserve to be heard." Maybe not, but who has the right to decide which ideas should be heard and which ones censored? Many people refused to listen to Martin Luther King, yet no one silenced Hitler. The point is that none of us has sufficient wisdom to dictate which ideas should receive a hearing. We best ensure our personal and social development not just by allowing, but by encouraging expression of diverse views.

Again we are reminded of the interactive nature of communication. Each person influences the other. Applied to freedom of expression, this suggests that your willingness to listen to others' ideas tends to increase their willingness to listen later to yours. But it is a willingness we earn anew each time we communicate. If we expect others to consider our ideas, we must consider theirs. If we do not listen fairly to others, we have no basis for asking them to attend to us. When we listen fairly and fully to others, we learn their views, the reasons behind them, and the meanings they attribute to their symbols. These understandings provide the essential foundation for continued interaction between people.

Value of self-determination. According to Nilsen, a major principle of democracy is belief in self-determination as a means to individual fulfillment.[11] People who commit to this belief do not try to control or exploit those with whom they communicate.[12] Instead, they assume that every individual is entitled to make free choices regarding personal convictions and behaviors.

Belief in self-determination implies acceptance of personal responsibility for your responses to communication. Suppose you become angry when listening to another person's opinions about nuclear energy. Is the anger caused by the person who spoke? If you accept the principle of self-determination, it is inconsistent to attribute your responses to the speaker. As a free, self-determining individual you select and enact your own responses to any situation. Responsible listeners neither blame nor credit a speaker for their own responses, because they realize those responses arise from their interpretations of the speaker's ideas and the meanings they have attached to the speaker's symbols. It is difficult to accept a genuine commitment to self-determination, because it strips away our rationalizations for behavior and emotions. "He made me do that!" "Your statement made me so angry, I couldn't help what I did." "If you hadn't talked me into going, this never would have happened." "You convinced me to do it." These are convenient and often comforting excuses, but they are inconsistent with a belief in self-determination. So part of effective listening is realizing that *you*, not someone else, controls your responses and feelings. The responsibility cannot be shirked.

Belief in self-determination has a second important implication for listeners. We want to select carefully those ideas, values, and goals that guide our lives. To avoid whimsical or expedient choices, we must expose ourselves to a variety of ideas and opinions. Ideally, our choices of attitude and action should be based on full awareness of all alternatives and their possible consequences. In reality, of course, such comprehensive knowledge is not possible. However, it is possible to enlarge knowledge of alternatives and their consequences by exposing ourselves to diverse points of view. Perry emphasizes this idea when he says people are "deprived of freedom in proportion as [they are] denied access to any ideas or [are] confined to any range of ideas short of the totality of relevant possibilities."[13] By actively seeking divergent views and by considering each reflectively, we construct solid foundations for our choicemaking.

The Marketplace of Ideas[14]

If there is free and unhampered expression of opinions, the many competing interests, by presenting their respective views and arguments and criticizing others, will provide the kind of information and critical appraisal that will make possible for the listeners the most constructive choices. This "marketplace of ideas" is fundamental to a democratic society.

There are limits to what can be expected of an individual speaker. If he has conscientiously informed himself, if he discusses the issues honestly and objectively, with a commitment to his listener's right to know and choose, we can ask no more. At the same time, a free society can ask no less. The responsible presentation and discussion of diverse views permits and fosters the kind of choice making that is the essence of a free society.

No one of course, can know of all the relevant possibilities; freedom is never absolute. Our effort must be to make this "freedom of effective choice" as great as possible.

Listening is based on an ethical commitment to the value and rights of individuals. This implies that good listeners value others, encourage freedom of expression, and believe in self-determination. Together these beliefs form a philosophy for the attitudes communicators hold toward one another and toward the process of human communication.

Dual Perspective

"Nobody understands my point of view." "Why don't you look at it from my perspective?" "You aren't even trying to see where I'm coming from." How often have you felt no one was trying to understand you? How often have others accused you of not trying to understand them? When people talk but do not attempt to understand each other, they talk past each other. Communication becomes a series of egocentric one-liners:

S: I'm really worried about choosing my major.
T: Yeah, I know what you mean. Do you think I can afford to skip my 10 o'clock class again Friday to go camping?
S: No big deal unless you have a quiz. My advisor says I need to declare my major this semester. How do I know what I want to do with the rest of my life?
T: It's tough, allright. Well, I gotta run—late for a study date. Catch you later.

In this example each person used the other as a sounding board. Neither person really attended or responded to the other. Genuine listening was absent, so the people talked past each other.

To avoid talking past each other, communicators should make a third commitment, to *dual perspective*. Dual perspective is recognition of someone else's perspective in addition to your own.[15] A listener with dual perspective not only understands her or his own views, but attempts to recognize the views of the speaker *from the speaker's perspective*. Because individuals attach different meanings to symbols, listeners don't necessarily understand what is meant by someone who is speaking. And it's insufficient to attach *our* meanings to others' words. That's listening to them through our own perspective. Instead, we need to try to discover what particular symbols mean to those who use them. To do this, a listener may need to "step out of his or her own perspective and temporarily "step into" the perspective of a speaker. If you have never had an unplanned pregnancy, you have no personal experience to help you understand the anxiety of a friend who is pregnant. Not having been in that situation, how can you respond thoughtfully to your friend's feelings and requests for support and help in deciding what to do?

To discuss the situation and to respond to your friend's needs, you must become aware of her perspective and what her situation means *to her*. This isn't a matter of deciding what it would mean to you. Instead, your initial goal has to be to learn what it does mean to her. When you can understand how she sees the situation as well as how you do, then you have dual perspective.

Many misunderstandings and hurt feelings result from a lack of dual perspective. Each person approaches the other from only a personal orientation, with little awareness of the other's orientation or even that there could be a viewpoint different from their own. Parents sometimes judge their children's behaviors by standards that prevailed 20 years ago. Children accuse parents of being "old-fashioned" or having "medieval mentalities" when their parents don't condone contemporary values. Teachers chastise students for being too grade-oriented and too career-focused in college. Since teachers have jobs and most attended school when the job market was less competitive than it is today, however, it's doubtful that they understand their students' perspective on the contemporary situation. Americans are quick to label attitudes and behaviors in other cultures as backward if they do not conform to those in our own country. The list could go on endlessly. In case after case we respond to others and situations from a highly personal perspective that does not incorporate the views of those whom we interpret. It is easy to view others from our own perspectives, but to do so is a disservice to ourselves and to them. To listen responsibly to another person we must attempt to discover and listen from that person's frame of reference. We cannot understand another's ideas or meanings outside of that person's perspective.

Carl Rogers on Communication[16]

The major barrier to mutual interpersonal communication is our very natural tendency to judge, to evaluate, to approve or disapprove, the statement of another person . . . . As you leave this meeting tonight, one of the statements you are likely to hear is, "I didn't like that man's talk." Now what do you respond? . . . Either you respond, "I didn't either. I thought it was terrible," or else you tend to reply, "Oh, I thought it was really good." In other words your primary reaction is to evaluate what has just been said to you, to evaluate it from your point-of-view, your own frame of reference . . . . There will be two ideas, two feelings, two judgments, missing each other in psychological space.

Achieving dual perspective is no simple task. Actually, none of us can ever fully see the world through the mind of another. Yet each of us can approach the ideal of dual perspective, and this increases our effectiveness as listeners. To achieve a realistic level of dual perspective, listeners need to be in touch with themselves and others. We must first be aware of our own feelings, attitudes, and biases regarding a topic of communication. Egan notes that "people who are out of touch with themselves keep stumbling over themselves as they try to communicate with others."[17] Egan means listeners must realize what is going on inside themselves so they can better understand and control their responses. We cannot listen to others until we have listened to ourselves. By recognizing our own perspective we prepare ourselves to listen openly and alertly.

Listeners should next try to understand what feelings, attitudes, and understandings others may have toward the topic of communication. Communication is interaction between people and the meanings they assign to their symbols. Each communicator is responsible for discovering the perspective of the other. Without this there can be little genuine interaction. To be effective, we adapt communication to the people and situation at hand. In turn, appropriate adaptation assumes awareness of the views, values, and general orientations of others. Skill in communication is directly tied to the ability to assume the perspective of others and to incorporate those perspectives into a total perspective on the situation.[18] Listeners who are in tune with themselves are more able to understand speakers. When listeners appreciate a speaker's perspective, they increase the likelihood of mutual growth through communication of high quality.

Dual perspective is essential to effective listening. Just as speakers need to be aware of listeners' meanings, so too are listeners obliged to consider speakers' meanings. When we aim for dual perspective, we show that we are concerned with what communication means to both ourselves and those with whom we interact. With dual perspective we avoid purely egoistic thought that begins and ends with ourselves: *I think. I feel. I mean. I believe.* Instead, we interact from an enlarged awareness of ourselves and those with whom we communicate.

Egospeak[19]

We seem to be so busy "speaking" to each other that we're not really "saying" very much. Conversation, or the art of such, is being "lost" only because no one is listening. And no one is listening to you because you haven't listened to the other guy.

Dual perspective is not just something we should do to be sensitive and fair to others. It also benefits us very directly. When you open you mind to learning how another views a situation, you enlarge your own perspective. You enrich the interpretive resources you have for understanding a situation and human responses to it.

Situational Sensitivity

Chapter 3 discussed situational awareness as a foundation of human communication. Naturally many of the ideas presented there apply to listening. Especially pertinent to our present concern with listening is sensitivity to situational purpose. As we noted then, there are a variety of communication situations, each of which has particular constraints that influence the form and content of communication. The purpose of a situation—the reason for interaction—suggests what kinds of talk are appropriate. Similarly, situational purpose influences the nature of listening effectively in a given set of circumstances.

There are many reasons why we listen to others: to gain information, to make decisions, to enjoy ourselves, to understand feelings. When we attend concerts or when we listen to comedy routines, it's appropriate to listen for pleasure. When we go to lectures, conferences, or training sessions, we listen to gain information. Listening to make judgments is appropriate when someone attempts to persuade us to buy a product, support a candidate or cause, or believe in something. We need to assess such persuasive attempts critically. We listen to understand feelings in situations involving therapy or interpersonal relationships. Here our goal is to understand and often to support a person whom we care about and who expects our compassion. The goals of listening vary, then, according to the purpose of a situation. Thus, while the four basic commitments we've examined apply to listening generally, the actual behaviors that are effective vary according to particular listening situations and purposes.

In addition to understanding situational purpose, good listeners realize that the other situational dimensions of environment and people influence communication. Chapter 3 presented detailed information on environment and how physical features of situations influence interaction. The colors in a room, arrangement of furniture, and presence or absence of background noise are a few of many environmental factors that constrain listening. People and relationships, a third situational dimension, affect listening. We listen one way when we are with a single other person, and another way when we are in the midst of an active group discussion involving six people. We can listen more sensitively—between the lines—to intimates than to casual acquaintances whose communicative styles and perspectives are not familiar to us. We tend to listen more critically to people we dislike than to people of whom we are fond. The three dimensions of situations—purpose, environment, and persons and relationships—influence the nature of effective listening. You might find it useful to reread portions of Chapter 3 from the perspective of a listener.

Effective listening does not come about from recipes or techniques. On a more fundamental level, listening involves making commitments to participate responsibly in communication, to honor the value and rights of individuals, to strive for dual perspective, and to be sensitive to diverse situations. It is out of these commitments that particular listening behaviors are motivated. In the next section we focus on the range of behaviors associated with effective listening in specific situations.

LISTENING BEHAVIORS

Our examination of listening behaviors will first identify behaviors that improve listening in general. Then we'll consider more specific behaviors appropriate for two broad listening goals of gaining information and understanding feelings.

General Listening Behaviors

A few behaviors contribute to effective listening in almost all communicative situations. Here we consider three generally useful listening behaviors: preparation, controlling biases and expectations, and determining the purpose for listening.

Preparation. It is difficult to listen well when we are physically or mentally unprepared. One of my colleagues refuses to teach classes at 11 a.m. or 4 p.m., because he claims by the middle of either period students are too hungry to listen well. A similar argument might well be made regarding 8 a.m. classes, when many students are too sleepy to listen (and many instructors are too sleepy to teach well). To listen effectively we need to be physically alert and comfortable. If we are tired or hungry, if chairs are uncomfortable, or if we have a headache, we cannot possibly give full attention to interaction with other communicators.

Listening requires mental as well as physical preparation. Distractions should be controlled to minimize competing demands for listeners' attention. Humans cannot attend fully to more than one activity at a time.[20] If your goal is to listen, you need to eliminate other stimuli in your situation. For instance, turn off a loud program on television, so that noise is not in the background when you try to listen. If you want to listen to someone but you are in a crowded, noisy room, move to a more quiet area where your mind is less likely to wander. Put aside your book or paper so that you are not tempted to give sidelong glances to them when your attention is better directed toward those with whom you interact. To listen effectively, you must mentally prepare by creating an environment that invites you to focus fully on the people with whom you are communicating.

Controlling biases and expectations. Personal attitudes, emotions, and beliefs can hinder effective listening. No one will ever be completely objective, but each of us can increase awareness of personal biases and thereby control them. For example, suppose you oppose capital punishment and you attend a debate on that topic. To listen effectively you need to recognize and compensate for your personal bias. You might work to see the arguments of the speaker favoring capital punishment to compensate for your own opposing stance. You might also attempt to be more critical, more skeptical of arguments presented by the speaker against capital punishment to counter your tendency to agree with that position. If your listening is to be responsible and if you are to grow from exposure to diverse ideas, it is important to compensate for your own biases on issues.

Human bias extends beyond the topics of communication. If we dislike someone's appearance, grammar, or mannerisms it is tempting to listen superficially, critically, or not at all. Again, we need to guard against these personal biases. We have little to lose and much that we might gain by hearing others with an open mind. Probably we've all had the experience of meeting someone who not initially impress us, but whose opinions we have come to respect highly. If we allow initial judgments and impressions to close us to interaction with others, we are the ones who lose out. To listen well, we need to identify and control biases regarding ideas and personal qualities of other communicators.

There's another, more subtle way in which our own perspectives can hinder effective listening. Often when we engage in communication we do so with a pre-set notion of what is going to happen. In other words, we enter conversation with our own agenda. This often leads us to impose our own expectations on interaction so that we listen through an interpretive filter that consists of what we predecided we were going to be communicating about. Sometimes we even force another person to adapt to our agenda for a conversation. We might say, "That's not the point." or "I'm not interested in that; what I want to know is. . . ." Responses such as these reflect a very egocentric, even arrogant, perspective on what communication is. They imply communication is what one person expects or wants, and others' interests and expectations can be dismissed if they don't suit our preconceived notions. Listening through our own expectations distorts communication by denying its nature as interactive—as something that happens between people.

It also robs us and those with whom we communicate of the possibilities of discovering what might happen in a conversation. A good example of egocentric listening and the problems it can cause is classroom teaching. Professors generally prepare for classes and enter them with expectations of what should and will be covered. This is necessary and generally useful in making sure that class meeting are productive. Yet, sometimes students' comments, questions, and interests are disregarded automatically. A professor might respond to a student's idea by saying "That's not my point, and we need to move on." In such a case the professor disregards the student's question, because it doesn't fit her or his preconceived agenda for the class period. Such a response also reflects a lack of dual perspective, since the student probably had a reason for thinking the idea was germane to what was being discussed in class. A lot can be missed when we limit what can happen in communication to what we decided in advance.

Determination of listening purpose. Humans do not act without purpose. Listening, like any other human behavior, occurs when directed by some specific purpose. Listening is enhanced when we define why we are listening and when we periodically remind ourselves of this purpose. Simple as this sounds, it's easier than you might imagine to forget the purpose of listening. Webb provides a familiar example of such forgetfulness: "When we attend a lecture we usually do so in order to obtain information; but it is possible to be lulled into inattention . . . or to be distracted by the person in the next seat." [21] Probably every student has had experiences similar to this one. The result may be failure to get information that you need for later parts of a course or for your own knowledge. It is also possible to listen inappropriately if we forget our purpose. Suppose you are assigned to interview public officials to find out the implications of a new local policy. In talking with these people you realize they are frustrated with their jobs and disappointed with the bureaucratic bumbling that surrounds the new policy. You listen to their feelings, focus on their problems, and leave without the information you were assigned to secure! Effective listeners need to be aware of their own goals throughout communication with others. Remind yourself during conversation that you have reasons for listening, that you have something in particular you want to gain from this interaction. This intrapersonal communication will assist you in responsible listening.

Three general behaviors consistent with good listening are to prepare mentally and physically, to control biases and expectations, and to remain aware of your purpose in listening. Once you define your purpose, additional behaviors can be selected to enhance your listening effectiveness in particular sets of circumstances.

BEHAVIORS ADAPTED TO PARTICULAR LISTENING GOALS

Listening goals fall into two broad categories: Information (gaining information, evaluating information) and understanding (attitudes, feelings). Different behaviors are appropriate to these two listening goals.

Listening for Information

In many situations listeners' primary concern is information. In educational and training settings, listeners need to understand and retain the content of communication; in persuasive situations, listeners should evaluate the arguments and reasoning in a message; in professional conferences, listeners aim to understand and integrate information that comes from several different communicators. In each of these examples the primary listening goal is to gain information. Whenever this is the case, four specific behaviors enhance listening effectiveness: motivate yourself, focus on content, hear out the speaker, and review content of communication.

Many people are poor listeners because they avoid difficult material or prematurely dismiss subjects as uninteresting. Both habits inhibit effective listening and both are based on the assumption that the speaker is responsible for making communication lively and interesting. Listeners can do a lot to motivate themselves. When listening for information, challenge yourself to follow difficult presentations, to discover what parts of a message could be of interest to you. Remind yourself that the information is valuable even if it is not being well presented—if it were not valuable to you, you would not be listening in the first place. Ask how you can benefit from the material—what is in it for you? You are listening because of your own goals, so those should be kept front and center in your mind during an informative presentation.

A second important behavior when listening for information is to focus on substance. A speaker's purpose is usually stated early in a presentation. Find that central idea and use it to guide your listening.[22] How does the speaker develop the central idea? Can you identify the pattern of reasoning? Is it logical? What evidence is adduced to support the speaker's theme? Is the research adequate? Good listening for information, especially critical listening, calls for constant attention to the substance of communication—how it is developed and supported. When you listen for information, this substance should be your major concern. Avoid focus on nonsubstantive matters such as the speaker's appearance, grammatical errors, or an odd accent. Keep your mind on content and how it is developed throughout a presentation.

A third suggestion when listening for information is to hear out the speaker. Give the speaker a full opportunity to develop and support ideas before you judge or respond to content. We cannot listen in a full, fair manner when we are busy planning our responses, our counterattack on the speaker's position. The tendency to plan responses interferes actively with careful listening and with retaining information. It is especially important to avoid premature judgments when a speaker introduces ideas or even words that offend you. Language or ideas we find repugnant invite us to "turn off" the speaker—to disregard anything that follows the offending part of communication. This response does not assist you in gaining information, and it might lead to your overlooking later parts of a presentation that you would find valuable. After a speaker has finished a presentation you may want to question material or to argue against certain ideas advocated. This is entirely appropriate as long as you wait until the speaker has had a full hearing. Then you are entitled to the same—a full hearing. You increase the effectiveness of your response if you have listened well enough to understand the speaker's material well and can adapt your response to it.

A final behavior that enhances listening for information is to review content during and after a presentation. Ideally, speakers should repeat key ideas, clarify connections among points in a speech, and summarize content. However, not all communicators provide this assistance to listeners so you may need to integrate and review content for yourself. As a speaker completes each idea, summarize in your head what was covered. Relate what has been presented to the announced purpose of the communication. Determine how the information fits together. If you detect gaps in information or faulty reasoning, listen with special care to the rest of the message to see whether the speaker provides additional information and argument. To increase your retention of any communication, review all of the material as soon as possible after hearing it. Understanding and retention of material is greatly aided by mental review of key ideas. This is why clinics that teach students how to study emphasize going over lecture notes immediately after classes.

After listening carefully to communication, it is appropriate to respond. When the goal of listening is to gain or assess information, two modes of response are most useful. First, a listener may question to gain further information or to gain clarification of ideas previously presented. Following are representative questions that seek extension or clarification:

What did you mean by the statement that . . .

What are your qualifications as an expert in this area?

Could you elaborate the third point of your lecture?

Do you have further evidence to support the claim that . . . ?

What was the source of the statistics you presented?

Does the person you quoted have a personal interest in supporting your position?

Could you clarify the distinction between the two positions you discussed?

In your opinion, what would be the implications of enacting the policy you advocate (or of not enacting it)?

Listeners may also offer personal opinion or information to support or challenge the speaker's position:

My experience is consistent with what you describe.

There is a recent research report that contradicts the study you cited.

You might want to check with Jane Doe who is working in an area similar to yours.

In your presentation, you noted only the positive outcomes of what you propose—would you identify some of the drawbacks as well?

Once a presentation has been concluded, listeners are entitled to comment on and question material and to discuss it with a speaker. Response is helpful to both communicators, since it can clarify and supplement the initial content of a presentation.

Listening for information is advanced by four particular behaviors. First, listeners should motivate themselves, rather than expecting a speaker to provide them with reasons for attention. Second, listeners should focus on the substance of communication—purpose, organization, and support. Next, listeners should allow a speaker a full, fair hearing before judging or planning any responses. A final behavior is active participation through mental integration and review of the information presented. Practice of these behaviors increases both understanding and retention of content. Further, the behaviors prepare listeners for constructive, insightful responses to the communication.

Listening for Understanding

Listening for information may be thought of as listening to the content level of communication. Our attention is focused on what is actually said—the literal, material meanings. As important as the content level is, you'll recall from Chapter 2 that there's another level of communication—the relational level of meaning. On many occasions we listen primarily on the relational level. We do this when we interact with someone we care about—a family member, friend, client, or intimate partner. In these situations we are not as concerned with the actual, literal content of communication as with understanding someone's feelings, perceptions, or attitudes.

Intimate partners need to recognize and deal with each other's emotions, problems, and personal disclosures. Friends expect openness and caring from each other. Family members need to acknowledge and work through shared problems and concerns. Listening to the relational level of communication requires that we focus on understanding feelings, perceptions, and attitudes, and that we demonstrate acceptance and support.

The behaviors we identified as promoting effective listening for information are not the ones that most advance relational level listening. When talking with an intimate about a problem, for instance, motivating yourself to attend is probably unnecessary and focusing on content is only a small part of what you should do. Because relational listening is distinct from content listening, different behaviors are appropriate. Three behaviors are particularly useful: recognizing the other's perspective, listening totally, and avoiding evaluations of feelings.

We can't understand other people's feelings from our own perspective. Instead, we have to try to grasp their perspectives—see the world as they see it, define the situation as they define it. To recognize another's perspective a listener must ask, "What does this mean to her or him?" Temporarily put aside what the issues mean to you and try to figure out what they mean to the other person. The immediate goal is to discover the other person's world of meaning and to enter it as much as possible. Of course, none of us can ever fully grasp another's perspective, but with genuine effort we can gain some insight into how another sees things. Rogers says that in counseling clients he asks himself, "Can I hear the sounds and sense the shape of this other person's inner world? Can I resonate to what he is saying, can I let it echo back and forth in me, so deeply that I sense the meanings he is afraid of yet would like to communicate, as well as those meanings he already knows?"[23] If we don't initially understand someone else's perspective, we can ask questions or ask them to elaborate to gain further insight into how that person views a situation and herself or himself within it. Of the many difficulties in listening from another's perspective, the greatest is probably lack of real commitment to do so. Why? One reason is that trying to enter into another's world is threatening to our own values and meanings. To participate fully in someone else's perspective, we must risk our own. People who are unwilling to take this risk protect their own value systems, but they also foreclose a major avenue to personal and interpersonal growth. They lose the opportunity to enrich their own ways of understanding experience, because they are closed to any way of seeing the world other than the one they already have. They also impede the growth between them and others. When we don't really try to understand our friends and intimates we lay the foundations for distance and lack of communication in the future. After several efforts to communicate with someone who will not respect our perspective on our experiences, we tend to get discouraged and to go elsewhere for understanding and support. So exercising dual perspective is critical to personal and interpersonal growth in relationships.

When the goal of listening is to understand feelings, it is insufficient to attend to just the words and surface ideas of communication. We need to listen totally, which means we must "listen with the third ear" to hear behind the words.[24] This is not as difficult as it may sound. We usually know the people who communicate with us about feelings. They are not strangers whom we must learn to interpret from scratch. We can draw on our history of interacting with them to pick up cues behind and between words: nervous gestures, unusual speech patterns, depressed voice, atypical eating or sleeping patterns, gain or loss of weight, volume and pace of talk. People who know each other have a sense of the range of behaviors typical of each person, and that range becomes a standard against which we can assess behavior in a present situation. If we really attend to others and commit to total listening, it is possible to pick up many of the subtle cues that suggest meanings behind and between words and that helps us understand the communication more completely.

If you find you can't understand what someone feels or how she views a situation, you can probe gently. Both paraphrasing and asking open questions encourage elaboration. So, for example, you might say to a friend, "You seem to be really uncomfortable with your father's attitude" (a paraphrase of what you think you've heard). You might also say, "I'm not really sure what you're feeling. Are you angry about your father's attitude or are you hurt or what?" Perhaps the simplest way of gaining greater insight into how another feels is to ask the straightforward question, "Can you explain a little more what you think is happening?" All of these responses show that you are listening and that you really care about understanding what is happening. Thus, they support the other person by saying "You matter to me."

Listening Totally[25]

One does not listen with just his ears: he listens with his eyes and with his sense of touch, he listens with his mind, his heart, his imagination. He listens to the words of others, but he also listens to the messages that are buried in the words or encoded in the cues that surround the words.

In addition to understanding the other's perspective and listening totally, it is important to listen without evaluating. When you want to discuss a problem or personal issue, do you seek out a listener who is quick to judge? When you want to disclose a weakness or a failure, do you go to someone who will pass evaluation on you? Probably not. Most of us become defensive when we sense others are judging us, particularly when we already feel somewhat worried, confused, or unhappy.[26] To listen for feelings, we must establish an open, accepting climate for communication. Without this, communication cannot progress and feelings cannot be shared. Rogers explains this way: "It is only as I understand the feelings and thoughts which seem so horrible to you or so weak . . . it is only as I see them as you see them and accept them in you, that you feel really free to explore."[27] If we evaluate someone's feelings ("That's a silly feeling"—"You shouldn't feel that way"—"I don't know why you doubt yourself—that's dumb"), we close the door on further sharing. We tell the other person that we don't accept or confirm her or his feelings. If, on the other hand, we listen openly and accept expressed feelings without judging, we pave the way for continued communication of high quality. We need not agree with another's feelings to accept them as genuine. We need not accept another's perceptions or attitudes for ourselves in order to recognize them as real for that person.

Judgment is generally threatening, and it is especially so when we already feel somewhat uneasy. All of us feel vulnerable when we talk about problems or feelings that upset us, even if we're talking to our intimates. Because we feel unsure of ourselves at such times, we're quick to clam up if we feel at all threatened. We want to be understood and supported, not judged. Thus, if you are listening to understand feelings, it's imperative to suspend judgment. Verbal and nonverbal evidence of evaluation interferes with communication about personal issues and feelings.

Accepting another's perceptions, feelings, and attitudes is an important foundation of listening for understanding.

Responding to feelings is as important as listening to them. Egan believes "the best evidence of your listening is the quality of your response to what others say both verbally and nonverbally."[28] Since feeling-oriented communication usually occurs in informal settings, listeners are able to respond throughout interaction. Nonverbal responses, in particular, can demonstrate that you hear, you understand, and you care. A head nod, a touch, or eye contact often conveys more involvement than verbal responses would. Nonverbal responses throughout listening encourage continued dialogue. In addition to nonverbal behavior, listeners will also want to use verbal responses that facilitate communication. Johnson suggests three kinds of responses that are particularly suited to feeling-oriented communication.[29] Supportive responses indicate involvement and acceptance of expressed emotions: "I understand." "I'm concerned." "I want to hear more." "I care about what you're feeling." Again, asking question often draws out the person who is talking and clarify feelings so that you as a listener can better understand the other's perspective: "You seem a little down today. Anything happen?" "Do you see this as a long-term problem or a temporary one?" "Have you ever felt like this before?" You may also respond with paraphrase to demonstrate that you understand the other person's perspective or the issue as she or he perceives it: "You're worried that your parents won't approve of your plans." If your boss would just let you explain the circumstances, you'd feel better." "You think you let your brother down when you didn't make time to talk with him, right?" Supportive, questioning, and paraphrasing responses indicate a listener is involved and is following communication. They contribute to building an open climate that fosters communication about feelings.

Listening for feelings is most effective when a listener recognizes another's perspective, listens totally to the words and the meanings behind and between the words, and avoids evaluation of feelings, perceptions, and attitudes. These behaviors, complemented by supportive responses, create an openness in which it feels safe to share feelings and concerns without defensiveness and in which problems may be discussed without fear of judgment. Listeners who foster such a climate ensure growth simultaneously in themselves and in those with whom they interact. Additionally, such sensitive listening enriches relationships by enhancing trust and understanding between partners.

SUMMARY

Listening involves commitments and behaviors that promote understanding, growth, and responses adapted to the particular situation at hand. When effective, listening is based upon commitments to responsible participation in communication, to the value and rights of individuals, to dual perspective, and to situational sensitivity. Listeners who embrace these commitments can cultivate behaviors that enhance listening.

In all situations, listeners should prepare mentally and physically, control biases, and determine their personal purposes for listening. If the listening purpose is to gain or assess information, recommended behaviors are to motivate yourself, to focus on the substance of communication, to hear the speaker out, and to review content during and after presentation. If the listening purpose is to understand feelings, perceptions, or attitudes, appropriate behaviors are to recognize the speaker's perspective and enter it as much as possible, to listen totally, and to avoid evaluation of expressed feelings. Supportive, probing, and understanding responses throughout interaction assist in creating a climate that encourages open communication.

There are no simple recipes for effective listening. Like other human activities, listening begins with self-reflection about personal values and commitments. The behaviors discussed in this chapter cannot be practiced genuinely unless they grow out of the commitments we identified. Those commitments are the foundation of effective listening which, in turn, is essential for a fully functioning and growing self.

As we've seen in this chapter, how we listen has considerable influence on climates of interaction. Through our listening style and the responses we make, it is possible to contribute to open, nonthreatening climates that free others to express feelings and problems. Similarly, when others listen sensitively to us, we feel safe disclosing personal information or asking for assistance from another. Because listening fosters supportive interaction climates, it is clearly related to individual, social, and intimate development. By listening well and responsively we can learn much about others and about ourselves. Thus we can grow—we can take risks that are essential to constructive change.

Effective listening is important in all communication contexts. It's very much a part of personal and interpersonal development as well as intimate relationships, all of which we discuss in Part II of this book. It's equally essential to public communication—group discussion, public speaking, and interviewing kinds of communication that we'll examine in Part 3. As you read the upcoming chapters, you will find that listening is of major importance in all communication. In fact, if public communication is to be effective, it must always precede from an awareness of and adaptation to listeners' perspectives, for they are as much a part of a communication experience as are those who speak.

REFERENCES

[1]Estimates vary. In *Listening Behavior*. Englewood Cliffs, NJ: Prentice-Hall, 1971, pp. 3-5, Larry Barker estimates 40 percent of communication time is spent listening. An estimate of 45 percent was made by Carl H. Weaver in *Human Listening: Processes and Behavior*. Indianapolis: Bobbs-Merrill, 1972, p. 13.
[2]Stuart Chase, "Are You Listening?" *Readers' Digest*, December 1961, p. 80.
[3]Wendell Johnson, "Speech Disorders of the Fluent." In Lee Thayer (Ed.), *Communication: General Semantics Perspectives*. New York: Spartan, 1970, pp. 261-265.
[4]Chase, p. 80.
[5]Gerard Egan, "Listening as Empathic Support." In John Steward (Ed.), *Bridges, Not Walls*. Reading, MA: Addison-Wesley, 1973, p. 228.
[6]Richard L. Weaver, II, *Understanding Interpersonal Communication*. Glenview, IL: Scott-Foresman, 1978, p. 99.

[7]Charles M. Kelly. "Empathic Listening." In Robert Cathcart and Larry Samovar (Eds.), *Small Group Communication: Theory and Practice, 3rd. ed.* Dubuque, IA: Wm. C. Brown, 1979, pp. 355-356.

[8]Roderick P. Hart and Don M. Burks, "Rhetorical Sensitivity and Social Interaction," *Speech Monographs, 24*, June 1972, 75-91.

[9]Carl Rogers, *On Becoming a Person.* Boston: Houghton Mifflin, 1961, pp. 62-65.

[10]Charles T. Brown and Paul Keller, *Monologue to Dialogue.* Englewood Cliffs, NJ: Prentice-Hall, 1979, p. 289.

[11]Thomas R. Nilsen, "Free Speech, Persuasion, and the Democratic Process," *Quarterly Journal of Speech, 44*, 1958, 235-243.

[12]Brown and Keller, p. 277.

[13]Ralph B. Perry, *The Humanity of Man.* New York: George Braziller, 1956, p. 105.

[14]Thomas R. Nilsen, *The Ethics of Speech Communication.* Indianapolis: Bobbs-Merrill, 1974, p. 54.

[15]The concept of dual perspective is best elaborated in Gerald M. Phillips and Julia T. Wood, *Intimate Communication: The Study of Human Relationships.* New York: Macmillan, 1985.

[16]Rogers, pp. 330-331.

[17]Gerard Egan, *Interpersonal Living.* Monterey, CA: Brooks/Cole Co., 1976, p. 92.

[18]George Herbert Mead, "The Genesis of Self and Social Control," *International Journal of Ethics, 35*, 1925, 251-277.

[19]Edmond G. Addeo and Robert E. Burger, *Egospeak.* New York: Bantam, 1973, p. 259.

[20]Magdalen D. Vernon, "Perception, Attention and Consciousness." In Paul Barker (Ed.), *Attention.* New York: Harper and Row, 1952, p. 60.

[21]Ralph Webb, Jr., *Interpersonal Speech Communication.* Englewood Cliffs, NJ: Prentice-Hall, 1975, p. 143.

[22]Irving J. Lee, *How to Talk With People.* New York: Harper and Row, 1952, p. 60.

[23]Carl Rogers, *Freedom to Learn.* Columbus, OH: Charles E. Merrill, 1969, p. 232.

[24]Theodore Reik, *Listening with the Third Ear.* New York: Grove Press, 1948, p. 125.

[25]Gerard Egan, *Listening as Empathic Support*, p. 228.

[26]Jack R. Gibb, "Defensive Communication," *Journal of Communication, 11*, 1961, 141-148.

[27]Carl Rogers, *On Becoming a Person*, p. 34.

[28]Gerard Egan, "Listening as empathic support", p. 231.

[29]David W. Johnson, *Reaching Out/Interpersonal Effectiveness and Self Actualization.* Englewood Cliffs, NJ: Prentice-Hall, 1972.

INTEGRATING FOUNDATIONS: A REVIEW OF PART I

We've covered a lot of material in the first six chapters of this book. Before moving on to our exploration of particular communication situations, it's probably a good idea to pause long enough to pull together the ideas presented thus far. So we'll take a few pages here to review the first part of the book and to suggest how it establishes foundations for what follows.

The overall goal of Part I is to explain symbolic interactionism as a perspective on communication and, therefore, on human nature. According to this theoretical perspective, communication is fundamentally a symbolic process through which we interact with others. Unlike other animals, we do not—in fact, cannot—respond directly to external objects, events, persons, and situations. Instead, our responses are inevitably mediated, usually by symbols. We use symbols to indicate external phenomena to ourselves and others. In doing this we define, organize, and attach value to our experiences. We also use symbols to establish our own goals and roles and to guide our behaviors in relation to our experiences as well as our visions of past and future. Thus, we never react directly to the phenomena of experience; Rather we build up responses through the meanings we construct for those phenomena.

Yet, as we've seen, meanings are not entirely unique to individuals. Inevitably they reflect social overtones. Because we are members of the human community, each of us participates in social interaction with others within a shared culture. Through this interaction we become aware of meanings that others hold for phenomena and, thus, we gain access to the common interpretations, values, and definitions of our society. Understanding the social meanings for experiences allows us to participate in the practices of our society.

As important as social overtones are, they alone do not explain the meanings we have for phenomena. Each of us must individually interpret our experiences. To do so we incorporate broad social meanings derived from interaction with others, but that's not the whole story. In addition we modify those meanings in unique ways: we add to them, subtract from them, and adjust, reorganize, and recombine them them in an ongoing process that blends our personal histories and interpretations with those of our society. As our experiences expand, we may revise both particular meanings and our ways of interpreting experience in order to make sense of our lives, thoughts, and feelings. In this ongoing process of blending personal and social meanings we continually adjust the chemistry that reflects the gamut of the interactions and experiences comprising our personal and social lives. Meaning, then, is both a social and individual product. It simultaneously reflects our membership in the overall community and the unique perspective wrought by our individual experiences and interpretations.

The interpretive process central to meaning depends at least primarily on symbols. We use them to define phenomena, to organize them into meaningful patterns of association, to evaluate them, to reflect on them as they are and might be, and to indicate their implications for us and our actions. Further, we use symbols to interact with others. Communication between people occurs through symbols that allow us to express ideas, values, and meanings and to construct common definitions of shared situations, experiences, events, and actions. Thus, we've come full circle in our understanding of meaning. The initial meanings for our experiences derived from interactions with others are modified and elaborated individually and, in turn, are channeled back into social interaction to revise common meanings. The creation of meaning is an ongoing process of interaction between individuals and society, carried on primarily through symbols. Symbolic interactionism provides a distinctive view of communication, as demonstrated in the preceding chapters and in this review. However, this is not all the perspective offers us. In addition, symbolic interactionism implies a particular view of human nature—what it means to be human and to act in human ways. At the core of symbolic interactionism is the belief that humans are proactive. We act upon our worlds. While other animals seem confined to relatively reflexive, automatic reactions to the existing physical world, humans rise above that level of existence. And we do so largely because we are symbol users. The meanings of our experiences interact with the symbols we use to define, organize, and evaluate them. As our experiences change, so do our symbols and our meanings for them; conversely, as we revise our meanings and the symbols we use to construct them, we come to perceive experiences in ever new ways. Through this ongoing process, humans interact with and through symbols to imbue their lives and activities with substance and value and to persuade themselves to changing definitions of themselves and their worlds.

Because humans are proactive, we have considerable control over the nature and quality of our lives, and therefore we have responsibility for the courses of attitude and action we select for ourselves. We need not accept what is in a given moment in time and space; instead, we may use symbols to create alternatives and to guide our actions in ways that realize those possibilities. In doing so we constantly reshape the universe in which we live. In any instance, we have choices regarding the interpretations we make, the ideals and values we use to guide our own conduct, and the broad goals we seek through our attitudes and actions. So, while symbol using elevates us to proactive status, it simultaneously makes us responsible for the choices we make—the choices we alone as humans *can* make about ourselves and our interaction with the world.

Symbolic interactionism maintains that in addition to being proactive, humans are social creatures. Despite the many differences among us, we are fundamentally similar in our humanity. Each of us is part of the human community. And each of us participates in creating and sustaining the meaning of that community. Only through interactions with others do we truly acquire our human character, because only through such interactions are we introduced to the definitions and value of our human society. Society in a sense creates individuals, teaching them what it means to be human and what kinds of values and actions are appropriate for humans; yet, individuals act back upon society to modify the very values and definitions it imparts to them. Individuals reflect the society with which they interact, and society also reflects the individuals who comprise it. In this ongoing dialectic, individuals and the social order constantly interact and, in so doing, constantly create and recreate each other.

The foregoing chapters should provide you with a clear understanding of symbolic interactionism and its implications for human communication and human life. At this point you should have theoretical knowledge that organizes your thinking about the communication process and you should appreciate the importance of situational awareness, language, nonverbal behavior, and listening in human interaction. With that foundation, we're now ready to progress to Part II, which explores the profound relationship between communication and our personal and interpersonal development. We first explore how communication creates the personal identity of each individual. Then we consider the ways in which communication contributes to our interpersonal development by instilling in us ways of responding to others and ways of understanding ourselves in relationship to others. Finally, we consider how communication creates intimacy between people by enabling them to share themselves with each other and to define and imbue with value a common, private world of intimacy.

Part II

Communication and Human Development

CHAPTER 7

COMMUNICATION AND PERSONAL DEVELOPMENT: THE INDIVIDUAL SELF

It is a symbolic order into which we are born, and as we become members of society [we] begin to enter the meanings which the symbols represent.

(Dale Spender)

The Nature of Self

Reflexivity
Self as object
Monitoring
Perspective taking
Bounding the ego
Forming interpersonal orientations

Propositions about the Self

The self arises in communication with others
The self is constantly in process
The self assumes multiple roles
The self is the anchor of all understandings

Communication and the Self

The self arises in communication with others
The self is constantly in process
The self assumes multiple roles
The self is the anchor for all judgments

How the I Limits Experience of the World
Communication and the Self

The self is established, sustained and altered through communication
The self influences how we construct and interpret communication

---

Improving the Self Through Communication

   Recognize change & knowledge as prerequisites for development
   Avoid the mind trap that I cannot change
   Accept yourself as in process
   How self-doubt cripples us
   Accept others as in process
   Self-disclose when appropriate
   Engage in constructive risk-taking

Who are you?
How are you unique?
Why are you the person you are?
Are there aspects of yourself you'd like to change?

You have probably thought more than once about questions like these. It's equally likely you'll continue to reflect on them for the rest of your life. We are concerned with our identity. We seek to understand who we are because for each of us the self influences our thoughts and actions, including our communication.

Symbolic interaction theory offers a distinctively sophisticated and rich view of human identity. While most theories of human nature adopt either the view that the self is largely an individual being or essentially a social creature, symbolic interactionism rejects this duality. Mead, the "father of symbolic interactionism," recognized that the human self is simultaneously individual and social. At once we are unique beings and members of a common social order. Mead further recognized that it is in communication with others and ourselves that both the individual and social aspects of the self develop. Since Mead's original work on symbolic interactionist theory, much research has confirmed and extended his germinal insights about the complex and fascinating nature of humans.

This chapter and the next one are companions. In this one we focus on the individual nature of the self. Chapter 8 elaborates the social nature of the self. This way of organizing material should not mislead you into thinking that the individual and social aspects of self are separate. They are not. Both develop and function simultaneously throughout our lives. So reading both chapters should provide you with an appreciation of the highly complex nature of every human as an individual actor and participant in the larger community.

In this chapter we explore the ways in which communication allows personal development. We begin by discussing the nature of self in terms of four abilities that comprise individuals. Next, we examine the dynamic interaction between communication and selfhood. Finally, we'll consider ways we can enlarge ourselves through communication. After reading this chapter you should have an increased awareness of who you are and greater insight into ways you can guide who you will become.

THE NATURE OF SELF

You've probably heard and used the term "self-concept" frequently. Symbolic interactionists, however, prefer the term "self," for two reasons. First, "self-concept" literally means concept of self, which implies only cognitive activity. By contrast, "self" is not restricted to cognition but includes behaviors of the self and feelings about the self as well. Clearly, what we do and how we feel about ourselves are important dimensions of who we are.

Second, "self-concept" seems to suggest a static, relatively unchanging view of the self" (a concept, after all, is generally, considered stable). Symbolic interactionists do not see the self this way. Instead, they think the self is constantly in process, always changing, becoming. In this chapter we use the word "self" to refer to an individual's ongoing interpretation and organization of experiences used to direct personal thought and action. Notice that we have defined the self not by things, but by action. This is fully consistent with the symbolic interactionist recognition of the self as process.

Most theories of human behavior give some attention to self, but symbolic interactionism regards it as especially important. From this perspective, self is viewed as central to human interaction and social life. It is self that links individuals and self that guides our actions so that we can participate in a shared society. For symbolic interactionists the self is not simply one of many aspects that make up a person. Rather, it is the essence of an individual—the center that defines and guides all of a person's behaviors, feelings, judgments, and goals. To understand better the symbolic interactionist view of self, we discuss four activities or processes that comprise individuals. After that, we consider four propositions that summarize the implications of a symbolic interactionist perspective on self.

Reflexivity

As we saw in Chapter 4, our symbolic abilities allow us to be reflective and self-reflective. This reflexivity means that we don't just exist. In addition, we think about our existence, we *think about* ourselves. In doing so, we constitute who we are. For symbolic interactionist the reflexivity in which the self engages leads to two related human abilities: the ability to take the self as an object, and the ability to monitor one's own experience.

Self-as-object. At first "self-as-object" seems an odd term. Some people dislike it, because they interpret it to mean detachment from self or to imply that the self should be treated as an object, rather than a person. Actually, neither of these meanings was intended by George Herbert Mead, who coined the term.[1]

Throughout his life Mead's enduring quest was to understand human nature and how humans are distinct from other life forms. One of the primary distinctions Mead saw between humans and animals was that humans are able to be self-reflexive—they can reflect on themselves. We can make statements such as "I have artistic talent," "I am a Christian," "I am short," or "I am eating too much." In each case the person expressing the idea is the same entity as the object to which the idea refers. We can "stand outside" ourselves and look at ourselves much as we might look at any other object. A person is able to view his or her self—perceive it, describe it, judge it, and respond to it. The object we perceive, describe, judge, and respond to is our own self. We are simultaneously the subjects and the objects of our experience. It is in this sense that Mead used the term "self-as-object."

For Mead and others who built on his ideas, the human ability to view self-as-object is crucial to communication. Because of this ability, we can monitor our own communication, an important skill introduced in Part I of this book. Let's return now to the idea of monitoring to see how it grows out of the ability to view self-as-object.

Monitoring.   Chapter Four defined monitoring as a process in which we observe and regulate our attitudes, feelings, and behaviors. Monitoring is such a constant activity that we are often unaware of it. Yet it is most important to communicating effectively as well as to personal growth. For instance, suppose your roommate tells you, "I really blew my chemistry test today," and you respond by saying, "Maybe you would have done better if you'd skipped the mixer last night and studied instead." As soon as those words come out of your mouth, you think to yourself, "Wow, that sounded really harsh. I ought to be more understanding and supportive." So you amend your initial statement with this additional comment: "Still, it was a great mixer, and you can always pull up the grade on the next test." When you heard your initial response, judged it inadequate, and decided to modify it with further communication, you were monitoring. You observed and regulated your own behavior. Incidents like this are taken for granted as parts of our daily experiences and interactions, but don't let this familiarity deprive you of realizing how important the skill is. Because we can monitor our own actions, we can adjust and readjust our communication to make it as effective as possible.

The ability to monitor is directly tied to the capacity to take the self as an object. As we engage in behaviors, we are actors, but as we observe our own behaviors, we become objects to ourselves. As far as we know, other forms of life have very limited ability to reflect on and change their own behaviors. By standing outside ourselves and observing our actions, we humans regard the self as an object whose behaviors we can analyze and regulate. Monitoring is possible because we are reflexive—able to look at ourselves as objects.

Perspective Taking

Because humans are symbol users, we reflect not just on ourselves, but on others as well. We are able to recognize that there are other people in the world and that they have perspectives, or viewpoints, different from ours. This ability is called perspective taking. It means we are able to take, or understand, ways of thinking and seeing situations different from our own. Perspective taking is valuable for a number of reasons. Notably, it allows us to grow personally. As we come to understand how others think, feel and interpret experience we expand our own range of interpreting and defining our world. Perspective talking is also valuable because it allows us to communicate more sensitively and personally than we could if we could only understand our own way of seeing things.

Perspective taking is a general ability—one we use to understand others,[2] be it a single friend or the society as a whole. Perhaps you're most familiar with using dual perspective which involves recognizing someone else's perspective in addition to your own. This doesn't mean you necessarily agree with the other's viewpoint, only that you recognize it and can see it as both distinct from and related to your own. As we'll see in Chapter 9, which deals with intimacy, dual perspective is the heart of effective interpersonal communication. It allows us to acknowledge the frame of reference held by another person with whom we are interacting. Without that ability, we couldn't understand anything outside of our own immediate experience. We could see the world only in our own limited terms.

Consider an example of how dual perspective operates. As Marylyn and Ben engage in an argument, he observes and evaluates what she says, notes his own thoughts on the topic, compares his perspective with hers to see where the two blend and differ, and advises himself on the best way of responding to her. The effectiveness of Ben's response depends largely on his ability to understand Marylyn's perspective. In turn, Marylyn's effectiveness is closely related to how well she comprehends the perspective from which Ben speaks. Thus, to understand another's perspective in its independent integrity is to exercise dual perspective—simultaneously to recognize our own and another's viewpoint.

Dual perspective is directly related to the ability to view self-as object. To assume dual perspective you stand outside of yourself—detach yourself temporarily from your role as advocate of your own ideas—in order to consider the perspective of another person. Further, as you come to understand the other perspective you are led to reconsider your own, which again requires you to stand outside of yourself and evaluate what you are doing. Finally, you (as actor) indicate to yourself (as object) what to say and how to say it. Viewing self-as-object is prerequisite to dual perspective.

Abilities to monitor and to employ dual perspective are central to effective, mutually satisfying communication. Both abilities are possible because we are able to view self-as-object. We can not only act, but reflect on our actions and thereby adapt them as necessary to increase our effectiveness.

Bounding the Ego

A third process made possible by our symbolic capacities is bounding our egos. A cornerstone in individual development is defining ego boundaries, which specify where the individual stops and others begin. Developmental psychologists believe this is perhaps the first task an infant must master in order to begin defining a distinct sense of self. According to scholars of child development, newborn babies have no sense of a distinction between themselves and the rest of the world. All experience—internal and external—flows together in what the child feels.[3] We think that if we put cold water on a baby's arm, the baby experiences the arm and the water as "the same"— not recognizing that the coldness comes from a source outside itself and it is having the sensory reaction of being chilled. Similarly, all others are merged with self at the beginning. The mother's nipple is as much as part of the baby's world as its own mouth.

Beginning in the early months, this starts to change. As parents and others who interact with the baby label it and themselves distinctly, the baby begins to recognize that it is in a sense apart from the flow of experience. Gradually, the infant gets more and more clear on what the boundaries of itself, its ego, are.

Particularly interesting is a difference in how boys and girls develop their ego boundaries. Male infants tend to define themselves as independent from others, while female infants usually define themselves as interdependent with others. While there are some exceptions, this is the general gender-differentiated pattern.[4] Researchers believe that these differences come about largely because of the different ways female and male children are treated. From the start, parents and others treat boy babies as independent and treat girl babies as involved in relationships with others. Parents leave boys alone more so they learn to think and act more independently than do girls who are more likely to be held, touched, and kept in close contact most of the time.[5] Through communicative interaction, boys learn to define themselves as separate from others while girls learn to define themselves in relation to others. Each reflects others' expectations and treatment.

One result of these two kinds of socialization is the tightness of the ego boundaries a person defines for self.[6] Because they come to see themselves within relationship to others, girls tend to develop somewhat permeable ego boundaries—ones that are not tight and that others can enter. For instance, a female is likely to feel hurt when someone she cares about is in pain—she feels the other's pain as her own. I still recall that my younger sister always cried *for* any of us who got shots from the doctor, because she felt our pain. She was not totally separate from others.

Males tend to develop more rigid ego boundaries. They generally have a quite clear sense of where they stop and others begin, and the two are independent. So a male is able to understand conceptually that another feels pain and to think about that pain, but he is less likely than a female to actually feel the other's pain as his own.

While males and females differ in how rigidly they define their ego boundaries, both distinguish between themselves and others in the world. This basic distinction was of keen interest to Mead.

As we've already seen, Mead was struck by the fact that humans experience themselves not only as objects, but also as actors. In further exploring this ability to take the self as object, Mead realized there are two aspects of self, which he called the I and the ME. The first dimension of self, what Mead called the I, is an actor, a doer, an agent. The I plans and enacts behaviors. The ME, on the other hand, is a thinker, an evaluator, a reflector. ME reflects on I's activities.

The I can be spontaneous, impulsive, even rash in its feelings and inclinations of how to behave. To temper this, there is the ME part of self that recognizes and operates from the perspective of others, not the I. The ME is sensitive to social rules and the perspectives of others in general. I is the individual, creative self. ME, on the other hand, is the social, analytical self. I wants to act in ways that are sometimes inappropriate in particular settings. ME works to adapt I's egocentric style. I and ME interact in a sort of inner forum to design behavior that meets I's goals but is moderated by ME's sense of what is appropriate. The spirit of this internal dialogue is well captured in Phillips and Metzger's explanation.[7]

> What ME does is conciliate between the urgencies that I needs gratified and the need that ME has to stay in that social system by hanging in with the norms. ME can tell I to go to blazes if it looks like I is giving orders that do not fit the norms of the situation. I can cool ME instantly if his behavior is making I unhappy. ME picks up the norms and constraints and tells I about them.

It would be a mistake to think of the I and ME as opposing forces. They are complementary, because they work together to guide communicative action. The I of one moment blends into the ME of the next moment. The internal conversations between I and ME allow us to rehearse possible communication strategies and try them out in our heads before we try them out in public. Through rehearsal we often find flaws in our initial ideas and develop more effective methods for public presentation. Consider this example of an internal dialogue between I and ME:

I:　　The next time that blasted Paul asks me to get him a cup of coffee, I'm going to pour it on his head! The nerve of him—treating me like I'm his maid, when we hold the same position in this company!

ME:　Hold on a minute there. It's not very smart to pour boiling coffee on someone whose cooperation you need, whether you like that or not. Surely we can figure out a more effective way of making the point—one that honors your identity without alienating a colleague.

I:　　I don't want a "more effective" method. I just want to burn him as much as his sexism burns me! I don't care if he is alienated. It would give me such pleasure to . . . .

ME:　Oh, come on, now. You're not a two-year old throwing a temper tantrum. You're a 28-year-old professional who has to find some way of handling a sexist colleague. Be adult and be professional in how you deal with Paul.

I:　　Well, maybe I could skip the physical violence. How about if I just tell him to quit acting like a sexist?

ME:　That's better, but still, you know full well that name calling is unprofessional and alienates others. Besides, it won't help anything. If you say that, then Paul's going to brand you "a radical feminist," and then where are you as two people who need to work together?

I:　　Alright, I get the point. How about this: What if I tell him that when he asks me to do service jobs, I feel he's treating me like his subordinate, not a peer?

ME:　Now, that's a lot more like it. If you approach Paul that way he might be able to hear you and then the two of you could have a mature talk about collegiality.

Notice how the I and ME work together to express the self. Both aspects are vital. The I provides the creativity and spark, while the ME stylizes I's impulses so that they fit within the social world. This understanding of the self recognizes both the individual actor and the socially conscious reflector. For symbolic interactionists a whole self cannot exist without both the I and ME. We recognize the self as a distinct ego—more so for men than women—an agent who acts upon the world as well as an object whose behaviors we can observe and regulate from the perspective of others or the social world in general. Neither self-as-actor nor self-as-object is a complete self. Working in concert, the two aspects furnish a basis for goal-oriented behaviors that are adapted to situational norms and constraints. Our communication reflects the constant interaction between I and ME, between our distinct ego and the world at large as we understand it.

The I and the ME[8]

Whatever I may be thinking of, I am always at the same time more or less aware of myself, of my personal existence. At the same time it is I who am aware; so that the total self of me, being as it were duplex, partly known and partly knower, partly object and partly subject, must have two aspects discriminated in it . . . . we may call one the Me and the other the I. I call these "discriminated aspects," and not separate things, because the identity of I with Me, even in the very act of their discrimination, is perhaps the most ineradicable dictum of common-sense.

The symbolic interactionist view of self recognizes that humans are highly individual actors and, at the same time, social beings. Each of us is unique, yet we are all members of a common society. The dual aspects of self guide our interactions and equip us to participate effectively in the social world.

Forming Interpersonal Orientations

A third activity or process that constitutes the self is forming an orientation toward others. Each of us develops a basic sense of our relation to others and a basic set of beliefs about how we should interact with them. As you may have already guessed, the interpersonal orientations we form are related to how we bound our egos. Thus, here again, we find there is a gender-associated difference in humans.

The distinctive interpersonal orientations of women and men have been studied by developmental scholars, notably Kohlberg and Gilligan. Kohlberg's work has clarified the pattern generally characteristic of males[9] while Gilligan has illuminated the orientation more typical of women.[10] As we consider each of these remember that what we know only describes generalizations about the sexes.[11] You may find that you don't follow the interpersonal orientation generally characteristic of your sex. That's fine too. What's most important is not the generalizable differences between men and women, but the distinctive perspectives people adopt toward others.

In general men tend to adopt what is called a fairness orientation toward others. Founded on the clearly defined and rigidly maintained ego boundaries, men tend to define themselves as separate from others. This leads them to seek autonomy and to regard independence as natural and desirable. They tend not to seek many highly intimate relationships with others and may, in fact, feel threatened by too much closeness. Of course, men still interact with others so they need some general guidelines for interpersonal behavior. Typically men adopt what is called a rights perspective in which they recognize and respect the fact that others have rights that are seen as generic (all people have these basic rights). Further, the source of these "rights" is external—they are defined by social codes, norms, rules and laws. In dealing with others, then, men's goal is generally to be *fair*—that is, to respect others' rights by following widely accepted rules and understandings.

Women, in contrast, generally proceed by what is called a caring orientation toward others. Because women tend to have more permeable ego boundaries, they see themselves and others as less independent than do men. Instead, women tend to feel connections with others are necessary to personal security and happiness. To be separated from others, to not have intimates, is to be unsafe and alone. Thus, for women independence is not as valued as interdependence with others. Women's sense of connection to others leads them to adopt what is called a "needs perspective" in dealing with others. They tend not to be concerned with what others are entitled to or have a right to. Rather, their priority is to meet the needs of others with whom they feel connected. This leads women to aim for caring, rather than fairness, as the basic interpersonal principle. They want to be responsive to others' needs, to show care. Needs, unlike rights, are not generic. Each person has unique needs. Further, needs are not externally defined by rules and the society. What someone needs is judged in its own context and in that particular individual's terms. What is caring in one context with one person may not be so in a different context with another person.

The caring and fairness perspectives are clearly distinct, so it's not surprising that we sometimes have misunderstandings in our relationships. For example, someone who operates from a caring perspective might say "I have to make more time for mother, because she's getting weaker and needs more help and support. I'll just have to rearrange my schedule in order to take more care of her." Someone from a fairness perspective might respond by saying, "You can't let your mother interfere with your own life. You're giving her all that she has any right to expect." To the person who believes caring is the titular interpersonal goal the notion of what the mother "has a right to expect" makes no sense. By the same token, to the person who defines himself or herself as independent of others and who aims to be fair, the notion of rearranging your life to meet another's needs may seem foreign and inappropriate. Neither of these perspectives is "right" or "wrong." They are, however, very different, and understanding this basic difference in human selves provides one important insight into individual identity and interpersonal relationships.

We've now seen that the individual self is formed and sustained through three symbolic processes. We engage in reflexivity about ourselves and our world; we take the perspectives of others; and we enact interpersonal orientations. All of these are basic to what the personal self is. We can appreciate further the symbolic interactionist view of self by exploring four of its important implications.

PROPOSITIONS ABOUT THE SELF

By now you've seen that self clearly occupies a central position in symbolic interactionist theory. Given this, it's only natural that there has been much thought about how the self develops, operates, and changes. Four propositions summarize much of this important thinking about the role of self in human conduct.

The Self Arises in Communication with Others

Each person's view of self arises out of communication with others. Newborn infants have no self in the sense of seeing self-as-object or of having ego boundaries. But infants are enmeshed within families and a larger social system that provides communication contexts within which the self can be developed. From the moment of entry into the world, human infants are involved in communication. Parents, siblings, and others who are significant to the infant interact with him or her. Children learn who they are from the way others communicate with them. If others ignore a child's preferences and constantly correct his early efforts to master language, he may define himself as ineffectual and introverted. If others interact frequently with a child and respond positively to her attempts to talk, she is likely to regard herself as socially competent and to become extroverted. If parents communicate through word and gesture that they love the child and regard it as an important part of the family, the child will probably develop solid self-esteem and a sense of self-worth. And, as we've seen, the tendencies of others to communicate gender expectations can recreate limiting roles for developing boys and girls.

Throughout our lives, others communicate their perceptions of us, and this is a primary foundation of how we see ourselves. The self, then, arises directly out of significant others' communication with an individual.[12] Because we learn who we are by observing how others define us, the self is said to be acquired rather than present at birth.

The Self Is Constantly in Process

The self is never a finished product. Instead, it is constantly in process, changing, evolving. In Allport's language, the self is a "being in the process of becoming."[13] What Allport means is that the self never stops growing. Although our early years have profound impact on how we define ourselves, they are not the only influence. As long as we are involved with others, our selves will continue evolving.

Throughout our lives we interact with others and reinforce or revise our views of self on the basis of their communication with us. Harry Stack Sullivan, a psychiatrist who studied the relationship between identity and interpersonal interactions, believed individuals reflect the appraisals others have of them. Earlier Mead expressed a similar idea when he said, "The individual experiences himself as such not directly, but only indirectly, from the particular standpoints of other individual members of the same social group, or from the generalized standpoint of the social group as a whole to which he belongs."[14] Because humans are by nature social, they are deeply affected by how others see them, as revealed in others' communication with them. Over time, our view of self reflects our interpretations of how others view us.

As we interact with others, our views of self are subject to alteration. For some people, changes in the view of self are gradual and relatively minor. Each new relationship provides communication that confirms and extends the view of self developed through previous interactions. The child who was encouraged to read and study and was rewarded for academic achievements becomes an adult who seeks the company of people who keep up with news and literature and engage in serious discussions. In such relationships the individual's acquired view of self-as-intellectual is reinforced. A child whose social accomplishments are praised while academic ones are ignored may grow into an adult who becomes part of a party crowd and thereby gets confirmation of the view of self-as-socializer.

Changes in the view of self are not always so gradual. They can be abrupt and major. Parenthood, for instance, brings about immediate and radical alterations in individual's goals, values, behaviors, life style, and self-definition. Marriage is another abrupt change because self gains an entirely new role with two words: "I do." Death of a loved one is a drastic change that can alter a person's view of self. Losing a spouse or parent simultaneously removes an individual and a relationship from your world, and, thus, substantially changes how you define yourself.

Through changes—great and small, gradual and abrupt—the self constantly develops. It is never finished, never fully or finally established. Ongoing communication with others exposes us to diverse appraisals of who we are, and we interpret these to confirm or change our own views of self.

The Self Assumes Multiple Roles

Symbolic interactionists see the self as having a large and changeable set of roles from which an individual selects appropriate ones for particular situations. This is not to say that we are artificial, consisting only of roles. As we have seen, self is reflective as well as active, so the self cannot be equated with the roles it assumes. Yet roles are an important part of who we are. Our interpretations of accumulated experiences provide us with a range of perspectives we can assume mentally as we debate with ourselves or interact with others. As we take a role, we project certain aspects of our self, but the decision of which role to take in a given situation is also made by the self. Rollo May explains the link between analysis and behavior as two parts of the self when he observes that self is not only the roles we take, but also "the capacity by which one knows he play these roles; it is the center from which one sees and is aware of these so-called different 'sides' of himself."[15]

There are two ways in which the self assumes roles: role taking and role playing. We consider each. To take a role an individual projects herself or himself into the viewpoint of another person to see the world from that other person's orientation. Role taking is a mental process. By contrast, to play a role a person enacts behaviors appropriate to the position. Performance is required. Roles can be played with or without understanding. Young children constantly imitate their parents. They play roles, initially with little or no understanding of the significance of the behaviors they enact. Later, children imitate with understanding, yet they still play out behaviors of the roles they imitate.

As we mature still further, we learn to take roles in our minds without having to perform them physically.[16] We gain skill in assuming the perspectives of others and we incorporate them into our minds to try out ideas and to plan courses of action. Through role taking we rehearse scenes, such as when you imagine how a job interview will go by taking the role of interviewer and asking questions of yourself. We also take roles to deliberate alternative actions we're considering. For instance, a person who thinks about dropping out of school may take his mother's role in a mental debate with himself. As he takes her role he argues all of the reasons for staying in school, tells himself how he will be viewed if he quits, and perhaps even threatens himself with withdrawal of financial support if he drops out. In his mind the student can represent two very different views of the issue. He can carry on an actual debate, because he has incorporated a perspective other than his own.

We also play a variety of roles in our relationships with others. We become many selves. This doesn't imply that people are merely chameleons who alter their "true identity" at the drop of a hat. What it does mean is that we understand a range of roles (sets of behavior) and we can think of ourselves in a range of ways. We have the capacity to select the role we think is most appropriate for each situation as we interpret it. This flexibility is necessary if we are to communicate effectively with very different people in diverse settings. Hart, Carlson, and Eadie explain further: "A person is a complex network of selves, only some of which are provided social visibility in a given exchange."[17] Only one version of yourself is called forth in a given situation; only certain aspects of yourself are presented. Because we can take and play roles, we are many selves. Each person has a broad repertoire of roles from which to select the most appropriate ones for particular interactions. The self, then, is multidimensional and flexible so that we can communicate in ways responsive to the varied interpersonal situations in which we find ourselves. We are able to do this because our symbolic capacities allow us to conceive ourselves and our situations and to use those conceptualizations to define goals and direct actions.

The Self Is the Anchor for All Judgments

As we saw earlier, symbolic interactionists award central importance to the self, which is regarded as the nucleus of a person's thoughts and actions. The self contains "anchoring attitudes," which are relatively stable frames of reference we use to interpret and judge objects, experiences, situations, and others. Anchoring attitudes consist of your accumulated roles (or views of yourself), interpreted experiences, interests, goals, beliefs, and self-appraisals. Together these form a basis for personal judgments.

Because the self has anchoring attitudes, we never approach situations neutrally. What we interpret in any situation is deeply colored by our anchoring attitudes. We understand the world through our own unique perspective. It both grounds and limits what we can experience. Consistency and predictability in human behavior result from the anchoring attitudes that frame and filter our experience of the world.

HOW THE I LIMITS EXPERIENCE OF THE WORLD[18]

We see the world through our idea of who we think we are. Our model of the universe is based on our model of ourselves. When we look at the world, all we see is our mind. Seldom do we experience an object directly. Little is allowed independent existence.

What is perceived is a function of the models we have—the mold into which we pour molten reality. The newness of each moment is compressed to fit our idea of ourselves. Our models freeze-dry the flow of experience into a "manageable" reality. They are our idea of the truth, not the truth itself.

In looking at the nature of self we have seen that the self is the individual's ongoing interpretation and organization of experiences used to direct personal thought and action. Within the perspective of symbolic interactionism "self" is centrally important for it is the foundation of both individuality and social experience. Symbolic interactionism recognizes that being a self involves reflexivity. We experience ourselves as objects, which allows us to reflect on our own behaviors. Selfhood also involves perspective taking, which allows us to understand others' ways of conceiving themselves and situations. As we engage in perspective taking, two aspects of the self, the I and the ME, allow us to understand both our own viewpoint and that of another or others in general. Finally, being a self involves enacting an interpersonal orienta- tion, a basic set of values and goals that guide how we respond to others. These processes that constitute the self encourage a complex understanding of the self as both a unique individual and part of larger social communities. Building on these ideas, we derived four propositions that summarize how the self functions in the world. First, we saw that selfhood arises in communication with others. As they communicate with us, we observe how they act toward us and what they seem to think of us, and this becomes part of our own view of ourselves. Second, the self is constantly in process. Throughout our lives, we communicate with others. As we do, we often gain confirmations of the self that we have defined. Sometimes, others' responses to us are not confirming of the image we have of ourselves, and this can lead us to revise how we define ourselves. Third, we saw that the self assumes multiple roles. Through role taking and role playing we learn to adopt varied perspectives on ourselves and our behaviors as well as situations. Finally, we recognized that the self is the anchor for all judgments. Anchoring attitudes within the self act as lenses through which we interpret the world and our experiences within it. You've probably already realized how deeply communication and selfhood are intertwined. In the next section of this chapter we look more closely at this connection and what it means.

COMMUNICATION AND THE SELF

Communication and self interact dynamically. Each is a vital, continuous influence on the other. The self is established, sustained, and altered in communication with others. In turn, communication is constructed and interpreted through the self. In the next few pages we examine how communication and selfhood interact in an ongoing, lifelong process. Ideas introduced in the first section of this chapter are elaborated here.

The Self Is Established, Sustained, and Altered Through Communication

As we saw in the first section of this chapter, the self arises in communication with significant others. It is not innate, but is acquired through our communicative inter- actions with other people. They literally tell us who we are and how important we are. We come to reflect the appraisals others make of us. We learn to regard ourselves as others indicate they regard us, which is the basis of self-fulfilling prophecy, discussed in Chapter 4. Most of us encounter a variety of people who provide diverse perspec- tives on who we are. Our own views of our identity tends to be most affected by the perspectives and definitions that come from people who matter significantly to us and/or people whose views of us are consistent with those we already hold.

Achieving Self[19]

The self is built almost entirely, if not entirely, in relationship to others. While the newborn babe has the equipment for the development of the self, there is ample evidence to show that nothing resembling a self can be built in the absence of others. Having cortex is not enough; there must be continuous interchange between the individual and others. Language, for example, would not be possible without social relationships. Thus, it is seen that man is necessarily a social being.

The self has to be achieved; it is not given. All that is given is the equipment and at least the minimal (mother and child) social environment. Since the self is achieved through social contact, it has to be understood in terms of others. 'Self and other' is not a duality, because they go so together that separation is quite impossible.

For instance, you are more likely to accept your best friend's appraisal of your worth than that of a casual acquaintance. You would probably believe your major professor's evaluation of your intelligence before you would accept an assessment from an instructor in an elective course. Throughout our lives we form relationships with others, and each of these provides communication that influences how we view ourselves. This raises an important issue about the kinds of relationships in which we choose to participate. The more you interact with another person, the greater power that person gains to affect your view of self. We should be careful to select friends and intimates who will be healthy influences on our selves. The most constructive relationships are those that encourage continued personal growth for all involved.

There is a second sense in which communication establishes self. Role taking, discussed earlier, is fundamental to selfhood, because it leads to expansion of the self. When we take roles we import the perspectives of significant others into ourselves. In so doing we add entire dimensions to our own identities. We consist of the roles we can take. For instance, I take those of my mother, a close friend, my husband, and a senior colleague whom I admire. With each of these people I have a significant relationship in which I have learned to understand their perspectives on many things. Thus, these four people are not external to me. They are part of me. I have incorporated some of their ideas, values, and ways of looking at the world into myself. I can observe my own actions (self-as-object) from the perspective of any or all of these people, then judge and guide my actions accordingly. This gives me a range of ways in which to view myself as I act in diverse situations. In professional situations I may choose to take the role of my senior colleague in order to monitor my actions. In intimate interactions I may take the role of my husband or friend to judge how I am coming across. In counseling interactions I usually take the role of my mother, since she provided a strong model of constructive counseling.

Each of us has imported others into the self and can take the roles of these others to observe and regulate personal behaviors. In private, mental conversations we take roles to view the self. This allows us to see ourselves from alternate perspectives and to conduct multifaceted evaluations of who we are and how effectively we're communicating.

The self is established, sustained, and altered in communication. Interaction with significant others continually tells us who we are in their eyes, which becomes part of how we define ourselves. Role taking is a second way in which communication affects self development. As we import others' perspectives into ourselves, we increase the ways we can perceive ourselves as well as the goals we can establish for our ongoing development as individuals.

The Self Influences How We Construct and Interpret Communication

Earlier in this chapter we noted that the self is an anchor for all judgments (proposition 4). We cannot experience the world objectively. Instead, we know it through the perspective of the self. How we view ourselves is a dominant influence on how we see other people, experiences, objects, and situations. How we view ourselves is particularly relevant to both the communication we construct to express ourselves and the way in which we interpret others' communication.

The self is expressed through communication. Others know us by the way that we interact with them. In conversation we define ourselves, project ourselves, tell others who we are. As we interact with others we make decisions about how we want to come across. To create the image we desire, we make choices about language, gesture, and demeanor—all toward the goal of persuading others to see us in the way we intend. It is communication through which the self is expressed. Further, it is through our prior symbolic interaction within ourselves (I and ME) that we define an image of ourselves to project in interaction.

Identity Creation[20]

As we act meaningfully we exercise our powers and create our identity. Self validation is only possible through meaningful interaction in a social context . . . . By the social exercise of linguistic power man creates his own identity and reinforces that of the other.

The choices we make regarding self-presentation reveal much about how we view ourselves. The collection of beliefs you hold about who you are establishes a baseline for the range of communicative options open to you. Some possibilities are foreclosed, because they are not congruent with your view of self. For instance, one of my students refused to act as leader of her discussion group despite the fact that the group members unanimously elected her. She could not engage in leading communication because, as she said, "I just can't see myself as a leader." All of us probably know people who seem preoccupied with physical appearance. They may select clothes to project the image of attractiveness and they may avoid activities that could jeopardize the desired self-presentation (water sports and camping, for instance, can mess up hair, make-up, and clothes). On the other hand, each of us seeks those communication situations that will confirm who we think we are or who we want to be. The person who sees himself as a vigorous, engaging conversationalist is likely to gravitate toward interactions that will confirm that view of self. He might, for example, join a college debate team. A woman who views herself as a naturalist might form friendships with herbalists in the community, join the Sierra Club, and go on backpacking expeditions with other naturalists. When we have a choice, we tend to select interactions that affirm and reinforce how we define ourselves.

Our communication reflects this view of self. People with positive views of self are likely to communicate in confident ways, indicating they expect to be heard and accepted. People who have low self-esteem and who regard themselves as somehow inadequate tend to communicate in self-effacing, passive ways, indicating they think little of themselves and anticipate similar judgments from others.[21] Through our communication we express not only ideas, but our view of self. We tell others who we think we are.

The self not only directs our communication to others, but also influences how we interpret their communication to us. We are most likely to interpret others' communication in ways that conform to our own view of self. We tend to focus on parts of communication that are consistent with our self-image and to screen out that which is inconsistent. Kelley vividly describes the process whereby the self guides our interpretations: "The self 'looks out' upon the surrounding scene largely in terms of its own enhancement or defense. It tends to extend in the direction of that which promises to make it better off. It withdraws from that which endangers it."[22] The self, in other words, chooses what to notice. As the self alters, so does its interpretation of others' communication. A good example of this is beginning teachers. Often new teachers are unsure of their abilities and fear they cannot earn students' respect. Thus, when students ask pointed questions or challenge course policies the new instructor may interpret the communication as personal affronts that indicate the students do not respect him or her. At the same time the teacher may overlook communication that indicates respect, such as attendance, good work, conferences about material beyond the course. Once the instructor learns the ropes and gains confidence in her or his own abilities, there are likely to be noticeable changes in how students' communication is interpreted. The change in self brings about changes in what is found in others' communication.

Let's consider a second example of how self-definition influences our interpretation of communication. An acquaintance of mine once prided herself on her physical attractiveness. This was of primary importance in how Ann defined herself. As a result, she actively sought and reinforced communication that was complimentary about her appearance, and she was particularly pleased when men flirted with her or indicated interest in her. Attracting men and playing the role of "femme fatale" were ongoing communicative goals for her. Then Ann entered law school where she met and interacted with a number of other law students. She quickly learned that physical attractiveness was not a major criterion by which her peers and professors appraised her. Further, she found the "femme fatale" role was not respected by many of her peers, male or female. As she interacted more and more with other law students and with the faculty, she gradually redefined herself. She remained attractive, but as one of her longtime friends commented, "She no longer traded exclusively on the 'traditional woman' image." Later, in describing this change to me, Ann said, "I realized I am more than just a pretty face and a good figure. I have a good mind, and that's considerably more important to who I am than my looks." As she redefined herself she also revised her social circles and activities. Now she prefers substantive conversation to flirting and idle cocktail party chatter, and she'd rather spend her time reading than having a facial. She's also changed her opinion about flirtation and now finds it insulting when men initially relate to her as a potential date. According to Ann, "When a man makes a pass at me, he's treating me as nothing but a sex object. He's not acknowledging me an equal or even as a whole person." Three years ago a man's interest would have confirmed her view of self and she would have regarded it positively. Now it's offensive. Clearly, Ann's view of who she is influences how she interprets others' communication. The same is true for all of us. Reflecting on the people and kinds of interaction you seek out and enjoy will give you insight into how you define yourself.

The self influences how we communicate and how we view others' communication. It acts as an anchor for our own actions and our judgments of others' behaviors. Because the self is always in process, it alters over time: We come to see ourselves differently. As we revise our selves there are corresponding changes in how we communicate and how we regard the communication of others. It's an ongoing, highly systemic process.

Self and communication are dynamically interrelated. Each affects the other constantly. Just as the self is developed in communication with others, so it is expressed in our interactions. Acting as an anchor, the self directs our interpretations of others' interaction with us.

So far we've discussed the nature of self and its vital relationship with communication. It should also be clear that a healthy view of self is important to effective interaction with others and to our own well-being. In the final section of this chapter we consider some specific ways of improving self through communication.

IMPROVING THE SELF THROUGH COMMUNICATION

A healthy view of self is both realistic and flexible. To be realistic, your view of self should be based on knowledge and understanding of the many aspects of yourself. To be flexible, it should change as a natural outcome of your interactions with new people in new situations. The next few pages focus on some guidelines that help us gain and maintain realistic, flexible views of ourselves.

Recognize Change and Knowledge as Prerequisites for Development

Adler, Rosenfeld, and Towne, a group of communication researchers, emphasize the importance of change and self-knowledge to personal development. They identify three ways to facilitate these as means of growth:

1. It's necessary to experience a new environment. As long as you deal with the same people in the same ways it's unlikely that you'll learn anything new about yourself.
2. You need to share information about yourself with others. By listening to yourself disclose you have the opportunity to learn who you are.

3. You need to hear others share their perceptions of you. Receiving feedback about yourself gives you the chance to test your own self-image with the way others view you.[23]

Underlying these three suggestions is the central idea that to develop ourselves we must be open to change. We can embrace change by putting ourselves in new situations and by listening to how we and others respond to what we say about ourselves. Whether physical or psychological, change seems essential to growth. We can change and we do. So don't fall prey to what Rusk calls the "mind trap" of believing you can't change.

Avoiding the Mind Trap that I Can't Change[24]

Acting differently in order to change and grow is not an attempt to deceive anyone. It is an attempt to transcend your lifelong identity. Acting in new ways which you believe would increase your self-respect *will* feel artificial. Your familiar self resists change. The combination of awkward discomfort and increased self-respect is evidence you are making a courageous and determined effort to face the identity crisis required for significant change.

The "People Don't Change" Traps are cowardly capitulations to the status quo. These mind traps perpetuate the past and deny the possibilities within a person.

Self-change is difficult. But anyone can change. No one is inalterably destined to act in a certain way. To change, you must be willing to try new attitudes and actions more likely to satisfy your needs and give you self respect *despite your fears*.

A while ago Joseph Luft and Harry Ingram created a model to represent the kinds of information or knowledge that affect our self development. They combined their two first names (Joe and Harry) and called their model the Johari Window.[25]

According to the Johari Window there are four types of information relevant to the self. Area 1 contains free or public information, which is known both to the self and

The Johari Window

	Known to Self	*Not Known to Self*
Known to Others	1 Free	2 Blind
Not Known to Others	3 Hidden	4 Unknown

to others. Examples are your name, physical appearance, and general information you would share freely, such as your birthday, major, nationality. Area 2 contains information about the self that the self is unaware of but that others know. We often do not realize we have certain nervous habits, for instance. We may not know how others feel toward us or how we come across in certain situations. Area 3 is knowledge that you have about yourself but hide from others. Examples are fears, insecurities, goals for the future, intentions for a relationship, vulnerabilities, past experiences. Area 4 is the unknown area, which consists of aspects of you that neither you nor others know. Here are your untapped resources, things that cannot be known because there has been no chance to discover them—or even to observe them. Your skill in managing crises, for instance, is unknown until you've been in a crisis. Your effectiveness in various professions is unknown until you enter them and "try your wings." What kind of a parent you will be is unknown until and unless you have a child.

These four areas describe kinds of knowledge about self that are possible for us to acquire and share with others. Since a healthy view of self rests on a base of self-knowledge, it's important to consider how we gain access to the types of information depicted in the Johari Window. We'll look at four basic ways to learn more about yourself and, thus, to create a firmer foundation for defining and pursuing changes that will enhance your self-respect. Directly or indirectly each of these paths to change involves communication, the primary means of self development.

Accept Yourself as in Process

Self-improvement begins with accepting yourself as in process. This implies two things. First, it's important for you to accept who you believe yourself to be now. Second, you should realize that the you of today will not be the you of tomorrow or next year, because you are in process and will continue to change.

Accepting yourself is vital. You do not have to admire everything about yourself (and few of us do!), but you can accept who you now are. The identity you have now results from interactions throughout your lifetime. Since we cannot alter our pasts, it's vital we accept them *as a starting point from which to go forward*. It's appropriate to recognize your imperfections, but try not to dwell disproportionately on them. Overemphasizing weaknesses harms you in a couple of ways. First, it can take your attention away from noticing your virtues, which are just as "real" as any imperfections. Second, dwelling on what you don't like about yourself weakens you further. It undercuts your belief in yourself, and you need that to believe you can change.

How Self-Doubt Cripples Us[26]

The effects of self-doubt go far deeper than an inability to accept one's talents and attributes. Self-doubt is a mental abscess which can penetrate to the very essence of your being. Like a slow-growing but highly adaptable fungus, self-doubt is a creeping rot that eats away at your sense of worth.

Introduced by painful experiences in childhood, self-doubt weaves itself into the fabric of your identity. There, disguised as the truth, utilizing the self-defeating attitudes (Mind Traps) it generates, self doubt asserts its poisonous influence over every aspect of life, from work to relationships. And you may find yourself sabotaging your own welfare.

Try to focus on just accepting you as you are, not in comparison to other people. The only realistic measure of yourself is in terms of your own development and not relative to others. After all, since others haven't had your experiences, they have naturally developed into different people who have strengths and weaknesses different from your own. Thus, they're unrealistic models for comparison. The only basis for sound evaluation of yourself is yourself. Focus on yourself as a baseline for judgment and you will more clearly see the growth you've already made.

Accepting yourself as in process also implies that you keep a forward vision of your identity. It calls on you to remember that you will change. Because our selves are in process, they are tentative—always becoming, always growing. If there are parts of you that you don't like, accept them as part of who you are, and resolve to work toward changing them. Realize that experiences yet to come will influence the direction of your development, and seek out those that will be most useful in helping you become ever more the kind of person you wish to become. Also consider the activities and relationships in which you now participate. Are any of them reinforcing aspects of you that you wish to change? If so, you might want to consider whether these people and habits are ones that are healthy for you.

To develop as an individual, you should accept who you are today and the experiences that have helped to shape that identity. Doing this requires that you view yourself as an object and acknowledge the many aspects of your identity—ones you like as well as ones you wish to change—and then consider what changes, if any, you wish to make in yourself. Accepting yourself is the foundation for personal strength and the courage to keep growing.

Accept Others as in Process

Just as we need to accept ourselves as we are now, so should we accept others as they are at the moment. Realize that their identities, like yours, were shaped by their life experiences and that they, like you, will continue to develop. Naturally, you may not like everything about other people, but accepting them is important for your own growth and theirs. As you accept others you enlarge the possibilities for interaction, which necessarily increases the bases of your own selfhood. Communication with others is the foundation of who you are, so it's important to expose yourself to a variety of other people. Sometimes we learn a great deal from people we don't particularly like. We interact with them, get glimpses of their perspectives, and so enhance our own understanding of the range of possibilities in human development. Every person represents an opportunity for our own growth, so we should be hesitant to reject anyone without first giving them and us a chance to learn from each other.

Accepting others happens inside your head. To have social impact, that acceptance must be demonstrated in your interactions with others. Since communication is the primary means by which we indicate we are open to others, we need to communicate in ways that convey our interest. The first step is to initiate conversation or to be receptive to others' invitations to talk. Once you've launched interaction, many other communicative choices will demonstrate your openness. Particularly important is listening, which we discussed earlier in Chapter 6.

Equally important is dual perspective, which we have discussed several times. When you communicate with others, try to imagine how they see the world, try to understand their unique perspectives on particular topics, themselves, and you. When you are able to do this, you enlarge the perspective that you personally have on the world. In taking others' perspectives, you may come to see possibilities that had never occurred to you before. Accepting tends to be reciprocal: As you reach out to others, they often reach out to you in return, which provides you with an empowering sense of acceptance.

Our focus on how your interactions have influenced your selfhood should not lead you to miss the obvious point that influence on personal identity applies to others too. Just as others affect your identity, you influence theirs. You have had and will continue to have impact on how others see themselves. To recognize your role in others' lives and health is to accept responsibility to assist them in their potential to grow. Willingness to interact with others is one way to meet this responsibility. Another way is to realize that, like you, they are in process. They can change and grow if they participate in rich relationships that encourage healthy development. You can be part of making this possible for them.

Self and other are intertwined. We are interdependent, each having a stake in how others develop and each having responsibility for the quality of interaction in which we engage. Accepting ourselves and others as in process is the first step in providing the strength to seek change in yourself and to encourage it in them.

Self-Disclose When Appropriate

Also instrumental to your personal development is self-disclosing communication. To self-disclose is to reveal, unveil, make known, or unmask the self to another person. It is to express information that we usually keep in the hidden area of the Johari Window. Of course, whenever we interact with others we reveal something of ourselves. Self-disclosure, however, is a special kind of communication that is more revealing than most. As a minimum definition of self-disclosure, Cosby says it is when one person intentionally tells something personal about herself or himself to another person.[27] Other researchers add that to self-disclose a person must reveal information that couldn't easily be obtained by another person.[28] Self-disclosure, then, happens when we deliberately tell another individual something personal that is unlikely to be discovered by other means.

Extensive research in this area suggests a number of potential benefits of self-disclosure. First, it tends to increase trust between communicators, which, in turn, often increases attraction, liking, and loving.[29] Second, self-disclosure seems positively related to mental health, probably because sharing ourselves with trusted others increases our self-acceptance and, therefore, our self-esteem. We tend to feel more secure and positive when our "hidden areas" are not overloaded with information we are afraid to expose. Third, self-disclosure is an important way to learn about ourselves. As we reveal personal information, we reflect on it ourselves and we get response from another person, both of which enhance our perspective on ourselves. In terms of the Johari Window we decrease our hidden areas by sharing private information and we decrease our blind areas by opening ourselves to feedback from others.

Despite all of the potential gains, self-disclosure is not always advisable. In order to be constructive, self-disclosure should occur in appropriate degrees and in a climate of mutual trust. This implies that there are levels of disclosure. It's usually a good idea to increase gradually the intimacy of information you reveal about yourself. Starting with low-level disclosures allows you to "test the water" before you reveal highly personal information. It's further advisable to self-disclose only with people who will respect your confidence and who are not likely to exploit private information. Because self-disclosures tend to expose our vulnerabilities, we need to be very cautious about whom we choose. Finally, self-disclosure should suit the context of interaction. It's generally not appropriate to offer highly personal information in a public bar or in the midst of a crowded party. Private contexts provide more control over how we disclose and offer others a better chance to respond openly and fully. The appropriateness of self-disclosure, then, depends on context, depth of information, and the relationship we have with those to whom we disclose.

In addition to thinking about conditions for appropriate self-disclosure, you should be aware of the risks entailed in revealing self. The primary reason many people avoid self-disclosure is fear of rejection. If others cannot or will not accept what we reveal, we may feel personally rebuffed. Other reasons for not disclosing include fear of damaging relationships, fear of presenting a negative part of self, and fear of losing control by exposing our weaknesses.[30] Sometimes we don't self-disclose because we don't want to have to acknowledge parts of ourselves we'd rather not face.[31] Sometimes we don't self-disclose because we fear it could increase our intimacy with another, and we feel unable to handle real closeness. Notice that the reasons we typically avoid self-disclosing center around our fears.

Why Am I Afraid To Tell You Who I Am?[32]

> I am afraid to tell you who I am, because,
> if I tell you who I am,
> you might not like who I am,
>   and it's all that I have.

While it's definitely prudent to exercise caution in self-disclosing, we shouldn't avoid it altogether. Self-disclosure aids in self-development, so it is worthy of consideration. When we reveal private things about ourselves to another, we necessarily call those things to our own attention. Although the term "self-disclosure" refers to unveiling self to others, in doing this we simultaneously reveal ourselves to ourselves. At the same time that we invite response from another, we give response to ourselves. We and the other person reflect on the information. When another person responds to self-disclosing communication, we gain new perspective on ourselves. This kind of feedback is helpful, because it aids us in making more realistic evaluations of ourselves. Furthermore, when someone accepts a self-disclosure, we often find it easier to acknowledge that part of ourselves. Personal weaknesses or fears may seem less severe to us if we discover that others can accept them without thinking less of us. Self-disclosures also tend to increase trust in relationships. If you reveal personal information to another who accepts it, you naturally feel more secure in the relationship. The other person tends to feel more secure too, because you have entrusted her or him with private knowledge and have opened the way for reciprocal disclosures to you. If you open yourself to another person, it's likely that person will be open to you in return.[33] When used cautiously, self-disclosure can be a valuable means to self-knowledge and growth. We need to be careful to make sure our disclosures are appropriate in terms of content, relationship, and context, and we need to consider realistically the risks involved in revealing ourselves to others. But we also should realize there are risks in not disclosing. We can become locked inside ourselves, selves whose growth is stunted by fear of interaction with others. Through careful self-disclosures we can increase self-knowledge and self-acceptance and we can enhance our relationships with others, all of which assist our personal development.

Engage in Constructive Risk-Taking

This is a summary suggestion. In opening this section on improvement of self we noted the necessity of change as a basic condition for growth. To develop and to know ourselves more fully we sometimes need to risk the security of how we see ourselves now in order to experiment with what we could become. To do this, we may seek new experiences and new relationships, we may attempt to take new roles, and we may place ourselves in familiar environments. Changes such as these tend to bring out parts of ourselves we had only dimly realized were there or to encourage us to develop completely new dimensions of self that were never before needed. In terms of the Johari Window, we can use change to reduce our unknown area.

The Fully Functioning Person[34]

According to psychologist Earl Kelley, "since life is ever-moving and ever-becoming, the fully functioning person is cast in a creative role. But more than simply accepting this role," the fully functioning person realizes that she or he is part of this creative process. He or she understands the dangers of "the static personality because it seeks to stop the process of creation to which, we owe our world and our being." The fully functioning person "exults in being a part of this great process and in having the opportunity to facilitate it. Life . . . means discovery and adventure, flourishing because it is in tune with the universe.

The theme of this chapter is that human self is established and constantly refined through communicative interaction with others. To keep developing, we need new forms of interaction. Without new experiences, people, and contexts the self becomes impoverished. Our growth is restricted to established sources and, thus, to established patterns. We settle for being less than we could become. The irony is that we will change anyway in response to alterations in our environments and the people who enter them. To settle for only change of this sort, however, is to give up our own control over personal growth. We then allow our development to be determined by fate or accident or the desires or others, instead of by our own goals and design.

You can direct the course of your self-development if you choose to venture into experiences, relationships, roles, and contexts that are new for you. Constructive risk taking seems especially valuable for people who are not satisfied with some aspects of themselves. Probably most of us fit into that category. You can set goals for positive change and then seek interactions and situations in which it's possible to engage in communication that helps you meet those goals. Observing others who have successfully changed parts of themselves may provide you with useful models of how to foster your own development. Many of the ideas and suggestions in this chapter offer additional guidance for taking constructive, prudent risks. Finally, your attitude toward change can assist you greatly. Try to realize that change can be opportunity. It represents adventure in which you can experiment with who you are and influence who you will become.

SUMMARY

The self is central to the symbolic interactionist theory of human communication. We began this chapter with a definition of self as an individual's ongoing interpretation and organization of experiences, thoughts, and feelings used to direct personal thought and action. The symbolic interactionist view of self rests on four basic understandings of the processes that comprise the ever-evolving human self. We are capable of reflexivity (taking ourselves as objects), taking the perspectives of others (ME), bounding our egos more or less permeably, and forming interpersonal orientations to guide our interactions with others. Working together, these capacities of the human self allow us seek our goals in ways adapted to the norms and constraints of particular situations and others with whom we interact. These four ideas form a foundation for basic propositions that maintain that the self arises in communication with others, is constantly in process, assumes multiple roles (perspective taking), and is the anchor for all of our judgments and actions.

The symbolic interactionist understanding of self recognizes the dynamic relationship between communication and selfhood. The relationship is interactive. On the one hand, communication establishes the self and, on the other hand, self directs communication. How we define ourselves is a major influence on how we communicate and how we interpret the communication of others.

Because the self directs our thoughts and actions, it is important to have a healthy, realistic view of self. We considered four ways to improve the self through communication. Accepting self and others as in process is the foundation of ongoing development of selfhood. In addition, we can self-disclose when appropriate and take constructive risks to explore who we are and might become.

The self is in process; in fact, the self is process. It is never in final form. This means that you have the power to change aspects of who you are and thereby direct your own growth. Perhaps the material in this chapter will encourage you to make an enduring commitment to learning about who you are now and to deciding who you want to become and how to achieve that.

REFERENCES

[1]This discussion is based primarily on George H. Mead's book, *Mind, Self, and Society*. Chicago: University of Chicago Press, 1934.

[2]Mead.

[3]N. Chodorow, *The Reproduction of Mothering*. Berkely: University of California Press, 1978; L. Kohlberg, *The Philosophy of Moral Development*. San Francisco: Harper and Row, 1981.

[4]Chodorow; J. B. Miller, *Toward a New Psychology of Women, 2nd. ed.* Boston: Beacon Press, 1986.

[5]J. Block, *Sex Role Identity and Ego Development*. San Francisco: Jossey-Bass, 1984.

[6]J.T. Wood and L. F. Lenze, "Gender and the Development of Self: Inclusive Pedagogy in Interpersonal Communication," *Women's Studies in Communication*, in press.

[7]G. M. Phillips and N. J. Metzger, *Intimate Communication*. Boston: Allyn & Bacon, 1976, p. 122.

[8]W. James, *Psychology*. Cleveland: World Publishing Co., 1948, p. 176.

[9]Kohlberg.

[10]C. Gilligan, *In Another Voice: Psychological Theory and Women's Development*. Cambridge: Harvard University Press, 1982.

[11]Wood and Lenze; J. T. Wood, "Different Voices in Relationship Crises," *American Behavioral Scientist, 29,* 273-301.

[12]Earl C. Kelley, "The Fully Functioning Self." In J. Steward (Ed.), *Bridges Not Walls, 2nd. ed.* Reading, MA: Addison-Wesley, 1977, p. 107.

[13]G. Allport, "Psychological Models for Guidance," *Harvard Education Review, 32,* 1962, 377.

[14]Mead, p. 138.

[15]R. May, *Man's Search for Himself*. New York: W. W. Norton, 1953, p. 92.

[16]H. Sullivan, *The Interpersonal Theory of Psychiatry*. New York: W. W. Norton, 1953, Part II.

[17]R. P. Hart, R. E. Carlson, and W. F. Eadie, "Attitudes Toward Communication and the Assessment of Rhetorical Sensitivity," *Communication Monographs, 47,* 1980, 2.

[18]S. Levine, *Who Dies*. New York: Anchor/Doubleday, 1989, p. 53.

[19]Kelley, p. 107.

[20]E. Becker, "The Self as the Locus of Linguistic Causality." In D. Brissett and C. Edgley (Eds.), *Life As Theatre*. Chicago: Aldine, 1975, p. 62.

[21]G. M. Phillips and N. J. Metzger, "The Reticent Syndrome: Some Theoretical Considerations about Etiology and Treatment," *Speech Monographs, 40,* 1973, 220-230.

[22]Kelley, p. 112.

[23]R. Adler, L. Rosenfeld, and N. Towne, *Interplay*. New York: Holt, Rinehart and Winston, 1980, p. 69.

[24]T. Rusk, *Mind Traps: Change Your Mind, Change Your Life*. Los Angeles: Price Stern Sloan, 1988, pp. 121, 122, 123.

[25]J. Luft, *Group Process: An Introduction to Group Dynamics*. Palo Alto, CA: National Press, 1963.

[26]Rusk, pp. 11-13.

[27]P. Cosby, "Self Disclosure: A Literature Review," *Psychological Bulletin, 79,* 1973, 73-91.

[28]L.B. Rosenfeld, "Self Disclosure Avoidance: Why Am I Afraid to Tell You Who I Am?" *Communication Monographs, 46,* 1979, 63-74.

[29]Cosby, 73-91.

[30]F. Steele, *The Open Organization: The Impact of Secrecy and Disclosure on People and Organizations*. Reading, MA: Addison-Wesley, 1975.

[31]L. J. Sherrill, *Guilt and Redemption*. Richmond, VA: John Knox Press, 1945.

[32]J. Powell, *Why Am I Afraid To Tell You Who I Am?* Niles, IL: Argus Communications, 1969, p. 12.

[33]D.M. Daher and P. G. Banikotes, "Interpersonal Attraction and Rewarding Aspects of Self Disclosure Content and Level," *Journal of Personal and Social Psychology, 33,* 1976, 492-496.

[34]Kelley, p. 117.

CHAPTER 8

COMMUNICATION AND INTERPERSONAL DEVELOPMENT: THE SOCIAL SELF

The human embodies the essence of culture, of relationships, of society, of mind.
Every form of social interaction begins or ends with a consideration of the human self.

(B. Aubrey Fisher)

In the last chapter we saw that self arises in communication with others whose responses to us become part of our own views of ourselves. Each of us becomes

159

unique, reflecting the range of interactions in which we participate throughout our lives. Because each of us is involved in our own relationships and interacts with particular others, each human is distinct, unlike anyone else in the universe.

Yet we share many values, beliefs, and codes of conduct with others in our society. In this sense we are similar to others. Among people within a given society there are regularities in attitudes and actions. We share understandings about agreed-upon ways of doing things and ways of thinking. With others we inhabit a shared world, so we are social beings. It is social interaction that enables us to develop our uniqueness and at the same time to recognize the ways in which we are like others. So, the self is at once individualized and socialized.

Chapter 7 focused on how the individual nature of self is established and altered through interactions. This chapter builds on those understandings to explore the social self. We focus on how we learn the basic "rules" of our society or, to paraphrase Mead, how society gets into the individual. This means we look at socialization, the process by which individuals realize and internalize the attitudes and norms for behaviors that characterize the society in which they live. As you may recall from Chapter 2, symbolic interaction theory recognizes humans as both individual and social beings. By extension, this means that a symbolic interactionist view of self must account for both the ways in which humans are unique and the ways in which we are common. To establish the direction for this chapter, we turn to what Mead said about the nature of self as a social being.[1]

> The self . . . is essentially a social structure, and it arises in social experience. After a self has arisen, it in a certain sense provides for itself its social experiences and so we can conceive of an absolutely solitary self. But it is impossible to conceive of a self arising outside of social experience.

This chapter elaborates on a number of the ideas suggested by Mead's comments. We begin by showing that social attitudes and behaviors are learned, not innate. Next we look at family interaction as the initial form of socialization through which we learn language, gender scripts, and life scripts. Then we consider peer groups and professional relationships as further socializing influences. Finally, we examine broad values that characterize contemporary American society, the basic social world in which we all participate.

As we proceed it will become clear that communication is the central force in human socialization. It is as we communicate with others that we acquire understanding of our social world and develop attitudes and behaviors that allow us to participate in it. Throughout our lives we are part of families, peer groups, and work organizations. Interaction in these settings equips us for membership in particular groups and society as a whole.

HUMAN INTERACTION AND SOCIAL DEVELOPMENT

Ghadya Ka Bacha—Wolf Boy[2]

In 1954 the staff at the Balrampur hospital in India received a most unusual patient—a young boy who was naked and starving and who showed no understanding of how to interact with the staff. Dr. Sharma examined the child and reported there were scars on the neck, probably made as the child was dragged by an animal, the child's incisor teeth protruded like an animal's, and both elbows and knees of the child had heavy calluses as if he had moved on all fours. The hospital staff began to suspect that he was ghadya ka bacha, the wolf boy.

The strongest evidence for this idea was the boy's behaviors. He spent his days curled in bed, playing with a stuffed animal, much like a baby wolf spends its time in the lair. The boy, named Ramu by the staff, had a keen sense of smell. Even though the hospital kitchen was over 100 yards from his room, he could smell raw meat and would howl for it. When presented with food Ramu tore it apart; when given fluids, he lapped them from a bowl. He once bit a nurse who was holding food.

Ramu was not happy at the Balrampur hospital. Most of the time he was quiet, playing with his stuffed animal. On two occasions, however, he displayed great excitement, once when taken to see the wolves at a zoo and once when a dog approached him. Most of the doctors and scientists who observed Ramu concluded he was indeed a wolf-boy who had grown up in the jungle and had been socialized by wolves. Ramu died after living 14 years in the hospital, roughly the length of time a wolf survives in captivity.

This factual account dramatically shows what happens to social development in the absence of interaction with other humans. Our attitudes and behaviors are clearly learned, not innate. We learn them through interaction with other humans. Children deprived of human contact do not develop values and behaviors we typically associate with human nature. In addition to Ramu, we know of other cases of children who developed in isolation from other people. In 1921 missionaries in India found two young girls living with wolves. One died shortly after being taken to civilization. Although the other girl survived for several years, she never learned language or any basic human abilities.[3] Another case involved an illegitimate child named Anna, whose mother hid her in a small dark room. Anna received essential food, but she was deprived of any meaningful interaction with other people and spent all of her time locked in the single room. When discovered, Anna was six years old and appeared deficient in basic human abilities of speech, vision, hearing, and movement. There were no physical reasons for these deficiencies—Anna simply had not learned how to use her senses. She was passive, almost a vegetable, and died before reaching her eleventh birthday.[4]

Ramu's behaviors seem strange to us because we do not expect a being with human form to lap beverages, rip into raw meat, and lope about on all fours. It would be understandable, though mistaken, to think Ramu simply wasn't socialized. Indeed, he was quite thoroughly socialized according to the values and behaviors that characterized his community—wolf society. His behaviors were as normal for him or any other wolf as use of knives, forks, and glasses is for us. The important point for us to realize is that Ramu learned his attitudes and behaviors from those with whom he interacted, presumably wolves. Even more striking is the case of Anna, who literally learned almost no behaviors because she had no one with whom to interact and, thus, no one to teach her a code of behaviors.

The social self that any of us develops reflects the values and codes of conduct in our culture. We learn those by participating in relationships where we communicate with others. Thus, it is primarily through our interactions with others that we develop an understanding of our social world and become aware of ourselves as members of a common social order. In this sense, a basic aspect of humanity—the social self—is acquired. We learn to be human because we develop in social, human contexts. The remainder of this chapter explores four relational contexts most important in our socialization.

SOCIALIZATION IN THE FAMILY

The nuclear family is the first and most important influence on human socialization. For a newborn baby the family is the entire world. It is the social environment in which the baby develops its initial views of self and others and its basic expectations for relationships with others. Through early interaction in families, infants learn what the human community is and how they can participate in it. To understand how this happens, we examine three major socializing processes that begin in the family: learning language, gender scripts, and life scripts. All of these have profound and enduring impact on how we see ourselves and others. In turn, how we regard ourselves and others is a primary influence on our interpersonal choices and actions within relationships.

Developing Language

Probably developing language is the single most important aspect of socialization by the family. It is in learning language—more generally, the ability to think symbolically—that children gain entry into the social world. Infants are born with the potential to learn language, but it is the family that is instrumental in realizing that potential. Children learn language and symbolic thought through a series of stages. Each stage involves a particular type of interaction with family members. The stages are progressive, each building on previous ones to bring the child closer to full membership in human society.[5]

Preverbal Interaction.   Before infants can learn language, behavior must have meaning. The first stage in language acquisition is behavioral interaction, what Mead called "the conversation of gestures." The infant learns to recognize basic patterns in its experience. Gestures of anger are accompanied by certain consequences, gestures of affection lead to different results, the feeding ritual involves yet another set of consequences, and so forth. The infant learns to make primitive distinctions among behaviors and their impacts on its world. Through initial interactions with family members, behaviors (gestures) come to have rudimentary meaning for the infant.

Language and development of "mind."   Language emerges out of the conversation of gestures. Once the child has attached meanings to behaviors, it learns to replace behavior with ideas about behavior with language. This is a crucial move: In learning to *think about* behaviors instead of just behaving and responding to behaviors of others, the child acquires what Mead called "mind."

At approximately six months of age, infants begin to vocalize. Over time certain sounds are rewarded and come to have meaning for the baby. "Ma" may be associated with food and comfort, "ba" with the bright, round thing that rolls. As more abstract words are learned, the child gains control of concepts and, thus, a whole new dimension of existence: the dimension of ideas. Fred Jandt explains the process well.[6]

> Language makes it possible to replace behavior with ideas. Though the mother can teach her child the meaning of "I am angry" only by behaving in appropriate ways, once the child learns the words, the mother need not behave in an angry fashion in order to communicate displeasure. Having learned what the words mean, the child now has the idea of anger. Because mother and child now share an idea, the child can respond to what the mother says as well as to what she does . . . . Furthermore, having the idea of anger, the child can think about his mother's anger; it can have meaning for him even when she is absent or not angry. Thus as the child acquires language he acquires mind.

In learning language the child is no longer restricted to concrete world of here and now. She or he is able to think beyond what is present in the given moment and to respond to ideas as well as to physical behaviors. Only as the child develops language does she or he enter the human world of ideas—the world of the mind.

Language and entry into the social world.   Just as language is the foundation of mind, so is it the foundation of the social self. As a child masters language, she or he can think about ideas and can reflect on personal behaviors in relation to other people. A child might, for instance, indicate to himself that crying causes anger in Father, that when Father is angry he behaves harshly, so crying should be avoided. Through reflection the child learns to direct his or her own behavior. Impulses to act (the "I" aspect of self) are now modified by an awareness of the social consequences of action (the "ME" aspect of self). The social self has begun to emerge.

Learning language is a primary focus for the next few years of life. Children quickly build up vocabularies to represent people, objects, and experiences. Learning words involves far more than simply understanding factual or descriptive labels. Language, as you may remember from Chapter 4, is not neutral; it is value-laden. In acquiring language, therefore, children learn the values that others attach to people, objects, and experiences. If parents become tense and raise their voices each time they point to things they call "dog," the child will learn not only what a dog literally is, but also a general attitude toward dogs, in this case fear. This process, repeated with each new word, ensures that children learn social meanings that influence their interactions and interpretations.

Children learn attitudes toward themselves in much the same way as they acquire attitudes toward other things. Children notice how others treat them, and adopt those attitudes toward themselves. Preschoolers internalize others' attitudes toward themselves by imitating others' communication. It's not unusual to overhear a toddler scolding herself ("Bad Annie. Dirt on dress. Bad, bad."), warning himself ("Be careful of stove. Burn Stevie."), or bestowing praise ("Very good. I drank all the milk."). Young children at first do not understand why dirt is bad, stoves are dangerous, or milk is good. Nonetheless, they imitate the attitudes of those people around them and use those attitudes to direct their own behaviors and attitudes. Through this process of role playing, children learn to respond to themselves as others have responded to them.

Gradually children progress beyond the imitative behavior of role playing. They begin to understand the attitudes and behaviors of other people. With understanding, children move beyond simple copying of roles they have observed. Now they can creatively extend others' dispositions and apply these in new situations. In order to extend another's role beyond the contexts in which the other has been observed, the child must grasp not only how the other acts, but the underlying patterns or rules for behavior. For instance, suppose a three-year-old girl sees her father groom the cat, straighten up the kitchen, pick up toys in the playroom, and vacuum dirt out of the family car. She generalizes that Daddy likes things neat, so neatness is good and clutter is bad. Later, playing in her treehouse, she may systematically clear away all twigs and leaves because she defines them as not neat and, therefore, not good. The little girl has taken her father's role toward neatness. She has never seen him in a treehouse, but she understands his general attitude toward neatness and can apply that attitude to her particular circumstances. Her understanding extends beyond concrete cases. She now comprehends the concept of neatness and can apply it in a range of settings.

With conceptual understanding, the child takes another giant step in social development. No longer is it necessary to act out every idea in a physical way (role playing). Because the child can think conceptually, she or he can imagine how another would would respond to objects, situations, and people. Thus, the child can mentally take the roles of others and consider how they would see various situations. This phase of development marks the onset of the inner dialogue we discussed in Chapter 7. The child symbolically tries out alternative ways of behaving to see how each would appear to others. Rehearsal precedes commitment to any physical action. This is a major step, since all advanced forms of communication depend on the capacity of a person to assume the roles of others and to plan personal actions with understanding of the probable responses of others to those actions.

Initially role taking occurs in reference to particular people who are significant to the child-parents, siblings, and the like. Thus, the child learns to observe situations and self from the distinctive viewpoints of specific other people. While taking the roles of others allows the child to interact with those people, it does not provide a basis for interaction in broader social contexts. Full participation in society hinges upon one further phase in symbolic development.

Over time, role-taking ability expands so that it's not tied only to particular individuals. Children learn to take the role of what Mead called the "generalized other," which is a composite of rules, roles, and attitudes endorsed by the whole social community of which an individual is part. Morris makes a useful distinction between taking the role of another and taking the role of the generalized other.[7]

> To the degree that the self has taken the attitudes of others into itself through the language process it has become the others, and the values of the others are its own; to

the degree that the self assumes the role of the generalized other, its values are the values of the social process itself.

In learning to take the role of the generalized other, children are socialized into dominant group values and norms. This, in turn, enables them to become members of society as whole.

The Generalized Other[8]

The organized community or social group which gives to the individual his unity of self may be called "the generalized other." The attitude of the generalized other is the attitude of the whole community . . . . If the given human individual is to develop a self in the fullest sense, it is not sufficient for him merely to take the attitudes of other human individuals toward himself and toward one another within the human social process, and to bring that social process as a whole into his individual experience merely in these terms: he must also, in the same way that he takes the attitudes of other individuals toward himself and toward one another, take their attitudes toward the various phases or aspects of the common social activity or set of social undertakings in which, as members of an organized society or social group, they are all engaged; only in so far as he takes the attitudes of the organized social group to which he belongs. . . does he develop a complete self or possess the sort of complete self he has developed.

The generalized other can be thought of as the ME part of self that we discussed in Chapter 7. The ME internalizes the attitudes of society in general and uses them to guide the self appropriately. Because these attitudes are now part of the self, the individual is part of the social world and it is part of her or him.

Our discussion of language development explains HOW we learn to interact with others and understand our social world and its values. With this as background, we can now ask WHAT we learn about who we are and how we should be and behave. Clearly families, especially parents, figure prominently in WHAT we learn about ourselves. Two primary kinds of content about identity that we learn first in families concern our gender roles and our life scripts.

Gender Scripts

A child's sex is known at the moment of birth: That's a matter of biology. Gender, however, is a matter of socialization. We learn to be feminine or masculine, and what we learn depends on the society in which we live. Different societies define feminine and masculine in different ways. In some cultures males are expected to be highly emotional, and females are expected to be dominant. Thus, how we define what it means to be masculine or feminine is a matter of what we are taught. In American culture gender is considered very important, so it's not surprising that learning to define self in terms of gender is one of the first and most profound aspects of self definition. According to scholars of child development, children have their gender scripts—rules about what it means to be male or female—by at least age 5. Many theorists think children learn this as early as 2 or 3 years.[9] How do we learn gender scripts? Again, the family is a primary socializing agent in the process of teaching gender.

Parents socialize children into gender scripts in two important ways. First, like all of us, parents have their own beliefs about what is appropriate for males and females. These beliefs are communicated to children in terms of expectations ("Son, you shouldn't cry." "Little girls shouldn't play so rough.") and the ways parents attribute gender stereotypes to their children ("You want to look pretty, don't you Suzie?" "Toby, you're so strong—such a little man.") Parental expectations and definitions regarding gender are also communicated through the clothes and toys that parents give their children—telling them how little boys and girls what appearance and kinds of activities are appropriate.

The Gender Game[10]

Recently arrived in toy stores is Heart Throb, the board game— recommended for "all girls who like boys." . . .

Walk into nearly any toy store and the toys are arranged by what appears to be gender appeal. A lot of the boys' toys are action-packed, while the girls' toys tend to have something to do with make-up or housekeeping.

The message is clear, says Rosemary Hornak, associate professor of psychology at Meredith College. "Girls are sweet and pretty and passive. Boys are go-getters." That's what worries Ms. Bratcher, who is director of community relations for the UNC Center for Public Television: "The toys carry certain perceptions about the world— about violence and sexism. They sort of transmit the prevailing culture."

Even the most well-informed and well-meaning parents may blindly pass on the lessons of their own childhoods. . . . children react to how their parents react to toys. . . .

The fault, dear parent, lies not in our toys but in ourselves. "Toys are influential but the toy itself is an inanimate object. It comes to acquire value depending upon the parents' reaction," says Dr. Hornak.

Research has shown that parents do have gender stereotypes that influence how they perceive and respond to their children. As this happens, the children learn the stereotypes too and associate them with themselves. One dramatic study showed that parents describe newborns of comparable size and activity levels quite differently depending on the child's sex. Newborn boys were described with words such as "strong," "solid," and "independent," while girls were described as "cute," "sweet," and "loving."[11] Thus, parents pass on their gender scripts to children as they communicate gender-based expectations and define what gender means.

A second way in which parents teach children gender scripts is through role modeling. Most children regard their mothers and fathers as primary models for many things, including gender. How your mother defined her own femininity and how your father defined his masculinity probably influenced your own views of what each gender is and is supposed to be.[12]

Part of social development—at least in contemporary American culture—is learning gender scripts that tell us how to look, think, and act in male or female ways. Parents are primary influencers in the process of teaching gender scripts.

Life Scripts

A number of years ago psychologists developed an intriguing approach to human communication. Called transactional analysis, it focuses on both the patterns and content of communication transactions between people to explain individual attitudes, behaviors, and views of self.[13] Basic to transactional analysis is the concept of *life scripts*, which provide rules for living. As the name implies, life scripts direct our lives. Like dramatic scripts, they define the roles we and others can play, our dialogue with others, and a plot for our lives. Most authorities believe life scripts are established quite early, perhaps by the age of five. At that age individuals have little charge over their worlds, so they cannot control the scripts being created for them. Most of us are not even conscious of many of the scripts we live by. This is because we learned the scripts so long ago and without awareness of what we were learning. We learned by observing how our family members treated us and each other and by unconsciously absorbing these patterns of interaction.

Life Scripts[14]

From out of all our early experiences, particularly from the messages-both verbal and nonverbal-received from our parents, we develop a psychological script for ourselves and, for the most part, follow this throughout our lives.

Individuals' scripts are generally "written" by the age of three; they provide us with specific directions for functioning within the larger cultural script . . . . Some children, for example, are told that they will be successes. Nonverbally, they are given love and affection; verbally, they are reinforced for numerous actions. Other children have been told they will never succeed. Statements such as, "No matter what you do, you'll be a success," as well as statements such as, "You'll never amount to anything," are extremely important in determining the script the child will assume in later life. Generally people follow the scripts their parents have written for them. But such scripts can be broken. We do not have to follow the script written for us by our parents.

We may have scripts for any number of areas in our lives. You might have a script that tells you how important status is, what kinds of professions are admirable, how families are supposed to be, and the importance of civic activity in life. Whatever your life scripts are, you can probably trace them back to communication in your family.

Sometimes our scripts work fine and we may never be aware that they exist. At other times they can create problems for us, because they lock us into attitudes and actions that are not appropriate for our present circumstances. The danger of living by an outdated script is illustrated in the following news report.[15]

St. Petersburg, Florida. When Mrs. Elsie DeFratus could no longer afford the cost of living, she died. She was nearly 80 years old, and she had survived Ed somehow for a long, long time on her meager widow's pension, frugally measuring it against the rising prices, scrimping and scraping and skipping meals, making do with less and less each day until finally, on a recent morning at an ancient hotel in this city, she crumpled quietly to the floor of her dark and tiny apartment.

She weighed 76 pounds. An autopsy found no trace of food in her shrunken stomach. "Malnutrition," the coroner concluded. . . . In New York, Detroit, Miami, and Chicago, there have been arrests of elderly citizens— some of them extremely feeble—for stealing groceries in order to eat.

"But Elsie would never have done that," said the manager of the hotel. . . . Instead, she chose to attempt to manage on her Social Security checks of less than $100 a month. . . . Her food allowance was down to less than 65 cents a day.

This is a tragic account. It illustrates that dire consequences can result when we don't control our life scripts. Ms. DeFratus did not employ her abilities to reflect and to change as necessary in a changing world. As this dramatic example shows, life scripts are very powerful, and they can be dangerous to us if we don't monitor and revise them appropriately.

We all have life scripts. Whether they are neutral, helpful, or harmful depends largely on whether we control them or let them control us. We need to understand that we do have scripts, learned from interactions with others, particularly our families, and that these scripts can deeply influence our attitudes and actions. Only then can we reflect on our behaviors, determine what our scripts are, and decide whether they are appropriate in our present lives.

Nuclear families are the first social groups to which we belong. Interaction within families proceeds through phases that allow development of language and, thus, symbolic thought. Through preverbal interaction—the conversation of gestures— behavior becomes meaningful, creating a foundation for the emergence of language. Acquisition of language creates mind, because it allows us to replace behaviors with ideas and to communicate about ideas with ourselves and others.

Language also creates the social self. Through symbolic interaction with others, children learn to play roles and later to take roles of particular others and, finally, to take the role of the generalized other. Through these stages of language acquisition the human child is moved from the narrow world of personal sensations and responses to an awareness of attitudes of others and, ultimately, to understanding of the generalized attitudes of the community as a whole.

As we interact within our families, we internalize attitudes toward ourselves and others, and we learn patterns of interaction. In short, we learn life scripts which direct our behaviors in a range of situations. Nuclear families have profound impact on our development as individuals, our views of self, and our ability to relate to others.

SOCIALIZATION IN PEER GROUPS

Important as the nuclear family is, it is not the only powerful socializing agent. Once children begin interacting outside of the home, peer groups assume increasing centrality in the socialization process. Between the ages of five and sixteen, peer relationships provide a "subculture" that teaches values and behaviors to its members.[16] As individuals mature, particularly during the teen years, the influence of the family recedes, while the influence of peer groups expands.

In our families we develop views of ourselves and our fit within the family unit. We test these views in peer relationships and experiment to find out where we fit in the larger social circles beyond our families. As we interact with peers we grow personally, because we observe a broad range of responses to us and, thus, gain an enlarged basis for our own views of oursleves. In peer relationships we also learn new behaviors and new roles, so that we increase the range of situations and people we can handle effectively.

The self established in the family is changed by interaction with peers. Some views of the self are confirmed by peers, while others are rejected. The youngster who commands center stage with Mommy and Daddy may not be such a star with peers and may learn to view herself as less important. The child whose parents regard him as second fiddle to his older sister may discover that peers accept him on his own merits and may gain a heightened view of self. Temper tantrums that are effective with parents may lead to ridicule from peers. Skills rewarded at home may be irrelevant in peer groups, while behaviors punished at home may earn status with peers. Thus we alter established roles and behaviors and develop new ones so that we can interact effectively with people outside of our immediate families and so that we can fit into those communities.

Peer relationships are a major source of socialization throughout our lives. Within peer interactions, two processes that most directly influence our social development are reflected appraisal and social comparison.

Reflected Appraisal (Looking-Glass Self)

As you may recall from Chapter 7, reflected appraisal is the process by which we come to understand how others see us. To varying extents, we reflect the appraisals of others who are important to us. A social scientist named Cooley came up with another way of thinking about this process when he suggested that others "mirror" who we are. We see ourselves through the mirror of their eyes. Cooley used the term "looking glass self" to refer to our interpretations of how we appear to others and how others judge that appearance, and our own response to the judgment we think others make.[17] For example, perhaps you think your best friend regards you as dependable (your interpretation of how you appear to another), you believe this friend regards dependability as a virtue (your interpretation of how this quality is judged), and you feel proud about this quality in yourself (your own response to the appearance). Your view of yourself is based on the you that you see in other's perspectives they are your looking glass or mirror.

The Looking-Glass Self[18]

The ability to see oneself as well-liked, easy to get along with, or pleasant . . . is the product of considerable intellectual and social development. It is only when the child is able to get beyond his own narrow view of the world that he can succeed in seeing himself as an object of observation of others, as one who *arouses in other people's minds a definite set of thoughts and feelings.* By taking the role of the other, the individual comes to *define* himself in terms of the reactions he arouses in the minds of others—as well-liked, popular, easy to get along with, and other looking-glass traits . . . .

At the heart of this change is the social factor of human communication. True communication involves the ability to adopt the viewpoint and perspective of the other . . . . It makes possible a quality of social relationships previously impossible to achieve and at the same time effects a major transformation in the structure and content of the self-concept.

Changes in how we see ourselves and how we choose to behave evolve out of our interactions with others. Even long-held views of self may be altered by the appraisals of us made by peers and reflected by us. Consider this example of how a peer group radically changed a young woman's view of herself:

A group of college men decided they would try to establish a shy and inept classmate as a social favorite. They saw to it that she was invited to all of the important parties, games and so forth. All of the men acted toward her as if she were a most desirable date and as if they felt fortunate to have her spend time with them. By the end of the year the woman had developed a self-confident style and an easy awareness of her own popularity. The men who had planned this soon discovered they were doing her no favors by asking her out—in fact, they had to wait in line. Other men—ones not "in" on the plan—were booking up her time![19]

Which was the "true" person—the shy, inept young woman or the popular, self-confident one? If you're even contemplating that question, you've not fully appreciated the symbolic interactionist view of self. The self is social as well as individual. Both aspects of self are real. For that reason, views we have formed of ourselves at one time are "valid," and so are views we construct based on others' responses to us. Also, symbolic interactionism tells us that how we define ourselves *is* who we are, regardless of the sources of that definition. In our example, the woman saw a new version of herself reflected in other's eyes, and she began to hold that view of herself. Reflected appraisal or the looking glass self shows how much our peers' attitudes toward us influence our own attitudes toward ourselves and our overall socialization. To become effective members of peer groups and the overall social world, we learn to observe and evaluate ourselves from the perspectives of other people. And we learn to use those perspectives to guide and sometimes to revise our attitudes and actions.

Social Comparison

While reflected appraisal explains how our perceptions of others' views of us affect how we see ourselves as individuals, social comparison describes how we learn to see ourselves in relation to others. Social comparison is a process in which we observe and judge ourselves in comparison to others. Two kinds of comparisons are made. First, we compare ourselves to others to see whether we are superior or inferior on some quality or skill. Compared to your peers are you more or less mature, more or less social, more or less attractive, more or less responsible, more or less athletic? A second form of social comparison focuses on similarity. Are we like others or different than them?[20] Are we similar in size? Do we have similar interests? Are we the same color? Do we have the same ethnic background, religious background? Is this person a liberal like me or a conservative unlike me? We assess similarity to discover where (with whom) we fit. We tend to be most comfortable with people like us, so this form of social comparison is a natural way of sizing up new acquaintances. Comparisons to others have major impact on how we view ourselves and on those with whom we are comfortable spending time.

Social comparisons strongly influence how we define ourselves. One implication of this is that our views of self change as we alter the people to whom we compare ourselves. Perhaps you experienced such a change when you started college. Many students suffer from deflated self-confidence for a while after they begin college. In high school they were regarded as socially and academically superior to most of their peers, and they came to regard themselves that way. The college environment frequently does not confirm this image of self. Other first year students were also above average within their high school peer groups, and those other above-average people are now the peer group for comparison. First-year students have to reassess who they are in comparison to this new group of peers. They have to discover what is required to "make it" in the interpersonal context of the campus. Each time you enter a group or relationship, you gain different bases for social comparison and, thus, varied ways of measuring yourself.

Reflected appraisals and social comparisons are two processes at the heart of our interactions with peers. Clearly, how we view ourselves is intimately tied to how we think our peers see us and how we see ourselves in relation to them. Because our self-images are linked closely to how others view us, we should select our friends and acquaintances carefully. Comparing ourselves with others is inevitable and it can be useful, but it's healthy only if we select others with whom it is realistic to compare ourselves. Similarly, it's natural to reflect others' appraisals of us, but we should exercise reasonable caution as to whose appraisals we accept, especially if those appraisals are negative.

Peer groups are a second major influence on our socialization. Through interaction with peers we expand our understandings of who we are, how others perceive us, and how to interact effectively with a range of people. By reflecting how others see us and by comparing ourselves with others, we enlarge the social context in which we exist. From the time we first venture outside the home until we die, we interact with peers. Thus, this source of socialization is continuous.

SOCIALIZATION IN WORK GROUPS

A third major socializing force is professional associates. Upon entering a work environment, an individual is confronted by an elaborate code of values, attitudes, roles, and norms of behavior considered appropriate in that context. The individual's success in this setting depends on how well she or he identifies and adjusts to the established social order. In other words, individuals are socialized into professional communities.

As in other contexts we've considered, socialization in professional environments occurs through interactions with others. We observe others, communicate with them, accept direct and indirect advice from them, modify our own behaviors, and watch how others respond to our adjustments. Through this kind of interaction we learn the tacit rules that govern attitude and conduct in the work place. We internalize many of these rules, just as we earlier incorporated social rules from interactions with family and peers, we learn how to think and act in professional settings.

Years ago, work socialization proceeded formally through an apprenticeship system in which a new worker trained with a "master" who served as a model. Modified versions of the apprenticeship system are still practiced in some fields such as medicine, where internship and residence prepare individuals for full membership in the profession. More informal socialization techniques include graduate study, in which students work closely with established professionals, and trainee and intern positions, which place new employees under the guidance of veterans. Some professions provide no official system of socialization for newcomers, so workers must discover for themselves the "rules of the game." The bottom line is that formally or informally, some kind of socialization accompanies entry into any new work situation. Newcomers are introduced to the values, attitudes, roles, rules, and expectations that form the normative assumptions of their occupations. Those who absorb this socialization fit in, while those who reject or don't understand the rules have trouble interacting effectively with colleagues.

Workers' Codes [21]

Between 1927 and 1932 a series of studies conducted at the Western Electric Company's Hawthorne Works in Chicago provided insights into the codes of conduct that govern employees'behavior. One particular study carried out by Roethlisberger and Dickson examined the rules followed by workers in a bank wiring operation. The researchers reported that there was a clear set of rules regarding appropriate and inappropriate behaviors and new members of the group had to be socialized into these rules. Among the most important rules were these:

1. Do not produce too much work or you will be regarded as a "rate-buster."
2. Do not turn out too little work or you will be regarded as a "chiseler."
3. Never tell a supervisor anything negative about another worker or you will be seen as a "squealer."
4. Do not be aloof or act like you are better than other workers. If you are an inspector or supervisor, you should not act like one.

The rules specify expected behaviors and further explain how colleagues appraise anyone who fails to act in the proscribed ways.

Professions are "mini-societies." Each is a unique social order into which individuals are inducted. Established patterns of attitude and behavior create and reflect distinct identities of various professions and provide for coordinated interaction among members who have learned to think and act along similar lines. Recent research in communication has focused on this idea by studying "organizational culture" and how individuals are socialized into it. According to scholars, the culture of an organization is communicated to individuals through several kinds of interaction, including rituals and storytelling.[22] Both of these define for new recruits the agreed-upon ways of "how we do things around here." Rituals recognize and sustain the organization just as anniversaries do for relationships and birthday celebrations do for individuals. Storytelling, too, is important. As an experienced professional tells stories about the organization and people in it, history and key values are often revealed. A newcomer, hearing about "the time we had to make a 20% cut in expenses in 1 month" will learn not only the "objective facts" of what happened, but also what values the organization embraced and what goals it prioritized: were people fired or were expenses cut in other ways? Did employees have any input into deciding how to make the cuts? Were people offered any options or did management simply decide and enforce its decision?

As we internalize the values and behaviors of a particular occupation, we become comfortable and find our place in our professional culture. If you observe new employees in any situation, you will notice that at first they don't quite fit in, regardless of how competent they may be. Then they "catch on" to the unspoken rules of conduct and blend into the context.

Initial awkwardness is not reserved for young people just starting careers. Even experienced professionals who change careers go through break-in periods. They resocialize themselves to harmonize with a new professional context. A social worker who becomes a realtor adopts attitudes and behaviors appropriate to his new career. A veteran homemaker learns new values and rules of conduct when she enters the business world. An older person returning to school catches on to patterns of interaction and attitude established by younger students, who comprise the majority of the population in that culture. It's probably more difficult to change occupations than to start a career initially, because in changing an individual must unlearn one set of rules as well as acquire a new set.

Most of us cannot neatly divide into discrete compartments the attitudes and behaviors appropriate to diverse areas in our lives. Inevitably we experience overlaps and, sometimes, conflicts among the various sets of rules we live by. The career you pursue will influence you personally as well as professionally. So much of our time is spent in the work world that our professional selves invariably sneak into our private areas. Doctors, used to hospital sanitation and order, may come to expect similar cleanliness and efficiency in their home lives. Executives, accustomed to a cadre of secretaries and assistants, may bark orders and treat family members as subordinates. Accountants and administrators, whose daily activities focus on details, may become picky and needlessly precise about personal matters such as whether a chair is one inch too far to the right or whether books are exactly even on a shelf. Military personnel have reputations for carrying professional emphases on regimentation into their private lives so that spouse and children have to "come to attention." Pat Conroy's novel, *The Great Santini*, superbly shows the potential tyranny imposed by a military man on his family. Teachers too often extend the professional activity of lecturing into social and personal contexts where monologues are less than appreciated by others. Just as our professional world seeps into our personal world, our personal life colors our professional activities. An individual whose interactions in family settings and with peer groups emphasized open, caring relationships may find it difficult to fit into an organization which expects employee relationships to be formal and distant.

Each of us has to become competent in diverse, often contradictory roles. We don't learn just one set of attitudes and behaviors, but a whole range of sets. Moreover, we either balance the demands in our personal, social, and professional worlds or establish priorities among these systems so that we know where we are willing to accept sacrifices and tradeoffs. The strain of trying to meet responsibilities in different spheres of life is increasingly an issue in dual-worker and dual-career families. Too often what happens is that the man continues to work his regular job and expect to relax at home. The woman too puts in a full day in her outside work, then comes home to the "second shift," where she assumes primary responsibilities for homemaking, cooking, and childrearing.[23] The gender scripts that prevail in our culture lead both husbands and wives to expect her to be in charge of the domestic sphere, even when she is as active in an outside profession as he. Challenging these scripts in ourselves and finding ways of achieving greater equity in relationships is one of the challenges of the 1990s.

Professional associates are a third source of individual socialization. Through interactions with colleagues we learn how to participate in work environments, how others perceive us as professionals, and how we need to alter our attitudes and behaviors in order to fit in. The impact of professional socialization on our total selves depends upon the degree to which we commit to our work. The greater our personal identification with our professions, the greater the influence they will exert on our overall views of who we are.

SOCIALIZATION THROUGH CULTURAL MEMBERSHIP

So far we've looked at families, peer relationships, and work groups as three specific sources of individual socialization. To tie up this chapter it's useful to expand our vision of socialization so that we understand culture as a broad context that establishes parameters on what we value, how we see ourselves, and how behave in particular settings such as the three we've considered.

As members of a single culture we all share basic knowledge, values, and undersandings about what various behaviors mean. In fact, culture is generally defined as a way of thinking, feeling, and believing. Because a culture has common understandings into which individuals are socialized, it guides our lives in large and small ways. From how we dress and what we disclose to friends to the kinds of ideals we hold, culture regulates our behaviors. Thus, the society into which we are born and socialized permeates our attitudes and actions.

It's difficult to realize how thoroughly your ways of thinking and acting are infused with cultural values—how deeply you reflect your society. People who travel report feeling out of place when they visit other countries. They don't understand the cultural patterns, so they have trouble participating in a foreign society. Many Western women find it difficult to operate in societies where women are often relegated to clearly subordinate status. Americans often become nervous in South American countries, where the pace of life is more leisurely than our own. By the same token, people from other cultures are frequently amazed by American life style.

They may see us as fast-moving, self-centered, impersonal, and loud. Until they are socialized into our culture we and they cannot interact effectively with each other. This has become especially clear to me recently since several foreign students have joined our graduate program. One woman who was from Taiwan was quite intelligent and hard-working, but I could not convince her to participate in class discussions. She explained that in Taiwan one demonstrates respect by being quiet and students should always show respect for teachers. Gradually she modified that attitude as a result of seeing how her peers contributed in class discussions. However, I was never able to persuade her not to call me "sir," which is the Taiwanese form of respectful address, nor was I able to convince her that it is "proper" for me to have a name different from my husband's. She could not understand that in America separate names are acceptable. Sometimes we gain the clearest insights into our own culture when we see it reflected in the eyes of someone from outside of it. We become more aware of patterns so normal to us that we do not notice them. In an apparent attempt to expedite socialization, the United States government once issued a booklet entitled *Basic Rules for American Living*, which was given to all Indochinese immigrants. Included in the pamphlet was the suggestion that undiapered babies are not appreciated in public![24]

Cultural Influences on Sex Role[25]

Definitions of masculinity and femininity are determined by culture, not biology. In Iran men are expected to be emotional and, in fact, they are distrusted if they fail to show their emotions. Iranian men enjoy reading poetry and place high value on human relationships. Within Iranian culture men are regarded as far more intuitively gifted than women and men are not expected to be logical or highly reasonable in their thought and action. Men embrace and hold hands. By contrast, Iranian women are considered coldly practical, logical and hard.

This pattern, a reverse of that in American society, offers support for the claim that we learn sex roles, rather than being born with inclinations and abilities based on our biological sex.

Each of us reflects our culture. Largely without conscious effort on our parts, we have learned basic American values, interaction patterns, role relationships—in short, the meanings of our culture. Because we've absorbed these gradually and generally without reflection, we're often only dimly aware of ways in which the overall culture influences who we are and what we do. Yet to increase self-knowledge and the control we exert on our own lives we should become more aware of how cultural values affect us.

Toward this goal, we'll consider six trends in contemporary American culture and explore how each pertains to us as individuals and members of various family, social, and professional groups.

Trends in Contemporary American Culture

Mobility.   American culture is highly mobile, and we become increasingingly so. The majority of adults in this country own cars which they drive freely, despite rising gas prices. We take for granted our freedom to go where we wish when we wish. Mobility, as a cultural trend, goes beyond modes of transportation. It is also evident in the number of moves we make. In the early 1970s the average American moved about 14 times in the course of life. The advent of two-career couples may affect the number of moves individuals will make in the future.

Because we are an on-the-move people, most of us will not spend our lives in one place. Consequently, we will enjoy few, if any, lifelong friendships. Both we and our friends will pick up and move every few years. And there's no reason to suspect we'll find stability in our professional relationships, since contemporary working people switch jobs every few years. To survive the consequences of increasing mobility we will need to generate new ways of adapting to our settings and our relationships. Alvin Toffler, a well-respected futurist, summarizes the issue this way.[26]

> When you live in a neighborhood you watch a series of changes take place. One day a new mailman delivers the mail. A few weeks later the girl at the checkout counter at the supermarket disappears and a new one takes her place. Next thing you know the mechanic at the gas station is replaced. Meanwhile a neighbor moves out next door and a new family moves in.

As we become ever more mobile, stable long-term relationships with people and environments will wane. We may need to learn how to form other kinds of bonds, ones that are erected around common interests and that are not expected to be permanent. Additionally, we may need to learn how to adapt rapidly to differing contexts which call for widely ranging behaviors and attitudes. Since mobility is a clear feature of contemporary American culture, we should begin to think about its implications for our personal, social, and professional relationships and for our individual senses of stability.

Acceleration. Fueled by mobility is our culture's accelerated pace of living. Transcontinental communication can be instantly achieved with phones and satellite technology. We eat instant food, take pictures that develop in 60 seconds, copy papers in a matter of minutes, acquire instant credit, use computers to produce our work at a fraction of the time typing and calculating required. It seems our culture emphasizes immediacy. More and more we come to expect speed in our lives. We want what we want when we want it—no delay!

Skimming Through Life[27]

> I think we're all engaged in a kind of hyperediting version of life. More and more, what I find is that you don't really live in the present anymore. You're never fully engaged in what you're doing at any given moment, because what you really want to do is finish it in order to get on to something else. You kind of skim along the surface of life. It's very frustrating.

Acceleration affects our lives, particularly our relationships. To maintain a healthy image of self and an adequate number of satisfying relationships, we'll need to think seriously about the fast-paced lifestyle and whether it entails more costs than we're willing to accept. We may need to find new ways of relating to others and, in fact, new ways of defining good relationships. Another alternative is to slow down—to decide that the culture's increasing push for acceleration does not fit us personally.

The Acceleration Syndrome[28]

Call it acceleration syndrome. Life in a state of constant overdrive. There's more information than ever to absorb, more demands to meet, more roles to play, the technology to accomplish everything faster, and never enough time to get it all done. . .

Perhaps it's not surprising that people who live in a state of constant acceleration rarely have much time for introspection. But stop them long enough to ask whether they're missing anything important by living so fast, and frequently the answer is yes.

For some, of course, it's just the time and efficiency to accomplish even more. Faster. But more often they'll say that what are being sacrificed are all those things that require concentrated time, particularly the unstructured time it takes to nurture relationships. Indeed, insufficient time for friendships—and even for spouses—is often accepted as inevitable.

But this *is not inevitable*. Unlike other animals, humans have will. They make choices about what they will and will not do. They decide what values will guide their lives. You, personally, will make choices as to whether to accept the acceleration syndrome or not, whether to make time for friends and romantic partners, or not. That's why it's important for us to think about the trends in our current society—so we can reflect and make informed choices about our evaluations of them and our actions.

Disposability ethic. Contemporary America is a "throwaway society." We increasingly think in the short term. We see things as temporary, to be discarded or exchanged when we lose interest or when a better model comes along. A few years ago CBS news reported there had been a drastic decline in the number of home cleaning supplies, especially ones for dishes, and—simultaneously—a great increase in the sales of plastic eating utensils and especially paper plates.[29]

Disposability is an accepted value these days, despite environmentalists' warnings about the long-term effects of overloading the planet with nonrecyclable materials. Just consider the number of disposable items in your everyday life: paper plates and cups and plastic utensils, disposable lighters, one-time containers, tissues instead of handkerchiefs, paper diapers, paper gowns instead of cloth ones in doctors' offices, shopping bags, and the vast amount of packaging on products. We're surrounded by throwaway items. So it's no wonder that we have few expectations of permanence. Cars, homes, furniture, careers, hobbies are increasingly regarded as temporary.

Throw-Away Society[30]

"Barbie," a twelve-inch plastic teen-ager, is the best-known and best-selling doll in history. Since its introduction in 1959, the Barbie doll population of the world has grown to 12,000,000-more than the human population of Los Angeles or London or Paris. Little girls adore Barbie because she is highly realistic and eminently dress-upable. Mattel, Inc., makers of Barbie, also sells a complete wardrobe for her, including clothes for ordinary daytime wear, clothes for formal party wear, clothes for swimming and skiing.

Recently Mattel announced a new improved Barbie doll. The new version has a slimmer figure, "real" eyelashes, and a twist-and-turn waist that makes her more humanoid than ever. Moreover, Mattel announced that, for the first time, any young lady wishing to purchase a new Barbie would receive a trade-in allowance for her old one.

What Mattel did not announce was that by trading in her old doll for a techno-logically improved model, the little girl of today, citizen of tomorrow's superindustrial world, would learn a fundamental lesson about the new society: that [our] relation-ships with things are increasingly temporary. . . .

Nothing could be more dramatic than the difference between the new breed of little girls who cheerfully turn in their Barbies for the new improved model and those who, like their mothers and grandmothers before them, clutch lingeringly and lovingly to the same doll until it disintegrates from sheer age. In this difference lies the contrast between past and future, between societies based on permanence, and the new, fast-forming society based on transience.

As this excerpt from Toffler's book, *Future Shock*, points out, the emerging throwaway attitude toward things may spread—ultimately affecting our relations with people. The cultural emphasis on temporariness may engender the attitude that other people are disposable or replaceable. Rising divorce rates and serial marriages are clear signs that increasingly we don't assume even our most intimate human relation-ships are necessarily permanent. If we do come to view relationships as short-term and disposable, we'll also need to alter both interaction patterns and some of our longstanding measures of self-worth. For instance, we may learn that dissolution of friendships or intimate bonds is not equivalent to personal rejection. On the other hand, we may choose to let most of our relationships be short-term, but to invest in a select few that are enduring and to concentrate our communicative energies into those few.

Rootlessness. Social critics describe our society as impersonal, machine-oriented, uprooted, and dehumanized. Contemporary Americans seldom enjoy the sense of rootedness that once characterized this country. High mobility and acceler-ation have ruptured community and family structures, two major sources of individual security. Most people no longer have a permanent community—geographic or inter-personal. Instead, we live a nomadic life, fitting in for awhile in one place with one group, then moving on.

In addition to the loss of community, many people feel personally rootless, sometimes even stripped of individuality by the technological nature of our times. Daily we are dehumanized by mail addressed to "occupant" and written by a computer. We identify ourselves with numbers, not names (When was the last time your name was sufficient on a check or form?). Many graduate and professional programs refuse to interview applicants—all they want is a transcript and test scores to summarize who the candidates are. We take jobs that could be filled by hundreds of other people and we live with the knowledge that many of today's jobs will be done by tomorrow's computers, displacing people.[31] It's hard to find indications that society will regain its former personalness or that enduring communities will re-emerge to provide rootedness. Instead of bemoaning the loss or engaging in nostalgia, we need to reflect in a sustained way to find or create new sources of personal security and fit for ourselves and new kinds of relationships that affirm our individuality and our personal worth.

Self-centeredness.   Americans, particularly younger ones, are often described as the "me generation," a label that implies concern for personal welfare overshadows other concerns. Most of us have heard maxims such as "Nice guys finish last," "Look out for Number One," and "Take care of yourself first." Expressions such as these reflect an attitude that encourages giving priority to personal interests, desires, and comforts. Popular books and workshops emphasize self-discovery, self realization, self fulfillment—SELF! We can also attend workshops that promise to teach us how to "win through intimidation," "succeed in business," and numerous other things designed to please, advance, and further individual gratification. Self-centeredness leads to pursuit of personal pleasure and material comfort. Nothing could make this more clear than public reaction to the energy crisis. Although some people have reduced their energy consumption, a great many continue to appease their personal desires with thermostats that read 78 in winter and 70 in summer. As long as individuals have enough money, many continue to drive large cars that waste gas and to travel at inefficient speeds. Obviously, a great many people regard their own comfort as more important that broad social needs. We spend more money on the frills of life than on charities and causes that help the larger community. We feel abused if we do not have the latest fashions and stereo equipment.

Excessive concern with personal gain is a foundation for competitiveness.[32] There are limited amounts of whatever is valued. Only so many As will be given, only a small percentage of applicants will be accepted in law school, only one promotion is available in the company, only one person can be president of the sorority, only one individual can be team captain. So we learn to compete for the prizes in life and to measure our success by how much we acquire and whether it's more than what the next person acquires. Keeping up with—or ahead of—the Joneses is still part of our way of life. We live in a self-centered era when hedonism and competitiveness are accepted, in many ways even encouraged.

In *Habits of the Heart*, an important book examining evolving American values, the authors make the point that the cultural trends we've been discussing affect both our public life and our intimate relationships.[33] In dual-career marriages, for instance, partners may find themselves enmeshed in subtle conflicts over which partner is advancing more quickly, which is making more money, which has more prestige in the community. To cope with cultural pressures to compete and put self first, we may need to separate our interactions into those where competitiveness is perhaps appropriate and those where it is not. In close relationships, self interest can be deadly. As we'll see in the next chapter, intimacy is based on a *shared* world, and that means partners must understand that WE can't work if we think constantly in terms of YOU and I. The lone self is ultimately a very lonely self. We need others to be fully human, and that means we need to commit to the kinds of communicative values and actions that nurture relationships. Inevitably, we will feel pressures to do otherwise, given cultural trends. Yet, we have the ability to reflect and to resist falling into whatever is currently popular. That is our choice and, relatedly, it is our responsibility.

Contemporary cultural trends represent challenges for each of us. How do we as individuals cope with a rapidly changing world? How do we learn to interact effectively and to form satisfying human relationships in a turbulent social world? We need to address these questions today if we are to prepare for living tomorrow.

SUMMARY

The uniqueness of self, which we examined in Chapter 7, is complemented by the social nature of self which we explored in this chapter. Each of us is at once highly individual and part of a common system of values, attitudes, and codes of conduct. For symbolic interactionists this dual nature of self is perfectly natural The individual must be viewed within social relationships and cultural contexts, because it is in communication with others that mind and self emerge, thus creating the individual. No individual could exist without society, and society could not exist without individuals.

Individuality and the Social Process[34]

The fact that all selves are constituted by or in terms of the social process, and are individual reflections of it . . . is not in the least incompatible with, or destructive of, the fact that every individual self has its own peculiar individuality, its own unique pattern; because each individual self within that process, while it reflects in its organized structure the behavior pattern of that process as a whole, does so from its own particular and unique standpoint within that process. . . . The common social origin and constitution of individual selves and their structures does not preclude wide individual differences and variations among them, or contradict the . . . distinctive individuality which each of them in fact possesses.

Each of us lives simultaneously in multiple social systems. We've learned both general information that makes us competent members of the overall society and more specialized information that allows us to participate in smaller social systems such as families, peer groups, and professions. Each system interacts with the others to form the overall social order, yet each is its own distinct mini-society. Culture, then, is a large system that influences the many smaller groups within it and that is influenced by them. Just as we are affected by the systems, so do we affect them by our individual actions and attitudes. We cannot be part of any social system, in fact, without changing its nature in some ways. So while we are socialized by family, peers, professions, and society, we also influence the character of each of those systems.

Of course we never stop interacting with others, so we never cease to develop as social beings. Socialization is a process that begins at birth and continues throughout our lives. As social values and codes of conduct alter, we absorb the changes and modify ourselves accordingly.

Each human relationship we enter affects how we view ourselves as well as the range of attitudes and behaviors we endorse. While we have little choice about the society and family into which we are born, we have considerable freedom to choose our own peer and professional relationships. In selecting these we exercise control over how we develop as individuals and members of shared communities. It is impossible to overestimate the impact of human relationships on personal and social growth. Choose your relationships wisely, and make careful choices about your communication within them. In so doing you take responsibility for a significant role in creating yourself and others.

REFERENCES

[1]G. H. Mead, *Mind, Self and Society.* Chicago: University of Chicago Press, 1934, p. 140.

[2]"Death ends India Wolf Boy Mystery Case." *Medical World News.* New York: McGraw-Hill, 1968; cited in F. E. Jandt, *The Process of Interpersonal Communication.* San Francisco: Canfield, 1976, pp. 87-88.

[3]J. A. L. Singh and R. M. Zingg, *Wolf Children and Feral Man.* New York: Harper and Row, 1939.

[4]Reported in K. Davis, *Human Society.* New York: Macmillan, 1949, pp. 204-208.

[5]This discussion is based on Mead, and H.S. Sullivan, *The Interpersonal Theory of Psychiatry.* New York: W.W. Norton and Co., 1953, Part II.

[6]Jandt, p. 93.

[7]C. Morris, "Introduction." In Mead, p. xxxii.

[8]Mead, pp. 154-155.

[9]J. Pearson, *Gender and Communication.* Dubuque, IA: Wm. C. Brown, 1985, p. 38; B. Bate, *Communication and the Sexes.* New York: Harper, 1988, Chapter 5.

[10]H. Selby, "Playing the Gender Game," *News and Observer*, Raleigh, NC, June 25, 1990, pp. 12-A and 12-C.

[11]J. Condry and S. Condry, " Sex Differences: A Study of the Eye of the Beholder," *Child Development, 47*, 1976, 812-819.

[12]Bate, pp. 117-118.

[13]T. A. Harris, *I'm OK, You're OK.* New York: Harper and Row, 1969; E. Berne, *Games People Play.* New York: Grove, 1964.

[14]J.A. Devito, *The Interpersonal Communication Book.* New York: Harper and Row, 1976, pp. 108-109.

[15]T. Steinfatt, *Human Communication: An Interpersonal Introduction.* Indianapolis: Bobbs-Merrill, 1977, p. 157.

[16]Jandt, p. 101.

[17]C. H. Cooley, *Human Nature and the Social Order.* New York: Scribner's, 1912, p. 152.

[18]M. Rosenberg, *Conceiving the Self.* New York: Basic, 1979, p. 222.

[19]E. R. Guthrie, *The Psychology of Human Conflict.* New York: Harper and Row, 1938.

[20]T. F. Pettigrew, "Social Evaluation Theory: Consequences and Applications." In D. Levine (Ed.), *Nebraska Symposium on Motivation.* Lincoln: University of Nebraska Press, 1967, pp. 241-311.

[21]G. C. Homans, *The Human Group.* New York: Harcourt Brace Jovanovich, 1950, p. 79.

[22]Bate, p. 178.

[23]"The Sexual Politics of Housework," *Utne Reader*, March/April 1990, pp. 65-89; J. T. Wood. "Maintaining Dual Career Bonds: A Note on Communication and Relational Structure," *Southern Journal of Speech Communication*, 1986, 267-73.

[24]"CBS Morning News," May 30, 1980.

[25]E. T. Hall, *The Silent Language.* New York: Doubleday, 1959, p. 50.

[26]A. Toffler, *Future Shock.* New York: Bantam, 1970, p. 103.

[27]T. Schwartz, "Acceleration Syndrome: Does Everyone Live in the Fast Lane Nowadays?" *Utne Reader*, January/February 1989, pp. 41-42.

[28]Schwartz, pp. 37 and 42.

[29]"CBS Morning News," February 19, 1987.

[30]Toffler, pp. 51-52.

[31]E. Fromm, *The Anatomy of Human Destructiveness*. New York: Holt, Rinehart, and Winston, 1973.

[32]G. M. Phillips and J. T. Wood, *Communication and Human Relationships*. New York: Macmillan, 1983, Chapter 3.

[33]R. Bellah, R. Madsen, W. Sullivan, A. Swindler, and S. Tipton, *Habits of the Heart: Individualism and Commitment in American Life*. Berkeley, CA: University of California Press, 1985.

[34]Mead, pp. 201-202.

CHAPTER 9

COMMUNICATION AND THE EVOLUTION OF INTIMATE RELATIONSHIPS

The grass is greenest where it's watered.

(Robert Fulghum)

Values of Intimate Relationships

The Meaning of Intimacy

The Process of Relational Evolution

    The escalating process
      Individuals
      Invitational communication (auditioning)
      Explorational communication
      Intensifying communication (euphoria)
      Revising communication
      Intimate bonding
    The shared world of intimates
    The navigating process
    The deescalation process
      Differentiating communication
      Disintegrating communication
      Stagnating communication
      Closing communication
      Individuals after intimacy

The private sphere is perceived, not without justification, as an area of individual choice and autonomy . . . . It is . . . only in the private sphere that the individual can take a slice of reality and fashion it into his world.[1]

Previous chapters explored how communication with others socializes us. From these interactions we gain basic views of ourselves, our world, appropriate values, and codes of conduct. Of course, we don't necessarily accept others' views of us or the world. Sometimes we use our own communication to challenge or modify the world "out there." Still, we are born into a preexisting culture and are largely talked into accepting and acting according to its norms. As individuals we have limited ability to define the general social order, how it will operate, or how it will expect us to behave.

In our intimate relationships, however, this is not true. As the quote opening this discussion suggests, in our private world we have considerable choice about what kind of relationships we will cocreate with our partners. We exert significant personal influence because we quite directly define our intimate worlds. We literally create these. Through intimate communication, partners create what in an earlier article I defined as their "relational culture."[2] This is a private world made up of partners' rules, roles, and definitions of themselves and each other. The relational culture includes issues such as who each partner is individually and in relation to the other, what the relationship is and stands for, who outside people are and in what ways they may associate with partners, what attitudes and behaviors within the relationship are expected, acceptable, and "out of bounds." By developing rules about these matters, partners define their intimate bonds. Within the realm of intimacy humans have great freedom to imbue their lives with order and meaning of their own choosing. Intimate relationships, then, provide especially intriguing insights into humans and their potential. This is so because, unlike social and public spheres, the realm of intimacy is created by individuals and, thus, it reflects their personal choices of how to act and be.

This chapter describes the evolution of intimacy. We first consider why intimacy is so valued and what it means to people. Then we focus intensively on how individuals develop relationships over time. Our attention will be on how individuals engage in communication to define and continually redefine their relationships and themselves within those relationships. Studying intimacy as evolution is important in reminding us that intimate bonds do not "just happen," nor do the values intimates live by evolve by magic. Instead, intimate partners communicate to build their relational cultures and to define the private world in which they will live. The process is one of human choice making. Learning how this happens will demonstrate dramatically that communication is the central means through which relationships are created, maintained, and—in some cases—dissolved. After reading this chapter you should appreciate the immense amount of control individuals have in constructing their relationships. Along with our control and choice comes responsibility. We have responsibilities to ourselves and our partners to be careful and thoughtful about how we communicate and what kinds of worlds we create.[3]

VALUES OF INTIMATE RELATIONSHIPS

Before we discuss how people construct intimate relationships, perhaps we should ask why they do so. To understand the value of intimate relationships, it is helpful to consider the context in which they exist: contemporary society. As we saw in Chapter 8 our society seems increasingly impersonal. People now move so frequently that neighborhoods are no longer stable communities that provide a sense of personal fit and history. Even nuclear families seldom remain intact or geographically near throughout an individual's lifetime. As technology expands, we too often find ourselves in the frustrating position of trying to reason with a computer rather than another human being. "Personal" letters we receive open with the salutation "Dear Sir or Madam," We get other mail addressed not to us, but to "Occupant." Our individual differences are frequently overlooked as we are lumped together to form an average. In many of our business transactions we are known not by our names, but by numbers, particularly the social security number, which has become the most popular means of personal identification. We no longer expect from our society at large much sense of security, recognition of our individuality, or confirmation of our value.

Yet, humans value personal identity and crave meaningful connections with other humans—ones that are more than superficial. And as proactive beings, we have will, which impels us to seek ways of satisfying our needs for closeness and intimate connection. We demand a place where we belong and someone with whom we belong, someone who knows us deeply and affirms our identity and worth as a unique individual.[4] Relationships with others enrich our lives: We need intimates. With our intimate friends and partners we can work to create special, relational cultures that affirm our individuality and in which our welcome is never doubted. Here we are not reduced to a number, an average, a "Dear Sir or Madam," or an "Occupant." Thus, our intimate worlds act as buffers against an overwhelmingly impersonal society.[5] Our private relationships, then, balance our world by offering an alternative to the lack of personal recognition and caring society at large offers individuals.

But we mustn't romanticize intimacy by recognizing only the ways in which it can enrich us. It's also true that they can be private hells. In too many cases, intimate worlds are not safe refuges from an uncaring world. Instead, they are arenas for venting anger, engaging in physical and psychological abuse, and waging chronic warfare. Intimates can wound each other far more deeply and cruelly than anything society can do. Perhaps the greatest form of pain and quiet desperation exist in intimate relationships is that of indifference. When indifference pervades a relationship, it is devoid of all emotion. Feeling is simply and profoundly absent. Divorce, spouse and child abuse, adultery, alcoholism, depression, and chronic discord are all grim testimonies that many intimate relationships do not enrich human life.

Clearly, our intimate worlds can be fashioned in ways that elevate and enhance us or in ways that debase us. Since it is through our communication that we build intimacies, the manner in which we communicate and the nature of what we communicate substantially influences the quality of our bonds. Throughout this book we have seen that humans are both the creators and the prisoners of their symbols. Applied to intimate bonds, this means that the ways we choose to communicate with our intimates and the quality of relational culture we create are directly related. We can build good or poor bonds, ones that liberate us to strive for ever stronger versions of ourselves or that restrict us to only a small portion of our potentials, ones that provide us a sense of security and value or that cause constant pain and self-condemnation. Whatever the quality of bonds we build, our own actions—particularly our communication with others and ourselves—will be responsible. Because we do directly control much of what happens in our intimate lives and because this sphere of our lives is crucial to our well-being, we should understand how we create and define our relationships through our symbolic interactions with others. By examining communication as the creative force in our intimate relationships, we should improve our abilities to build bonds that can provide the kind of personal worlds we desire.

THE MEANING OF INTIMACY

There are many types of intimacy. The abstract term, "intimate relationship" includes the love between siblings, the bond between parent and child, the closeness and caring between best friends, and the deep commitment between romantic partners.

This chapter focuses on one particular kind of intimacy—that between romantic partners. The material we consider applies to gay and lesbian partnerships as well as heterosexual ones since research indicates that the basic nature of romantic love is more alike than different for people of varying sexual preferences.[5] But what is the "basic nature of romantic love?" Perhaps you recall the list of things love may mean that appeared in Chapter 4. That just scratches the surface of what love can mean to us. One useful perspective on what love is comes from a psychologist named Brehm. According to her intimacy or love consists of at least one and often two or three of three qualities:[6]

- *Interdependence:* Partners have mutual impact on each other that is strong, frequent, and enduring.
- *Fulfillment of Psychological Needs:* Intimates share their feelings, worries, and concerns. They care for each other and accept nurturance from each other. They assist each other, and they reassure each other of personal worth.
- *Emotional Attachment:* Partners feel loving and closeness for each other.

While not all romantic intimacies have all three of these qualities, it's difficult to conceive of any that don't possess at least one of them. So Brehm offers us a minimum definition of romantic love. Yet intimacy is more than love. It's also a commitment, an expectation of continuing to be intimate. Intimacy, then, is not only a matter of feelings in the present; it's also an intention to be together in the future. Thus, to Brehm's definition, we need to add the idea that partners intend to continue caring deeply for one another. Putting all of this together we can define intimacy as *a voluntary commitment to an extended future of emotional attachment, interdependence, and/or fulfilling partners' psychological needs.*[7]

This definition highlights fundamental similarities common to all intimate relationships.

However, pointing out these commonalities certainly doesn't mean that all intimacies are the same. Your own experiences will quickly convince you that isn't true. There is great variety in what different people consider intimate and even a lot of range in how any single individual is intimate in different relationships.

Rosa may show emotional attachment by kissing and hugging Jose while Ben is very physically inexpressive of his deep feelings for Tommy. Ellen may fulfill Jerry's needs for nurturance and reassurance of worth while Jerry tends to satisfy her needs for assistance and concern about her worries. We show intimacy in different ways, and we feel different things within the broad latitude of the definition we constructed.

It's also important to realize that differences in intimacy are not entirely individualistic; that is, they aren't all explained by saying people are different. There are some general patterns of difference—some relatively predictable factors that influence what intimacy means to us. While research has not established many clear links between personality factors such as esteem and love, it has demonstrated that gender is an extraordinarily important influence on what love means and how we enact love.

Love and Gender[8]

Probably the most powerful individual difference that affects how we experience love is that of gender. A considerable body of research shows that males and females construct their realities of love in very different terms.

From extensive research we know several ways in which gender affects the experience of love. First, males, especially young ones, are more romantic than females. Second females tend to make greater distinctions among feelings such as liking, loving, and feeling romantic than do males. Females are also more likely than males to idealize romantic partners, particularly during early stages of intimacy. Finally, it seems that women perceive love as more rewarding than men, a finding that is especially interesting given the fact that women report more experiences of unrequited love.[9]

From these specific differences in how the sexes experience love it's possible to draw two general portraits of what love means. In general it seems that for women love is a central focus and goal in life, one that remains so even after an intimate commitment is made. Women tend to see intimacy as a process, something that grows over time and requires ongoing effort, investment, and work. One important dimension of this investment for women is communication. Far more than men, women want to talk to their partners and not just about "big events," but also about daily matters. They also seek conversation about the relationship itself. Finally, women tend to invest their personal self in love relationships; thus, their identities are substantially interwoven with their relationships.

For men, a distinct general portrait emerges. While love relationships are important to most men, they are not necessarily the center of men's lives. Socialization teaches men to define themselves by what they do—their work and achievements—so careers tend to be more central foci in their lives. It also seems that men see intimacy more as a quest, a goal to be achieved than as a process. Once a firm commitment has been made, many men tend to assume that the issue is settled and they can focus their primary effort and attention elsewhere. In general men don't see either the need or the value of extensive communication about daily issues and about the relationship itself. Their feeling seems to be, "When there's some problem, we should talk about the relationship. Otherwise, let's not analyze it." Finally, while men do invest importantly in relationships, their investments tend to be more instrumental than do women's: Men do things (make money, take care of the cars, take the kids to and from school, etc.) while women are more likely to invest by being emotionally responsive and demonstrative.[10]

So what does love mean? Clearly it means different things to different people. To that we can add the fact that gender is one major influence on what love means and, thus, what we expect to invest in and receive from intimate relationships. And what we expect to give and receive in intimacy influences the entire process by which relationships evolve. Understanding that process is the focus of the rest of this chapter.

THE PROCESS OF RELATIONAL EVOLUTION

Intimate relationships typically develop through a process that is fairly generalizable across people.[11] We'll examine this process considering 12 stages that comprise it. Yet you should realize that the term "stage" can be misleading in suggesting distinct and separate points in what is really an ongoing process. It's important to understand these stages are not really discrete or entirely independent junctures. People tend to move gradually through one stage and blend slowly into the next. Frequently partners in a relationship are between stages, neither entirely out of one stage nor completely into another.

While presenting relational evolution in terms of stages achieves clarity, it does imply a linearity which is not really descriptive of how relationships develop. In many relationships, partners move back into stages previously experienced. For instance, couples who have intimately bonded frequently revisit the intensifying stage in which they enjoy renewed excitement about their bond. Moving back and forth through stages is not unusual.

A more serious situation exists when partners move through stages at different rates. Problems generally arise, for instance, when one partner is assessing the merits of the relationship (Revising Stage) while the other partner is still in the intensifying stage, in which the relationship is seen idealistically. Partners in different stages have differing goals and expectations, which may create tension, misunderstandings, and awkwardness. These problems are alleviated, though not entirely resolved, when we understand what is happening. If partners realize they are moving through stages in a nonsynchronized manner, they at least understand what is going on. Thus, they're less likely to misinterpret each other's communication.

As you read about the stages in relational development, it's also important to remember that, like any model, they provide only a general description of how people build intimacies. There are numerous exceptions to the process we will consider. Many relationships do not follow the exact sequence we present here. Other relationships may entirely skip one or more of the stages we consider. Despite exceptions such as these, the developmental approach to the study of relationships is useful in imposing some conceptual order on what often seems like a very chaotic process.

Finally, we should realize that most people are unaware of the stages through which relationships evolve. This does not mean that relationships do not proceed through these stages. Instead, it suggests that we often don't see the patterns in our own behaviors. In learning the developmental process my students frequently comment, "I never thought about relationships this way before, but it's so obvious now!" Since we can exercise control only in areas we understand, one value of learning about relational development is increased understanding of how we build our bonds with others. Given that rationale, let us move on to consider how we construct our relationships.

The Escalation Process

Intimacy does not come about suddenly and in full form. Rather, it is created through a process of communication that takes place over time. This will become clear as we explore the six stages in the escalation process, by which we move toward intimacy: individuals, invitational communication, explorational communication, intensifying communication, revising communication, and bonding. For each stage we'll identify what it "looks like" and how our communication serves to explore, test, and define relationships at each stage of their development.

Individuals. Relationships cannot be formed without individuals. Further, the nature of individuals establishes basic constraints on all later aspects in relational development. Thus, when we think about how relationships evolve, we must first think about the individuals who create them.

In our book on intimacy, Gerald Phillips and I noted that "the way people define themselves directly affects their choices of . . . partners, as well as their behavior toward other people in general."[12] So self-definition is an important aspect of individuals—one that critically influences whom we form relationships with. For instance, if Maria defines herself as very traditional and a born-again Christian, then it's likely that she will be interested in partners who share her social and religious values. Conversely, it's unlikely Maria would try to build a relationship with an atheist or a staunch liberal. If Dwayne sees himself as a politically and socially progressive person, he'll look for partners who fit with those values, not Republicans and conservatives. How we define ourselves, then, entails implications for how we define potentially suitable partners for us.

Individuals also have a number of "standards" they use to evaluate others with whom they might form relationships. Most of us aren't aware of these standards, and we don't tend to use them consciously. Nonetheless, research makes it clear that we do have and use three standards to judge others.[13] First, there is the *Comparison Level.* This is a cumulative measure of relationship quality, and it is based on all of our past experiences and observations. The comparison level may be thought of as a personal norm for relationships. It is relatively stable since it is based on cumulative experiences that define how satisfying relationships are generally expected to be for an individual. If Fran has had many good and very satisfying relationships, she'll have a high comparison level. If Rich has had only bad relationships, he'll have a low comparison level. Thus, it will take more to satisfy Fran than Rich in the next relationship either enters.

A second standard individuals use to evaluate others is the *Comparison Level of*

Alternatives. As the name implies, this is a measure of a given relationship against the perceived alternatives or options to it. This standard is not as stable as the comparison level. It shifts as new options appear on the scene. Fran may be very satisfied with her relationship with Joey until she begins graduate study and finds that she wants to be alone to work intensively on her research. For her the alternative of independence becomes preferable to what had been a satisfying relationship. Peter may think Wendy is the greatest woman he's ever known until he meets Jennifer. If he finds Jennifer more exciting, attractive, and so on. than Wendy, Mark may break up with Wendy. Thus, both other people and independence from intimacy are alternatives that we weigh against any given relationship.

Finally, individuals have what's called a *Relational Quota.* This is a standard that defines what a given person finds a satisfying degree of overall involvement with others. Marilyn may enjoy being involved in several serious relationships simultaneously, while Brent feels much more comfortable being in only one relationship at a time. Marilyn's relational quota is higher than Marks, and she might well be interested in forming new relationships even though she's already involved.

We all use these three standards to guide our choices of whom to interact with and to try to form relationships with. In addition, how we define ourselves is a major influence on how we define appropriate partners for ourselves. Understanding these aspects of individuals is essential to making sense out of all else that follows in relational development.

Invitational Communication (Auditioning). To launch a relationship we have to communicate with another person. Of the many people each of us encounters daily, we approach and speak to only a very few, because only those few attract us. The primary influences on initial attraction are proximity, physical attraction, and similarity. Proximity is the "bottom line" for initial attraction, since we can only approach people who are around us. Further, we're more likely to strike up conversations with people we see frequently.[14] In addition to proximity, other situational factors may foster or hinder interaction. For instance, interaction may be inhibited or even precluded in formal settings such as courtrooms, funeral parlors, and so forth. By contrast, interaction—talking to new people—is encouraged in situations like mixers where the implicit goal is to mingle and meet people. So, while situational factors do not directly cause interaction, our interpretations of them can advance or diminish our interest in communicating with others.

But why do we interact with some people rather than others within a situation? The initial choice of a particular person with whom to interact is closely related to physical attractiveness.[15] Each of us has distinct preferences regarding physical characteristics: "I like blondes." "I like men with glasses." "I dig earthy types." "The foxy ones get me every time." "Someone who is smiling attracts me." Our criteria for physical attractiveness vary according to our goals: One set of criteria for friends, another for dates, and yet another for roommates. We also know that there's a gender-based difference in the importance attached to physical attractiveness. As your own experiences may suggest to you, men say physical attractiveness is more important to them in dates than women say it is to them. Bearing this out is the related fact that women judged physically attractive tend to date more than women judged as less attractive.[16] It's unfortunate that we rely on such clearly superficial and inadequate criteria for our initial choices of whom to approach. Despite this, the fact remains that our initial decisions about interaction are significantly influenced by surface cues that we indicate to ourselves.

A final important criterion of attraction is similarity. You've probably heard that "birds of a feather flock together." But you've probably also heard that "opposites attract." These two adages imply quite different kinds of choices about whom we find interesting and want to interact with. On which is more accurate the research is quite clear: The overwhelming evidence is that similarity is much more likely to lead to attraction than is complementarity. In general (and probably all of us do know of exceptions), we are attracted to people who are similar to us in demographic characteristics (background, race, status), personality, attitudes and values, and level of physical attractiveness.[17]

Now that we know something about what attracts us to others, we can turn our attention to the communication that occurs during the invitational stage of relationships. Once we've decided to approach a particular person, we issue an invitation to converse: "Hello." "Want to dance?" "I see you're reading the Norton anthology. I had that course last term." And most people have worked out "lines" they think are particularly good in hooking another's interest. Sometimes we take a few minutes in my class to share these opening lines. Here are several my students have volunteered as their favorites: "Weren't you in Psych. 100 [mass course] last semester?" "You remind me of my best friend from high school." and "Hi. My name's Brad. How am I doing so far?" To understand what this kind of communication is really about, you have to consider its relational meaning, not its content meaning. The literal content of the lines is largely irrelevant. What's important is the relational level message that "I'd like to talk to you." The basic intent of these invitations is to open the lines of communication, to see whether another person is willing to interact with us. If our invitation is met with rejection or indifference, further interaction is discouraged.

On the other hand, if we receive encouragement or signs of interest, avenues for continued dialogue are opened. Communicators move into what's called "conversational fishing," in which they search for common ground: "Do you like sailing?" "I was born here. Where are you from?" "I'm into Bluegrass music; are you?" Through conversational fishing people are able to check out the possibilities of further interaction by defining points of identification between them—areas of similarity.

Communication during the invitational stage is largely governed by prevailing norms for the situation in which conversation occurs. At neighborhood get-acquainted functions, for example, popular topics include "Which is your house?" "Where did you live before moving here?" "Do you have children?" "Have you seen the new tax assessments for our area?" The minutes prior to the first meeting of a class stimulate different topics: "Had any other courses in this department?" "What do you know about this prof?" "I'm just not ready for classes to start." The situation often suggests the appropriate content for initial communication, and the form of communication tends to be relatively superficial, confined to the realm of small talk.

Several outcomes may result from invitational communication. One or both of the people may lose interest and foreclose further development of a relationship. The people may choose to keep the relationship at a level of casual acquaintances and future interactions will be friendly but will remain on a superficial level. A third potential outcome is a decision to explore further the possibilities of a relationship.

Explorational communication.   After deciding to pursue a relationship further, people want to learn about each other. During this stage people typically engage in a variety of activities and types of interaction that allow them to explore each other and the relationship. Whereas invitational communication is highly superficial, explorational communication becomes more open, more personal, and more revealing. Early conversation that was formal and restricted to safe topics now gives way to communication that's more informal, personal, and in depth.[18] Although few of us are likely to venture controversial opinions and highly personal disclosures in initial conversation with a stranger, most of us are willing to risk honest, even unpopular statements as we get to know someone better. And, as you'll recall from Chapters 7 and 8, risk is necessary to discover another person and to build a relationship.

Explorational communication serves two important purposes in relational development. First, it provides each person with information necessary to decide whether to continue the relationship. Second, by communicating each person begins to declare individual identity and to recognize the perspective of the other. Thus, dual perspective begins at this stage in relationships.

A relationship is not sustained by the situational and physical factors that led to the initial interaction. Individuals need a firmer basis for continued interaction. The strong positive correlation between similarity and interpersonal attraction that we mentioned before continues to operate during this stage of relational development. In fact, similarities seem the single most influential factor in enduring attraction between people.[19] Explorational communication is directed toward gaining information about possible similarities: how the other person feels about ecological and environmental issues; how much she values money and prestige; to what extent he enjoys reading, helping others, sports; whether he believes in God; where she stands on various public issues such as energy regulation, family leave bills, and governmental support of particular leaders in other countries; how he values family and friends; and so on. Through conversation we explore these and hundreds of other topics and we gain information needed to judge our similarity to another person. One primary function of explorational communication is giving and gaining cues about attitudes, beliefs, values, and personality so communicators may assess their compatibility.

Explorational communication also allows us to construct initial images of each other. Throughout interaction, the other person interprets all that we do and say and weaves it into a portrait that symbolizes us—our identity as the other sees it.[20] As a simplified illustration of this process, consider the following description that contains information we would typically gather during explorational communication:

> Laurie goes out a lot with both girlfriends and dates. In fact, she's seldom alone. She's an informal kind of person, preferring a tee-shirt and track shorts to anything more dressy. Much of her conversation revolves around social issues, especially the need for environmental consciousness: "It's not just throwing out aerosol cans and gestures like that. It's a whole new attitude of respect for the environment that we need." Another favorite topic for Laurie is the Animal Protection Society which gets her volunteer

services for at least ten hours each week. Not able to bear the thought of any animal's death, Laurie has so far adopted three dogs and seven cats who had run out of time at the local pound. "Somebody has to care about them. After all, it's not their fault they're unwanted." Her five housemates have learned to tolerate this zoo. Right now Laurie is unsure of her future plans, but she isn't worried—worrying just isn't her style: "Maybe I'll get a job that lets me travel or maybe I'll marry rich and raise a bunch of kids in the country. Heck, maybe I'll even start a kennel. I have lots of options."

Even on the basis of this sketchy description, Laurie emerges as a distinct personality. From this information we form some impressions of Laurie. Perhaps we'd describe her as compassionate (caring for animals and the environment), informal (dress, living arrangements, conversational style), extroverted (always with others), socially conscious (interest in the the environment and political issues), and a go-with-the-flow kind of person (lack of worry about the future, flexible life style). The point is not whether you agree with these inferences about Laurie. Rather, it's that you formed some impression, some image, of Laurie.

In a similar manner we construct images of people we interact with. At the same time, of course, those people are busily interpreting our actions and expressions to form their own symbolic representations of us. In essence, we assign meanings to each other. This is a crucial process, because through it we move each other from the category of people in general and into the more private, personal realm. We no longer view each other as role players in a "cast of thousands." Instead, we begin to recognize each other as distinct, unique human beings. Naturally the images we construct will be modified and elaborated as we gain additional information through continued inter-action—it's an ongoing process begun during the extended stage of explorational communication.

Interaction during the explorational stage may have several outcomes. Either or both persons may lose interest and reject the relationship entirely. Alternatively, the people may decide to maintain a relationship based on a defined interest. Tennis-mates, research colleagues, and backpacking partners are examples of such defined relationships. A third possibility is a decision to escalate the relationship's intensity by moving into intensifying communication.

Intensifying communication (euphoria). Marking this stage of relational de-velopment is a dramatic increase in both tone and tempo of interaction. Entry into this stage is predicated upon a tentative commitment to a serious relationship, since each person now believes something worthwhile can be built. Interaction now moves even further away from reliance on social norms, as people begin generating their own private rules for conduct. During this stage people are also likely to idealize each other and the relationship, seeing it through the proverbial "rose-colored glasses": "He is the best friend I have ever had." "She just doesn't have any faults." "We're the two musketeers!" A third feature of this stage is the use of communication to symbolize the relationship as an actual entity and to define it as valuable and unique. Interestingly, research shows that men are more likely than women to first say "I love you" and to fall in love more quickly.[21]

As the name implies, during this stage interaction is intense. Typically the individuals get together frequently and for long periods of time. They may even decide to live together to maximize interaction. As individuals intensify their bond, they develop rules and roles for their relationship and themselves. If one person tends to make decisions for both and the other accepts these decisions, a superior-subordinate role relationship is established. If one person adopts the attitudes and hobbies of the other without reciprocal action, a rule is generated for future attitudes and actions. If disagreements involve harsh, abusive language, a destructive pattern of conflict resolution is set in motion. If evenings are spent watching television, the individuals inculcate a habit of minimum interaction during evening hours. If each partner accepts an equal share of household tasks, a pattern of balanced responsibilities is formed. While this list could be extended indefinitely, the point should be clear. During the integrating stage, partners slip into interactional roles and rules which quickly become patterned. In turn, these form expectations for future interaction within the relationship. [22]

An overused but fairly accurate saying is that "love is blind." During integration, this is almost the case. Partners in a relationship are infatuated with each other and their union. Because they are so caught up in this mutual excitement, they literally don't see a great deal of what is happening within the relationship. Partners tend to overlook each other's flaws and exaggerate each other's virtues. This leads to an ironic condition: The patterns and rules of a relationship are developing just at the point when partners are least able or willing to control them. The critical process of generating rules and roles for the relationship thus proceeds almost without awareness, much less reflection. As we'll see shortly, partners may at a later stage negotiate and redefine some of these rules.

Now that we have a general idea of what happens within this stage, let's consider the nature of integrating communication. Self-disclosures and relational communication are the two unique communicative features of this stage. As partners spend more and more time together and as their attraction grows, their communication becomes increasingly personal and revealing. A developing sense of trust encourages partners to risk self-disclosing in ways that are more and more revealing.[23]

Additional areas of each partner's self are unveiled as partners share the intensely personal worlds of memories, dreams, and hopes. As we noted in our earlier discussion of self-disclosure, each revelation made and accepted increases the sense of safety and the sense of commitment between people. The relationship becomes richer. Self-disclosures are critically important to a relationship's growth, because they allow partners to integrate previously separate worlds into a single, shared universe that represents a kind of merging of individuals.[24]

During the intensifying stage, partners develop their own language to reflect their awareness of their relationship. Partners begin to think of themselves as a team, not two separate people, and their language reflects this: "We" replaces "you" and "I."[25] Partners make up nicknames which symbolize their identities within the relationship: "Two wild and crazy guys!" Private meanings are attached to ordinary words and terms, serving as reminders of past experiences or values. Partners also use their communication to share perceptions of what the relationship is and where it is going. Because integrating is the stage of idealization, descriptions of the relationship tend to be euphoric and unabashedly positive: "Our friendship is just incredible! We must have the most open relationship ever." "It's so unusual for two sisters to be this close—

we're really special." "It's hard to believe how close we've become in just three months of dating." Talking about the relationship further intensifies partners' interest in a long term bond. It is really a cyclical process. Individuals create rich, strong images of their relationships and begin to think of the relationships as animated, living realities. For example, here's how one person, a young man completing his junior year of college, described his relationship with his partner:

> I was kind of messed up before the relationship came along, but it helped me pull my act together. It made me grow a lot and gave me a sense of direction for myself. Sometimes when I'm down about grades and stuff, our relationship really pulls me back up again. It helps me keep things in perspective. Carole and I have talked about the future and we know the relationship is too strong to end. It will keep going.

During integrating, partners come to believe in the relationship as a "being" that has existence and power. Partners use communication to create symbolic images that represent both of them and extend beyond either of them. Once begun, the dialogue about the relationship continues as long as the partners stay together.

Intensifying communication escalates a relationship. During this stage, partners increase their knowledge and understanding of each other and begin generating rules and roles to govern their interactions. Because partners at this stage are idealistic about the relationship, they tend to do little critical monitoring of these emerging patterns. During the next stage, however, partners will give extended consideration to the patterns.

Revising communication. While the previous phase consisted of intense inter-action between partners, revising proceeds more privately within each person. The individuals need time to think over what has happened, to get back in touch with themselves, and to consider the desirability of continuing the relationship. During this stage the relationship is in a lull of sorts while each person is engaged intensely in reflection on self and the relationship as a long-term prospect. Many relationships that are satisfying, even exciting in the short term, are not ones that can endure: It is entirely possible (and also tragic) to love someone you cannot live with comfortably. And this is the issue during the revising stage: Can we/should we commit to each other for the long haul?

A primary function of the revising stage is evaluation of the relationship. Any problems not noticed and doubts that were pushed aside during the intensifying stage now receive serious contemplation. At this point, individuals ask questions such as "Can I tolerate particular habits of language permanently?" "Does she require more time than I want to give to a relationship?" "Will his dependence make me resentful over time?" "His moods really irritate me—I wonder whether I want to put up with that full time." Not only is the partner evaluated, but the relationship is as well: "How good is this relationship compared with others I've been in?" (comparison level). "Am I gaining enough from it, given what I am investing?" "What are the alternatives to this relationship—are there any better prospects in sight or would being alone be better?"[26] In answering questions such as these, each partner assigns a value to the relationship as it has evolved thus far and decides whether it merits further invest-ment.

Individuals also evaluate the personal consequences of committing to the relationship. Involvement with another inevitably changes us. We may begin thinking of ourselves in relation to our partners.[27] Before entering a relationship an individual has perceptions of personal strengths and features, but, once in a relationship, these are compared to those of a partner: "Am I less intelligent than Frank?" "Is Shelley more attractive than I am?" "Paul seems more generous than I do." "She's so organized and efficient compared to me." Partners become reference points for self-evaluations, and this changes the way we see ourselves. Further, our values, attitudes, and behaviors are modified by involvement with another. How a partner thinks and feels modifies how we think and feel about issues, people, ideas, and conditions. During the revising stage each person steps back to take stock of changes such as these. We ask who we're becoming by being in a relationship and whether we like the changes. Sometimes we decide a relationship has helped us grow into better versions of ourselves. In other cases we realize that a relationship is restricting our development. If we think the relationship is undesirable or is having undesirable effects on us, we usually end it at this stage. But if we decide the relationship, upon careful thought, is good and is good for us personally, we generally seek to intensify further our connection with the other.

No matter how good a relationship has been, after evaluation partners usually wish to modify or revise it in some ways before making a commitment to an enduring future.[28] Partners begin negotiating for changes in each other and the rules of interaction. Each person may make a number of changes in attitudes and behavior in response to stated or implied requests from the partner: "I wish you'd get more involved with social issues." "Your grammar really is atrocious!" "You'd look and feel better if you lost ten pounds." "I'm not willing to commit permanently to someone who smokes." "I wish you wouldn't spend so much time with other guys." "We don't handle our differences effectively. I think we need to talk to a counselor about how to manage conflict if we want to stay together." Each request suggests a change in one or both partners, a revision that's pertinent to at least one partner's interest in continuing the relationship.

We also negotiate rules of interaction, revising these to suit our preferences for the sake of an enduring relationship: "You ought to pay attention to me when I'm talking." "Why do you always try to dominate every conversation?" "You're going to start doing your share of the work around here or else." "I really wish we could spend more time talking with each other instead of partying all the time." Through such communication partners clarify and, in some cases, revise the rules governing their interaction so that each is more comfortable with the patterns and more confident that those patterns of the relational culture are ones that would be satisfying in the long term.

Predictably enough, communication during this stage may reflect tension, even conflict at times. Requests for personal changes may create defensive feelings. If these aren't handled with sensitive communication, conflict can spiral destructively. At this juncture it's easy for partners to drift into patterns of cross-complaining and negating each other.[29] "What's wrong with the way I dress? At least I'm not still wearing banlon shirts!" "Who are you to choose my friends, anyway? And as long as we're on the topic, I don't think your friends are anyone to brag about." "I'll clean up my language just as soon as you get rid of your ##!"! beergut!" On the relational level, the meaning of such communication is deadly—it disconfirms the worth of individuals. Yet this danger can be reduced at least somewhat if we monitor how we express our needs and requests for change. Also, it's important to understand that negotiations are normal at this stage—their occurrence doesn't mean something is fatally wrong with your bond. So even if they do tend to make us feel a bit defensive, as if our adequacy is being questioned, with reflectiveness and care in communication, we can find ways to make this kind of discussion productive for the relationship. To do this is to apply basic principles of supportive communication and good listening that we discussed in prior chapters. These along with an open attitude can make negotiation sessions productive and minimally threatening for both partners.

Revising is a stage that prepares individuals for intimate bonding. Partners assess their relationship's strengths and weaknesses and then negotiate for changes that will improve the bond. They work out logistics and details of being a team. The major goal of revising communication is to coordinate and stabilize the partners' images of each other and the shared relationship. Any tension and conflict may be minimized by sensitive, supportive communication between partners.

A number of outcomes may follow the revising stage. One or both partners may choose not to make personal changes, so the relationship may falter. Conversely, one partner or both of them may be unwilling to make changes the other wants and may leave the relationship. In either of these cases partners may terminate the relationship entirely or may move it back to a previous level. A third possible outcome is the decision to bond intimately.

Intimate Bonding. Unlike previous stages, bonding is not a process, because it doesn't occur over time. Instead, bonding is an event. It represents the culmination of the entire escalation process and it sets the tone for the future of a relationship. Intimate bonding is partners' voluntary commitment to a common and indefinite future of sustained intensity. Bonding may occur privately between partners or it may be public, as in a ceremony. This definition of bonding is very important, so let's take the time to examine what the terms in it mean.

First, the word commitment is crucial to the nature of bonding. Commitment is not the same thing as love. We may (and usually do) love people to whom we commit, but the two are not equivalent. Commitment is an intention to stay together. It involves an act of will, a pledge, an expectation that ties us to the other not just in the present, but in the future as well. Love, on the other hand, is a feeling, an intense emotional attachment. Research demonstrates that love and rewards we receive are the critical factors that attract us into a relationship. Yet the likelihood that we will *stay* in a relationship over time is more closely associated with commitment and investments. When we invest in a relationship (our time, efforts, money, hopes, emotions), our commitment increases; and the more committed we become, the more we're willing to invest, which, in turn, increases our commitment. In short, there's a mutually positive association between commitment and investment, and neither is equivalent to love.[30] Of course, this isn't to say that love's not important, only that it's different than commitment.

The term "voluntary" is also important in our definition of bonding. It stipulates that the commitment we make is freely chosen. It is not mandated or biological (siblings, for example). Our definition also stipulates an indefinite time frame. This does not necessarily mean the relationship will last "till death do us part," but it does mean that at the time of commitment neither partner foresees a point at which the relationship will end. This commitment, however expressed or implied, is the bonding communication. It symbolizes the rich past and the expectations of the future.

The Gift of Future[31]

In western society at least the most prized possession we can give to another is our future.

In examining the escalation process we've seen that communication is central in building relationships. Individuals employ communication to construct images of each other, to integrate previously separate worlds and personalities, to define a relationship and its rules, and to symbolize commitments to the future. Communication, then, is the primary means of creating and refining our intimate relationships. It is also the heart of maintaining bonds over time, and that's what we want to explore now.

The Shared World of Intimates

Throughout the escalation process, individuals progressively build a shared world, a relational culture created by them and for them. Of course, this doesn't mean individuals are "swallowed up" in a relationship. Indeed, the ideal is that individuals are enlarged by their participation in an intimate bond. In very important ways involvement in a relationship can enrich individuals and actually heighten their individuality. Murray Davis, who wrote a most insightful book on intimacy, explains how individuality can be enhanced by participation in close relationships:[32]

Although it is necessary, for both intimates to establish a common being in order to create a personal relation of the highest order, it is not necessary for each of them to lose all individuality,. . . in fact, in acquiring a more focused ground against which to contrast himself, each intimate actually sharpens his self.

To be with another person intimately invites growth in self. Our consideration of the escalation process has emphasized the construction of a shared world as central to intimacy. Through their symbolic interactions partners establish their unique relational culture, which consists of understandings, patterns, roles, and identities that define their private world.

The Shared World of Intimates[33]

Each social world may be viewed as a peculiar moral order . . . . Contained within it are special views of self, unique vocabularies of meaning and motive, and, most important, symbol systems that have meaning only to the participants involved. In relationships of long duration rules surrounding the following dimensions will be developed. First, rules specifying acts of deference and demeanor . . . alone and in public. Second, mechanisms regulating knowledge, secrecy and personal problems . . . . Third, task structures to specify who does what, when, where and with whom. Last, specifications concerning . . . proper conduct . . . when not in each other's presence. These are interactional dimensions which . . . give order, rationality and predictability to the relationship.

This description from Norman Denzin, a sociologist, makes it abundantly clear that we cannot think of intimate relationships as a simple sum of the involved individuals. Intimacy is the partners plus the shared world created through their symbolic interactions. So, once again, we are confronted by the systemic quality of human interaction. As we have seen, this shared world comes about through communication, the creative force in constructing an intimate relationship.

We have elaborated the concept of shared world and we have seen how it arises in communication. Now we're are ready to examine the Navigating Process that follows intimate bonding.

The Navigating Process

Falling in love is easy and fun. Staying committed is more difficult and requires considerable effort. I hasten to add that navigation can also be a great deal of fun! This stage represents the real challenge of intimacy: making it work well over time.

Navigation is the most extended stage in enduring relationships. As the name implies, navigating is a matter of keeping intimacy on course over its (hopefully) long journey. The term "navigation" suggests movement. This is appropriate since during the stage partners constantly adjust in large and small ways to guide their bond on a rewarding course and to keep the course as smooth as possible. Ideally, this is the stage that we should be in for the bulk of time in intimacy.

Most characteristic of navigation is the effort to balance two sets of needs: partners' desires for both autonomy and connection, and the bond's need to both change and have stability. It is working out the balance between these two sets of demands that is the crux of navigating communication.

During navigation partners deal with the ebb and flow of intimacy. They constantly adjust themselves, each other, and the bond as they interact with each other and with systems (society, professions, etc.) that are also changing. As an example, consider Lloyd and Teresa, who married after four years of dating in college. Both found jobs, she as an environmental consultant and he as a computer analyst, and suddenly , everything changed. In college they had spent most evenings at parties or with friends, frequently staying up until 2 or 3 A.M. This pattern was no longer viable, since Teresa began work at 8 and Lloyd at 8:30 each day. Besides, most of their college friends had graduated and left the area. Even the hours Lloyd and Teresa did have each evening were spent in low-keyed activities, because both were tired after a full day's work. From our earlier discussion of systems you may realize that these changes reverberated throughout the system of Lloyd and Teresa's marriage, causing more changes. The hours spent apart and the fatigue from work reduced the amount of time they had to be together and talk. As they communicated less, they began to lose touch with aspects of each other's worlds, which were changing rapidly. As they felt somewhat distant from each other, it became more difficult to communicate. And so it goes with any kind of system—one change triggers others in an infinite interaction. Obviously, Teresa and Lloyd had to adjust their expectations and interactions to sustain the relationship in the face of such changes.

All relationships change; all individuals change; all systems change; and all of these changes interact constantly, compounding the dynamics of regulating a relationship. To deal with these changes, partners engage in two types of regulating communication: ritual and redefinition.

Rituals are patterned interactions that provide security and/or predictability. Anniversary celebrations are obvious examples of an institutionalized ritual. So are second honeymoons, in which partners symbolically relive the time when they began their shared life. We engage in everyday rituals too: Friday afternoon, every Friday, a pitcher of beer with a friend at the local pub, Sunday afternoon with our family, going out to dinner one night each week, a walk at dusk each evening. Each of these rituals affirms the value intimates place on spending time together, so these are confirming rituals.[34]

Revitalizing rituals serve a slightly different purpose. Rather than affirming the continuing value of the bond, revitalizing rituals are used to revive a relationship that is faltering or to invigorate a solid bond that has become too routine and unstimulating. Some long-married couples go through mock courtship to renew the excitement and mutual appreciation in their bond. Friends sometimes develop a new shared hobby to recement their relationship. Such rituals intensify partners' awareness of shared values and affections and, thus, they, revitalize the relationship.[35] So, on the one hand, rituals (confirming) anchor a bond, keeping it grounded in its own heritage, and, on the other hand, rituals (revitalizing) expand the dimensions of relational culture. Both are important in navigating intimacy successfully.

A second type of navigational communication is *redefinition*, which counterbalance rituals by deliberately introducing change into the bond. The roles and rules that governed the relationship at one point may become less viable as the partners grow and their needs and interests change. For example, a close friend and I have redefined the nature of our roles and the focus of our interaction. Sue and I met in graduate school, and we quickly formed a fast friendship based largely on concerns, problems, and interests common to us as graduate students. The bulk of our communication focused on academic issues, and our roles were those of emerging professionals. When we completed our programs and moved to different parts of the country, we had to redefine both our roles and the focus of interaction in order for the friendship to survive and grow. No longer were we participants in a shared physical and social sphere; no longer were our sole concerns professional ones. In our letters, calls, and occasional visits we worked to establish new foundations for a relationship by interacting on personal and social levels more and interacting less over academic topics. Today the friendship remains strong, and for that to be the case we had to navigate it in ways that make it now distinct in nature from the original bond.

Constant change is the nature of enduring intimacy. As an extended stage, navigation is inherently dynamic. It is an ongoing process of adjusting. To the extent that partners adapt themselves and their bond as needed or desired, they continue to grow as individuals and as a couple. If, however, partners are unwilling or unable to adapt functionally, they will slide into the deescalating process of relational evolution.

The Deescalation Process

There is a danger in discussing the deescalation process. To organize ideas, we must impose a sequence that suggests a certain inevitability: once a relationship begins deescalating, it might seem, there is no turning back. Fortunately, this is not the case. Many relationships that enter the first stage or stages of deescalation are revitalized. Partners realize their bond is deteriorating and they work to rebuild it. They confront problems, renegotiate rules and roles, get back in touch with each other, explore the changes they have undergone, and revise or redefine their shared world so that it is comfortable for the people they are now. Quite frequently a "rebuilt relationship" is even stronger and more exciting than the original, because the partners have recommitted themselves. So the deescalation process does not necessarily signal the imminent ending of a bond. In the following pages we will consider the deescalation stages comprehensively.

As you read, remember that at any stage in deescalation partners may choose to reverse the process and begin rebuilding on their intimacy.

Differentiating communication. The earliest stage of deescalation is often difficult to detect because it has no clear "red flags" to signal danger and because it is so similar to aspects of navigation. Often partners find they're differentiating without ever consciously realizing they entered this stage.

Perhaps the clearest way to explain how this happens is by thinking back on our previous discussion of the balances of navigation. Both partners need a sense of autonomy, of personal independence; equally, both seek a sense of intimate connection. Typically during navigation periods of intense closeness alternate with periods of distance and independent activity. What's important is that partners establish a balance over time that satisfies both needs.

When autonomy and connection get out of balance, partners tend to become increasingly independent. When this continues long enough to jeopardize the sense of connection between partners, differentiation begins. The term "differentiate" literally means to become different, and that's precisely what occurs in this stage. In this phase of deescalation, partners often seem to start just "drifting apart," in a gradual way that may escape notice at first.

Just as partners once sought to harmonize their identities (intensifying stage), they now differentiate themselves. Their identities become increasingly distinct and separate. Partners tend to accent differences rather than similarities and to think of themselves independently more than jointly. During differentiation, communication becomes constrained, formal, and frequently tense.[36] Each partner becomes more involved in activities, associations, and thoughts external to the bond and, consequently, less involved with interaction within the bond. As this happens, people tend to think of themselves increasingly as individuals, not partners in a relationship. Once self is defined independent of the bond, the foundation for further deescalation is laid.

Disintegrating communication. As the name suggests, this is the stage when the relationship begins disintegrating. Whereas differentiation concerned largely the individual partners, disintegration focuses on the bond itself. Typically, this stage is foreshadowed by changes in partners or their systems, changes that are not navigated effectively. As partners change they will naturally grow apart or differentiate unless they consciously communicate about these changes and their implications for the bond. Without careful navigating communication, partners may drift away from the bond, either because better alternatives appear or because the bond itself is no longer interesting or rewarding.[37] Disintegrating communication acts to disassemble the shared world—to unravel the values, expectations, and patterns that comprised the relational culture which was the nucleus for the bond.[38]

Typically, communication becomes less frequent and less intense than in previous stages. Murray Davis uses the phrase "uncoupling intersubjectively" to describe this process whereby partners dissolve their perceptions of a shared world and themselves as an unbreakable unit.[39]

When disintegrating partners do communicate, often conflict arises. Partners may try to push each other into changes that only one wants, may find fault and blame, and may otherwise act in ways that are negative modes of coping with conflict. Alternatively, partners may handle their disagreements and problems with compassion, caring and effective communication. If so, the prospects for revitalizing intimacy are very good. Women and men generally adopt distinctive responses to relationship conflict. Women are more likely to handle conflict in one of two ways: Either they don't "ripple the waters," and simply hope things will get better, or they initiate discussion by talking with their partners about perceived problems in the bond. Men more generally employ two contrasting responses to conflict: Either they neglect it by ignoring and denying problems, or they simply exit by leaving the relationship.[40]

Stagnating communication. This stage is more optional than most. Partners in a deteriorating relationship may skip this stage altogether and move to end the bond. Yet many couples do enter stagnation, which is really a standstill stage, a point of marking time. Partners neither work to improve their bond nor work to end it finally. Sometimes parents do this, believing they should stay married for the sake of their children. Sometimes people do it for other reasons: For devout Catholics divorce is not an option; for highly career-focused individuals, having a languishing relationship may be unimportant; for many people the familiarity of the relationship, even in its diminished state, is preferable to the unknown of ending it. As you might expect, stagnating communication tends to be low keyed and superficial. Partners do not deal with or talk to each other as intimates any longer.

Closing communication. The purpose of this stage is to end the relationship clearly and officially. Partners need to settle logistical matters (property, custody of the dog, "your" half of the rent) and erect psychological barriers to create distance between themselves. Communication during this stage is in many ways similar to invitational communication: formal, governed by social norms, constrained to safe or superficial topics. If partners slip from that style, conflict may erupt, perhaps initiating another period of disintegrating communication. Understandably, communication may be awkward, since people who have been intimates lack rules for interacting as nonintimates.

Individuals after intimacy. We could not end our discussion of relational evolution without giving some attention to the individuals who emerge from intimate bonds. When a relationship ends, its participants are not simply back where they were prior to the beginning of the intimacy. The individuals have been changed by their participation in the bond. Each person has gained insights into his or her own needs and values and expectations of relationships: "Next time I won't get involved with a workaholic." "I need someone less dominating than she was." "I didn't realize how much I value my private time and space—that must be understood the next time I live with someone." "I need to mature a lot more before I'll be ready to make a lasting commitment." "I didn't realize how easily I could slip into a dependent role." Involvement in an intimate relationship teaches us about ourselves and it alters the criteria we will use to judge our future relationships. The relationship that has been closed is a lasting point of reference for us and our potential future intimates.

SUMMARY

Intimate relationships are as good as we make them—no better, no worse. Whatever their nature and quality, we are responsible. At each stage in a relationship's evolution, partners have the ability and the responsibility to monitor what is happening so that they may together build a satisfying relationship or determine that intimacy is not a viable goal for them. This is preferable to allowing ourselves to "drift" with the tide in the hope that things will turn out well.

In this chapter we've considered a sequence of stages that is typical of the evolution of intimacy. As we noted at the beginning of our discussion, this sequence is not absolute. Many friendships and loverships chart courses different from the one we've examined. Some people seem to follow cyclical patterns, in which they go through certain stages several times before moving on. For instance, one couple I know cycled through intensifying and revising stages repeatedly, eventually bonded, and now they're cycling through navigation and disintegration-back and forth, back and forth. Other people seem to follow an almost random pattern, perhaps starting with integrating, moving back to exploration and then onto another stage. And many people roughly follow the sequence we've explored in this chapter. While variability in patterns is great, most relationships pass through each of the stages in some way and at some time.

Like other types of communication we have considered, intimate communication is highly complex and dynamic. It involves the individuals, plus their shared world, plus the systems in which they exist. Constant interactions and changes in all of these make intimate communication one of the most interesting and dynamic forms that exist.

Central to our analysis in this chapter is the concept of a relational culture, a private, idiosyncratic sphere constructed to meet and reflect the particular needs, values, self-conceptions, and behavioral preferences of partners in a relationship. This relational culture conjoins individuals, transforming previously separate lives into one that can be shared. Communication, as we have seen, is the force by which this shared world is developed, sustained, revised, and, in some cases, dissolved. Over time the shared world expands and becomes an ever more central way of knowing through which partners interpret themselves, their relationship, and their experiences outside of the bond. Through their ongoing communication, partners construct shared perceptions which unify them, allowing concerted attitudes and conduct both within the relationship and beyond it.

REFERENCES

[1]P. Berger and H. Kellner, "Marriage and the Construction of Reality." In D. Brissett and C. Edgley (Eds.), *Life as Theatre*. Chicago: Aldine, 1975, pp. 222-223.

[2]J.T. Wood, "Communication and Relational Culture: Bases for the Study of Human Relationships," *Communication Quarterly, 30*, 1982.

[3]G.M. Phillips and J.T. Wood, *Communication and Human Relationships*. New York: Macmillan, 1983, Chapter 3.

[4]H. S. Sullivan, *Interpersonal Theory of Psychiatry*. New York: W.W. Norton and Co., 1953.

[5]S. Brehm, *Intimate Relationships*. New York: Random, 1985, pp. 128-140.

[6]Brehm, pp. 4-5.

[7]Phillips and Wood, p. 141.

[8]Brehm, p. 99.

[9]Brehm, pp. 99-105.

[10]A. W. Schaef, *Women's Reality*. St. Paul, MN: Winston Press, 1988.

[11]Phillips and Wood, Chapters 6, 7, 8.

[12]Phillips and Wood, p. 85.

[13]Phillips and Wood, pp. 87-90.

[14]Brehm, pp. 58-60.

[15]Murray Davis, *Intimate Relations*. New York: Free Press, 1973; Phillips and Wood, pp. 125-126.

[16]Brehm, pp. 60-69.

[17]Brehm, pp. 70-74.

[18]I.A. Altman and D. A. Taylor, *Social Penetration: The Development of Interpersonal Relationships*. New York: Holt, Rinehart and Winston, 1973.

[19]Brehm, pp. 71-72.

[20]Davis, p. 104.

[21]Brehm, pp. 101-102.

[22]Phillips and Wood, pp. 131-135.

[23]Joseph Luft, *Of Human Interaction*. Palo Alto, CA: National Press Books, 1969.

[24]Wood; P. C. Cosby, "Self-Disclosure: A Literature Review," *Psychological Bulletin, 79*, 1973, 73-91.

[25]Davis, Chapter 3.

[26]J. W. Thiabaut and H. H. Kelley, *The Social Psychology of Groups*. New York: John Wiley, 1959; H. H. Kelley, E. Berscheid, A. Christensen, et al. (Eds.), *Close Relationships*. New York: Freeman.

[27]M. D. Scott and W. G. Powers, *Interpersonal Communication: A Question of Needs*. Boston: Houghton Mifflin, 1978, p. 265.

[28]Phillips and Wood, pp. 138-141.

[29]Brehm, Chapter 8.

[30]Brehm, pp. 191-194.

[31]Davis, p. 204.

[32]Davis, p. 170.

[33]N. K. Denzin, "Rules of Conduct and the Study of Deviant Behavior: Some Notes on the Social Relationship." In G.J. McCall, M. M. McCall, N. K. Denzin, G. D. Suttles, and S. B. Kurth, *Social Relationships*. Chicago: Aldine, 1970, p. 71.

[34]Davis; Berger and Kellner; Wood.

[35]E. Durkheim, *Elementary Forms of Religious Life*. New York: Collier Books, 1961, pp. 337-461.

[36]Phillips and Wood, pp. 192-195.

[37]Brehm, Chapter 11.

[38]Wood.

[39]Davis, p. 269.

[40]C. E. Rusbult, I. M. Zembrodt, and L.K. Gunn. "Exit, Voice, Loyalty and Neglect: Responses to Dissatisfaction in Romantic Involvements," *Journal of Personality and Social Psychology, 43*, 1982, 1230-1242.

Part III

Communication and Personal Influence

CHAPTER 10

PROBLEM-SOLVING GROUP COMMUNICATION

. . . our life in contact with others is a constant process of spinning a linguistic self-system and placing it in relation to our understanding of the self-systems of others. Through this process of interaction, we become human. . . . Interaction with others in groups represents the most pertinent elements of human life. . . .

(G.M. Phillips and E. C. Erickson)

The Nature of Problem–Solving Group Communication

    Values of group problem solving
    Limitations of group problem solving

Guidelines for Using Problem-Solving Groups

Influences on Communication in Problem-Solving Groups

    Values of participation
    Influences on participation in problem-solving groups

Individual Attitudes & Communication in Problem-Solving Groups

    Individual attitudes
    Individual communication

Organizing Problem-Solving Discussion

    Values of organization
    Standard agenda for problem solving

Some people enjoy working in groups. They enjoy interacting with others and find that an exchange of ideas stimulates them to their best efforts. Other people avoid group situations whenever possible. They complain that groups waste time, crush individuality, and produce watered-down decisions. Actually, there's some truth to each point of view. Group interaction does stimulate ideas—often better, more creative ideas—than individual thought. On the other hand, group work is time-consuming and—if it is mismanaged—it can indeed suppress individuals or lead to inferior decisions. So the reasonable conclusion to draw is that groups themselves are neither good nor bad; rather, groups can be used well or poorly. Whether groups are effective or ineffective depends largely on members' skills and understandings of group dynamics, two topics we will consider in detail in the following pages.

Language and Situational Definition in Task Groups

The members of [President Johnson's advisory group on Vietnam war] adopted a special vocabulary for describing the Vietnam war, using terms such as body counts, armed reconnaissance, and surgical strikes, which they picked up from their military colleagues. The Vietnam policy makers, by using this professional military vocabulary, were able to avoid in their discussions with each other all direct references to human suffering and thus to form an attitude of detachment similar to that of surgeons.

(From Irving L. Janis, "Groupthink Among Policy Makers," in Nevitt Sanford, Craig Comstock, and Associates (Eds.), Sanctions for Evil (San Francisco, CA: Jossey-Bass, 1971), p. 73)

Communication is the lifeblood of group work. What happens in groups occurs as members communicate with each other to establish meanings for themselves and their collective activities. Thus, theoretical material presented in Parts I and II relates directly to understanding how groups operate and how you can participate effectively in them. Particularly pertinent is Chapter 4's focus on the implications of human symbolic abilities, such as the use of symbols to name or define our experiences. In small group discussion common definitions arise out of members' symbolic interactions with each other and language. Communication defines a group's situation in relation to external people and forces. In one group, members may talk about "fighting the establishment," while in another group members discuss ways to "ally ourselves with the powers that exist." Distinct group situations are defined by these two lines of conversation. Within groups, communication also establishes values. As members talk they, define what goals they will pursue, what issues they will regard as important and which as insignificant, what attitudes they should adopt regarding issues they address, and the fundamental meaning and value of their group ("another silly committee," "a powerful board," "just an informal group," etc.). Out of interaction in groups, members' identities are established. Each person's status and role arise out of communication with others in the group, out of their responses to the individual. Interaction further serves to organize the content of deliberations and to create an interpersonal climate that suggests what kinds of attitudes and actions are appropriate within the context of the group. Communication establishes meanings for all of a group's activities. As you read this chapter and as you participate in groups, notice how communication creates symbolic environments that provide definitions of situation, task, members, and group climate.

This chapter focuses on problem-solving group communication. We'll begin with a general examination of problem-solving groups in contemporary society. Next we'll look at group characteristics that influence communication in problem-solving discussion. Third, we'll consider how individuals influence discussion through their attitudes and communication as members and leaders of groups. Finally, we'll discuss how

group communication can be organized to promote effective, high-quality deliberations. Learning the material in this chapter should increase your understanding of
problem-solving discussion and should provide a basis for your future participation in
task groups.

THE NATURE OF PROBLEM-SOLVING GROUP COMMUNICATION

There are many types of groups, including family, social, educational, professional,
and therapeutic ones. In Chapter 8 we saw how individuals are socialized through
communication in some of these groups. This chapter is about another kind of group,
the problem-solving or task group. Problem-solving groups engage in goal-directed
communication designed to solve problems, make decisions, offer policy recommendations, or perform other specific tasks. Problem-solving groups consist of individuals
who interact face-to-face and who are dependent upon each other to achieve collective goals. In Western society, problem-solving groups serve a variety of purposes
including addressing social issues and work problems.

In private life, individuals organize themselves into groups to deal with issues of
common concern. Neighbors band together to solve community problems. Parents
work cooperatively to improve local schools. Citizens unify their efforts to push for
social programs. People pool their energies to oppose siting of nuclear plants near
cities. Through such private groups, Americans have gained the ability to exert more
power than they can as individuals.

Citizen groups are gaining the respect of official policy makers. Presidential task
forces routinely include one or two "average citizens." Many government grant
programs require citizen participation as an integral part of planning effective social
policies.[1] Whether self-organized or appointed, citizen groups play important roles in
solving social problems and in planning policy. It is probable that citizen groups will
increase in number and power in the decades to come.[2]

Problem-solving groups have also become prevalent in business and industry.
This was not always the case. Until the early part of this century, businesses were run
by one or two executives while workers performed their individual jobs. Moves
toward work groups and worker participation in management resulted from studies
conducted between 1924 and 1950.[3] Researchers compared the productivity and
satisfaction of people who worked in groups and people who worked individually.
From these studies we learned that group work has a positive impact on both
productivity and personal satisfaction. Analysis of group dynamics shows that groups
provide employees with a sense of community or "fit" within an organization. This
increases job satisfaction and reduces turnover and absenteeism.[4] Membership in a
work group also increases employees' identification with their organization. By virtue
of their positions, managers and executives identify with their organizations, but line
workers have less basis to see themselves as part of a particular company. As they
work together in groups, workers identify themselves with others who are part of an
organization. Out of interaction with peers a sense of community arises, transforming

workers' definitions of their jobs from "necessary chore" to participation in a human community.[5]

Group work has advantages for businesses as well as workers. From pioneer research we learned that people working in groups often do better jobs than people working alone. Compared with individuals, groups tend to be more productive and to do better-quality work.[6] Additionally, when people work in groups they tend to create a cooperative constructive atmosphere that enhances productivity. By contrast, when people work individually competitive relationships tend to emerge and interfere with productivity.[7]

Impressed by how much groups can increase productivity and interpersonal climates, researchers wondered whether groups might have other values in work settings. They launched experiments to see what would happen if workers were given voices in the design of policies traditionally handled by management. The first major finding was that group decision-making increases workers' commitment to decisions. When people work together to solve problems and achieve tasks, they tend to become committed to what they have done. Participation in decision making heightens workers' involvement in policy issues and increases their willingness to carry out decisions.[8] Another advantage of group decision making is superior outcomes. Often far better decisions and policies arise from groups composed of workers and management than from management alone. Workers have distinctly valuable ideas to offer in group decision making, and they take pride in making contributions. Findings such as these led to participative management, a system of organizational management in which employees at various levels participate in designing policies and procedures that govern the organization. Instead of passively accepting executive dictates, employees in participative management systems actively help shape policies pertinent to their jobs and work situations. In the years since this early research, participative management has gained popularity with both workers and managers. Most contemporary managers believe in some degree of worker participation in policy making, and most contemporary employees expect to have a voice in some of the decisions that affect them and their work. Participatory decision making has clear benefits for all concerned. Thus, group problem solving is an important part of contemporary organizational structure.

The Workers Know Best[10]

Boosting productivity and morale with IMPS and VIPS

Like the jowls of an aging Hollywood star, U.S. productivity is sagging, and the blame has been placed on everything from Government regulation to declines in business investment. But experts increasingly believe a primary reason is that remote corporate bureaucracies have isolated workers from all decision making, turning many of them into uncaring automatons.

To change that, more and more U.S. companies are returning the responsibility for solving factory floor problems to the factory floor itself. On the premise that the workers often know best, the firms are forming "quality circles." These are groups of five to 13 employees who volunteer to gather for perhaps an hour each week, on company time, in brainstorming sessions that focus on what can be done to improve output per hour worked. Supervisors lead the discussions and help put the recommendations into practice. The result: bonuses and more job satisfaction for workers plus higher profits and productivity for firms.

The idea is hardly new. The Japanese developed circles after World War 11, borrowing ideas from U.S. business theorists, and such groups are considered to be an important contribution to Japan's productivity. Among the U.S. corporations now using quality circles are General Motors, Ford, American Airlines, 3M and Martin Marietta. One of the most enthusiastic, Westinghouse, is expanding the use of circles after experimenting with the idea for 16 months at its Defense and Electronic Systems Center near Baltimore. Notes Executive Vice President George Beck: "This is one of those rare programs that benefit everyone."

The Baltimore workers have christened their circles with such acronyms as VIPS (Volunteers Interested in Perfection), IMPS (Improved Methods and Products Seekers) and TOPS (Tuned Onto Productivity and Savings). By any name, they have already generated savings of at least $800,000. Examples:

> > A group of people who use wire-bonding machines suggested that if a single worker came in 15 minutes early each morning to warm up all the machines, everyone could start work as soon as he arrived. The saving: about $22,000 a year.

> > Another circle, of people who use color-coded tapes to assemble transformers for radar systems, recommended that each worker be given his own tape machine rather than sharing on a three-for-one basis. The twelve extra machines cost $174, but the company saves some $11,000 a year in production time.

> > A purchasing-department circle noted that when supplies were ordered, many vendors routinely sent more than requested. The company either paid the bill or shipped the parts back at its own expense. The group tallied all the overcharge costs and found them startling. The solution was to inform suppliers that the company would either keep the extra material or charge for returning it. The saving: $636,000 a year.

> >For a cost-saving idea, the top award that members of a Westinghouse circle split up is $25,000. Says Earn Crehan, a vice president at the Baltimore plant: "The circles motivated our people. Unless management provides an environment of participation, we will not survive." Adds Georgette Schaefer, the supervisor of one circle: "They have all become minimanagers. They now take the job home with them."

Values of Group Problem Solving

Extensive research comparing individual and group decision making shows that groups have some distinct values. When the goal is to solve a problem or make a decision, groups are superior to individuals in four respects: They have more resources, are more thorough, are more creative, and have greater implementation power.

Increased resources.   The most obvious advantage of groups is that they have more resources than individuals. There's something to the old adage that "two heads are better than one." When a variety of people work on a task there will be diversity of ideas, points of view, skills, and backgrounds. There will also be more time and energy from five people than from one. In most cases the lone individual is restricted by her or his personal perspective on issues and by a limited amount of time to devote to solving problems. Group problem-solving increases the physical and psychological resources brought to bear on issues.[11]

Increased thoroughness. In group problem solving a "check and balance" system evolves, so that members screen each other's ideas and compensate for each other's weaknesses. Any individual will overlook some aspects of a problem, but it's unlikely that all members of a group will do so. If one person endorses an unrealistic solution to a problem, other members of a group are likely to see its flaws. In group interaction others' responses to our ideas provide a basis for modifying our own contributions as appropriate. We can monitor our ideas from the multiple perspectives furnished by other members of a group.

Initially the increased thoroughness of group deliberations was regarded as an averaging effect whereby extreme opinions were weeded out and a middle position emerged. Careful study, however, showed that group decisions are not a simple average of members' ideas. Instead, the superiority of group problem solving results from interaction that promotes detailed analysis of information and ideas. In discussing issues with each other, group members become more thorough and critical than when thinking issues through on their own.[12] The result is decisions that reflect more comprehensive, critical analysis than those typically made by individuals.

Increased creativity. Compared with individuals, groups are more creative in solving problems and making decisions. Any single person eventually runs dry of ideas on a topic, but a group can generate ideas indefinitely.[13] Interaction seems to stimulate creative thought, so groups are not only more potentially creative than individuals, but more creative than all of the individual members put together. In discussion you volunteer an idea which sparks an insight in someone else, which leads a third person to yet another idea. Members build on each other's contributions to create perspectives none could develop alone. Communication within groups stimulates more ideas and different ideas than would be developed by individuals. In problem solving this is important, for it increases the options available for understanding and resolving problems.

Implementation power. Decisions reached by groups tend to be implemented more effectively than those determined by individuals. As we saw earlier, people commit to decisions they take part in making. People believe in their own ideas and those they participate in building, so they naturally work hard to put them into practice. Support for new policies is essential to their effectiveness. If workers are opposed to one of management's policies, they can thoroughly sabotage it. If citizens dislike a local ordinance, they will find ways to undercut it. If people cannot see the value in a proposal, they refuse to go along with it. Without support, few decisions can be effective and many will not work at all. Any decision's effectiveness is directly related to the extent that the decision-making process has included those whose acceptance will be needed for implementation. A decision, policy, or program proposed by a group starts off with a built-in constituency to support it and to garner additional support. Implementation is further assisted by the increased resources a group commands. There are several people who understand the intricacies of the decision and how to carry it out most effectively. Finally, group problem solving results in superior implementation because a group of people can design policies with fewer practical problems than those proposed by an individual. Because a group has varied perspectives and because groups are more thorough in analyzing issues, group decisions tend to be better thought-through and more pragmatic.

In summary, group decision making has four values not inherent in individual decision making. Groups have increased resources, conduct more thorough analysis, are more creative, and have greater power to implement decisions effectively. Because of these strengths, group discussion is a popular method of solving problems and designing policies.

Limitations of Group Problem Solving

The advantages of group problem solving must be weighed against potential disadvantages. There are two important limitations on the effectiveness of group problem solving: time and conformity pressures.

Time. Anyone who has ever worked in a group knows that discussion takes time. An individual can efficiently consider information and alternatives to reach a decision. Not so with groups. In discussion the ideas of several people are thrown on the table and must be explained, evaluated, and related to other ideas that have been voiced. Each idea is considered from the diverse perspectives of all members. Time is required to present and clarify information, to coordinate individual views into a common perspective, and to make sure that all members stay on a shared line of thought. In this respect groups are less efficient problem solvers than individuals. There is a tradeoff between values of increased resources, thoroughness, creativity, and implementation power and the cost in time required to reach decisions.

Conformity pressures. Perhaps the most frequently cited weakness of group discussion is its potential to suppress individual thought. Conformity pressures can operate in groups and, if they do, the integrity of the process and its products is compromised. There are two kinds of conformity pressures that group members need to understand.

The most commonly recognized conformity pressure is that of majority opinion. When the majority of members agree on some issue, they may apply pressure to the member or members who disagree. Tactics to induce conformity include persuasion ("Really our plan is the best because. . . ."), bargaining ("If you'll go along on this, we'll support you on the other issue"), threats ("If you don't want to cooperate, we'll report you") and exclusion from the group ("If you cannot see it our way, we think it would be better for you to leave the committee").[14] These are strong pressures for any individual to withstand, and they often induce conformity.

A second line of conformity occurs when a single prestigious group member pressures others to go along with her or his ideas. From experimental research we know that a person with high status can sway others' opinions. The prestigious individual may not intend to influence others' judgments; in fact, there may be no deliberate pressure at all. What tends to happen frequently is that members place too much trust in a prestigious person's ideas and accept them without adequate scrutiny.[15] They define an idea as good because they identify it with a member they view as powerful or important. President John F. Kennedy, for instance, was so highly respected that even his top policy advisors tended to go along with his ideas without first examining them critically. President Kennedy did not intend to exert such influence on others' judgments and his advisors did not intend to let the President shape their views; it happened nonetheless.[16]

This example as well as research findings make it clear that individuals' suppression of their ideas is not always conscious or deliberate. Some interesting research pertinent to this issue suggests that males are more likely than females to not be aware of doubts they have—to be unaware of important reservations and questions that should be voiced about topics under discussion. Women, in contrast, seem more likely to be aware of doubts and to express them to others.[17] While the reasons for this difference are not yet entirely clear, one plausible interpretation is that males are socialized to be assertive and confident, which could lead them to speak in ways that reveal no equivocation. Women's socialization, however, teaches them to doubt ideas, including their own, so they might be expected to be more aware of reservations and to voice them in groups. Unfortunately this tendency, which is vital to critical thinking in groups, is too often interpreted as evidence that women are indecisive, rather than that they are cautious. Because the tendencies to conform are heightened in groups, it's important for members to recognize and guard against tendencies to define ideas from prestigious members as automatically good and to not question ideas that come before the group.

Both types of conformity pressures are injurious to effective problem solving. Group decisions suffer whether a minority member is pressured to accept majority views or an individual with high status influences majority judgment. In group problem solving, members and leaders must continually guard against deliberate and nondeliberate interference with independent thought.

Group problem solving has, then, two potential disadvantages. Clearly groups take more time than individuals to analyze issues and make decisions. In addition, as people interact in groups they risk having other members influence their individual judgments. Recognizing these problems is essential if you are to guard against their occurrence in groups that you work with.

GUIDELINES FOR USING PROBLEM-SOLVING GROUPS

We've seen that groups have strengths and weaknesses, just as individuals do. In some respects group problem solving is superior to individual problem solving, while in other respects the reverse is true. So we cannot conclude that groups should or should not be used universally; rather, we arrive at a qualified conclusion that groups should be used in some situations, but not in others. To identify when groups should be used, we can build on our previous examination of values and limitations of group discussion. There are four general guidelines regarding when to use groups rather than individuals to solve problems and make decisions.

Complex tasks. Group problem solving is appropriate for complex tasks that allow for division of labor. Routine and mechanical tasks are more efficiently handled by a single decision maker. Much time is wasted when groups are assigned to do what an individual could accomplish efficiently and with less frustration.

Ambiguous tasks. Groups are effective in dealing with ambiguous tasks where there are no clear-cut answers. A single person can solve problems that require only computation or the collection of information. An individual is less effective than a group, however, in solving problems that don't have solutions that are clear or can be deduced in a logical way from existing information. When diverse perspectives must be recognized and incorporated into a solution and when values (rather than just information) must be considered, group problem solving is in order.

Because communicative interaction allows us to appreciate perspectives beyond our own individual ones, group discussion can enlarge our understandings. They are more likely than individuals to analyze a problem from multiple viewpoints and to identify a wide range of alternative ways of solving it. As we know from symbolic interactionism, it is through human interaction that we gain access to multiple perspectives, multiple ways of understanding issues and their implications. So talking with others allows people to understand facets of a problem and possible solutions that might not occur to an individual within that limited personal perspective.

Nonemergency tasks. Group problem solving should be used only when there is sufficient time for effective group interaction. It's often more advisable to let one person handle emergency decisions, because group problem solving cannot work well when faced with tight time pressures. When forced to make quick decisions, groups may engage in superficial deliberation or rash conformity. Effective group problem solving requires substantial amounts of time to identify and examine diverse views. If decision making must be rushed, individuals are more effective than groups.

Broad acceptance needed. Most of us resent having ideas and policies imposed on us without any effort to seek our input. We want to have some say over matters that affect us. For this reason, group problem solving is advisable in those situations where there must be broad acceptance of a decision in order for it to work. By allowing various sectors of an organization or community to participate in problem solving, support for decisions is built into the process. Individuals can make decisions that do not require human acceptance in order to work. For instance, technical matters can be resolved by experts. However, group problem solving is advisable whenever effective implementation depends upon broadly based support for policies or decisions.[18]

Goodmeasure Incorporated[19]

Goodmeasure, Inc. is a management consulting firm that emphasizes the quality of work life. The founders are Yale Professor Rosabeth Moss Kanter and her husband,

Barry Stein. Both Kanter and Stein believe it's important to maximize employees' satisfaction with their work and that this will pay off in productivity and, thus, company profits. One of Goodmeasure's favorite techniques of organizational improvement is the "diagonal task force," which is a working committee that includes members from different levels in an organization. The diagonal task force works with Goodmeasure to diagnose problems in an organization and to find solutions. Participation from all levels of an organization is the key to the effectiveness of the diagonal task force. According to Kanter, "With representation, employees are more likely to use what's generated."

No tool is very effective when used for something it isn't designed to work on. This rule holds true for group work. Groups tend to be effective only when they are used for those tasks that call for the particular abilities of groups, rather than individuals. Inadequate understanding of when to use group problem solving is at the root of much ineffective group work. Group problem solving is appropriate for complex tasks that can be divided among several people, for ambiguous tasks that involve values and on which there are multiple perspectives, for tasks where there is time available, and for making decisions that require broad acceptance in order to work. Group problem solving is only effective if it is employed under conditions that maximize its strengths and minimize its potential weaknesses.

INFLUENCES ON COMMUNICATION IN PROBLEM-SOLVING GROUPS

Understanding when group discussion is appropriate is the first requirement of effective problem solving. A second requirement is knowledge about the dynamics of participation in small groups.

Think about task groups to which you've belonged. Chances are that your behavior differed from group to group. In some you felt comfortable and contributed actively, while in others you were hesitant to participate. Probably in some groups all members contributed, while in other groups one or two people dominated interaction. How important is participation? Should it be relatively balanced among members? Does it influence the quality of a group's work and members' satisfaction? The next few pages address these questions.

Values of Participation

A number of researchers have studied the impact of participation on group decisions and member satisfaction. From these investigations we know that better decisions tend to result from groups with relatively balanced participation than from those in which a few people do the majority of talking. When discussion is dominated by one or two members, a group loses one of its primary potential strengths: increased resources. Participation from all members leads to greater perspective on issues and possible solutions to problems.

We also know that participation in discussion directly influences members' satisfaction with group process. Through interaction with others, individuals identify with a group and gain a sense of their own value to the group. People who do not participate experience little satisfaction with group membership. Participation is also closely associated with members' commitment to group decisions. The more ideas and efforts members invest in discussion, the more committed they tend to be to what the group decides. Individuals who don't participate have little personal stake in final decisions.

Clearly these values of participation need some qualification. Not all talk is useful; not all is even sensible! We've probably all known people who like to talk but who contribute very little by occupying the air waves. You've probably seen examples of this in classes as well—some students always make some comment on any topic, regardless of whether it really adds anything to the class discussion. So while everyone should probably be allowed to voice some opinions and to participate proportionately, there's no presumption that all contributions are equally valuable. Further, there's no reason why a serious task group should tolerate extended commentary by a member whose ideas are weak. Even with this qualification, however, the generally advisable course of action is to encourage fairly even communication from members, because it has such important values. Balanced participation in discussion is desirable because it directly affects the quality of problem solving, members' satisfaction, and members' commitment to decisions reached by a group.

Influences on Participation in Problem-Solving Groups

Clearly, participation is important to problem solving. Therefore, we should understand the conditions that foster and inhibit balanced interaction. Why is it that some groups seem to invite open communication, and others seem to discourage it? What is it about some groups that makes us feel our ideas are really wanted, while in other groups we sense nobody cares what we have to say? A number of factors account for such differences. We will examine five characteristics of groups that most directly influence participation: size, participation norms, cohesion, power structure, and seating patterns.

Group size. The number of people in a group influences how much they contribute. Several studies have shown that the ideal size for discussion is five or seven members. With five or seven people, sufficiently diverse views are represented, and there is ample opportunity for everyone to interact yet the odd number prevents deadlocks. In groups with eight or more members it's difficult for everyone to contribute, so one or two people tend to dominate discussion. In addition, as groups increase in size members tend to define the discussion situation as more formal, so relaxed interaction is less likely to occur. It becomes increasingly difficult for members to take into account the perspectives of all other members. Through interaction we can discern the perspectives of a few others, but it's nearly impossible to understand the perspectives of 8, 10, or 12 other people.

Participation suffers in different ways when groups are too small. With fewer than five members, discussants may hesitate to voice strong ideas that could alienate others—it's risky because alienating even one person severely reduces the group! Further, with fewer than five members discussion tends to lack the diversity of viewpoints so important to problem solving. Insufficient perspectives are brought to bear on issues of deliberation.

Though discussion groups should have five or seven members, this ideal is not always met, so you need to think about how you should deal with groups that are too large or small to encourage maximum participation. If you find yourself in a group with more than seven members, you might make special efforts to invite broad participation. If you're in a group with fewer than five members, on the other hand, it is important for you to encourage expression of differing points of view, perhaps by initiating some constructive debate yourself. The size of a group influences members' definitions of a group situation. By understanding how perceptions of size affect interaction you can guide your own communication behaviors to compensate for situations when size is not ideal.

Participation norms. All groups have norms, which are patterns of attitude and behavior. Norms are useful because they provide order and stability and they serve to coordinate interaction in groups.[20] Norms may regulate anything from meeting time to members' attitudes. One of the most important group norms is the one for interaction behaviors. The understood rule may be that everyone should participate, that anyone may participate, or that only certain members have the right to offer ideas. Each of these norms naturally leads to a distinct kind of participation.

Norms develop out of interaction. For example, one person speaks up and others listen; another person offers an opinion and others respond; pretty soon there is a participation norm that suggests members respect each other's right to speak. In another group, perhaps the first person who volunteers an idea is cut short by a second member, who is interrupted by a third; the leader addresses all comments to one other person in the group and listens only to that person's ideas; after a few meetings only two people participate seriously—the others quit trying. Here the participation norm is that only two people have the right to enter discussion. Any hope for balanced participation goes out the window and the two participating members push through their ideas. These two examples provide an important insight into how participation norms evolve. They develop very early in interaction, so group members and leaders should try to establish communication patterns that promote balanced participation. Ways to do this include listening and responding to any comments offered, presenting your own ideas without talking too often, asking for opinions from quiet people in the group, and stimulating interaction between members by pointing out possible relationships between ideas. Actions such as these build healthy participation norms that encourage effective problem-solving interaction.

Cohesion. A third influence on participation is group cohesion. Cohesion is difficult to define precisely. It's best thought of as members' feeling of "weness" or team spirit. In cohesive groups, members think of the group as a community, rather than just a collection of individuals. By contrast, in noncohesive groups members think of the various individuals rather than the group as a whole. Membership in cohesive groups is more satisfying than is membership in noncohesive groups, which often splinter or disintegrate.

Cohesion and participation are interrelated. Participation builds cohesion, and cohesion encourages healthy participation. As members interact they learn how to work together as a team, which, in turn, leads to continued participation. In cohesive groups, members generally respect one another and take pride in their group. Consequently, communication tends to be friendly and positive.[21] One danger here is that in the effort to preserve the friendly atmosphere, members may suppress controversy and insist on unified opinions among members.[22] When the desire to be harmonious gets distorted into pressure for conformity, poor decision making tends to happen. Thus, a balance has to be maintained between efforts to get along and insistence on critical thought and discussion of differing ideas and opinions. We should note here a relevant gender-related difference. Women in many contexts, including groups, tend to be more cooperative and more concerned with maintaining friendly relationships than men.[23] This prosocial behavior is clearly valuable in advancing cohesive group relationships. Yet, women may be somewhat more prone than men to avoid differences of opinion or to try to smooth over disagreements that seem to jeopardize pleasant interaction. When problem solving is the goal, differences need to be encouraged and discussed, though of course with diplomacy.

Cohesion and healthy participation are related, each affecting the other. The value of cohesion as a stimulant to productive communication, however, should not be taken to the extreme of encouraging conformity among members.

Power structure.   A fourth influence on participation is group power structure, the varying levels of status attributed to members. Status may be gained by demonstration of abilities or may be a function of the meanings others attach to an individual's title or position. If all members have relatively equal status, power is distributed throughout a group. If some members have high status while others have little or none, a hierarchical power structure exists.

Power structure directly affects communication in discussion. Members with high status tend to contribute actively and to be addressed frequently by others in the group. Members with lower status talk less often and are talked to less often. As status increases, there is a corresponding rise in a person's influence on group judgments, so that members with low status tend to direct their communication to people of higher status, a communication pattern that has been called "social climbing."[24]

Particularly in the early stages of a group's life, there's often a negotiation over power—who will occupy what position in the group's hierarchy? The tendency to be concerned about one's place and to try to gain and hold a position of influence seems considerably more pronounced in men than in women. Men also seem less willing to share power with others than do women. In groups, as in other situations, women appear not to regard having power as particularly important. Further, when women do occupy positions of power, they seem quite willing to share it by inviting others into discussion and demonstrating they value others' ideas.[25] Knowing about these gender-related tendencies is helpful when you try to understand some of the dynamics at work in small group discussions.

How is power structure established in groups? A primary influence on power relations is communication among members. Out of interaction roles arise and levels of power are defined for each participant in group process. An initial concern of each member is to establish an identity within a group, to define a role in relation to the other members. Your communication directs others' interpretations of your status. At the same time, how others respond to your communication will guide your self-definition in a group situation. Just as communication shapes your identity within a group, so does your communication influence the identity of other members. As you respond to members, you indicate how you view them and how you regard their ideas. This is the relational level of communication we first discussed in Chapter 4. Thus, you contribute to a definition of their roles within a group. If you consistently label a member's comments as "inadequate" or "unrealistic" or if you ignore a member's ideas, that person may view himself or herself as unworthy in the situation. On the other hand, if you approve a members' comments, encourage elaboration of ideas, and otherwise indicate that person's importance, you foster definitions of that person as a significant member. Members' responses to each other affect each person's definitions of self in a group situation and establish the overall power relations in a group.

When communication flows in one direction—toward high status members—an asymmetrical kind of participation exists. This impairs both problem solving and member satisfaction. Obviously problem solving suffers if ideas are judged on the basis of who contributes them rather than on their intrinsic worth. Good information may be discarded because it comes from members with low status, and poor ideas may be accepted because they are contributed by prestigious members. If a rigid hierarchy exists, members with low status tend to be excluded from participation, so naturally they become dissatisfied with the group and less committed to its goals and decisions. To guard against these problems, it's advisable to minimize discrepancies in power. All members should be encouraged to participate actively and all ideas should be examined with equal care. High-status members should not be allowed to dominate discussion, and low-status members should not be forced to withdraw from interaction.

Seating patterns. A final influence on participation is seating arrangements. Members may adopt a centralized seating pattern, in which one person occupies the key position, or a decentralized pattern, in which no member is prominent. The two patterns have impact on group communication, because they tend to guide members to quite distinct definitions of the group situation and, thus, of appropriate interaction in the situation. Researchers report that decentralized arrangements promote balanced participation and, consequently, satisfaction with membership. Centralized patterns, by contrast, tend to result in imbalances in participation and satisfaction. More surprising is the finding that for problem-solving interaction, decentralized arrangements are more effective and more efficient than centralized patterns.[26]

Participation is additionally influenced by the physical placement of particular members. The further members are from the center of a group the less actively they tend to participate, probably because they define themselves as somewhat removed from the group. Members who define themselves as "fringe" participants will make

Seating Patterns

		x x x	
Centralized	x	xxx	x
Patterns	xxxxx	xxx	x x
		xxx	

	xx		
Decentralized	x x	x	x x
Patterns	x x	x x	x x
	xx		x x

few comments and may not be included in others' communication, because the others may similarly define them as outside of the hub of discussion. Of course, in truly decentralized groups there are no peripheral members. Yet sometimes it's impossible for a group to adopt a decentralized pattern. Fixed furniture may dictate a centralized arrangement. In situations where the overall pattern cannot be controlled, careful positioning of members can encourage healthy participation. For instance, members who tend to be less outspoken should be invited to sit toward the center or head of the group, while highly active members may be asked to take more removed positions. A potential dominator may be deliberately placed in a peripheral spot. Knowledge about the probable effects of seating patterns can also be used to control participation. For example, you now know that members at the edge of a group tend to be less fully included in discussion. If you find yourself in a centralized group you can take care to direct comments to people who occupy outer positions and to include them in your nonverbal communication.

Interaction is the heart of problem solving, so it's important to understand how group dynamics affect the level and quality of participation. We've considered five influences on how members communicate in groups: group size, participation norms, cohesion, power structure, and seating patterns. Each of these has impact on members' perceptions of a group situation and, thus, on their interaction behaviors. Members guide their communication in groups by indicating to themselves what the situation is and what is appropriate within it. In turn, communication is the basis of problem-solving effectiveness, members' satisfaction with the discussion process, and members' commitment to group decisions.

INDIVIDUAL ATTITUDES AND COMMUNICATION IN PROBLEM-SOLVING GROUPS

We've seen that effective problem solving depends on knowledge of when to use group discussion and how group characteristics influence participation. A third influence on problem-solving quality is participants' attitudes and communication. Each person in a discussion group has vital impact on the problem-solving process and the outcomes it produces. The next few pages summarize the orientations most appropriate for members and leaders of problem-solving groups.

Individual Attitudes

As we've emphasized throughout this book, individuals act on the basis of their attitudes and commitments. This is as true for how people act in groups as it is for other contexts we've already considered. To tailor this general point to group discussion, we will consider five attitudes that underlie effective participation in task discussion.

Rhetorical sensitivity. Central to effective group discussion are members' orientations toward communication. Of the various orientations possible, rhetorical sensitivity seems best suited to the problem-solving context. Rhetorical sensitivity regards communication as a dynamic, flexible process which must be consciously managed in order to achieve personal and collective goals.[27] In another book with two colleagues, I drew out the implications of rhetorical sensitivity for group discussion.[28]

First, rhetorically sensitive group members respect themselves and others, so they promote their own ideas and at the same time encourage others to argue for theirs. This suggests each member should listen actively in order to adopt dual perspective, striving to understand how others define a situation and its implications for the group. Rhetorical sensitivity further implies a commitment to common goals, so members should demonstrate the relevance of their communication to group objectives and should avoid comments that reflect strictly personal concerns. As you speak in groups, show that you are aware of others' perspectives as well as your own views. Third, rhetorically sensitive members recognize communication as a means of building relationships with others; thus, they employ dual perspective to design communication in ways that others can understand. Even good ideas will be dismissed if they are presented unclearly or if they are not adapted to the particular concerns and abilities of other members. Finally, rhetorical sensitivity calls for continued openness to interaction with others, so members should show they are willing to extend discussion, to talk further to clarify ambiguous ideas, or to continue participating even when a personal preference has been overruled. Rhetorical sensitivity is a basic attitude that guides communicative interaction with others. It promotes conscious management of communication to build understanding with others and to accomplish personal and collective goals. It is fundamental to effective participation in groups.

Cooperativeness. Problem-solving discussion is a cooperative enterprise. A group's success depends upon individuals' willingness to work together. Members share a common goal that can be attained only through concerted efforts. Each person's effectiveness is directly related to every other person's effectiveness.[29] The interdependence of members calls for cooperative attitudes that promote unity within the group. Competitiveness is inappropriate in the task group, because a member who "beats" others also beats the group. There is no room for grandstanding, hogging center stage, or one-upmanship. Given the research just discussed on gender-related differences in comparative and competitive styles, this point is one that men may need to work harder to internalize than women. All members should have cooperative attitudes that reflect respect for the team as a whole. Cooperative attitudes are evident when communication is open to others and their ideas and when communication indicates support for the entire group. In effective problem-solving groups, members have cooperative attitudes that enhance their ability to work together. These attitudes arise in and are reflected by communication that is open, respectful, and oriented toward common goals.

Responsibility. For problem solving to be effective, every member should adopt a responsible attitude toward participation. Members with responsible attitudes recognize and meet their obligations to the group. In addition to preparing outside of meetings, each person is expected to take an active role in actual discussion. This means that when presenting ideas members should be well prepared, clear, and concise. When listening to others' ideas members should be thoughtful and responsive. In group work every member is responsible to the group as a whole, and members count on each person to meet this responsibility. If one member fails to contribute to the discussion, the entire group loses valuable perspective. If one member neglects an assigned task, everyone suffers and the entire group is set back.

Unfortunately, responsible attitudes do not always guide participation in groups. When individual members are irresponsible, problem solving falters. Little gets done, because each member waits for someone else to collect information, contact resource people, check the quality of evidence, organize discussion, and so on. When individuals abdicate personal responsibilities to the group, inferior problem solving is the inevitable result. Situations in which members are irresponsible are the basis for the often-heard complaint that nothing gets done in groups. The claim has a grain of truth in the sense that groups are not magically productive. The process is as effective or as ineffective as those who engage in it. Members who commit to responsible preparation and participation bolster the integrity of group problem solving. Group norms as well as individual attitudes arise out of communication among members. If one person's irresponsible conduct receives an unfavorable response from others, irresponsibility is defined as unacceptable and is unlikely to continue. Communication within a group establishes definitions regarding appropriate conduct.

Reflectiveness. A reflective attitude is thoughtful and tentative. It is open-minded, avoiding the extremes of dogmatism on the one hand and wishy-washy positions on the other. Reflective members are open to ideas presented by others, even when those ideas contradict personal positions. They give fair hearing to all views because they realize this is essential to rational deliberation. Further, reflective individuals are able to reflect on their own positions; they listen to criticism or questions of their opinions and, when appropriate, modify their original ideas. Reflective attitudes allow us to suspend judgment until we have considered a range of information and perspectives. Only when members are reflective can problem solving reach its potential as a process that culls the best aspects of varied viewpoints.

Reflective attitudes show up in communication. Participants indicate an interest in hearing opinions different from their own, a willingness to alter personal stances when appropriate, an openness to continued interaction over controversial material. This kind of communication establishes participation norms that invite vigorous, thorough deliberation among members. Naturally, such animated interaction sometimes results in conflict, so members need an attitude that allows them to approach conflict constructively.

Respect for conflict. A fifth attitude appropriate for problem solving is respect for conflict. Conflict is not a dirty word, despite the fact that many people think it has no place in discussion. Actually, conflict is integral to effective problem solving; without it, discussion cannot be maximally effective. When conflict is properly managed it stimulates thought, increases the intensity of analysis and deliberation, and invigorates the interaction climate. These are important values that are appreciated by individuals who have a respectful attitude toward conflict.

Since well-managed conflict materially assists problem solving, group members should learn how to handle it constructively. To make conflict productive, members should first establish a cooperative climate that emphasizes common goals. Throughout discussion members' communication should reflect a commitment to participation, an interest in all ideas, and a nonthreatening style of questioning opinions offered by others. Differences should be confined to issues, avoiding personalities, and disagreements should be understood as ways of increasing everyone's perspective on issues.[30] Adoption of dual perspective is especially important in conflict. It is insufficient to realize that a difference of opinion exists. Members need to understand the nature and basis of alternative perspectives on an issue. Each member should make a genuine effort to discover how others define issues. Only by understanding each other's perspectives can members hope to resolve differences in legitimate ways. How you and others treat conflict will influence the meanings attached to it. Thus, you can contribute to your group's effectiveness by communicating your respect for conflict as a natural and valuable part of productive problem solving.

How individuals participate in problem-solving discussion is based on their attitudes toward group work and human communication. Five attitudes especially conducive to high-quality problem solving are rhetorical sensitivity, cooperativeness, responsibility, reflectiveness, and respect for conflict. Productive, satisfying discussion is probable when members and leaders embrace these attitudes and demonstrate them through their communication.

An Unspoken Contract for Serious Group Problem Solving[31]

I am here for a purpose, and I suspect that the others here have a purpose as well. I do not expect them to agree with me or to support me in all things I do, but I expect them, like me, to be reasonably dedicated to the accomplishment of the group task that brought us here in the first place.

I have the obligation to speak up, to make my point of view known. If I just sit here, I will waste my time and the time of others, I must present my ideas clearly so that others can understand them well enough to criticize them sensibly, and I must listen to the ideas of others in a critical, but not hostile way.

I have the obligation to defend my points of view when necessary. I have no right to be truculent, to polarize the group, or to attack my fellow members. Furthermore,

I am not compelled to curb my own personal moral commitments or understandings. Still, I cannot be dogmatic; I cannot demand my way and concede nothing to others. Although I know that agreements are generally imperfect, I must do my share in forging agreements. When I am wrong I must concede it, and I must understand that my ideas may deserve modification just as much as the ideas of my fellow members. Still, controversy is often useful, and I must respect it and learn from it even though it may take a great deal of time.

Each new group, each new problem, is its own challenge. There is nothing in history or science that will predict the outcome. And that is the pleasure I take in the process, for I know that I can contribute, and to do so makes me feel more of a human being.

Individual Communication

As we've seen throughout this chapter, interaction is the heart of discussion. It influences problem-solving quality as well as members' satisfaction and commitment to group decisions. But what is good participation? What determines whether interaction is effective or ineffective? The bases of effective participation are knowledge of group processes and awareness of options for personal communication. The first requirement for effective participation (knowledge of group processes) is met by experience in group activities and by study of how groups work. This chapter should also introduce you to much of the knowledge necessary for effective participation in problem-solving groups.

The second requirement (awareness of options for personal communication) is met by learning about your alternatives as a member or leader of task discussion. The possibilities for participation may be classified into four broad areas: task, procedural, climate, and egocentric.[32] We'll examine each kind of communication to see how it influences problem solving.

Task communication. Every discussion needs task communication to provide and evaluate information. Task communication is used to give and seek information, ideas, and opinions, to clarify and interpret comments that are initially ambiguous, to evaluate information, and to make sure evidence and reasoning are solid. Task communication focuses on the content of problem solving and aims to provide the group with a definition of the problem situation and sufficient information for decisions.

Procedural communication. Procedural communication is needed to keep problem solving efficient and organized. Procedural communication serves to maintain an agenda for problem solving, to coordinate ideas expressed by various members, to test for agreement on issues so the group can progress, and to keep records of deliberation. Procedural communication directs and orders discussion so that individuals' contributions are integrated into unified lines of thought.

Climate (relationship) communication. Through their communication, group members define their situation—the overall climate for their interaction. Effective climate communication serves to regulate participation so that all members have opportunities to participate and so that no member dominates, to stimulate interaction by emphasizing progress and by demonstrating enthusiasm for the group and its work, to acknowledge contributions so that members will continue to participate, to reconcile disagreements by keeping conflict constructive and by looking for legitimate compromises among positions, and to relieve tension by introducing humor or calling for breaks when interaction becomes strained. Effective climate communication builds a satisfying atmosphere that invites participation and commitment and that promotes in members a sense of community.

From the research we've noted throughout this book, and especially in this chapter, you might suspect there are some gender-related tendencies relevant to these different kinds of communication. If so, you'd be correct. Typically, the differences are summarized by saying that males tend to be more task focused and females tend to be more climate-, or relationship-, focused. Yet, this generalization needs an important qualification. It tends to be true of *mixed-sex* groups. So when a group consists of men and women, the likelihood is that men's talk will pertain more to the task itself and women's will be more focused on interpersonal relationships among members and group unity. However, when single-sex groups meet to solve problems, both men and women demonstrate both task and climate behaviors. Thus, it seems that when the sexes are together, differences in their styles are promoted. Perhaps what's most important to note here is that both women and men are able to contribute the range of constructive behaviors needed for task discussion, even though situations may make it more or less likely that they will demonstrate their full range.[33]

Symbolic Interaction in Groups

The fundamental nature of any group is established through members' communicative interactions. As they talk with each other, meanings arise and become shared within the group. Through communication, members create a social order, complete with rules that guide interaction. They define values that infuse deliberation and decision making. They establish identities for individual participants and the group as a collective. Communication in groups, then, is the process through which values and meanings arise and, in turn, are used to construct shared definitions of the group situation. Membership in a task group, like membership in any society, imposes certain responsibilities, notably the responsibility to acknowledge the impact of symbols on human attitudes and actions and to make communicative choices in accordance with that knowledge.

Egocentric communication. The fourth kind of communication does not enhance discussion, because it detracts from group morale and achievement. As the name suggests, egocentric communication is self-centered. It advances personal interests, rather than group concerns. The goals of egocentric communication are to block others by putting down their ideas or by degrading the group's work, to call attention to oneself by boasting of personal accomplishments, to gain special treatment by taking up group time to disclose personal problems and feelings, to dominate interaction, to socialize by joking or rambling extensively, to plead for special causes that are not in the group's best interest, and to withdraw from discussion and, thereby, deprive the group of ideas and perspective. Egocentric communication operates at the expense of the group. It interferes with productive, efficient interaction because it diminishes members' sense of a unified working team.

Effective problem solving results from combining the first three kinds of communication and avoiding the fourth. Task, procedural, and climate communication complement each other. They work together to make discussion productive, organized, and enjoyable. To be an effective participant you should master all three kinds of communication. Most of us seem naturally skilled in at least one of these. Some people have a talent for presenting and clarifying ideas; other people know how to impose order on discussion; still others have a knack for creating supportive interpersonal climates. Native ability in one or two areas is valuable, but it is not sufficient. To be ideally effective you should cultivate skill in all three types of communication so that you can contribute whatever kind is needed at a given time in discussion. To do this you must first understand and experiment with your alternatives for communication. The options for participation that we've considered here serve as a list of possibilities open to you as you interact with others to solve problems. Review this section to decide which communication skills you've already mastered and which ones need further development. Then, as you participate in groups, experiment a little, try to enlarge your range of communication competence. You will derive personal satisfaction from your abilities to contribute productively to problem solving. Further, you will gain the respect of others as they recognize your versatility in problem-solving communication.

ORGANIZING PROBLEM-SOLVING DISCUSSION

The final topic we will discuss in this chapter is organization of problem solving. One of the major causes of unproductive group work is poor organization. Group members and even leaders often do not understand the importance of organization and the ways to achieve it. This leads to inefficient interaction. To prepare yourself for effective participation in task discussion you should understand why organization is needed and how it affects the substance of problem solving.

Values of Organization

A primary value of organization is that it provides common procedures for problem solving. Individuals approach issues and solve problems in different ways. When several individuals form a group, they need a collective method of going about their business. To coordinate group discussion, members must designate procedural guidelines that allow individuals to align their actions in relation to those of other members. Organization is essential to coordinated group work.

Effective collective organization also increases the efficiency of group work. An agreed-upon approach to problem solving discourages tendencies to wander away from the topic or to deal prematurely with various issues in problem solving. A collective approach to problem solving encourages focused, productive discussion.

A third value of organization is its impact on the substance of problem solving. Organization and content are interrelated. The order in which issues are addressed and the focus of analysis influence members' interpretations of the problem and the options for resolving it. Well-organized discussion ensures careful definition of problems, comprehensive analysis, and informed evaluation of alternative solutions. On the other hand, poorly organized discussion may result in failure to apprehend the full dimensions of problems, superficial analysis, and haphazard selection of solutions. Either way, organization has impact on content. If you learn how to organize problem solving well, you enhance the substantive quality of discussions.

Organization, then, is clearly important to problem-solving discussion. We turn now to a method for organizing group deliberation, the standard agenda for problem solving.

Standard Agenda for Problem Solving

One of the most respected and most widely used methods of organizing problem solving is called the standard agenda. This method describes five sequential stages in careful, effective group problem solving.[34] As we examine these stages, notice how their order as well as their substance influences both the process and outcomes of problem solving.

Stage One: Define the problem. The first step in problem solving is for members to reach agreement on exactly what the problem is. Although this is clearly a logical start, most people do not naturally begin with it. Typically members assume they agree on what the problem is and that they all see it in the same way. Given what we've seen about individual interpretations and perceptions, this is obviously not a very prudent assumption.

Without instruction in how to organize problem solving, people tend to start by focusing on solutions. The opening comment in many discussions is something like, "Well, I think the answer is . . ." or "The way to solve this issue is. . . ." Premature focus on solutions ruins problem solving. Before a group can consider solutions, it must deal with a number of preliminary tasks. The first of these is reaching agreement on what the problem is. Through communicative interaction, members establish the meaning of their problem, its dimensions and significance. It is the communication in this initial stage that defines the basic problem-solving situation in which members will work.

Four criteria guide members as they formulate their problem. First, the problem should be limited to a manageable size. "How can America become energy efficient?" is an important question, but it's far too broad for productive discussion. A more limited question might be "What can be done to minimize energy use in dormitories?" A second criterion is that problems should be clearly phrased, so all members understand at the outset what the task is. "How can the college experience be made most meaningful?" is a question that cannot be answered because it contains unclear terms. Does "college experience" refer to academic, extracurricular, or housing issues? What does "meaningful" mean? Is an experience meaningful if people like it, learn from it, or what? How would a group determine the meaningfulness of college experiences? To engage in productive discussion, the terms in this question would need clarification. A third criterion for well-defined problems is minimum bias. Language of course is inherently value-laden, so it's impossible to define a problem in an absolutely neutral, unbiased way. Nonetheless, members should take care to minimize the bias in problem formulation. "How can the public be convinced of the superiority of solar energy?" is heavily biased because this question assumes solar power is superior and assumes the public should be convinced of this. "How can tuition be lowered to a reasonable level?" is biased because it assumes tuition should and can be lowered and it implies that current tuition costs are unreasonable. A final criterion for defining problems is openness. Problems should be phrased to leave open a wide range of possible solutions. "Are current curriculum requirements fair to students?" is a closed question because it allows only two answers: yes or no. "Should women be drafted?" is also closed. "Should the government support nuclear power or solar power?" is closed because it limits answers to two options out of many that might be considered. An open question on the latter topic would be, "To what extent, if any, should the government support alternative energy sources?" Open questions invite members to consider a range of alternatives and to look for creative ways of solving problems. Well-defined problems are limited, clear, minimally biased, and open.

Stage One is the most important step in the entire problem-solving process, because out of this interaction members construct initial interpretations of issues that will guide all subsequent phases of analysis and resolution. A problem can be defined in numerous ways, each of which leads to a distinct view of the issues involved and the appropriate stance of the group regarding those issues. Stage One establishes the foundation for problem solving. The rest of the process will be only as strong as the foundation beneath it.

In defining a problem, group members establish the substantive context for all that will follow. The way that a problem is defined influences members' attitudes and commitments, the issues that will be considered or ignored, and the kinds of solutions that will be examined and approved.

Stage Two: Analyze the problem. The second step in problem solving is to collect and analyze information needed to understand the problem. To do this, members break down the overall problem into a series of smaller issues, which they investigate through interviews, library research, observation, and information gathering. To determine the present status of the problem, a group must find out how extensive it is, what its symptoms are, who is affected, what policies currently exist relevant to the problem, and—if possible—what has caused the problem. To learn more about problems, groups should investigate their history: How long has a problem existed? Have there been previous attempts to solve it and, if so, why didn't they work? Has the problem changed in nature or importance over time? To lay groundwork for later talk about solutions, groups should check out how similar problems have been handled by other groups. If you're trying to solve the parking problem on your campus, for instance, it's a good idea to see how other universities meet their parking needs.

After researching the problem and its history, members meet to discuss findings, evaluate information, and decide what should be done next. Each member is responsible for presenting any information he or she has obtained and for listening critically to information provided by others. On the basis of thorough analysis of facts the group may refine the original definition of the problem or may decide there really is no serious problem and the group should disband. If the information that has been collected and analyzed confirms the existence of the problem, however, the group is ready to proceed to the next stage.

Stage Three: Establish limitations and criteria for solutions. The purpose of Stage Three is to establish a collective frame of reference to judge possible solutions to the problem. Discussion first focuses on limitations that constrain the group's efforts. Limitations may be legal, institutional, financial, moral, or persuasive.[35] Discussion of limitations helps groups avoid recommendations that are unrealistic or impractical.

Once limitations are clear, members establish criteria, which name requirements that any acceptable solution must meet. Primary sources of criteria are the group's goals, the information gathered in Stage Two, and the values endorsed by members of the group. Someone in the group should keep written records of limitations and criteria, so they can be used in the next stage of discussion.

It's easy to become impatient during Stage Three and to push for talk about solutions. However, without thorough work on limitations and criteria, solutions are likely to be superficial, impractical, or otherwise flawed. Discussion in Stage Three paves the way for informed, pragmatic deliberation over solutions.

Stage Four: Evaluate solutions. The goals of this stage are to generate alternative solutions and to test each against the limitations and criteria established previously. Members should not be satisfied until a wide range of solutions have been proposed and examined.

There are two major sources of solutions. First, review research and discussion. Suggestions may come from experts interviewed in Stage Two or from investigation of how others have dealt with similar problems. Investigation of the problem's history may expose previously tried solutions that could be modified to work effectively. A second source of solutions is brainstorming, which is a technique to encourage a free flow of ideas. Members volunteer solutions, even far-fetched ones. Each idea is written down, but no criticism is offered until all members are through generating solutions. Then the group resumes serious deliberation to pare down the list to only the useful ideas. Brainstorming is not always advisable, because it requires valuable group time and can result in a number of unrealistic proposals. However, it is useful in situations where members are temporarily blocked and need creative stimulation.[36]

Once a number of solutions have been suggested, members must evaluate them. To do this, each alternative is measured against the preestablished limitations and criteria. Sometimes one solution emerges clearly as the best, because it meets all limitations and criteria or comes far closer than any other solution. At other times, the choice is less clearcut. No single solution may meet all requirements, so members patch together the best parts of several solutions.

There are a number of ways that members may reach their final decision of which solution to advocate. Ideally, the decision is reached through consensus, which occurs when all members talk through ideas long enough to reach a unanimous agreement on which one they collectively support. Consensus, however, is not always possible. Sometimes differences among members are sufficient to make agreement impossible. Sometimes there is simply not enough time to work through all differences until a common agreement is forged. So, methods other than consensus are sometimes appropriate during this stage. In a separate essay I analyzed the relative values of voting and negotiation arbitration as alternative methods of reaching group decisions. I defined the conditions under which each method is appropriate as well as the advantages and disadvantages associated with each of the three.[37] The decision stage of problem solving is complete when members agree on a solution, through whatever method they use, that meets their criteria, is within their limitations, and that they can collectively support.

Stage Five: Implement and Monitor the Solution. The last stage of problem solving determines how a solution will be carried out and how its effectiveness will be measured. To make sure a solution is well implemented, members need to spell out procedures such as who is responsible for implementation (the group or some other person or group), when and how implementation should be achieved, and what special resources will be needed for effective implementation (money, personnel, media coverage, etc.). Many groups have failed because they concluded their work with a statement such as "We think X is the best solution and recommend that it be implemented as soon as possible." Such a conclusion is a copout, because it undermines all of the investments made in problem solving. After working through all stages of standard agenda a group is familiar with a problem and is in a good position to specify exactly how a solution should be enacted.

Problem-solving groups have one last responsibility: to specify how the solution will be monitored. Monitoring provisions are methods to measure the effectiveness of a solution once it is implemented. For instance, a group may recommend a poll to measure satisfaction with a solution three months after implementation or a count of how many people use a proposed new system. Too often solutions are implemented and then forgotten until new problems arise. Monitoring is like preventive health care; it builds into the system periodic checks on a solution's effectiveness. Minor "bugs" can be worked out before they grow into major problems.

Standard agenda is a widely recommended method of problem solving. Following the five stages of agenda encourages thorough, productive discussion of issues. As members work through agenda, they supply the content of problem solving. At every stage members interact to establish the meaning of their work by creating a symbolic context that suggests the appropriate values and attitudes for members and that defines the issues of discussion. Understanding standard agenda helps members organize group discussion and highlights the impact of organization on content.

SUMMARY

Since the early 1900s group discussion has become increasingly popular as a method of resolving problems and deciding policies. It's likely that you will participate in a variety of task discussions during your lifetime, so you should learn how to operate effectively in groups.

In this chapter we've examined a variety of influences on group problem solving, including factors such as group size, participation norms, cohesion, power structure, and seating patterns. Each of these is important because it influences how members define a group situation; in turn, definitions of a situation guide members' communication in groups. The foundation of group work is communication. This is the single most powerful influence on group processes and outcomes. Through their communication, members define themselves, each other, the group situation and problem, and the overall climate in which discussion occurs. Members' interaction establishes meanings for all group activities and for members' actions within groups. The more conscious you are of the relations between communication and group process, the more effectively you can make communicative choices that, in turn, enhance the effectiveness of groups in which you participate.

A major theme of this chapter is that group discussion is a cooperative, collective activity. It involves individuals acting in relation to one another. As you act, you take others into account; you acknowledge their perspectives and construct your own communication in ways designed to reflect your awareness of their views and values. Each member makes individual contributions while keeping others in mind. Through such rhetorically sensitive interaction members transform themselves from a disparate collection of individuals into a unified, coordinated task-team engaged in concerted problem solving. When this happens, group discussion can be an extremely exciting and empowering kind of communication through which individuals work together to exercise real impact on their worlds.

REFERENCES

[1]Currently over 137 federal grant programs require citizen participation as part of the grant process. See Federal Regional Council, Citizen Participation (Washington: Community Services Administration, 1978).

[2]Philip B. Coulter and W.H. Stewart, "The Status of Citizen Participation in Formulating Public Policy." In E.M. McMahon (Ed.), *Public Action and Social Change*. University, AL: Dept. of Communication, 1979, pp. 29-39.

[3]The Westinghouse Studies are summarized in Elton Mayo, *Human Problems of an Industrial Civilization*. New York: Viking, 1933, pp. 74-94.

[4]Keith Davis, *Human Relations at Work*. New York: McGraw- Hill, 1967.

[5]Mayo.

[6]F.J. Roethlisberger and W.J. Dickson, *Management and the Worker*. Cambridge, MA: Harvard University Press, 1943.

[7]N. C. Morce and E. Reimer, "The Experimental Change of a Major Organizational Variable," *Journal of Abnormal and Social Psychology, 52*, 1956, 120-129.

[8]Kurt Lewin, "Forces Behind Food Habits and Methods of Change," *Bulletin of the National Research Council, 108*, 1943, 35-65.

[9]Lewin; Morce and Reimer; Julia T. Wood, G. M. Phillips, and D. J. Pedersen, *Group Discussion: A Practical Guide to Participation and Leadership*. New York: Harper, 1986.

[10]*Time*, January 28, 1980, p. 65.

[11]M. E. Shaw, "A Comparison of Individuals and Small Groups in the Rational Solution of Complex Problems," *American Journal of Psychology, 44*, 1932, 491-504.

[12]D. C. Barnlund, "A Comparative Study of Individual, Majority and Group Judgment," *Journal of Abnormal and Social Psychology, 58*, 1959, 55-60; J. R. Cox and J. T. Wood, "The Effects of Consultation on Judges' Decision-Making." *Speech Teacher*, 1975, 118-126.

[13]Shaw.

[14]S. Schachter, "Deviation, Rejection, and Communication." *Journal of Abnormal and Social Psychology, 46*, 1951, 190-207.

[15]B.M. Bass and C. R. Wurster, "Effects of the Nature of the Problem on LGD Performance." *Journal of Applied Psychology, 37*, 1953, 96-99.

[16]I.L. Janis, *Victims of Groupthink.* Boston: Houghton Mifflin, 1977.

[17]B. Bate, *Communication and the Sexes.* New York: Harper, 1988, pp. 151-152.

[18]N. R. F. Maier, "Improving Decisions in an Organization." In Stewart Tubbs (Ed.), *A Systems Approach to Small Group Interaction.* Reading, MA: Addison-Wesley, 1978, pp. 293-304.

[19]L. L. Small, "Goodmeasure: Selling Corporations on Change." *Ms*, July 1980, pp. 53-55.

[20]C. A. Kiesler and S. B. Kiesler, *Conformity.* Reading, MA: Addison-Wesley, 1970.

[21]D. Cartwright, "The Nature of Group Cohesiveness." In D. Cartwright and A. Zander (Eds.), *Group Dynamics.* New York: Harper and Row, 1968, p. 105; Schachter.

[22]Wood, Phillips, and Pedersen, chapter 7.

[23]J. C. Pearson, *Gender and Communication.* Dubuque, IA: Wm. C. Brown, 1985, p. 317.

[24]H. H. Kelley, "Communication in Experimentally Created Hierarchies," *Human Relations, 4*, 1951, 39-56.

[25]Pearson, pp. 317-318.

[26]M. E. Shaw, "Communication Networks." In L. Berkowitz (Ed.), *Advances in Experimental Social Psychology, 1.* New York: Academic Press, 1964, pp. 111-147.

[27]R. P. Hart and D. M. Burks, "Rhetorical Sensitivity and Social Interaction," *Speech Monographs, 24*, 1972, 75-91; R. P. Hart, R. E. Carlson, and W. F. Eadie, "Attitudes Toward Communication and the Assessment of Rhetorical Sensitivity." *Communication Monographs, 47*, 1980, 1-22.

[28]Wood, Phillips, and Pedersen, pp. 69-72.

[29]Wood, Phillips, and Pedersen, pp. 15-16.

[30]J. T. Wood, "Constructive Conflict in Discussion: Learning to Manage Disagreements Effectively." In J. W. Pfeiffer and J. E. Jones (Eds.), *1977 Group Facilitators' Annual Handbook.* LaJolla, CA: University Associates, 1977, pp. 115-119.

[31]Wood, Phillips, and Pedersen, p. 130.

[32]D. Benne and P. Sheats, "Functional Roles of Group Members." *Journal of Social Issues, 4*, 1948, 41-49.

[33]J. E. Baird, "Sex Differences in Group Communication: A Review of Relevant Research." *The Quarterly Journal of Speech, 62*, 1976, 179-192; Pearson, p. 316.

[34]The standard agenda seems to have been first proposed as a method for group problem solving in J. H. McBurney and K. G. Hance, *Discussion and Human Affairs.* New York: Harper and Row, 1939.

[35]Wood, Phillips, and Pedersen, Chapter 11.

[36]Wood, Phillips, and Pedersen, Chapter 12.

[37]J. T. Wood, "Consensus and its Alternatives: A Comparative Analysis of Voting, Negotiation and Consensus as Methods of Group Decision-Making." In G. M. Phillips and J. T. Wood (Eds.), *Emergent Issues in Human Decision Making.* Carbondale, IL: Southern Illinois University Press, 1984.

CHAPTER 11

PLANNING PUBLIC DISCOURSE

To be "liberally educated" is to be personally and socially effective, and being able to interact purposively with other people through speaking and listening is a significant part of being "personally and socially effective."

(John F. Wilson and Carroll C. Arnold)

A Symbolic Interactionist Perspective on Public Discourse

Purposes of Public Discourse

    All communication is persuasive
    Listeners' purposes must be considered

Selecting and Limiting Topics

    Selecting topics

        The speaker
        The listeners
        The situation

    Limiting topics

Analyzing Listeners

    Rhetorical analysis: Bases of identification

        Listeners' self-definitions
        Listeners' definitions of topics
        Listeners' definitions of their relationship with topics

    General methods of audience analysis

        Demographic analysis
        Motivational analysis

Throughout this book we've seen that communication is a primary means through which individuals develop personally and build relationships with others. Nowhere are these functions of communication more pronounced than in public discourse. Here one person assumes primary responsibility for creating relationships with others through human communication. This and the following chapter focus on public discourse-communication that is planned, developed, and presented by one person and in which a group of listeners participate. Before we deal with specific aspects of preparation for speaking, however, we need to establish our perspective on public discourse.

A SYMBOLIC INTERACTIONIST PERSPECTIVE ON PUBLIC DISCOURSE

Perhaps you already have ideas about public discourse. If you're like many people, you may regard it as stilted, formal—almost a performance activity. This is a common misconception. The kind of public speaking appropriate in contemporary society is neither stilted nor formal, and it certainly shouldn't resemble a performance. Rather, public discourse should be unpretentious interaction. One scholar defines public speaking as "enlarged conversation."[1] This is a good, basic definition, because it reminds us that effective speeches are similar to effective kinds of communication with family, colleagues, and friends. Like these other kinds of communication, public discourse requires situational awareness, sensitivity to interactions among language, thought, and behavior, and—of course—a keen appreciation of others' perspectives. These are foundations of public speaking just as much as they are foundations of self-communication or interpersonal or group communication. In basic nature, then, public speaking is more like other kinds of communication than it is different from them.

Another frequently held misconception is that public discourse is an activity reserved for only a few people, such as politicians, lecturers, spokespersons, and ceremonial directors. This may have been true once, but it is no longer the case. Today public speaking is widely practiced by individuals in professional, civic, and social settings. Professors Wilson and Arnold emphasize this when they point out "public speaking is with us now more than ever. . . . People increasingly are required to 'take a few minutes to report: to 'sell ideas,' to 'raise the problem,' to 'speak to this point,' and to engage large and small audiences in countless other *public* ways."[2] Throughout your life you will have opportunities to speak in public. To the extent you do so effectively, you will enhance your professional prestige and mobility, and you will help shape civic and social issues through your ability to influence others' opinions. Public discourse is vital, dynamic communication in which each of us will engage during our lives.

But what is the nature of public speaking? What is involved in extended public communication? At one time public speaking was conceived as something speakers did to listeners. Listeners were viewed as persons who absorbed and reacted to what speakers did. From this orientation, effectiveness in speaking was almost entirely the responsibility of speakers. This view led to guidelines that speakers were advised to follow. Presumably, a speaker could virtually ensure success by following "recipes" for organization, use of evidence, and so forth. Many contemporary communication scholars realize this is a simplistic and distorted view of what public speaking is, and they have developed a more realistic, interactive understanding of the process.

From a symbolic interactionist perspective, public discourse is a process of creating identifications among speakers, listeners, and topics through the language that links them. Speeches, like any other communication, are made up of symbols which, by definition, require interpretation by others—those who listen. Effective speeches encourage listeners to identify their own experiences, values, attitudes, and perceptions with the symbols employed by the speaker. A speaker's goal, then, is to invite this kind of identification.

The primary means by which identification is made possible is the symbols through which listeners and speakers interact. Language allows us to organize and express our ideas in ways that others can understand in terms of their own perspectives. Thus, it is through language that people are linked, that they can participate jointly in a communicative, human experience. In designing a speech you aim to portray ideas vividly and persuasively. You make careful choices regarding organization, content, and language, knowing that these choices will influence listeners' perceptions of your ideas and you personally. No less than an artist sculpting a statue, you engage in a creative process, one in which you ask listeners to participate fully and freely.

In public speaking listeners and speakers engage in sustained interaction. Because your objective in speaking is to influence listeners, nothing short of their complete participation will allow you to achieve your goals. If listeners are to be moved by your presentation, they must involve themselves with it. Hence, one of your priorities is to understand your listeners' perspectives. You take the role of your listeners to discern how they see themselves, your topic, and you. From their perspective (which may differ from your own), ask what makes your topic interesting, important, compelling of *their* thought and attention. Why should it matter to listeners? How does it affect them and their lives? What will they find persuasive? The more familiar you are with your listeners, the more skillfully you can adopt their perspectives and design a speech that incorporates their values and views. Even when you don't know listeners well, you can assume the perspective of the generalized other to gain considerable insight into the views of people in general. Sometimes it is difficult to step outside of your own perspective and into that of others. This is particularly true with public speaking, because speakers generally speak on issues about which they have strong personal feelings. Nonetheless, if you wish to have impact on others, you must assume responsibility for discerning and adapting to the perspectives they hold. To the extent you do this, you make it possible for listeners to identify themselves with your ideas.

When you speak publicly you attempt to achieve a goal through symbolic interaction with others. Your success depends largely on your ability to select and organize symbols in ways that invite listeners to interact with your ideas and to construct meanings similar to those you hold. When this happens, a speaker has effectively built bridges between his or her phenomenal world and those of listeners. Achieving this is a goal worthy of the time, thought, and effort required to plan, develop, and present a public speech.

Now that we've established an overall perspective on public discourse, we can consider more specific issues that arise when you plan a speech. Planning is the first stage in public speaking. It is an extended process in which a speaker thinks seriously about ideas to be presented and ways of expressing them most effectively to particular listeners. In the pages that follow we'll turn first to examination of the purposes involved in public speaking. Next we'll consider how to select and limit topics effectively. Finally we'll discuss what is perhaps the single most important aspect of planning: analysis of the listeners for whom a speech is intended. To organize our thoughts, each of these areas will be explored separately. In actuality, however, public discourse is a dynamic, systemic process, so these three aspects of planning interact— each constantly affects the others. These interrelations should become clear as we examine the issues involved in planning public communication.

PURPOSES OF PUBLIC COMMUNICATION

Traditionally public discourse has been classified according to three distinct purposes: to inform, to persuade, and to entertain.[3] This trichotomy is of doubtful value for two reasons. First, it suggests rigid distinctions among informing, persuading, and entertaining. Second, it focuses on only the purposes of the person presenting a message.

All Communication Is Persuasive

We can't draw absolute distinctions among informing, persuading, and entertaining. Given our understandings of how people interact with symbols, such distinctions are inaccurate. No message can be purely informative. Information, facts, ideas themselves are inevitably persuasive. A new idea—information we had not previously known—stimulates us to think in new ways, to understand or believe something we did not formerly believe, or to cease believing in something we had held to before interacting with the new ideas. But what of messages labeled "entertainment"? Are these to be considered persuasive as well? Again, from a symbolic interactionist perspective, what is entertaining can also clearly be persuasive. Think of Jonathan Swift's classic satire, "A Modest Proposal." Amusing though that essay is, it is also a powerful piece of persuasion, perhaps especially so because the persuasive arguments are cloaked within witty prose. The popular comic strip Doonesbury is amusing, to be sure; nonetheless it invariably conveys persuasive messages about political and social issues. Even the purely comedic speech is a form of persuasion, since jokes are used to expose our human foibles or to let us recognize problems and issues that are too threatening for us to deal with in a straightforward manner. Because symbols are inherently valuative, they always carry persuasive force. The intent and impact of persuasiveness may vary, but where there are symbols there will be persuasion.

We realize, then, that the general purpose of communication (private as well as public) is persuasion. In addition, we may identify three persuasive foci that may, separately or in combination, underlie a message:

to alter listeners' perceptions of some phenomenon (e.g., Marijuana is not as dangerous as alcohol);

to alter how listeners perceive their relationship with some phenomenon (e.g., Your decision to donate blood might one day save your life or that of a loved one, since your donation entitles you to transfusions);

to persuade listeners toward certain perceptions of the speaker (e.g., I have your interests in mind, I am an expert on this topic, I can be trusted).

Persuasion attempts to alter the ways people perceive phenomena surrounding them, themselves, or their speaker. These persuasive possibilities will be elaborated in Chapter 12 as we discuss ways to develop public messages.

Listeners' Purposes Must Be Considered

A second problem with classifying speaking purposes is that it is based solely on the perspective of the individual who is speaking. Listeners may or may not have similar purposes. All too often discussions of public speaking focus exclusively on speakers' purposes, as if listeners' purposes either do not exist or are unimportant. The implication of this view is that a speaker "does something to an audience,"[4] which is considered essentially passive and amenable to the speaker's intentions. As we've seen throughout this book, it's inaccurate to regard listening as a minor part of communication; listening is as integral to communication as speaking. Further, communicators simultaneously listen and send messages. Although we will use the terms "speaker" and "listener" for clarity in these chapters on public discourse, remember that both roles are really dual, involving both initiating and responding to communication. Because listening is central to effective communication, the person planning a speech should devote considerable thought to listeners' purposes.

Why do people listen? What purposes guide their participation in communicative interactions? In an early study Ralph Nichols, a professor of communication whose special interest is listening, reported 14 factors that influence listening. Interest, curiosity, and significance were among the most important reasons.[5] The person preparing for public communication may recognize listeners' purposes by planning to arouse their interest and curiosity and by selecting topics that listeners will consider significant. To expand Nichols' general observations Professors Wilson and Arnold identify nine factors that increase listeners' readiness to attend to a message:[6]

1. activity, physical or verbal
2. proximity in time or space to listeners
3. realism and vividness from physical or verbal action
4. familiarity and its opposite, novelty
5. conflict and suspense-drama
6. vitality—direct concern with listeners' lives
7. specificity in detail and description
8. intensity of language and action
9. humor, including exaggeration, irony, and the unexpected

While this list certainly is not exhaustive, it should assist you in thinking about the kinds of content that you will need to plan and develop in order to meet your listeners' purposes. Effectiveness is achieved when speakers' and listeners' purposes work in concert: As you recognize listeners' purposes, they recognize yours.

To summarize this section, we may say that public communication presupposes purpose. We recognize the general persuasive force inherent in all symbolic interactions and the more specific persuasive purposes of altering the ways in which people perceive phenomena, themselves, or a speaker. Finally, we realize that preparation for public communication demands attention to listeners' purposes—factors which influence their involvement in communicative situations. Public communication, like its less formal relatives, involves interaction among people, all of whom have purposes.

SELECTING AND LIMITING TOPICS

Selecting topics

Topics for public communication may be assigned or may be selected by speakers. Often a general subject is suggested for a speaker by a program chair, a boss, or an individual inviting a speaker. In such cases the speaker retains considerable leeway in deciding how to develop a particular message within the specified area. In classroom situations students are usually encouraged to select their own topics, with few limitations imposed by the instructor. Whether a topic or topic area is designated or self-selected, basic considerations should guide an individual's selection of content. These considerations pertain to the speaker, the listeners, and the situation in which the communication will take place.

The speaker. To develop an effective message, your first concern must be yourself. A primary guideline is to choose a subject in which you have interest and knowledge or experience. Adherence to this advice will assist you in several ways. First, you will be enthusiastic when you talk about something that matters to you, and enthusiasm is contagious: Listeners will sense and respond to your interest. Second, being acquainted with a subject gives you a headstart in developing your message. Because you already have a general knowledge of the area, you know its various aspects and some of the resources for additional information. You need not devote large amounts of time to basic background research. Instead, you begin with a focused interest.

The listeners. Because speaking—when effective—builds a relationship between communicators, a topic must be selected and developed with attention to listeners' interests, knowledge, and experiences. People will not pay attention to a message that seems irrelevant to them. In selecting a topic, then, speakers should either choose one which has immediate and recognized importance to listeners or establish the topic's relevance to listeners. One of my students faced this when he chose a subject in which he knew listeners had no immediate interest, so his initial task was to convince his listeners they should attend to his ideas. This is how he opened his speech:

> Today I'm going to talk about basketball. Since I am on the basketball team you probably aren't surprised by my interest in this topic. However, you may be surprised by your own interests in basketball. In the next few minutes I will show you that basketball is important to every one of us, whether we are players, fans, or just students. It's important because the basketball team generates the largest amount of alumni contributions. And alumni contributions are used to support all students' interests—the campus newspaper, the student union and academic scholarships which many of you need to attend this school.

Within the first minute of his presentation this speaker gave his listeners persuasive reasons to listen.

In addition to relating content to listeners' interests, messages must adapt to listeners' expectations of the speaker. People who are particularly known as experts in certain areas are expected to speak accordingly.[7] Our expectations would be violated if we attended a presentation by Ralph Nader in which he discussed natural childbirth. Similarly, we would feel misled and perhaps angry if we traveled to a program featuring former Secretary of State Henry Kissinger and he presented his views on real estate investments. Because Nader and Kissinger are recognized for their expertise in, respectively, consumer rights and international diplomacy, they are expected to speak on these topics. Most of us do not have reputations which so seriously constrain our selection of speaking topics. Still, listeners will have some expectations about you as a speaker. They will expect any speaker to be knowledgeable about his or her topic. This means you should alert listeners to your expertise, your knowledge, if they are not already aware of it. A former student began a speech on reforming the penal system by demonstrating his knowledge of the topic:

> I want to convince you of the need to improve rehabilitation programs in our state's prisons. To make this point I could quote various government reports and statistics. But I won't do that. Instead, I'm going to give you a detailed description of the inadequate rehabilitation programs that currently exist in our state's prisons. This will be a very personal description, because I just completed a three-year sentence myself.

That opening established the speaker' qualifications and gained listeners' rapt attention. Although listeners sometimes assume a speaker's credibility on the basis of reputation, the general rule is that speakers should demonstrate their expertise in their topic areas.

The situation. Decisions about what to communicate are influenced by situational factors, many of which we discussed in Chapter 3. Occasionally the selection of a topic is commanded by the nature of the situation. For instance, someone invited to speak on a program commemorating a university's founding would surely design a presentation that focused on the importance of higher education and the strong role played by the particular university being honored. Testimonials, funerals, and nominating sessions are additional examples of situations that literally define the appropriate content of communication.

More often, situational factors suggest guidelines for topics and how to manage topics. Situations usually encourage a *mood* which influences listeners' expectations and, therefore, the speaker's decisions regarding topic selection. A person speaking at a political rally will be expected to offer a vital, partisan, enthusiastic message in keeping with the mood of that situation. Someone giving an address in a very formal ceremony, by contrast, will be expected to present measured, restrained remarks consistent with the mood of a ceremonial situation. The general advice is well summarized by Professor Bradley: "If the subject of the speech is inconsistent with the mood of the occasion, the listeners will have a difficult time shifting their mood to coincide with that of the speech."[8]

Another important situational factor is *time limitation*. Time limits should always be honored by speakers. Listeners resent speakers who exceed the specified time and they tend to judge such speakers as inconsiderate, unprepared, or both. Speakers need to know how much time is allowed, because this affects what can wisely be said. For instance, we can discuss a much broader topic in 30 minutes than we can in five. We plan coverage with attention to the amount of time allowed.

The *overall program* is a situational consideration of importance in planning communication.[9] Understanding who else will speak and what topics will be covered is important information. Speakers may include references to subjects and speakers who come before and after their own presentations. If a program consists of several serious speeches, speakers should anticipate the possibility of listeners' fatigue. Additional interest or drama can then be planned for the speaker's presentation so that listeners' attention will be held. From awareness of the overall program a speaker may also gain ideas for the content of a message.

A final situational consideration is the *physical setting* for communication. Large rooms call for more volume and animation than do small rooms; speeches given outside must be even more vital. Some settings include or allow for special equipment such as a blackboard, a stand for visual aids, or a screen and an overhead projector. If not, the speech must be planned so no visual aids are required for clarity and interest. How and where the listeners are situated is important. If they will be distant from the speaker's position, the speaker will need to plan ways of bridging that psychological distance. Comfortable seating may encourage listeners to relax (particularly if the speech follows a large meal), so the speaker will need to plan communication that keeps listeners alert and interested. By contrast, stiff chairs may make listeners restless, so a wise speaker might recognize this constraint and plan abbreviated remarks.

In summary, communication should be planned with attention to the situational factors of mood, time, program, and physical setting. Each of these has bearing upon the selection of a topic that will encourage listeners' involvement.

Limiting topics

We've seen that considerations of speakers, listeners, and situations influence the selection of subjects for public communication. These same factors assist speakers in limiting a topic in ways that are appropriate. Once a speaker has chosen a general topic, it is still necessary to limit or narrow the material to be covered. No one can, for instance, deal successfully with a topic so broad as religion, government, or higher education. Speakers must narrow their topics by choosing a particular focus within the larger subject area. This is achieved by analyzing self, listeners, and situation to determine what will be most interesting, expected, feasible, and appropriate. Consider the following example of how one student limited the broad topic of euthanasia to manageable size:

Self-
Considerations:

1. As a nursing student and a volunteer in the hospice am well informed about terminal illness and how it can affect patients and families.
2. I know several patients and doctors whom I could interview to get expert opinions supporting legalized euthanasia.

Listener
Considerations:

1. Most listeners will not be immediately concerned with a topic about death. I'll need to establish relevance.
2. Since my listeners are not especially religious, I need not focus on religious objections to legalizing euthanasia.
3. To demonstrate my knowledge of the topic to listeners I should explain my major and volunteer experience.
4. In previous speeches these listeners have shown their belief in freedom of choice for people, so they might be more interested in voluntary than involuntary euthanasia.

Situational
Considerations:

1. In keeping with my topic, I want to establish a mood that is serious, but not somber or sad.
2. I have only ten minutes, so I can deal effectively with only one form of euthanasia: voluntary-active, voluntary-passive, involuntary active, or involuntary-passive.
3. People may be tired, since I'm speaking at the very end of the period.
4. Since the speech before mine is about first amendment freedoms, I could open by saying I'm interested in another type of freedom—choice in how one dies.
5. A stand will be available for aids.

In this example the speaker was able to use selection factors to limit her topic in several ways. Time limitations constrained her to deal with only one form of euthanasia, and audience interest suggested the most appropriate type would be voluntary. The speaker also learned she need not devote speaking time to religious arguments, so she could focus on other issues that would be more important to her particular listeners. Additional information gained in this review could be used later in developing the message. In a similar manner, most broad topics can be limited by considering carefully the speaker, the listeners, and the situation.

At this stage in planning, your goal should be to formulate as specific a statement of purpose as possible. Your statement of purpose should specify what your persuasive goal is. The speaker in our last example formulated this statement of purpose:

I want to persuade my listeners that individuals should have the freedom to end their own lives if they suffer from a terminal illness. (I am not attempting to convince them to personally choose euthanasia, only to support it as a freedom of choice for people in general. I will know I have achieved my purpose if two-thirds of the listeners will sign a letter I have written to our state legislators.)

Notice this statement of purpose indicates the specific topic the speaker will present, the speaker's stand on the topic, and a measure of persuasive effectiveness. All three elements are necessary to a specific statement of purpose. The purpose statement is primarily for the speaker's use. It helps a speaker focus thought and research as he or she plans communication. Keep in mind, however, that you may adjust this purpose as you discover additional information about your listeners and your topic. Such adaptations are to be expected throughout the planning and development of public communication.

Once a topic has been selected and limited, a speaker engages in the last stage of planning: analysis of listeners. As you have probably realized by now, each of these planning areas is intricately related to the others. In thinking about selecting and limiting the topic, for instance, we have already touched upon issues related to listeners. In your own planning you will discover that your purpose, your topic, and your listeners constantly interact in ways that affect each other.

ANALYZING LISTENERS

The fool persuades me with his reasons, the wise man with my own.

This idea is as insightful today as it was thousands of years ago when an ancient Greek rhetorician is said to have used it in a lecture to his students. The statement suggests effective persuasion is always mindful of listeners' attitudes, values, and concerns. Communication must be adapted to listeners' phenomenal worlds if it is to affect them. In this section we will examine available methods for analyzing and adapting communication to listeners. We first discuss rhetorical analysis as the overall process of analyzing listeners. Then we consider two more general kinds of audience analysis which can assist speakers in achieving the broad goals of rhetorical analysis.

Rhetorical Analysis: Bases of Identification

You persuade a man only insofar as you can talk his language by speech, gesture, tonality, order image, idea, identifying your ways with his.[10]

This advice from Kenneth Burke, a philosopher-critic of language and human conduct, is fundamental for anyone wishing to persuade others to some action or attitude. Like many other scholars of human communication, Burke realizes effective persuasion depends upon establishing relationships or identifications: identifications between speakers and listeners, listeners and topics, speakers and topics, and communication and situations. To be effective, persuasive communication must bring about precisely these sorts of identifications. Chapter 12 gives detailed attention to means of developing these identifications through organization and evidence. In the present discussion, however, we are concerned with a preliminary question: How does a speaker discover the bases of identification? A clue is offered by Faules and Alexander, who advise that "a communicator who wishes to appeal to certain motives must first discover the defining process of the other person" [11] To do this a speaker analyzes the ways in which listeners define themselves, the selected topic, and their relationship with that topic.

Listeners' self-definitions. As you recall from our discussion of self-development, individuals carve identities for themselves. For each of us our selfhood, as we individually define it, is our most prized creation. Consequently, we want our chosen identities confirmed. We respond favorably to communication that confirms our self-definitions and, by contrast, we respond negatively to communication which ignores or denies those definitions. Speakers must be concerned with how listeners define themselves, so that the developed message can honor these definitions.

While no speaker can hope to understand the intricate details of others' self-definitions, speakers can gain some insight through careful thought about listeners. As we noted in earlier chapters, one primary basis of self-identity is reference groups. Speakers gain valuable information by discovering listeners' reference groups.[12] Are they members of a profession? Do they identify themselves with regional, political, religious, or social organizations? In thinking about listeners' reference groups, speakers will also want to consider what people's opinions will be valued by listeners: What opinion sources do they respect? What opinion sources do they reject? Third, reference groups may provide insight into listeners' value structures.[13] What inferences may be drawn from listeners' associations? Do listeners' activities, lifestyles, and allegiances suggest priorities in values? While these questions surely do not exhaust the pertinent lines of inquiry, they do suggest the kinds of issues that help a speaker understand how listeners define themselves. A brief example should highlight the importance of this phase of analysis. One of my students gave a speech on private enterprise in which she relied almost exclusively on articles and broadcasts by William F. Buckley. The listeners, students at a liberal university, were not persuaded by the speech. In fact, the listeners were notably unimpressed. In frustration, the speaker told us she had been quite effective when she gave the same speech to the Civitan Club in her hometown the previous week. A bit of questioning revealed this information: The speaker's hometown was rural and politically conservative, whereas class members were not generally from rural backgrounds and were decidedly liberal in political leanings; members of the Civitan Club were middle-aged citizens with vested interests in economic issues, while class members were 18 to 24 years old, with little personal awareness of national economic issues. Quite predictably William Buckley commands respect from the first audience but would be distinctly unpersuasive to the second. The class audience did not define themselves in a manner that identified them with Mr. Buckley or even with the issue of private enterprise. The speaker had not recognized and adapted to her different listeners' self-definitions. As a result the speech was ineffective.

Listeners' definitions of topics. To prepare persuasive messages we need more than an understanding of listeners' self-definitions. We also need to know how they define the specific topic we plan to present. Speakers and listeners define topics differently, because they have differing phenomenal worlds. Speakers must discover listeners' definitions in order to develop communication with which listeners can identify. To discover how listeners define a topic a speaker must first determine listeners' knowledge of the topic: Are they well or poorly informed? What aspects of the topic do they recognize? Are they aware of information and arguments on both sides of the topic or are they aware of only one side? Speakers should also analyze the sources of how listeners define topics: What newspapers, magazines, and broadcasts are favored by these listeners? How have the favored sources treated the topic? Are listeners likely to have had personal experiences with the issues in the message? Have listeners defined the topic on the basis of peer values and attitudes or have they personally read about, thought about, or had involvement with the topic? Questions of this type allow a speaker to anticipate listeners' definitions of the topic. This, in turn, allows a speaker to develop a message that identifies with and speaks to listeners' views of the topic.

Listeners' definitions of their relationship with topics. The final task in analyzing listeners is to determine how they define themselves in relation to a particular topic. To develop a persuasive message we must understand how our concerns can be identified with those of our listeners. Any topic has a wide range of aspects and implications, but only some of those can be related to a particular group of listeners. One of a speaker's most important tasks is to discover which of a topic's many angles and ramifications can be made meaningful to the particular people for whom the discourse is intended. For instance, consider the campaign to persuade people to adhere to a 55-mile-per-hour speed limit. Several different strategies were designed to create identifications between different groups of people and the issue. For some individuals "STAY ALIVE AT 55" was effective in appealing to concern for safety. Other people, who did not perceive a strong relationship between the speed limit and their safety, were persuaded by "SAVE GAS AT 55," an appeal which identified with an economic motive. Still other people were persuaded by the warning that the speed limit would be strictly enforced and by the concomitant increase in speeding tickets, an appeal designed to identify with entirely different motivations. No single appeal could have created identifications with the diversity of people whose cooperation was needed. In your own persuasive communication, your goal is to find the way or ways in which you can create identifications between your listeners and your topic.

To discern how listeners define their relationship with your topic, you must first determine the topic's salience to listeners: How important do listeners regard this issue within their overall schema of priorities? Is the topic perceived as of central or peripheral importance? Under what conditions and/or for what reasons would the topic become more salient to listeners? Second, you want to discover the intensity of listeners' positions on your topic: Do listeners initially agree or disagree with your position, or are they neutral? How intense are their positions (very strongly agree, agree somewhat, etc.)? Third, you need to locate probable implications of this topic for your listeners: How does, will, or could this issue affect listeners personally? Which parts of the topic are most closely related to listeners' motives, values, and interests? How would listeners benefit by endorsing your ideas or, by contrast, how would they be harmed by not endorsing your ideas? Finally, you want to discern existing and possible identifications between listeners and the topic.[14] What individuals and organizations respected by listeners share your position? What values of listeners are met by the position you advocate? Which interests of listeners are represented by the topic and your position on it?

Questions of the type raised here assist a speaker in discovering the bases for identifications among self, listeners, and topic. Once identified, these bases of identification can become the foundation of effective public communication.

It's easier to understand the importance of rhetorical analysis than to conduct it. Discovering listeners' bases of identification is a difficult task, especially since speakers often have little opportunity for direct interaction with their listeners. This difficulty is compounded by the fact that there are many listeners who have multiple perspectives. How does a speaker discover and adapt to the varied perspectives of listeners with whom it is impractical to talk directly prior to a speech?

Of necessity, a speaker must make some generalizations about listeners. It's possible to analyze listeners as a group if you focus on what they have in common. What do they share in terms of knowledge, experience, environment, concerns, hopes, ideas, attitudes, and values? Despite important individual differences, listeners will have many commonalities, including those that have brought them together at one time and place to hear your speech. As a speaker you want to build from these commonalities in planning your communication.

To carry out the overall process of rhetorical analysis, speakers often employ methods of general audience analysis that are particularly helpful in situations where speakers and listeners have little or no direct interaction prior to a speech. We now consider these general methods of audience analysis.

General Methods of Audience Analysis

There are two ways to conduct a general analysis of listeners. One method—demographic analysis—focuses on identifying general characteristics of your listeners, while the second method—motivational analysis—stresses discovering the motivations of listeners relevant to your topic.

Demographic analysis. This method is an examination of the general features of a group of people. Demographic characteristics include age, sex, religion, cultural background, occupation, race, political preferences, socioeconomic level, geographic identification, family size, and educational level.[15] Demographic information is most frequently gathered by opinion pollsters (How does the public feel about Senator Edward Kennedy's running for President? How many people are in favor of tax reform?) and by advertising strategists (What kinds of people could be interested in particular products?). Demographic information helps speakers identify similarities among listeners. Knowledge of listeners' educational level, for instance, informs a speaker about the appropriate kinds of language for a message. Knowledge of age informs a speaker about major events and personalities with which listeners are likely to be familiar. Use of demographic information to draw inferences may also assist the speaker. in some cases, for example, a speaker may infer listeners' attitudes on specific topics by assessing the values esteemed by the society in which listeners participate.[16] Inferences such as these are necessarily probabilistic; that is, they are generalizations which may or may not apply to particular listeners. In planning communication, demographic analysis provides only very general information about listeners.

Motivational analysis. This second method of thinking about listeners involves examination of the broad motivations of humans. Perhaps the best known theory of human motivation is the hierarchy of needs, proposed by Abraham Maslow, a contemporary psychologist. According to Maslow all people have five kinds of needs, which are arranged in a hierarchy. The most basic needs or motives must be satisfied before we are able to attend to more abstract needs and motives. At the most basic level, all humans have physiological needs for food, water, air, sex, rest, and exercise. A second level of human need is security and safety, from danger, threat, and deprivation. The third level of need, belonging, involves social interactions from which we gain feelings of acceptance and affection. On the fourth level, humans have motives for esteem and ego satisfaction, which are met by achieving respect of self and others and by senses of competence and status. Fifth, humans have needs to self-actualize by realizing their unique potentialities in creative and personal ways.[17]

Thinking about these general motivations identified by Maslow can be helpful when you're planning public discourse. You might ask, for instance, what needs and values are salient to your listeners and how what you have to say can relate to those. Thinking about the relationship between your topic and your listeners' motives may also cue you into which aspects of your topic might be most directly pertinent to the needs and motives your listeners are likely to feel. Inquiry into human motivation is a useful way of thinking about broad goals that underlie human values and actions. Thus, it provides a speaker with basic insights into listeners. On the basis of motivational analysis, a speaker moves on to ask more complex questions about listeners:

> What connections can be defined between your topic and the human motives of your listeners? To which level(s) of human motivation can you appeal in your discourse?
>
> How can your speech invite listeners to identify their own motives with what you advocate? How can the connections you see between your ideas and listeners' motives be made clear and persuasive to them?
>
> How can you design your message so that it guides listeners to define what you advocate as a meaningful way of fulfilling motives important to them?

These kinds of questions take you beyond the general information ascertained through demographic and motivational analyses and move you toward the overarching concerns of rhetorical analysis, in which you seek ways of identifying with listeners through ideas expressed symbolically.

THE HIERARCHY OF HUMAN NEEDS

Least Basic Needs	Self Actualization To develop individual potential, express ourselves creatively and personally

Ego and Esteem Needs
To earn respect, status, and reputation;
to be competent, successful, and admired

Belonging Needs
To belong to groups, families, and be in relationships; to be accepted by others and to experience
giving and receiving affection and love with others

Security and Safety Needs
To be safe, protected, to be sheltered from dangers
and deprivations; to feel comfortable and secure

Most Basic Needs	Physiological Needs To have air, water, food, rest, exercise, sex, and any special needs upon which life depends (e.g., insulin)

We've now considered several ways to analyze listeners so that a speech can be designed in ways that invite their participation. Rhetorical analysis provides a way of thinking about your listeners and the potential relationships that can be built between their perspectives and your own. Through rhetorical analysis you locate bases of identification among yourself, your listeners, and the ideas through which you and they will interact. Both demographic and motivational analyses further inform rhetorical analysis by helping a speaker discover and draw upon commonalities that exist among listeners.

SUMMARY

This chapter discussed the first phase of public communication: planning. In a sense this is the most important part of public communication, because it is the foundation for the later stages of development and presentation. Speakers who devote adequate time and effort to careful planning have the information and understanding required for skillful development of persuasive messages.

Planning begins with attention to the purposes of public communication. Speakers will want to think about both their own purposes and the probable purposes of their listeners, since both must be served if communication is to be effective. To select and limit topics it is useful for speakers to consider the nature of their own interests, listeners' interests, and the communication situation. Attention to these issues allows speakers to formulate specific purpose statements, which then guide thought and research pertinent to the message. After selecting and limiting a topic, speakers need to center attention on listeners. While demographic and motivational methods of analysis provide useful general information, their basic function is to support rhetorical analysis, which focuses on the bases of identification that will enable speakers to develop effective persuasive messages. It is through rhetorical analysis that we are able to establish identifications, or relationships, among ourselves, our ideas, and those with whom we communicate.

Perhaps you have been a bit surprised by the amount of attention devoted to listeners in this chapter. Perhaps your expectation when you began the chapter was that the dominant concern would be with the speaker. To an extent, they are one and the same. In order for speakers to be effective in meeting their own persuasive goals, the goals and priorities of listeners must be addressed. If a speaker cannot identify a topic with listeners, the topic should not be developed. It is inappropriate. Every speaker is obligated to provide listeners with something of value in exchange for their attention. In a sense, public communication may be thought of as a contract between those who speak and those who listen. As expressed by Professors Wilson and Arnold, this means that effective communicators realize that "speaking is behaving in relation to other people and that the behaving must show that the speaker is thinking about his listeners as well as about content . . . . Every speaker operates in what his listeners expect to be a genuine, personal relationship.[18] This kind of relationship is best achieved through constant thought about listeners and their concerns, not only in planning, but also in developing and presenting ideas.

Before proceeding to the next chapter, which deals with developing public discourse, make sure you have completed the initial tasks of effective planning. The information gained during this first stage is essential to the next one. The checklist that follows identifies the information you should obtain as you plan for public communication.

PLANNING PUBLIC COMMUNICATION: A CHECKLIST

I. Determine Purpose
- What is your persuasive goal?
- What angle of development will you pursue?
- How will you measure your effectiveness?
- Are you meeting listeners' purposes?

II. Appropriate Selection and Limitation of Topic
- Do you have interest, knowledge, and/or experience pertinent to the topic?
- Do listeners have interest, knowledge, and/or experience pertinent to the topic?
- Will this topic meet listeners' expectations of you, particularly your expertise in the area?
- Will this topic be appropriate for the mood of your speaking situation?
- Can the topic be adequately treated in the time allowed?
- How can your topic be related to other people and events in your program?

- What aspects of the physical situation may influence how you deal with your topic?
III. Analyzing Listeners
   - Are any general characteristics of your listeners important for your message?
   - Can you identify motivations of your listeners and, if so, can your communication address these?
   - What are your listeners' reference groups, opinion leaders, and value structures?
   - What does this imply about your listeners' self-definitions?
   - What do listeners already know about your topic?
   - How (from what sources) did listeners gain information about this topic, and what sort of information was probably gained?
   - How do your listeners perceive their relationship to your topic?
   - How initially salient is the topic to listeners?
   - How intensely do they feel/think about the topic?
   - How does or could your issue affect the lives and values of listeners?
   - What identifications exist or can be created between your listeners and your topic?

Because communication is dynamic, the issues in the above chart interrelate. You may wish to deal with the questions in an order other than the one presented here.

REFERENCES

[1] James A. Winans, *Speechmaking.* New York: Appleton-Century- Crofts, 1938, pp. 25-28.

[2] John F. Wilson and Carroll C. Arnold, *Public Speaking as a Liberal Art,* 4th ed. Boston: Allyn & Bacon, 1974, p. 3.

[3] These distinctions date back to the 19th-century "faculty psychology," which held that there were distinct regions of the human mind, each region suited only for certain kinds of thought.

[4] Raymond Bauer, "The Obstinate Audience: The Influence Process From the Point of View of Social Communication," *American Psychologist, 19,* 1964, 319.

[5] Ralph Nichols, "Factors in Listening Comprehension. Speech Comographs," *15,* 1948, 154-163.

[6] Wilson and Arnold, pp. 62-64.

[7] Bert E. Bradley, *Fundamentals of Speech Communication: The Credibility of Ideas,* 2nd ed. Dubuque, IA: Wm. C. Brown, 1979, p. 83.

[8] Bradley, p. 84.

[9] Bradley, p. 85.

[10] Kenneth Burke, *A Rhetoric of Motives.* Berkeley: University of California Press, 1962, p. 55.

[11] Don F. Faules and Dennis C. Alexander, *Communication and Social Behavior: A Symbolic Interaction Perspective.* Reading, MA: Addison-Wesley, 1978, p. 145.

[12] Paul D. Holtzman, *The Psychology of Speakers' Audiences.* Glenview, IL: Scott-Foresman, 1970, pp. 73-79.

[13] C. Wright Mills, "Situated Actions and Vocabularies of Motive," *American Sociological Review, 5,* 1940, pp. 904-913.

[14] Burke, pp. 55-59.

[15] Theodore Clevenger, Jr., *Audience Analysis.* Indianapolis: Bobbs-Merrill, 1966.

[16] Edward Steele and W. Charles Redding, "The American Value System: Premises for Persuasion," *Western Speech, 26,* 1962, pp. 83-91.

[17] Abraham H. Maslow, *Motivation and Personality,* 2nd ed. New York: Harper and Row, pp. 35-52.

[18] Wilson and Arnold, pp. 4 and 6.

CHAPTER 12

DEVELOPING AND PRESENTING PUBLIC DISCOURSE

. . .form is the creation of an appetite in the mind of the auditor, and the adequate satisfying of that appetite.

(Kenneth Burke)

Researching Topics

> Personal experience
> Library materials
> Interviews

Organizing the Body of a Speech

> Values of organization
> The body
> Designing an introduction
> Designing a conclusion
> Building in transitions

Supporting Ideas

> Values of support
> Types of support
> Hypothetical examples

Outlining Public Discourse

Presenting Public Discourse

> Oral style
> Styles of presentation
> Practicing public communication
> Speaking anxiety: Elimination or control?

The last chapter focused on planning public discourse, a process in which you think seriously about the ideas you want to present and how they may be most effectively related to the concerns and values of our listeners. Your thought during the planning phase should provide you with a clear and limited sense of your speaking goal and an understanding of your listeners' perspectives on themselves, the topic, and you. You're now ready to build on this knowledge as you develop and present your speech.

Development of a public speech involves research, organization, and support. As you pursue these three tasks your attention should remain riveted to the overall goal of building a presentation with which listeners can identify themselves and their values. As you conduct research you'll want to take the role of your listeners, so that you can include information they deem important and consult sources whom they consider trustworthy. Then as you organize your speech you'll want to be especially sensitive to ordering and grouping materials, knowing these will influence listeners' perceptions of what you say. Organization, as you saw in Chapter 4, affects meaning, so you'll need to think carefully about the kind of organization that will most effectively suggest relationships you perceive among ideas in your speech. Next, you'll turn attention to supporting your claims with material that increases the force of your ideas in listeners' minds. To select support that invites listeners' involvement you'll need to consider your listeners' perspectives on the topic, an understanding gained from your analysis during the planning stage.

After you've developed your speech, you move into the final tasks of outlining it and presenting it to listeners. Through outlining you crystallize organization so that you can reflect on the ways you've related ideas and how they will guide listeners' understandings of your presentation. In the final stages of practice and delivery you'll make decisions about language and presentational style, both of which affect listeners' perceptions of your ideas and you as a spokesperson for those ideas. Your choices regarding language and speaking style will influence the sense of interaction that exists between you and your listeners during the communicative experience.

At each step in developing and presenting a speech your choices should reflect a keen awareness of those with whom you will communicate. The more fully you can take the role of your listeners and use that perspective to guide your development and presentation, the more likely it is that your speech will encourage your listeners' involvement and interaction. And, of course, the more you promote their interaction, the more effective you can be in achieving your own goals.

Before moving on, it's important for you to understand the intent of the suggestions these chapters provide regarding how you plan and present public discourse. Public communication can't be reduced to a paint-by-numbers formula. There are no sure fire recipes for effective public speaking. As you conceive, develop, and deliver discourse, regard material presented here as a guideline not as a straightjacket and not as a guarantee. The best public communication reflects awareness of general guidelines such as those presented here. In addition, effective public discourse shows imagination and innovation that goes beyond the guidelines. Ideally, speaking should be a highly creative process that engages speakers and listeners in focused, purposive thought.

Every speaker has an opportunity to enrich the lives of those who listen by offering them new conceptions of themselves and their experiences. This is especially true of classroom speaking, where speakers address peers on subjects of shared concern. During my years of teaching I've seen the power of student speeches. One student developed an exceptionally strong speech on the dangers of smoking, and she persuaded three of her classmates to "kick the habit." Another student convinced a number of his peers to volunteer for a Homelessness walk that raised unprecedented funds that were used to start a shelter for people who have no homes. Recently a student spoke on the desperate lack of human eyes and other organs for people who are blind, have kidney disease, and so forth. The speaker explained how we could designate ourselves as organ donors upon our deaths and thereby improve the lives of others. Many of us, myself included, were persuaded to do this, and we now carry our organ donor cards with us and have our wish to donate included on our driving licenses. Clearly, classroom speeches need not be idle exercises conducted only for grades. They can be—and should be—genuine efforts to affect how others think and act. Commit yourself to this goal and you may be surprised by the impact you have. A speech that is well thought-out, well-developed, and well-delivered can make a difference in the quality of your listeners' lives. So the thought, time, and effort required for such impact are worthwhile investments. Combine the material in this and the previous chapter with your own creativity, and you will design presentations that earn respect from yourself and your listeners.

RESEARCHING TOPICS

Once you select a topic and analyze listeners, you need to research your speech. Research usually proceeds in two stages that serve distinct purposes. You begin with general thought, conversation, and reading to define the boundaries of your subject and the range of information available to you. In the second phase you focus more specifically on particular aspects of the topic you've chosen to develop for your presentation. For both stages there are three sources of research: personal experience, library materials, and interviews.

Personal Experience

Your personal experience and knowledge are the first sources to draw upon as you develop your speech. These provide lots of ideas if you follow the last chapter's advice to select a topic with which you have some experience. Think about your relationship with this topic. What is your experience with it? How did you become involved with it? What do you know about it? How has your experience or knowledge affected you? Why is the topic important to you? To your listeners? Questions such as these stimulate your thought about personal experiences and perceptions. As you think about your involvement with the topic, jot down ideas and anecdotes as they occur to you. Later some of these will go into your speech.

Personal experience is a valuable source of content for several reasons. Obviously, you understand your own knowledge and can discuss it comfortably with others. Most speakers are relaxed and engaging when they talk about their own interests. As a speaker you will be at ease talking about personal experience. A more important value of personalized content is that it increases listeners' perceptions of your knowledge on your topic.[1] Listeners tend to place more confidence in what you say if you demonstrate you have direct knowledge of the topic. Naturally listeners are more likely to be persuaded by speakers they regard as qualified to speak on a topic than by speakers whose qualifications they don't respect. One study compared the persuasive impact of speakers who used direct experiences and speakers who referred to others' experience or knowledge. The results showed clearly that personal information is more effective than indirect information in enhancing listeners' perceptions of speakers' competence and trustworthiness. Because listeners place high confidence in personal experience, they will be more persuaded by speakers who include these.[2]

Personal experience is an important source of content for speeches. When you include personal experience and knowledge you identify yourself directly with your topic, a move that enhances your competence in listeners' minds.

Library Materials

A review of personal knowledge is a good way to find out what you already know about your topic and what you yet need to find out. Given your speaking purpose and your own experiences, what information do you need to build your speech? Libraries provide a wealth of resources to help you find content for your speech.

First consult your library's general resources, which furnish useful background information on current topics. You might begin with the card catalog to see what materials your library has related to your subject. Next check out encyclopedias and abstracts of journals to find general summaries of your topic or aspects of it. Many speakers rely on *The Readers' Guide to Periodical Literature* to discover articles about their topic in over 125 popular magazines such as *Time, Ebony, Newsweek, The Christian Science Monitor, Working Woman, Fortune,* and *Harpers.* Pamphlets, books, and materials about public affairs are indexed in *The Public Affairs Information Service Bulletin. Facts-On-File* summarizes world news. Because it comes out weekly, you get up-to-the-minute information on your topic. Other indices reference specific materials, such as research in the humanities and government publications. Ask your librarian to point out general indices and guides most appropriate to your topic.

General sources provide a broad perspective on topics. In addition, speakers often want specific kinds of information or want in-depth material on certain aspects of their topics. Libraries have several resources that provide specific factual information. One excellent publication is *Statistical Abstracts of the United States*, which summarizes statistical information on over 30 aspects of American life, such as education, employment, population, and economy. This publication comes out each year, so you can get current statistics and can compare information from various years to discover trends. An especially good resource for international topics is *Statesman's Year-Book*, another annual publication, which gives statistical profiles on every nation in the world. Other reliable sources of specific information and facts are *The World Almanac and Book of Facts* and *What They Said.* If these sources do not provide all of the information you need, talk to the reference librarian, whose special skill is tracking down hard-to-find materials.

A third library resource is biographical publications that furnish background information on authorities you may want to quote in your speech. Among the better biographical directories are *Who's Who in America, Who's Who of American Women, Biography Index, International Who's Who,* and the *Directory of American Scholars.* Whenever you quote other people or refer to their opinions you should indicate their credentials, so listeners know that your sources are qualified. The biographical publications assist you in identifying your sources.

Through library research you gain general and specific information about your topic and the credentials of authorities whose ideas you may include in your speech.

Interviews

A third source of content for your speech is interviews with people who have special knowledge or experience pertinent to your topic. Depending upon your subject, you may interview only one key person or you may engage in a series of interviews. You may need to select from several experts on your topic. If so, interview the person or persons whom your listeners will find most credible and persuasive. Consider the possible sources from the perspective of your listeners to decide which of the potential experts will most effectively engage them. When you call to schedule an appointment, explain your purpose and what you want from the interviewees, so they can prepare materials and ideas for you. It's a good idea to plan interviews sufficiently late in your speech preparation that you have a solid grasp of your topic and can use interviews to gain information unavailable from other sources. To make interviews productive and efficient, prepare specific questions in advance. That way, you won't forget important questions and you'll be able to keep conversation moving. During interviews, allow interviewees to initiate ideas not on your list-because they are experts, they may know information that you wouldn't think to ask about. It's generally wise to let the interviewee do most of the talking. Your job is to guide discussion enough to make sure basic topics are covered. Then sit back and let the experts inform you. Take notes as necessary, but don't become so focused on your notes that you neglect interaction with interviewees. To acknowledge interviewees' time and help with your research, you should send short notes of appreciation to them.

Personal experience, library materials, and interviews are three sources of content for your speech. Research drawing from these sources provides you with a range of material which you then organize into a coherent presentation.

ORGANIZING THE BODY OF A SPEECH

Once you have collected information pertinent to your speaking purpose, your next step is to organize your presentation. In Chapter 3 we saw that symbols allow us to organize experiences in ways that construct meanings. Now you have an opportunity to use that ability to its fullest as you make choices about how you will order and group your materials. In organizing a speech, you segment the experiences about which you speak. You guide your listeners to perceive the overall topic in a particular way, to apprehend relationships among your ideas, to discern patterns among experiences. In short, the way you arrange your material will influence how listeners experience your topic. In the next few pages we consider the values of organization and we discuss some of the more popular ways to organize public communication.

Values of Organization

Organization is a primary influence on how listeners evaluate speakers and their presentations. Research documents five distinct values of well organized speeches. First, organization satisfies listeners' desires for structure.[3] Unorganized presentations frustrate listeners, because they find it difficult to follow speakers' trains of thought. They become confused and may lose interest or resent speakers for wasting their time.

> *Quintilian on Organization*[4]
>
> Speech, if deficient in that quality arrangement [organization], must necessarily be confused, and float like a ship without a helm; it can have no coherence; it must exhibit many repetitions, and many omissions; and, like a traveler wandering by night in unknown regions, must, as having no stated course or object, be guided by chance rather than design . . . . just as it is not sufficient for those who are erecting a building merely to collect stone and timber and other building materials, but skilled masons are required to arrange and place them, so in speaking, however abundant the matter may be, it will merely form a confused heap unless arrangement be employed to reduce it to order and to give it connection and firmness of structure . . . .

A second value of organization is that it directly and indirectly affects the meanings listeners construct as they interact with a a speaker's ideas. It guides listeners' thoughts in particular ways. Form and substance interact to arouse meanings, so the way you structure ideas influences listeners' understandings of what the ideas are and what their significance is.

Third, organization affects listeners' comprehension of speeches. The more clearly organized communication is, the more quickly and accurately listeners will understand and remember the central ideas.[5] A fourth value is that organization is positively related to attitude change. Listeners are more persuaded by well-structured speeches than by the same content presented in unorganized fashion.[6] This makes sense, given other values of organization. Listeners are more likely to be persuaded by a speech that does not frustrate them, that is meaningful to them, and that can be understood by them. Finally, organization influences listeners' evaluations of speakers. A well-structured presentation reflects positively on the speaker, and, conversely, a poorly organized speech reflects negatively on the speaker.[7] When messages are disorganized, listeners tend to regard speakers as incompetent and, therefore, unreliable sources of information and attitude change.

Organization is vital to effective speaking. It directly affects listeners' satisfaction, meanings, learning, attitude change and evaluation of speakers. These values justify keen attention to the process of organizing speeches.

Among speech communication teachers there's an adage about organization: Tell listeners what you're going to tell them; tell them; then tell them what you told them. Roughly translated, this means a well organized speech has an introduction, a body, and a conclusion. We'll consider each of these major parts of a speech and a fourth part called transitions. We'll begin with the body of the speech, since this is the heart of the presentation and requires the most time and thought from speakers. The body is developed first; then introduction, conclusion, and transitions are built around it.

The Body

The body of a speech develops the thesis or central idea of the speaker. Chapter 11 explored ways to select and limit topics so that a speech has a single, clear central idea. Once you formulate that idea, break it down into several aspects that will serve as the points of your speech body. Most experienced speakers have learned they can cover only a few points well in a single presentation. Short speeches (those of less than 20 minutes) should have a maximum of three major points, and two points are often sufficient to develop a thesis.

The major points in the body are organized into an overall pattern that directs listeners' thoughts in ways consistent with the speaker's purpose. There is no finite number of patterns for speeches, nor is there a recipe for "correct" patterns. However, there are some patterns that frequently appear in speeches and that represent an initial array of alternatives for you. Each pattern defines content in a distinct way and, thus, each encourages in listeners particular interpretations of ideas.

Time (chronological) patterns. Time patterns organize ideas temporally in a progression. They are appropriate for speeches that trace developments, histories, or sequences of events. Time sequences could develop theses such as these: "The process of strip mining depletes target land and then causes erosion of surrounding areas." "Nuclear reactors' safety is assured by the steps involved in the cool-down process." "The LeBoyer method of birth is ideal because it prepares the mother before labor and teaches her to assist during birth." "Current quota systems that increase minority enrollments are necessary to compensate for past discrimination" With the time pattern, emphasis is on progression, development, or change. A well-developed time pattern gives listeners a sense of movement regarding the topic. They experience the topic progressively, perceiving one idea as leading to another.

Space patterns. Space patterns organize ideas according to physical relationships. They are appropriate for speeches that demonstrate relationships among parts of objects or situations, explain the geography or layout of something, or establish how various parts of something are affected by something else. Space patterns are effective with topics such as these: "Aerosol sprays progressively destroy the three layers of the atmosphere." "Plant life varies among piedmont, coastal, and mountain regions of this state." "Open classrooms are functionally divided into areas for individual study and group learning." "To work effectively, solar-powered homes have special features in floors, walls, and roofs." Space patterns call attention to relationships among parts of a whole or to overall physical arrangements. They encourage listeners to apprehend relatedness. When you use this pattern you guide listeners to notice connections among ideas, to appreciate how one aspect of a topic is related to others, to perceive an overall unity among ideas that you present.

Comparison (analogical) patterns. Comparison patterns compare two or more things. Through comparison the speaker shows likenesses among things, identifies differences, or argues the superiority of one thing over another. Topics that can be developed with comparison patterns include the following: "Socialized medicine is superior to private practice in cost, convenience, and quality of care." "The British system of managing heroin is more effective than the American system." "Baseball is run similarly to any other business." "Laetril is less effective than traditional methods of cancer treatment." "Breast feeding and bottle feeding are equally effective for both mother and child." "Fission and fusion are very different sources of nuclear energy." Comparative patterns emphasize relative merits, qualities, or effectiveness of something. They encourage listeners to think about one thing in direct relation to others specified by the speaker. This pattern provides listeners with a specific perspective within which to think about the speaker's topic. Comparison patterns are especially useful when you want to assist listeners to understand some new idea, event, or process by identifying it with one with which they are already familiar. This is strong organizationally, because it draws directly on listeners' existing experiences to establish an unfamiliar idea. Thus, this pattern, more than some others, invites active participation from listeners.

Classification (topical) patterns. Classification patterns divide topics into several categories or classes. Speakers resort to this pattern when their topics break down naturally into two or three separate areas not related by time, space, or comparison. Classification structures are appropriate for theses such as these: "There are three advantages to increased control of firearms. . . ." "Student fees fund social, academic, and extracurricular activities." "The U.S. government is divided into executive, judicial, and legislative branches." The classification pattern is less internally unified than others we've considered, so it should be used only for topics that do not lend themselves to other patterns of organization. As an organizational format it has limited power to unify ideas in ways that help listeners experience a speech as an organic whole.

Problem-solution patterns. Problem-solution patterns divide topics into two major areas of presentation: discussion of the problem and proposal of a solution. A speaker begins by showing the nature and severity of some problem and then explains a solution to it. Many subjects are well suited to this pattern: "The current need for organ transplants can be met if more people become donors." "Thousands of deaths could be prevented each year if motorcyclists were required to wear helmets." "Genetic counseling is one way to reduce the chance of having a deformed child." "Court backlogs would be reduced drastically if victimless crimes were misdemeanors." The problem-solution pattern is psychologically satisfying to listeners, because it provides balance and completeness. If they acknowledge the problem presented in the first part of your speech, they're ready to entertain a solution. The organization has allowed listeners to participate with you in developing the topic from identification of some inequity to resolution of it. Thus, listeners have a sense of involvement and often a willingness to further their investment in the topic through personal actions you may recommend in the latter part of your speech. Problem-solution organization is a particularly effective choice when your goal is to move listeners to some form of action.

Cause-effect and effect-cause patterns. Cause-effect and effect-cause patterns suggest that a direct relationship exists between two or more things, one being the cause of the other. Sometimes speakers want to show what has occurred or will occur (effect) as the result of a particular phenomenon (cause). Topics that could be developed along this line include the following: "Affirmative action hiring guidelines (effect) are necessary because of years of discrimination against minorities (cause)." "The rise in day-care centers (effect) has been brought about by the increase in the number of women who work and men who do not assume active roles in child rearing (causes)." "Current unemployment levels (effect) result from inflation and unrestricted foreign competition (causes)." The effect-cause sequence encourages listeners to perceive the basis for some phenomenon, to indicate to themselves a direct association between two phenomena (effect and cause) that may previously have been unrelated in their minds.

Sometimes speakers decide it will be most effective to demonstrate how certain things (causes) will affect other things (effects). Cause-effect patterns could be used to develop theses such as these: "Legislated minimum wages (cause) will lead to lower worker productivity and a sluggish economy (effects)." "Ownership of handguns (cause) increases accidental shootings, suicides, and crimes of passion (effects)." "Violence on television (cause) results in violent attitudes and behaviors in children (effects)." With the cause-effect sequence you encourage listeners to link one phenomenon causally with another, to perceive a direct and strong relationship between the two.

It is difficult to establish or prove causal relationships. However, speakers can use organization to link one phenomenon with another in listeners' minds to suggest causality. These two patterns can be quite persuasive in showing listeners the consequences that will follow from certain policies or events and in convincing listeners of relationships between phenomena that may have been previously unconnected in their minds. Causal patterns of either order guide listeners to define an association—real or potential—between one thing and another. Thus, with these patterns you can create identifications that listeners did not previously recognize.

These six patterns represent varied ways to organize ideas. Select the one that advances your purpose by how it guides listeners' understanding of the issues you will discuss. Not only does the pattern guide listeners' perceptions, it also guides yours. You use the process of self-indication to direct your own perceptions of issues—what fits with what, which ideas come first and which later, how one point relates to another, which material can create the best foundation for other material. Keeping your overall organization firmly in mind, review your ideas and research to see where each item fits within your organization. Most speakers find they have more material than they can possibly use in a short speech, so you next task is to sort material. Decide what information best develops each major point in your speech, and discard anything that does not relate directly to one of your points. If you lack sufficient material to develop a particular point, more research is in order. Each item you keep should have a clear bearing on your purpose and should fit naturally within your overall organization. Anything that does not meet these two criteria should be eliminated.

Organization is vitally important to effective public communication. Your goal is to create an order of presentation that transforms a collage of ideas into a unified whole that will encourage listeners to perceive patterns in your material similar to those you discern. In achieving this goal you offer listeners not only ideas, but, more importantly, a perspective on those ideas, a way of seeing, understanding, and interacting with the ideas. If listeners can experience the topic as you do, they are likely to find themselves persuaded to the point of view you represent. How you organize your speech will have direct bearing on the probability of listeners' experiencing your ideas in ways consistent with this objective.

Once you've created an overall pattern and arranged your materials within that framework, your attention turns to other aspects of organization: the introduction, conclusion, and transitions for your speech.

Designing An Introduction

An introduction is your first opportunity to involve listeners with your topic, to persuade them to interact with your ideas through the symbols you use. To do this effectively, an introduction achieves three important goals. First, it arouses interest and attention in listeners. To do this you may open your talk with a strong, vivid quotation, example, or statistic that highlights the heart of your speech. A question or comment directed to listeners is also effective, because it encourages their personal involvement with the presentation. Reference to your experience with the topic may capture interest and establish your qualifications to speak. Humor can also open a speech effectively as long as it pertains to the topic and is successful—a joke that "bombs" devastates the speaker and negatively impresses listeners. When time allows, a speech may begin with a detailed example to personalize issues and to help listeners identify with the topic. These are five of the most frequently employed methods of arousing listeners' initial interest in your topic.

The second task of an introduction is to announce the purpose of the speech. State your thesis in a single, clear sentence that is as short as possible. Your goal here is to give listeners your theme so they can focus their attention from the start. To make sure listeners recognize your thesis, you may want to frame it with phrases such as "This morning my goal is to . . . . . . or "In the next few minutes I will show that. . . ." Phrases such as these cue listeners to listen well; they act as oral underlining. The more explicitly you state your thesis, the better-prepared listeners will be to follow your ideas and, thus, to be persuaded.[8]

The third purpose of an introduction is to preview content and organization. The preview comes immediately after the statement of thesis. It tells listeners what you'll cover and how to follow your ideas. They get an advance sense of how you plan to develop your thesis, and so they are prepared to move with you as you talk. To preview a speech designed to persuade listeners that prison reform is needed (thesis), a speaker could say this: "I will first document inadequacies in existing prison systems and then I will demonstrate the positive impact of administrative reforms as illustrated in two model prisons in Arizona." From this statement listeners know the basic content of the speech and the organizational pattern (problem-solution). Thus, they are prepared to follow the speaker's development of the thesis. You want listeners to experience your speech in a particular way, yet they do not begin with your understanding of how ideas are related. With a preview you define how you perceive the material, so that they can understand that perspective and, thus, participate in the speech as you have conceived and designed it. Because previews direct thought and invite participation, they enhance listeners' comprehension of communication.[9]

Well-designed introductions tune listeners into speeches. A complete introduction arouses listeners' interest, states the thesis, and previews content and organization. Time, thought, and effort are required to achieve these three goals in less than 10 percent of total speaking time, the average length for introductions.[10]

Designing A Conclusion

The importance of a conclusion is that it establishes final impressions of speaker and message. To be effective, a conclusion summarizes content and provides closure, and it does both very concisely, since conclusions usually take less than 5 percent of the total speaking time![11] In concluding a speech, the speaker's first responsibility is to review major ideas one final time. This is your last opportunity to identify your perspective with that of your listeners. To summarize your speech you'll want to restate your thesis and each major point you developed. One or two sentences are sufficient to highlight key ideas.

The second function of a conclusion is to provide closure or completeness to the communication experience. An otherwise solid speech can be weakened by an abrupt conclusion in which the speaker says, "For the reasons I've explained, a peacetime draft is advisable" and sits down. Listeners are not ready for the speech to end. In fact, with a conclusion like the one above the speech doesn't really end—it stops cold! Bradley explains the importance of closure: "The speaker who quits on his last main idea runs a risk of leaving his listeners frustrated and dissatisfied by a feeling that the task was not completed. A conclusion gives the impression that there are no loose ends remaining; everything has been tied up in a nice neat bundle."[12]

There are several ways to provide closure. One of the most effective is to return to an idea initiated in the introduction. If you open with a detailed example, you might end with reference to that same example or with an extension of it. If you begin with a quotation or statistic you might conclude with a related datum, a twist on the opening information, or even with emphatic repetition of the original idea. For instance, a speech on alcoholism could open with a statistic on the number of college social drinkers who later develop drinking problems. An appropriate conclusion would include a summary and a return to the opening idea: "As I said earlier, most alcoholics began as social drinkers and it's estimated that 25 percent of college students who drink socially today will have drinking problems later in life. According to that statistic, 15 of the 60 people in here will have trouble with alcohol. Let's try to beat those odds." This concluding statement provides closure on the speech, which has come full circle from opening to closing.

Sometimes it is inappropriate or inconvenient to return to the opening idea, so closure must be provided in other ways. Speakers may end with quotations, statistics, or examples that drive home themes developed in their speeches. Another option is to close with an appeal for action from listeners. Ask them to write their Congressional representatives, to sign a petition, to give blood to the Red Cross, to carry an organ donor card, or to do whatever is appropriate action in response to your speech.

Effective conclusions tend to be brief and tightly focused. They summarize content and provide closure on ideas so that listeners have a sense of completeness.

Building in Transitions

A final organizational concern is transitions, which connect ideas and unify a speech. In order for your speech to be effective you must keep listeners within your perspective, so you need to provide cues as you move along. Transitions alert listeners that you are progressing from one idea to another; they create bridges linking ideas so that the movement seems natural. Bradley suggests the need for transitions when he notes that "Organization may exist in the mind of the speaker and may even have been transferred to paper . . . but to be effective that organization must be clear . . . to listeners."[13] Transitions should occur between major parts of the speech (introduction, body, and conclusion) and between points,

> Transitions are like signposts. They tell your audience where you have been, where you are, or where you intend to go.[14]

within the body of the speech. They move your listeners from one idea to the next. Transitions may be words, phrases, or sentences. Within points, transitional words such as "therefore," "finally," "consequently" help listeners follow the flow of your thoughts. Transitional phrases often used to connect points include "My first point is . . . My second point is. . .," "This brings me to the next major idea . . . ." "In addition to X, we must consider Y On the other hand. . . ." Sometimes speakers use full sentences to move listeners from one idea or part of a speech to the next: "The most obvious effect is X. . . . Although X may be the most obvious, Y is also important . . . . Yet another effect is Z." "Now that we've examined the problem, let's turn to a possible solution." "We've explored the history and present status of unionization, so let's now speculate about its future." Variety in transitions is advisable in order to maintain listeners' interest, so speakers should use a combination of words, phrases, and sentences to unify ideas.

Transitions are vital to the coherence of your presentation. Without them, listeners may perceive your speech as a "laundry list," a string of ideas not clearly tied together. With transitions, you link ideas together into a unified, progressive whole that listeners can identify and follow. Transitions allow you to take a collection of ideas and facts and transform it into an organic, internally related whole, in which your listeners can participate.

Organization is essential to effective speaking. It bears directly on listeners' understanding of ideas and their evaluation of both speech and speaker. An organized speech has an introduction, a body, and a conclusion which transitions weave into a coherent whole. By building transitions into your speech, you guide listeners to interact with ideas within the overall perspective you designed for your presentation.

SUPPORTING IDEAS

Once you've selected and organized the basic ideas for your speech, you'll want to think about how you might develop them most effectively. How can you make what is now a skeleton of material interesting to listeners? How can you make it persuasive? What can you do to maximize their involvement and interaction with this material? To answer these questions we will consider the nature and value of support, or evidence, in public communication.

What is support or evidence? Traditionally, it has been regarded as material that proves a speaker's claims. From this orientation, support is a stimulus that has predictable effects on listeners; that is, it makes them believe a speaker's claims. Symbolic interactionists take issue with the traditional view of support, because it portrays listeners as essentially passive, subject to the effects of a speaker's evidence. As we've seen in previous chapters, listeners are active participants in communication. They interact with a speaker's ideas through symbols which they interpret to construct meanings. The complex processes of interpretation cannot be reduced to stimulus-response models. Evidence is but another way of inviting listeners to participate in communication—another means of encouraging their interaction with ideas through language.

Support, then, is material designed to increase listeners' involvement with ideas by encouraging them to be interested, persuaded, and moved. From this perspective, the effectiveness of evidence is not entirely a matter of a speaker's perception of its worth, or even of its "objective" quality. Effectiveness is also tied directly to listeners' acceptance of the evidence. Clearly, you would not want to use evidence that you regard as inadequate, nor would you want to include evidence that is distorted, misleading, or false. To preserve your integrity and that of your ideas, you will want to consider only evidence that is reliable, valid, and intrinsically worthy. Yet this is not enough. In addition to screening out evidence that is not sound, you should also avoid support that will not be persuasive from your listeners' perspectives. No matter how "true" a piece of evidence is, it will not influence listeners if they do not accept it. We can think of evidence, therefore, as material used in an effort to increase the force of ideas in listeners' minds. Your selection and use of evidence should be guided by understanding of your listeners' perspectives—by what they are likely to find credible, interesting, persuasive.

Values of Support

Support invites listeners' involvement with material on several levels. First, it can invite their understanding and interest by making ideas more clear, vivid, or memorable to them. For instance, a well-developed example of child abuse will stick with listeners far longer than the straightforward claim "Child abuse is brutal." Use of an extended example or photographs of child abuse tends to make the basic claim vivid, more impressive, so listeners are more likely to become involved with the idea.

A second goal of support is to invite listeners to believe in what you say. Carefully selected evidence encourages listeners to share your belief in the truth and importance of your arguments. In many instances your opinions are insufficient to convince listeners of a point, so you need to support your ideas with evidence that will be compelling to listeners. A claim that alcoholism is on the rise can be supported with statistics comparing the number of alcoholics in 1980 with the number in 1991. To back up an argument that retarded citizens can assume responsible roles in society, you might quote an expert who has worked directly in vocational placement of retarded citizens. That expert, if accepted as credible by listeners, substantiates your argument with opinion based on personal experience. By providing evidence supportive of your claims you increase the chance that listeners will accept your ideas and will experience lasting attitude change.[15] Presumably, this is because in interacting with your claims and in identifying those claims with good reasons (your evidence), listeners convince themselves of what you argue; thus, the opinions they form will hold up against opposing opinions they may later encounter.[16]

A third function of support is to encourage listeners to evaluate speakers favorably. When a speaker incorporates listener-adapted evidence into a presentation, listeners associate the support with the speaker—an identification is made between the person advocating something and reasons for the advocacy. The quality of the evidence reflects back upon the speaker, adding to his or her credibility in listeners' minds. Many speakers, particularly novices, begin their speeches without reputations as experts on a topic. During the speech, however, much can be done to create a perception of expertise through the use of evidence that listeners find sound. If you support each of your ideas carefully, using material that involves listeners, your listeners will come to see you as an informed, knowledgeable individual.[17] Through your use of evidence you have established your own personal reputation as a person qualified to speak on a topic.

Support is essential to effective public communication. Through the use of support you invite listeners to become involved in your ideas—to understand and care about what you say, to believe in the truth and importance of your ideas, and to perceive you as a competent spokesperson. All of these values of evidence increase the overall force of your presentation in listeners' minds, because they heighten listeners' involvement with your topic. In order to realize these values of evidence it is necessary for you to make thoughtful decisions regarding when to use evidence and what kind of evidence will be most effective. The central guideline for such decisions is to consider your listeners' perspectives. Ask whether they will understand a point, believe a claim, see you as a credible source on some argument. If not, then you need support. What kind of support will be most likely to involve your particular listeners? Whom will they see as credible sources? What kinds of examples will be arresting and involving for them? Questions such as these help you select evidence that is likely to be effective, because it comes out of the perspectives of those whom you wish to influence.

Types of Support

It is one matter to decide you need evidence at certain points in your speech and quite another matter to figure out exactly what kind of evidence to use. You may find it helpful to break the broad concept of evidence into more specific units. We can think of evidence in terms of five types: quotations, examples, statistics, analogies, and visual aids. We'll examine each of these types to see how it encourages listeners' involvement with a speaker's ideas.

Quotations. Quotations—also called testimony—are exact reports of statements made by others. In speeches, quotations may clarify or substantiate claims, depending on how speakers use them. An expert's testimony may explain an idea more thoroughly than the speaker could, so testimony here would clarify. In other cases controversial claims may be backed up by supporting opinions from respected sources. Because speakers cannot be experts on all aspects of their topics, they often incorporate the opinions of people who have special expertise. To be effective, quotations must meet three criteria. First, they must come from sources who are qualified to speak on the topic. It is insufficient for a source to be an expert in some area or a well-known person; she or he must be qualified in the particular area involved. Whenever testimony is used, the speaker should cite credentials so listeners will know why the source is qualified. Second, quotations should come from unbiased sources. For instance, spokespersons for the tobacco industry are poor sources to support the claim that smoking is unrelated to cancer. The sources are biased; they have a vested interest in supporting that claim, so their opinions are subject to suspicion. Listeners are seldom persuaded by biased testimony. Third, quotations should come from sources respected by listeners. This is the crucial test of testimony. No matter how qualified a source is, testimony is only persuasive if listeners accept it. To persuade listeners, you must select sources with whom they identify.

Examples. Examples—also called instances and illustrations—are single cases used to prove a point or add vividness to an idea. Examples may be undetailed, detailed, or hypothetical. Undetailed examples are brief references that take up little speaking time and remind listeners of instances they already know of or inform them of instances that are immediately understandable. Detailed examples are more elaborate. Speakers use these to introduce cases listeners will not already know about or to present cases in great detail so that they will stick with listeners. Detailed examples provide verbal pictures that include three dimensional characters with whom listeners can identify. Time is required to present detailed examples, but their interest value often justifies the time. Hypothetical examples are nonfactual, so they cannot prove claims. However, well-developed hypothetical examples clarify and enliven ideas and enhance the emotional impact of a speech. They can personalize facts and statistics by putting them into story form. Examples—undetailed, detailed, or hypothetical—add substance and interest to speeches.

Hypothetical Examples

To support his proposal for Medicare, President John F. Kennedy used this hypothetical example:*

> Let's consider the case of a typical American family—a family which might be found in any part of the United States. The husband has worked hard all of his life, and now he has retired. He might have been a clerk or a salesman or worked in a factory. He always insisted on paying his own way. This man, like most Americans, wants to care for himself. He has raised his own family, educated his children, and he and his wife are drawing social security now. Then his wife gets sick, not just for a week, but for a very long time. First the savings go. Next he mortgages his home. Finally he goes to his children who are themselves heavily burdened. Then their savings begin to go. What is he to do now? Here is a typical American who has nowhere to turn, so he finally will have to sign a petition saying he's broke and needs welfare assistance.

Statistics. Statistics are numerical facts or figures that summarize many examples or show relationships among phenomena. The use of statistics is a most efficient way to support ideas, because it presents large amounts of information in very concise form. The function of statistics is more to provide substance than interest. When well used, they enhance the persuasiveness of a speech. Unfortunately, statistics are often confusing or boring to listeners. When they are, it's because a speaker used them poorly, not because statistics are intrinsically dull. To employ statistics effectively, follow several guidelines. First, choose a few good figures rather than a battery of numbers. Listeners resent speakers who spew out streams of statistics, and well they should. Speakers who do this have devoted inadequate time to making their data interesting. Second, avoid using a series of statistics. Try to intersperse numerical data with other kinds of support. After presenting one set of numbers, use an example or quotation; then, if appropriate, cite your next statistic. Third, translate numbers into terms listeners will understand immediately. Round off large figures to facilitate comprehension: "three million" is more clear and forceful than "2,979,985." Compare numbers to provide perspective for listeners. A documentary film made this comparison: "Each year Americans spend 14 billion dollars on alcohol, 9 billion on tobacco, 2 billion on pets and only 200 million on juvenile reform."[18] The small amount spent on juvenile reform is dramatized by comparing it with amounts spent on other, less vital items. To present that information more effectively, a speaker might break the large numbers down into smaller units: "For every dollar we spend on juvenile reform, we spend 70 dollars on alcohol, 45 on tobacco and 10 on pets." Statistics are powerful aids to speakers. They allow you to present a maximum of information in a minimum of time. To realize the persuasive impact of statistics, use them well, making sure they are clear and interesting to listeners.

Analogies. Analogies are comparisons of two things that are essentially similar in important respects. Literal analogies compare things within a class. Comparisons

---

*Speech delivered at Madison Square Garden rally of The National Council of Senior Citizens, May 19, 1962.

between Toyotas and Datsuns, Irish setters and German shepherds, racquet ball and squash are literal analogies. Because literal analogies compare members of a single class (cars, dogs, athletics), they produce conclusions that can support claims. For example, we can prove the claim that Toyota Camrys are fuel-efficient subcompacts by comparing the mileage of Camrys with those of other subcompacts.

Figurative analogies, on the other hand, compare things in different classes. Comparisons between the human body and a machine, war and a game, the mind and a computer are figurative analogies. These analogies cannot prove claims. Instead, their persuasive function is to clarify or dramatize ideas by comparing something familiar to something unfamiliar or by providing a new perspective on one thing by likening it to another. Listeners identify with the new idea or perspective, because the speaker has associated it with something they already understand. Analogies add a lot of interest and originality to speeches. Years ago after the Watergate scandal that rocked the capital and led to Richard Nixon's resignation from the President, Representative Hungate opened the Watergate hearings with an analogy designed to compare the events of Watergate to the experiences of typical Americans: "What if your mayor had tapped the phones of your neighbors? What if your mayor had misspent your tax monies to refurbish his home? What if your mayor had evaded his own taxes?" Hungate's analogy placed Watergate in a perspective that invited average American citizens to identify with the issues at stake. In a similar way an Air Force officer explained how he felt when Congress refused to finance B-1 planes by comparing that to the more common experience of not getting a desired new car: "It's like owning a Model T and saving money 'til you have enough for a Cadillac and then being told you really don't have enough and to keep the Model T."[19] Most people lack experience with different kinds of Air Force planes, so they might not have understood the officer's feelings had he not used an analogy that drew upon common experiences with cars.

Analogies are useful forms of support. Literal analogies provide substantive evidence for a speaker's claims, while figurative analogies add clarity and interest. When your speech will include unfamiliar ideas, analogies are especially valuable, because they invite listeners to draw upon their existing experiences as a basis for understanding something new.

Visual aids.   A final type of support is visual aids, which include charts, graphs, maps, photographs, models, and real objects. The primary purposes of visual aids are to reinforce and clarify information presented verbally. For instance, the statistics cited earlier on expenditures for juvenile reform could be reinforced effectively with a bar graph that dramatizes comparative investments. Diagrams and models help listeners understand complex descriptions such as how nuclear reactors work or the layout of spacecraft. Maps are valuable for speeches that involve geographical relations with which listeners may not be familiar.

There are a few guidelines to follow when using visual aids. Be sure to make them large enough for everyone to see clearly. Nothing is more frustrating than a picture or chart that listeners cannot see. Numbers, words, or other symbols on a visual aid must be made sufficiently large to be read by people in the very back of a room. A second suggestion is to keep visual aids simple. Cluttered charts may confuse listeners and are

Claim: For every $1 we spend on juvenile reform, we spend $70 on alcohol, $45 on tobacco, and $10 on pets.

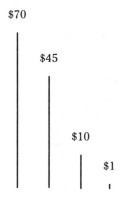

less attractive than simple ones. Restrict visual information to what is absolutely pertinent to your claims. Finally, do not let visual aids interfere with your interaction with listeners. A common mistake of novice speakers is talking to charts, with their backs to listeners. Always maintain visual contact with your listeners and be sufficiently familiar with your aids that you don't need to read them. It's a good idea to keep visual aids out of sight or covered with blank paper when not in use. That way, listeners will not be distracted by a visual aid when you want their attention elsewhere. Keep listeners' attention focused on you until you are ready to use visual aids. When preparing the aids, make them sturdy so they don't flop over and don't require you to hold them up. You want yourself free to interact with listeners at all times. Visual aids are important forms of support; they clarify information and add substantial interest to speeches. To be effective, however, they must be carefully prepared and presented.

One-Sided or Two-Sided Support?[20]

Should speakers present only evidence that favors their points of view or should they examine opposing points of view as well? Phrased another way, should speeches be one-sided or two-sided? Classic studies conducted during World War II provide these answers:

A one-sided approach can be effective if: listeners already believe the point of view advocated by the speaker
listeners are unaware of an opposing point of view and will not be presented with counter-arguments
only temporary change of attitude is sought by the speaker

A two-sided approach is advisable if:

listeners initially disagree with the speaker's position
listeners know of or are likely to be exposed to a position opposing the speaker's
listeners are well educated and regard themselves as mature, critical thinkers

When using a two-sided approach, speakers should present and support their own positions before introducing opposing views. This sequence establishes the speaker's position strongly at the outset and predisposes listeners toward that position so that they are less likely to find competing views attractive.

Effective speeches include support to clarify and substantiate claims and to add interest to information. By furthering listeners' involvement with a speaker's ideas, solid evidence adds to the persuasive impact of the speech and the personal credibility of the speaker.

When you have organized your ideas and decided how to support them, you're ready to consider the final step in developing your speech: the outline.

OUTLINING PUBLIC DISCOURSE

As long as your ideas are in your head or scribbled randomly on paper, it's impossible to tell how well they will actually work when you present them publicly. As a final step in preparing your speech, you should construct a written outline. Doing this provides a check on the quality of your preparation. As Verderber points out, "Outlining is a test of the organization. Through an outline we can test to see whether the speech is logical, whether it really does what we intended it to do, and whether it really covers all that needs to be covered in the speech."[21] When you write an outline, you can reflect on your choices of how to develop and unify ideas, and you can make changes if appropriate.

Think of the outline as the skeleton of your speech. It is not the whole speech. In fact, it's generally unwise ever to write out all that you intend to say, since that would diminish the spontaneous character of your presentation. You don't want the speech to sound "canned" so keep the outline brief. An outline should have three headings: introduction, body, and conclusion. Under each of these headings write out major points, supporting material, and transitions. Try to write in full sentences, but avoid paragraphs, since that promotes a canned quality in the final speech. Many speeches include quotations, statistics, or other evidence that must be presented verbatim. In such cases the material may be written out in full on the outline or may be written on separate note cards which are kept with the outline. On the following pages a sample outline is presented.

Not only does an outline test your preparation, it also assists you when you practice and deliver your speech. In most situations speakers talk from outlines. All key ideas are written out so that a speaker is unlikely to forget major points or to become blocked. Yet, because the outline is brief, it does not require constant attention; hence the speaker remains free to interact with listeners throughout the presentation.

Constructing an outline should be easy if you've been thorough in your preparation. It's simply a matter of formalizing in writing what you've already through through. When you've constructed your outline, look at it carefully Is your overall organization clear? Are transitions included between all points? Is each claim supported in ways your listeners will find persuasive? Will your introduction arouse attention, clearly announce your thesis, and preview content and organization? Will the conclusion provide both summary and closure? If you can answer affirmatively to each of these questions, you have an outline that proves the quality of your work so far and that will assist you as you practice and deliver the speech.

SAMPLE OUTLINE

1. INTRODUCTION
   A. Attention
   1. Of the 20 million elderly Americans, 1 million live in nursing homes(3).
   2. This is relevant to each of us.
      a. We may one day need to decide how to care for family or friends in their old age;
      b. We may ourselves enter nursing homes when we are elderly.
      c. As we become taxpayers it is our money that supports many of these nursing homes.
   B. Thesis Statement: One of the greatest problems in nursing homes is inadequate personnel, which results in unsafe living conditions and inadequate medical care.
   C. Preview: In the next few minutes I will inform you about the deficiencies in nursing home personnel and I will describe the effects of these deficiencies on living conditions and medical care.
II. BODY (Cause-effect pattern)
   A. The majority of nursing homes in America have inadequate personnel.(causes)
   1. Most nursing homes are understaffed.
      a. Comparison between ideal staff-patient ratio and actual ratio (2). (statistical analogy)
      b. Examples of nursing homes that do not have personnel in certain key positions: nutritionist, counselor, physical therapist (2). (undetailed examples)
      c. Clair Watkins complains that she can seldom find anyone to help her when she wants to leave her room or move to a different place in her room (6). (detailed example).
         (Transition) In addition to being understaffed, nursing homes too often have unqualified personnel.)
   2. Most nursing homes employ persons who lack necessary training and experience.
      a. Many patient attendants have the training in health care (1). (statistics)
      b. Man nursing home employees have no training in the special problems and needs of older people (1). (statistics and expert testimony)
      c. There are cases in which staff lack training essential to the performance of their particular jobs (2, 5). (undetailed examples)
         (Transition & Internal Summary): Now that I've shown that many nursing homes are understaffed and have unqualified employees, let's consider the effects of these inadequacies.)
   B. Inadequate personnel in nursing homes leads to major problems in patient care and comfort. (effect)

1. Poor personnel fail to provide satisfactory living conditions for patients.
   a. Adequate standards of sanitation are not maintained for patients (1, 4). (undetailed examples)
   b. Meals may be served at odd times and may be cold by the time they reach patients (3). (undetailed examples)
   c. Routine maintenance of facilities is too often neglected (2). (undetailed examples) (visual aids: photographs of rooms in disrepair)
   d. In emergencies there aren't enough staff people to take care of patients—example of fire in Ohio nursing home when 32 patients could not be gotten outside in time (4). (detailed example)
      (Transition: Inadequate personnel cannot provide safe, comfortable living conditions, as we've seen; but there's an even more serious consequence of poor staff unsatisfactory medical care for patients.)
2. Poor personnel in nursing homes furnish unsatisfactory medical care for patients.
   a. Comparison of ideal doctor-patient ratio with actual ratio in nursing homes (4). (statistical analogy,)
   b. Cases of widespread carelessness in prescribing and administering medication (4). (undetailed examples)
   c. Cases of withholding or cutting back medication to minimize expense of patient care (2, 4). (undetailed examples)
   d. Cases of patients who became ill because of improper diets (2, 6). (detailed examples)
   e. Quote from Ben Maxwell, resident of a nursing home, on superficial medical examinations that are common practice (6).(testimony)

III. CONCLUSION
   A. Summary of speech: The majority of America's nursing homes have too few employees and have employees who lack essential training for their jobs. As I've shown, these staffing deficiencies lead to serious problems in the living conditions and medical treatment for patients.
   B. Final Appeal: The problems I've discussed will not go away on their own. It is up to us to eliminate them through informing ourselves and through active support of efforts to improve the quality of nursing home personnel. Our involvement is necessary if we are to care for our loved ones and—one day—perhaps you yourself.

REFERENCES

1. Manard, B., Kart, C., and van Gils, D. *Old Age Institutions.* Lexington, MA: Lexington Books, 1975.
2. Mendelson, M. *Tender Loving Greed: How the Incredibly Lucrative Nursing Home Industry is Exploiting America's Old People and Defrauding Us All.* New York: Knopf, 1974.
3. *Time.* June 3, 1988.
4. Townsend, Claire. *Old Age: The Last Segregation.* New York: Grossman Publishers, 1971.
5. Vedder, Clyde B., and Lefkowitz, A. (compilers). *Problems of the Aged.* Springfield, IL: Chas. C. Thomas, 1965.
6. Interviews with Clair Watkins, Ben Maxwell, and Rona Jacobs, residents of Restview Nursing Home, October 4 and 6, 1989.

PRESENTING PUBLIC DISCOURSE

So far, we've focused on what a speaker says. We now turn attention to how a speaker communicates. Presentation, the final step in public speaking, is the speaker's actual delivery of a speech. Effective delivery depends upon effective oral style, selecting an appropriate style of presentation, practicing, and managing any speaking anxiety that is experienced.

Oral Style

Perhaps the most common problem in presentation is speakers' tendency to employ written style rather than oral style. Many speakers—both novice and experienced— insist on writing out their complete speeches. This technique virtually guarantees poor delivery. Writing out a speech is inadvisable because it encourages written style, which is not generally suited to oral communication.

Writing and speaking are distinct modes of communication. A good essay will not necessarily be a good speech, nor will a solid speech necessarily be a solid essay. To deliver effective speeches you should learn about oral style and how it differs from written.

The primary distinctions between oral and written style are personalness and immediacy. Writers and readers need not interact personally to communicate. Speakers and listeners do interact personally. Because speaking involves direct interaction between people, it calls for a more informal, conversational style than would be appropriate for writing. The second distinction is that oral presentations are more immediate than written ones. Spoken ideas must be comprehended as uttered, whereas in written presentations ideas are absorbed at the reader's own pace. If readers miss important points, they turn back a page and review. Listeners do not have this option—they must grasp ideas as they are presented. It follows that effective speaking will be more repetitious than writing—restating central ideas is the speaker's way of reviewing for listeners.

Oral Style[22]

John F. Wilson and Carroll C. Arnold, scholars of public address, identify 16 ways in which oral style differs from written style:

1. More personal pronouns
2. More variety in kinds of sentences
3. More variety in sentence lengths
4. More simple sentences
5. More sentence fragments
6. Many more rhetorical questions
7. More repetition of words, phrases, and sentences
8. More monosyllabic than polysyllabic words
9. More contractions
10. More interjections

11. More indigenous language
12. More connotative than denotative words
13. More euphony
14. More figurative language
15. More direct quotation
16. More familiar words

Because speaking is more personal and immediate than writing, it requires its own style. Specific features of oral style, such as those identified by Wilson and Arnold, lead to four general guidelines for effective oral language: appropriateness, clarity, vividness, and personalness.

Appropriateness. This is the bottom line for effective speaking. Language should be adapted to suit particular situations and listeners. Language appropriate to one group of listeners may be poorly suited to another. With an audience of chemists a speaker can and should use technical terms in a presentation on biological warfare. Discussion of the same topic with laypersons calls for elimination of technical language wherever possible and definition of any specialized terms that must be kept. A speaker needs fewer details and elaboration for listeners already knowledgeable on a topic than for listeners who lack background.

Language should be appropriate to the particular situation in which it is used. A speaker can be highly informal with a group meeting for social reasons, but may be more formal in business contexts. Large auditoriums with large audiences require speaking volume (or special equipment such as microphones) that would be inappropriate in smaller rooms with fewer listeners. Boldness of gesture and motion too are influenced by setting. Dramatic, sweeping movements are well suited to large settings where small gestures would be lost; in smaller settings, however, grand motions may appear overly dramatic, even stagy. Highly formal occasions call for speech that is less conversational than is generally desirable. Effective oral style adapts to the particular situation in which it occurs and the particular listeners being addressed.

Clarity. A second fundamental quality of good oral style is clarity. Listeners should understand ideas as they are spoken. If they have to stop to figure out what words mean or to unravel lengthy sentences, the language is unclear and, therefore, ineffective. Clarity begins with familiarity. Use language your listeners will understand. Avoid jargon, technical terms, and uncommon words whose meanings may not be known to listeners. "Brave" is more clear than "valorous;" "thoughtful" is more clear than "pensive"; "dog" is more clear than "canine." If you must use some technical words, define them quickly for listener.[23] In addition to familiarity, clarity is enhanced by concrete language. Whenever possible, select words that are specific and concrete, rather than general and abstract. "African daisy," is more clear than "flower," just as 'five-year-old boy," is more clear than "child." Replace general words such as "things," "people," and "events" with more precise references. Short sentences and phrases additionally increase clarity. Complex sentences with multiple clauses may, be appropriate for writing, but they are not appropriate for speaking. Long sentences, when spoken, have less clarity and force than short ones.[24]

Clarity is basic to effective oral style. To consider and perhaps accept your ideas, listeners must first understand what you say. Clear language is familiar, concrete, and simply expressed. It represents ideas as precisely and directly as possible.

Vividness. Effective oral language is vivid, which means it is lively and interesting. Language should create images in listeners' minds, make the content of a speech jump to life. You can achieve vividness in several ways. First, use language to evoke images in listeners' minds. "A fire that burns a building" is unlikely to create as strong an image as "a roaring blaze that consumes an isolated cottage." Look for words that build vivid images, that create vibrant pictures of your ideas. Vividness is further enhanced by details that add depth to expressed ideas. "Prison" creates no mental image; "the large grey building with narrow windows filled in by straight, black bars" does create a picture—we get a sense of starkness and coldness. A third aid to vividness is use of connotative words, ones that arouse subjective, personal meanings in listeners. "Home" connotes more than "house"; "tiny, speckled puppy" connotes more than "dog"; "mother" connotes more than "woman." A fourth way to enhance vividness is to use active language. Consider the difference between these sentences:

It is thought by most experts that hypertension tends to result from both genetic and environmental factors.
Experts think both genetic and environmental factors contribute to hypertension.

Increasingly, drugs are consumed by average citizens.
Average citizens increasingly consume drugs.

Guns are misused by people.
People misuse guns.

In each case the second sentence is sluggish. It is passive and unlikely to arouse interest in listeners. The sentences on the right are active, hence more direct and forceful. Oral style should emphasize active language. Finally, delivery influences vividness. Good speakers use their voices and bodies to "underline" ideas. Inflection, repetition, variation in pitch and volume, and physical motion all increase vividness of presentation. Vividness is important in public speaking because it makes ideas more involving to listeners. When you design a presentation that is vivid, listeners are likely to be drawn into interaction with your ideas.

Personalness. Chapter 11 opened with the idea that effective public speaking is "enlarged conversation." This means that good speaking tends to be personal, informal. A conversational style of delivery, establishes a sense of interaction between speaker and listeners. By contrast, formal speaking style acts as a barrier between communicators. To personalize your speaking, use personal pronouns such as "you," "we," "our," "I," "me," and "us." Don't refer to yourself as "the speaker" or to your listeners as "the audience," because these terms create distance between you and your listeners. Whenever possible, use language that involves listeners directly in your presentation. You want them to identify themselves with you and your ideas.

"Some people think grades are a poor measure of their learning" is less effective than "You may think your grades don't reflect what you know." The second sentence invites listeners to participate in the speech. Another way to personalize speaking is to ask questions of listeners. "Do your grades really reflect what you've learned?" "Do you know how your student fees are used?" "What will you do if the person next to you starts choking? Would you know a simple maneuver that could save a life?" Questions such as these generate interest. Listeners mentally consider and answer the questions, so they participate in the communication. References to shared experiences and understandings also increase conversational tone in speaking. Try to find commonalities between you and your listeners, then draw upon those to emphasize your relationship. "We've all spent too many hours in the registration lines." "Remember taking the SAT exam? We lost a whole Saturday morning, then waited for six weeks to find out how we did." "If you've ever visited the infirmary here, you probably share my feeling that you'd have to be pretty desperate to go back!" Pertinent common experiences, understandings, and values represent potential bonds between you and your listeners.[25] The more conversational and personal your language, the more listeners are likely to identify with you and your topic. Oral style is more personal and immediate than written style.

To achieve effective oral style you should strive for appropriateness, clarity, vividness, and personalness. These features of good oral style increase your speaking effectiveness. The essential point is that speaking is not writing. To speak dynamically you must modify what you have learned about written expression. Years ago James Winans humorously made this point when he said, "A speech is not an essay on its hind legs!" Remembering this should help you achieve an engaging oral style.

Styles of Presentation

As we saw in the preceding section, effective oral style is appropriate to its context. Presentational style appropriate for Congressional testimony will not work well for classroom speaking, sales reports, or political rallies. Speakers should select a style of presentation that suits their speaking situation and purposes. There are four styles of presentation, each of which is effective in some situations.

Impromptu Style. Impromptu speaking occurs with little or no preparation. Speakers think on their feet, organize as they go, and rely upon information they already have. You speak impromptu when you respond in class, contribute ideas in a group discussion, answer an unanticipated question in an interview, explain your beliefs to a friend, or convince a salesclerk you are entitled to a refund. In these situations there is no time for preparation or rehearsal.

Veteran public speakers sometimes give impromptu speeches. Through years of experience they've honed skills in organization and expression, so they can speak "off the cuff." Even for seasoned speakers, however, impromptu speaking has drawbacks. Without preparation, ideas cannot be fully developed or supported. Research is needed to back up claims and add interest to any presentation. Impromptu speaking also tends to increase rambling and the use of filler words such as "and," "uh," "you know," and "um." Impromptu style is best reserved for situations where preparation is impossible or where only a short statement will be made. As a general rule, ideas sufficiently important to merit a speech and an audience also merit preparation and practice.

Extemporaneous style. Extemporaneous speaking involves preparation and practice, but precise wording is not determined prior to actual delivery. To speak extemporaneously, speakers research, organize, support, outline, and practice. They prepare notes and visual aids to assist them. Yet a complete speech is not written out and practice is limited so that the speech retains its spontaneous character. Ideas are learned, but a formal text is not. The extemporaneous style allows time for preparation and practice but still leaves room for natural, adaptive delivery. This style promotes informal conversational tone and increases the sense of interaction between speaker and listeners. These advantages make extemporaneous style the most popular among both novice and experienced speakers.

Manuscript style. As the name implies, manuscript style is speaking from a manuscript, a word-for-word text. A speaker writes out the entire speech, then uses the manuscript to practice and deliver the speech. The outstanding values of this style are that it provides absolute security to speakers and ensures precise phrases and language. Manuscript speaking finds its primary uses in diplomatic and official situations where there is no room for ambiguity or mistakes; exact wording must be worked out in advance and adhered to in presentation. Situations such as these also call for rather formal speaking, which tends to result from manuscript style.

Manuscript speaking has some substantial disadvantages. Most notably, it limits the speaker's freedom to adapt content and language to listeners during presentation. The speaker is locked into the manuscript and finds it difficult to adjust expression in response to cues from listeners. Manuscript speaking is further limited by individuals' skill in writing speeches. Most people who try to write speeches lapse into written style. The result is an "essay on its hind legs," which is, of course, a poor speech. Effective manuscript style requires an ability to write for the ear. Not only must a manuscript be written in oral style, but also the speaker must read conversationally, a difficult skill to master. Few of us naturally read aloud in an animated, vivid manner. in fact, most people who rely on manuscripts or even extensive outlines lose contact with listeners— their eyes lock onto what is before them and they do not interact fully with listeners. Much practice is required to speak well from a manuscript. As a general rule, speakers should not start out using manuscripts, because this fosters dependence on notes and a less interactive style of delivery than is desirable. These habits are difficult to correct later in a speaking career.

Memorized style. Memorized style is an extension of manuscript speaking. A speech is completely composed in advance and usually written out in full form and then memorized. Speakers use no notes, not even an outline. The advantages of memorized speaking are the chance to prepare exactly what will be said (as in manuscript style) and the freedom to look at listeners while speaking. These values, however, are generally insufficient to balance the limitations of memorized style.

Speakers who try to commit an entire speech to memory may forget a word or phrase. Instead of substituting similar words or referring to an outline, they become stuck and may be unable to continue. Furthermore, memorized speaking lacks the spontaneity of extemporaneous speaking. Because it has been so heavily rehearsed, the speech sounds canned, dry, unnatural. Frequently students assigned to speak extemporaneously will memorize speeches, thinking memorization will not be detected. Usually a memorized speech looks and sounds like a memorized speech. It lacks the informality and freshness of an extemporaneous speech. With memorized style there is only superficial interaction between speaker and listeners. The speaker's primary attention is riveted to retrieving detailed information from memory, so listeners get only peripheral attention. Because of these disadvantages, few speakers choose to memorize their presentations.

Impromptu, extemporaneous, manuscript, and memorized styles are options available to speakers. Knowing the advantages and disadvantages of each provides a basis for deciding when to use a particular style. For the majority of speaking situations the extemporaneous style is most effective. It combines adequacy of preparation and practice with spontaneity and conversationality in presentation.

Practicing Public Communication

Practice is important for effective public communication. Once you've developed your speech, become conscious of oral style, and selected your presentational style, you're ready to practice. Practice should begin at least several days prior to your presentation. Before you actually rehearse your speech, read over the outline to familiarize yourself with both content and form. You may want to read it several times. Then stand up with the outline in front of you and go through the speech. Try, to use rate, volume, inflection, and gesture as you plan to use them in your presentation. Go through the entire speech without stopping, even if you make mistakes or want to alter the outline. You need to get a sense of the overall speech—its unity, rhythm, and progression. After this first practice, indicate any changes on the outline and run through the entire speech again, this time noting when you start and finish. If your speech is too long, decide what material to delete; if it's too short, develop ideas more fully or support them more extensively. Practice once again, making sure you're within the time limit. Then put the speech aside for at least a few hours, and come back to it with a fresh perspective. Practice a few more times with several volunteer listeners. Friends or roommates can usually be drafted, and they can offer you valuable responses that may help you refine your presentational style. As you practice, look at your listeners as you speak to accustom yourself to seeing people listening to you. After you've given the entire speech, seek their impressions and suggestions. Ask if they found it easy to follow your ideas, if they found your evidence interesting and persuasive, if they felt involved in the communication. Incorporate their suggestions into your speech and practice again. It's a good idea to take breaks between practice sessions since this allows you to come back to your material with a fresh perspective. Practice until you know your material well. THEN STOP!! Too much practice is just as bad as too little. You do not want to rehearse to the point that you wind up memorizing the speech, since that would destroy the spontaneous quality of your presentation. Many speakers like to practice a final time an hour or so before their presentations—it refreshes content and improves confidence.

If you prepare thoroughly and practice well, your presentation should be effective. It will reflect your sensitivity to the communication process, your respect for listeners, and your commitment to the ideas you present. The only potential hindrance that remains is speaking anxiety, a topic we will now consider.

Speaking Anxiety: Elimination or Control?

Many beginning speakers identify nervousness or speaking anxiety as a major problem. Actually, speaking anxiety is seldom a serious problem, but misunderstanding of anxiety can be. The problem arises from two common misconceptions about speaking anxiety. First, many people assume speaking anxiety is unusual, a difficulty peculiar to them or novice or poor speakers. Nothing could be further from the truth. Most speakers—no matter how experienced, famous, or effective—feel anxiety when they make public presentations. In fact, two separate studies report that over 75 percent of prominent speakers experience anxiety before presentations.[26] If you don't believe the research, ask people who speak frequently. Most of them will admit the same kind of nervousness you feel. Seasoned speakers—teachers, ministers, performers, and the like—experience nervousness each time they speak. If you feel nervous about speaking, be assured you've got company and lots of it! A degree of anxiety is entirely normal.

A second misconception is that speaking anxiety is undesirable, something to be overcome or eliminated in order to be effective. This too is false. Speaking anxiety is absolutely essential to dynamic presentation. Nervousness is caused by adrenalin, a substance the body produces to increase physical and mental performance in stressful situations. Our bodies release extra adrenalin when we confront physical dangers, such as a car swerving toward our lane or an attacker. Adrenalin is also produced when we're in emotionally stressful situations, such as interpersonal conflict, a tough job interview, or public speaking. A lot is on the line, and the body gives us extra adrenalin to cope well and to perform at peak levels. We need the extra energy to meet unusual challenges. Without this adrenalin we would surely feel less nervous, but we'd also perform less well. Just as athletes must be "psyched" to play their best games, so must speakers by psyched to communicate their most effectively. Without some tension, speakers lack the essential alertness to speak with vitality and dynamism.

The Physiology of Speaking Anxiety[27]

Just as it would be wasteful and inefficient for an automobile engine to use all its 350 horsepower when the car was going 25 miles an hour, so it would be wasteful and inefficient for the human body to operate at peak efficiency under normal circumstances. When an emergency is perceived, however, these organs are ready to go into operation. The adrenal gland pumps adrenalin into the system. The arrival of adrenalin at the muscles restores their vitality and increases their reaction time.

Larger quantities of sugar are released into the blood from the reserves in the liver and insulin is released from the pancreas to convert the sugar into energy, giving the body greater strength to cope with physical problems. Numerous red corpuscles are discharged into the blood stream from the spleen. Breathing is quickened, thus bringing in more oxygen and expelling the carbon dioxide more rapidly. The pulse rate speeds up . . . . The brain is thus capable of thinking with greater clarity, greater perceptiveness, and greater quickness; the muscles are capable of exerting a more intense physical effort; the central nervous system is capable of reacting more quickly. Because of these physiological changes, the human body can perform at a much higher level than under normal conditions.

Because nervousness spurs you to your best efforts, you do not want to eliminate it. However, you do want to control it so that it works *for* you. Control begins with understanding. You should first realize that your anxiety is normal, natural, and helpful. Veteran speakers regard it as essential to their maximum performance. Nervousness is not just in your head. It is a physiological response to challenge, and it's evident in physical reactions such as weak knees, shaking hands, perspiration, and dryness of mouth. Second, make sure you prepare and practice thoroughly so that your nervousness will be limited to appropriate levels. You do not need the additional anxiety that results from not knowing what you will say or whether your ideas are coherently developed. Thorough preparation gives you confidence in yourself and your material. Third, channel your nervousness constructively. Don't let your excess energy create only "butterflies" and shaking hands—there are better ways to use it. Make that energy work for you. Incorporate gesture and movement into your speech. Plan to move from one place to another as you speak, perhaps as you make a transition between major points in your speech. Use your hands to emphasize key ideas and to point out items on visual aids. As you engage in physical activities you use up the excess energy in ways that enhance your effectiveness. A fourth way to control anxiety is to focus on your content and your listeners instead of yourself. To manage any personal nervousness you feel, remind yourself of your reasons for choosing your topic, its importance to you and your listeners. When you speak, concentrate on listeners: Are they following you? Do you need to clarify an idea? Do you need to inject some questions to to spark interest? Remember that you and they are involved in a relationship sustained by the force of your ideas. Finally, remember that your listeners are far less aware of any nervousness you feel than you are. Chances are that most listeners won't even realize you are nervous unless you emphasize it.

Some anxiety is normal, natural, and necessary for effective communication. While you should not try to eliminate it, you do want to control it. To direct your anxiety constructively you should understand its nature and causes, prepare thoroughly for speaking, channel energy into constructive actions, focus on content and listeners, and remember that your nervousness is far more obvious to you than to anyone else. Don't call attention to it and most listeners will never notice you are nervous.

SUMMARY

This chapter focuses on ways to develop and present effective speeches. Development begins with research, including review of personal experience and knowledge, checking library resources, and conducting interviews with experts on your topic. After you research your topic, material must be organized into a coherent, logically developed speech that listeners can follow with ease and interest. The next step is to support ideas with evidence. Quotations, examples, statistics, analogies, and visual aids increase the force of your ideas in listeners' minds. When you've organized and supported ideas, outline your speech to make sure your organization is clear and your support adequate.

Delivery is the next consideration. Effective delivery begins with sensitivity to the distinct nature of oral style, which emphasizes appropriateness, clarity, vividness, and personalness. Consider the advantages and disadvantages of presentational styles and decide which style is most appropriate to your particular situation. In most cases the extemporaneous style is highly effective, since it emphasizes both thorough preparation and conversational, spontaneous tone.

The final step in preparing to speak is practice. Practice enough to be familiar with your ideas, but avoid overpractice, which can result in memorization. As you practice and deliver your speech, remember that some anxiety is normal and natural and that it actually enhances your effectiveness once you learn how to channel it constructively.

From this and the previous chapter you should realize that effective public speaking requires substantial thought, time, and effort. If you make these investments, you can create presentations that benefit you and those who listen to your ideas. For all of us, our attitudes and actions arise out of our interactions with language. When you speak to others you ask them to interact with your language and, thus, your ideas. This is a tremendous responsibility and challenge. It's also an exciting opportunity to have some real impact on others.

REFERENCES

[1]Bert E. Bradley, *Fundamentals of Speech Communication: The Credibility of Ideas*, 2nd ed. Dubuque, IA: Wm. C. Brown, 1978, pp. 249-250.

[2]T.H. Ostermeier, "Effects of Type and Frequency of Reference Upon Perceived Source Credibility and Attitude Change." *Speech Monographs, 34*, 1967, 137-144.

[3]A.R. Cohen, E. Stotland, and D. M. Wolfe, "An Experimental Investigation of Need for Cognition." *Journal of Abnormal and Social Psychology, 51*, 1955, 291-294.

[4]H.E. Butler, trans, *The Institutio Oratoria of Quintilian, vol. 3, book 7*. Cambridge, MA: Harvard University Press, 1950, pp. 2-3.

[5]D.K. Darnell, "The Relationship between Sentence Order and Comprehension." *Speech Monographs, 30*, 1963, 97-100; C. Spicer and R.E. Bassett, "The Effect of Organization on Learning from an Informative Message." *Southern Speech Communication Journal, 41*, 1976, 298; J. P. Parker, "Some Organizational Variables and their Effect Upon Comprehension." *Journal of Communication, 12*, 1962, 27-32.

[6]J. C. McCroskey and R. S. Mehrley, "The Effects of Disorganization and Nonfluency on Attitude Change and Source Credibility." *Speech Monographs, 36*, 1969, 13-21.

[7]E.E. Baker, "The Immediate Effects of Perceived Speaker Disorganization on Speaker Credibility and Audience Attitude Change in Persuasive Speaking." *Western Speech Journal, 29*, 1965, 148-161; H. Sharp and T. McClung, "Effect of Organization on Speaker's Ethos." *Speech Monographs, 33*, 1966, 182-184.

[8]D. Sears and J.L. Freedman. "Effects of Expected Familiarity with Arguments on Opinion Change and Selective Exposure." *Journal of Personality and Social Psychology, 2*, 1965, 420-426; Bradley, pp. 160-168.

[9] J.E. Baird, Jr., "The Effects of Speech Summaries upon Audience Comprehension of Expository Speeches of Varying Quality and Complexity." *Central States Speech Journal, 25*, 1974, 124-135.

[10] E. Miller, "Speech Introductions and Conclusions." *Quarterly Journal of Speech, 32*, 1974, 124-125.

[11] Miller.

[12] Bradley, p. 196.

[13] Bradley, p. 175.

[14] J.F. Wilson and C. C. Arnold, *Public Speaking as a Liberal Art*, 4th ed. Boston: Allyn & Bacon, 1974, p. 171.

[15] J. C. McCroskey, "A Summary of Experimental Research on the Effects of Evidence in Persuasive Communication." In J. W. Gibson (Ed.), *A Reader in Speech Communication.* New York: McGraw-Hill, 1971, pp. 297-306.

[16] J.C. McCroskey, "The Effects of Evidence as an Inhibitor of Counterpersuasion." *Speech Monographs, 37*, 1970, 188-194.

[17] J. A. Kline, "Interaction of Evidence and Reader's Intelligence on the Effects of Short Messages." *Quarterly Journal of Speech, 55*, 1969, 407-413.

[18] "Cage Without a Key." Documentary film on NBC television, March 15, 1975, 9-11 p.m. EST.

[19] "NBC Nightly News," October 27, 1977, 6-6:30 p.m. EST.

[20] R. L. Rosnow and E. J. Robinson, *Experiments in Persuasion.* New York: Academic Press, 1967, pp. 69-70 and 99-104.

[21] R. F. Verderber, *Communicate.* Belmont, CA: Wadsworth, 1975, p. 170.

[22] Wilson and Arnold, pp. 225-226.

[23] T. Carbone, "Stylistic Variables as Related to Source Credibility: A Content Analysis Approach." *Speech Monographs, 42*, 1975, 99-106.

[24] J. W. Black, "Aural Reception of Sentences of Different Lengths." *Quarterly Journal of Speech, 47*, 1961, 51-53.

[25] C. F. Vick and R. V. Wood, "Similarity of Past Experience and the Communication of Meaning." *Speech Monographs, 36*, 1969, 159-162.

[26] W. A. Kniseley, *An investigation of the phenomenon of stage fright in certain prominent speakers*, Ph.D. dissertation, University of Southern California, 1950.

[27] Bradley, p. 391.

CHAPTER 13

EFFECTIVE INTERVIEWING

The small talk at the beginning of an interview has vital importance. . . . [It] tends to identify the conversation as a human one rather than a mechanical one.

(Ken Meltzer)

Interview Purposes

    Information-giving interviews
    Information-getting interviews
    Persuasive (advocative) interviews
    Problem-solving interviews
    Counseling interviews
    Employment (hiring) interviews
    Complaint interviews
    Performance reviews
    Reprimand interviews
    Stress interviews
    Exit interviews

The Anatomy of Interviews

    The opening stage
    The substantive stage
    The closing stage

Styles of Interviewing

    Formality
    Power balance
      Mirror (reflective) interviews
      Distributive interviews
      Authoritarian (directive) interviews
      Stress interviews

The Question-and-Answer Process

    Open questions
    Closed questions
    Mirror (reflective) questions
    Hypothetical questions
    Probing questions
    Leading (loaded) questions

Preparing for Interviews

    Research
    Mental review

The Interview Process and the Law

    Laws
    The EEOC Guidelines
    Court cases involving the interview
    What cannot be asked in an employment interview

Probably you've participated in several interviews, either as an interviewer or as a respondent, and it's likely that you'll take part in many more. Perhaps your most immediate concern is with employment interviews. For most college students, getting an initial job will depend largely on what happens in the relatively brief interaction of an interview, and that first job may affect the course of your entire professional career. It's appropriate, therefore, that you be concerned with interviews and with gaining skills that will enhance your effectiveness in interviews. Do you know how to prepare for an interview, what to expect in an interview, how to adapt your communication to various interviewing styles, how to respond to different types of questions? If not, you'll want to read this chapter carefully, because it will help you develop communicative understandings and skills necessary for effective interviewing.

Interviewing is, of course, communication. Thus, material from previous chapters pertains to communication in interview settings. Interviewers and respondents interact with each other through symbols to establish meanings for themselves and their joint concerns. Content and form of symbols are the essential influences on participants' perceptions of an interview and each other and on the overall effectiveness of interaction. As we'll see, dual perspective and monitoring are communication skills of special importance in interviewing, for they help participants interact in productive, coordinated ways.

Yet interviewing is a specialized form of communication, different from other kinds of communication we've considered. An interview is purposive communication between at least two people, each of whom participates actively primarily through a question and answer process. The distinctive character of interviews will be clearer if we break this definition down. First, interviews are purposive, not casual, interactions. Although unplanned events surely occur, an interview has a specific purpose, known in advance to at least the interviewer. Because interviews are purposive, they require preparation. Both interviewer and respondent should plan for interviews. A second feature of interviews is the balance of communication in them. Neither interviewer nor respondent has sole responsibility for interaction, and neither talks to the exclusion of the other. In most interviews talking and listening roles switch back and forth rapidly. Finally, a question-and-answer format characterizes interviews. They proceed primarily—though not entirely—by a series of questions, responses, and follow-up questions. While interviewers tend to ask most questions and respondents tend to answer, both participants may pose and respond to questions. Preconceived purpose, balanced interaction, and question-and-answer format are features that distinguish interviewing from other kinds of communication.

This chapter explores five topics that should enhance your ability to participate effectively in a variety of kinds of interviews. First, we consider the range of interview purposes and how they shape the content of interaction. Second, we analyze the anatomy of interviews to understand how communicative structure affects content. Third, we discuss four styles of interviewing, each of which establishes its own communication climate. Fourth, we examine the question-and-answer process at the heart of interviewing. The final topic is preparation for interviewing. The material in this chapter emphasizes understandings and skills that should increase your your effectiveness in communicating in interviews.

INTERVIEW PURPOSES

Many people regard interviews as synonymous with job hunting. Naturally employment interviews are especially salient to you now, but they aren't the only kind of interview. In fact, we can identify 11 distinct purposes served by interviews.[1] The chances are good that you'll participate in several of these during your lifetime.

Information-Giving Interviews

Information-giving interviews are set up when one person intends to give information or instruction to another person or persons. Doctors tell patients how to administer medicines; advisors explain to students the steps involved in appealing a grade; supervisors clarify expectations to new employees. In each case the purpose is to give information or instruction to others.

Information-Getting Interviews

In information-getting interviews interviewers gather information, opinions, attitudes, values, and beliefs from respondents. Public opinion polls, research surveys, and census taking are well-known examples of information-getting interviews. In addition, there are many other uses of this kind of interview. To gain information for a speech or group discussion, you might interview an expert on your topic; journalists spend substantial time interviewing sources of information for stories they publish;

students sometimes confer with advisors or instructors to gain information that helps them plan coursework; doctors and therapists interview patients to get information about medical or psychological problems.

Persuasive (Advocative) Interviews

Sometimes interviews are designed to influence others' attitudes and actions. The prototype of the persuasive interview is a sales pitch, in which the salesperson (interviewer) tries to convince the customer (respondent) to buy some product or service. Ideas can also be sold through persuasive interviews. For instance, after problem solving, discussion groups often appoint a spokesperson who attempts to persuade others to act on the group's recommendations. Perhaps you've tried to convince your parents to accept your choice of a major, your decision to join a house, or your intention to rent an apartment. Each of us tries to influence others' attitudes and actions, just as others attempt to influence what we think and do.

Problem-solving Interviews

Interviews may be conducted to analyze and solve problems. In many ways this kind of interview is like a two-person problem-solving discussion in which participants begin by defining and analyzing a problem and progress to some resolution of it. Students and instructors frequently engage in problem-solving interviews when they attempt to diagnose why a student is not doing well in a course and how the two of them can work out a plan to improve the student's performance and grade. Professional colleagues confer to decide how to increase sales, raise morale, improve product quality, or plan effective programs. In problem-solving interviews participants work together to resolve mutual problems.

Counseling Interviews

Counseling interviews are similar to problem-solving interviews, since in each type participants work cooperatively to solve a problem. However, in counseling interviews the problem is not mutual at least not initially. One person (client) has a problem and seeks professional help. Personal problems that lead individuals to seek counseling include phobias, lack of assertiveness, inadequate study habits, grief, depression, shyness, and relationship tension. Professional advice may also be sought for less personal problems. For instance, we seek a lawyer's counsel on legal issues and consult a member of the clergy on religious problems. In counseling interviews experts advise individuals on ways to manage or resolve problems.

Employment (Hiring) Interviews

Employment interviews allow prospective employers and job candidates to evaluate their mutual fit. Most employment interviews have both informative and persuasive dimensions. The interviewer gives information to the candidate (respondent) about the position and seeks information from the respondent about past experience and qualifications. Candidates exercise persuasive skills as they try to convince interviewers of their credentials. Recruiters too may engage in persuasive strategies in an effort to win over top candidates who have several job offers. Employment interviews give participants information on which to base their decisions.

Complaint Interviews

In a complaint interview, one person hears and responds to another's complaints. Many firms have departments whose purpose is to attend to consumer complaints and to minimize dissatisfaction. Here the firm's representative (interviewer) gains information to determine the nature of the complaint and gives information about the firm's policies, including what can and cannot be done to satisfy the consumer. Frequently the interviewer tries to persuade the consumer to a particular course of action pursuant to the complaint.

Performance Reviews

Performance reviews—also called appraisals—are conferences between superiors (interviewers) and subordinates (respondents) about subordinate's work performance. A superior generally reviews a subordinate's work to date, comments on progress, identifies strengths and weaknesses, and helps the subordinate establish goals for future performance. The subordinate should offer perceptions of progress, assets, and liabilities and should inform the superior of any special circumstances or problems pertinent to performance. Appraisal interviews allow superiors and subordinates to check perceptions periodically and to agree on expectations for future work.

Reprimand Interviews

Reprimand interviews typically occur when a superior perceives some problem in a subordinate's work. Ideally these interviews should be informal and constructive, so that participants can talk cooperatively. To open a reprimand interview a superior may begin by getting information about the subordinate's perceptions of performance as well as the subordinate's attitudes toward work. Once the problem is defined and understood and both participants have explained their perceptions of it, the superior typically moves into persuasive communication to motivate improved performance from the subordinate.

Stress Interviews

Stress interviews are designed to apply pressure to a respondent. Sometimes an interviewer needs information from a person who does not wish to divulge it. Lawyers confront this situation with reluctant or hostile witnesses. Parents, guidance counselors, and prison personnel encounter reluctance when people do not wish to "rat" on others. In other cases, stress interviews are used to find out how well a person can withstand pressure. Employers may deliberately create stress in interviewing candidates for jobs that involve constant or intense pressure. Typical stress tactics are rapid-fire questions, probing, deliberate misinterpretation of responses, and communication that belittles the respondent. Unlike most other types of interviews, stress interviews are not primarily concerned with information. Instead, the interviewer attempts to make an assessment of the respondent's psychological stability and strength.

Exit Interviews

In the last decades exit interviews have become increasingly used in academic and corporate settings. The purpose of an exit interview is to gain insights and impressions from someone who is leaving. Typical examples are employees who retire or move on, students who have completed their work at a university or in a graduate program, volunteers who are ending their work with an agency. This kind of interview clearly involves aspects of others, especially information giving and getting interviews. What is unique and especially valuable about exit interviews is that the former associate is no longer constrained by the need to please others in the system: She or he can speak with a degree of openness and honesty that most people would not dare in situations where others could retaliate later. Thus, exit interviews can yield honest and very useful information about problems in a company, program, or agency. Wise executives rely on these to learn what needs improvement.

These are the 11 most common types of interviews. As you can see, interviewing is not just an occasional or rare event. It's actually a major form of communication that serves a variety of purposes. Now that we've established the range of interviewing communication, we'll examine its typical structure.

THE ANATOMY OF INTERVIEWS

Maybe you've had the disconcerting experience of participating in an interview that seemed disorganized. The interviewer rambled, topics seemed unrelated, lines of thought were not developed. Afterwards you probably felt frustrated because you didn't have a chance to present yourself or your ideas well. Occasionally interviews are disorganized, and this reduces their effectiveness for both interviewer and respondent. Fortunately this is the exception. In most cases interviews are structured. Even interviewers who lack formal training tend to organize conversation in relatively standard ways. To insure effective interaction, interviewers should understand the nature and function of each stage in interviews. Respondents need to know what to expect if they are to participate effectively, so they too should understand the anatomy of interviews. The next few pages explain the three basic stages in interviews and the purposes served by each.

The Opening Stage

Interviews begin with an opening stage. Its functions are to establish participants' identities in relation to each other and to designate the purpose of interaction.

In the opening moments of an interview each person's primary concerns are to construct a definition of the other and the joint situation and to define self positively to the other. Initial definitions of self, other, and situation arise out of the communication between interviewer and respondent. Each person's opening comments provide guidance for these definitions, which will be refined throughout an interview.

Most interviewers' initial concern is to help the respondent relax. Comfortableness is essential if the respondent is to express opinions freely and provide appropriate information. A basic degree of trust and rapport should be built between interviewer and respondent. To do this, interviewers generally begin with social conversation about impersonal topics such as weather, news, or geography or with personal conversation designed to discover respondents' interests, talents, and background. Opening remarks are those of invitational communication, the first stage in relational development. After all, interviewers and respondents are in the first stage of a relationship which may or may not progress to higher stages. During the initial moments of an interview typical questions include these:

> I see you're from Chicago. Are you a Bears fan?
> It's been a while since our last conference. How have you been keeping yourself busy since then?
> Have you been to the club that just opened on Franklin Street?
> How are things going for you these days?

Opening dialogue attempts to create a relaxed atmosphere that makes interviewer and respondent comfortable with each other.

After several minutes the interviewer should move on to explain the purpose of the interview. This provides a transition between social conversation and business. Respondents usually have some idea of an interviewer's purpose, but that idea may or may not coincide with the interviewer's idea.[2] To make sure that both parties share understanding of an interview's purpose, the interviewer should explain the exact reason for the interview, what will be covered, and why and how the interaction will affect the respondent. Following are two examples of well-constructed explanations of purpose.

> I asked you in today, Sheila, so that we could review your first six months with the company. I want you to fill me in on what you've done and your impressions of our organization, and I'll share my perceptions of your work so far. Then we'll try to chart some goals for your work during the next six months.

> As you learned when you signed up for this interview, IBM is looking for some young people with good business training to fill management trainee positions that will come open this June. I want you to elaborate the information on your vita and we'll try to find out whether our needs and your qualifications are compatible. If we're mutually interested, we'll set up a second interview for later this month.

Both examples provide useful orientation to the respondent. They clarify the purpose of the interview, preview topics that will be discussed, and indicate how the interview will affect the respondent.

The opening stage of an interview is important, because it sets the tone for all that will follow. Interaction during this stage should establish a relaxed climate conducive to open communication and should orient the respondent to the purpose and content of the interview.

The Substantive Stage

The second stage of an interview deals with substantive information. During this stage participants use communication to designate issues that merit attention and to define themselves in relation to those issues. Communication is very important here since how participants use language and nonverbal behaviors will shape perceptions of topics and themselves. During this stage, participants focus on information relevant to the purpose of the interview as defined in the previous stage. In an employment interview, communication focuses on the respondent's professional training and experiences and goals and how well the respondent's values fit with those of the hiring organization. In a counseling interview, the substantive stage ferrets out information about the client's problem, its causes, and its impacts. A reprimand interview tends to concentrate on how the respondent failed to meet expectations and what might be done to improve performance. During the substantive phase the interviewer seeks information needed to solve a problem, make a decision, clarify expectations, chart a course of action, or accomplish whatever is the purpose of the interview.

The substantive phase takes up the majority of time in an interview, so it should be carefully planned and focused. Often interviewers prepare notes in advance to guide discussion. During interaction they may also make notes or record answers for future reference. Unless the interview is intended to be stressful, interviewers should minimize disruptions such as incoming phone calls and drop-in visitors.

The substantive stage tends to progress from surface information to in-depth probing. Using a technique known as the *funnel sequence*, interviewers begin with general questions and move gradually into more and more specific probes.[3] Typical of employment interviews is this funnel sequence:

Tell me about your long-term career plans.
Do you intend to return to school for additional training at some point?
Would you expect your employer to finance your graduate education?
If your employer were to finance or partly finance advanced training, would you be willing to stay with the company?
If your employer would not contribute to your education, would you leave the company?

The funnel sequence may be repeated with each topic covered during the substantive stage. Interviewers must build gradually to pointed or threatening questions, a goal easily achieved with the funnel technique. Questions become progressively more specific, detailed, and demanding. As Cannell and Kahn point out, "early questions should serve to engage the respondent's interest without threatening or taxing him before he is really committed to the transaction . . . . The most demanding of questions might well be placed later."[4]

Once interviewers cover planned topics, they often invite questions from respondents. it's a good idea for respondents to come prepared with a few questions that demonstrate alertness and initiative. In an employment interview, a respondent might pose questions such as these:

> I understand your company is getting ready to manufacture a new colorcopying machine. If I am offered a sales position, would I have an opportunity to market this machine?
>
> I've noticed your branches are concentrated in the Southwest region of the country. Given the national appeal of your products, are there plans for expansion?
>
> This firm has a reputation for providing educational seminars for employees. How would I qualify to participate in these?

Someone interviewing for admission to a graduate or professional program might ask questions like these:

> One of the impressive features of this school is the computer facilities it commands. As a graduate student would I have access to these for my research?
>
> Do you encourage graduate students to do some actual research during their academic program?
>
> Would it be possible for me to work with some of the faculty in designing instructional materials?

Questions such as these serve two important purposes. First they gain information for the respondent. Second, they demonstrate initiative. They show the respondent is enthusiastic, a go-getter type. Most interviewers respond favorably to such an image.

QUESTIONS FOR THE INTERVIEWEE

I. For interviewees applying for positions with firms, industry, and institutions

1. How do you evaluate performance here?
2. What would you say are the biggest problems in your department (or agency)?
3. How will the (economy, recent government action, suppliers' strike, energy shortage, etc.) affect your operations here?
4. Who would be my supervisor? Who would be his or hers?
5. What is your philosophy on promoting from within the firm?
6. How much authority and responsibility would I have in (planning, budgeting, decision-making, etc.)?
7. What sort of personnel turnover have you experienced here?

8. What is management's (or the organization's) policy (feeling) regarding employee participation in community and civic activities?
9. What happened to the last person who held this position?
10. Describe the organizational structure. Where would I fit in?
11. Are the various departments within this firm (agency, organization, etc.) mutually cooperative or competitive?
12. Your firm has a reputation for providing seminars and related opportunities for its personnel. How does one qualify for participation in such programs?
13. I've noticed your branches are concentrated in the Southeastern area. Is there some reason why you have not expanded, since your products are of national use?
14. I understand your firm is getting ready to manufacture a new color-copying machine. If I am offered this position, would I have the opportunity to work on the marketing campaign for it?
15. In addition to your present programs (products, policies) what kinds of new proposals (programs, policies) are you currently considering?
16. To what extent does this agency (firm, etc.) seek public or citizen input when making its policies (designing its products) (planning its programs)?
17. How does your agency (firm, etc.) feel about its personnel's engaging in research projects?
18. How long and how comprehensive is your training program?
19. How did you become interested in this field?
20. What do you see as the future of this field? What new areas will come under its purview and what current areas (products, programs) will be outdated?

II. For Interviewees applying to graduate and professional programs

1. Do you encourage a broadly based program or specialization?
2. What kinds of careers have your graduates traditionally followed?
3. Do you encourage your graduate students to get some actual field experience during their academic programs?
4. Would I have any opportunity to teach or assist in classes?
5. To what extent are your graduate students invited to participate in research with the faculty? One of the impressive features of this school is its computer facilities (or whatever). As a graduate student would I have access to these?
6. What kinds of theses and dissertations have been produced by recent graduate students in your department? Quantitive?
7. What is your department's policy on minor programs?
8. I have been following Dr. S's research on the relation between age and liberalism. Is she still engaged in that program?
9. Why doesn't your department require theses of its candidates?
10. What is the normative length of time required to complete this program?
11. Does your department have a comfortable relationship with the anthropology (chemistry, medical, linguistics) department? My research interests might involve me in that department.
12. Are you contemplating any changes in the courses listed in your catalogue?

The substantive stage provides the interviewer with pertinent information about the respondent. The questions posed as well as their sequence influence the nature of information that is acquired and the overall climate for interaction. When the interviewer has sufficient information and has answered the respondent's questions, the final stage of interviewing begins.

The Closing Stage

The last and usually briefest stage of an interview is the closing. Here the purpose is to arrive at final definitions of participants and the information dealt with during the interview. Thus, closing communication should summarize information that has been covered and should doublecheck for accuracy. In addition, this last stage of interaction should reaffirm the relationship between interviewer and respondent. To accomplish this, an interviewer may reinitiate social topics or may offer an expression of good will toward the respondent. Whenever possible, the interviewer should indicate future interactions or implications that will follow the current encounter. Following are two examples of appropriate closing comments by an interviewer:

> Well, I've learned a good deal about you in this short period. It seems that your qualifications are right in line with what we're looking for. Your experience in marketing plus your advanced coursework certainly prepare you for the position. I'll need to talk with a couple of other people at the home office and then I'll be back in touch with you about a second interview. I've enjoyed talking with you.

> This has been a most informative meeting. I think I have a better understanding of some of the problems you're encountering in your work. There may be some ways that I can reduce your frustration by reorganizing our procedures. I'll be back in touch with you on that matter. Meanwhile, I wish you continued good luck in meeting the new objectives we've agreed on today. Let me know if I can help out at any time.

The closing should provide a smooth ending for the interview by summarizing content and suggesting what next steps may be expected.

Most interviews follow the three-part sequence discussed here. However, this is not always the case. There are no guarantees that interviewers will adhere to this structure. An interviewer may plunge immediately into the substantive stage with no preliminary comments to set a tone, or may engage in prolonged social conversation before moving into the substantive stage. Understanding of the content of each stage tells you what stage you are in at any given time and, therefore, suggests what kind of communication is appropriate for you. You may need to adapt expectations rapidly in the flow of actual interviews.

With this information in mind, we're ready to proceed to consideration of styles of interviewing and how each style affects the communication climate for interaction.

STYLES OF INTERVIEWING

Every interview has a style or tone—the overall flavor of interaction. An interview's style depends on the degree of formality and the power relationship, both of which arise in communicative interaction between interviewer and respondent.

Formality

Interviews vary in degree of formality.[5] A highly formal style is established when interviewer and respondent adhere rigidly to general norms of social interaction. In such cases participants do not acknowledge each other's individual identities. Instead, they treat each other as social roles. Communication occurs between employer and job candidate, between superior and subordinate, between citizen and pollster. The interviewer treats all respondents similarly, making minimum adaptation to personal differences. Often in formal interviews the interviewer follows a standard set of questions. Respondents tend to give stock responses, based on generalized assumptions about appropriate communication. Participants address each other by titles or last names (Ms. Smith, Mr. Jones, Madam Chair, Mr. Secretary). Nonverbal behaviors further define formality. Interviewer and respondent follow formal dress codes, usually somewhat conservative. A stiff handshake is the formal greeting ritual. Participants maintain a fair amount of space between themselves, adopt standard seating patterns, and interact in conventional settings such as offices. In highly formal interviews communication is standardized, leaving little room for spontaneity but ensuring efficiency.

At the opposite end of the continuum is the highly informal interview style. Rigidity is replaced by flexible, relaxed interaction. Participants treat each other as individuals, rather than as social roles. Communication thus becomes more adaptive, more personal. Ms. Baker may screen ten job candidates in a single day, but each interview will be unique, because she recognizes individual differences and attempts to adapt her communication accordingly. informal interviewers may prepare questions or have a set of standard topics; however, they are unlikely to become locked into any preestablished plan. Instead, informal interviewers feel free to depart from prepared agendas, to pursue worthwhile lines of talk, even if those were unanticipated. In response to this style, interviewees tend to loosen up and to deviate from highly standardized answers to questions. The interaction resembles focused conversation more than structured conference. First names may be used, often at the suggestion of one participant ("Please call me Ben."). Informality is defined by nonverbal behaviors as well as verbal communication. Participants may dress casually or even adjust attire during interaction by loosening ties or removing jackets. If participants are seated, more relaxed and unconventional seating positions prevail. Sometimes informal interviews occur during walks or golf games or at social gatherings where people are not seated. While informal interviews may occur in offices, they are just as likely to be held in homes or other nonbusiness settings. Informal interviews promote relaxed interaction and allow for considerable spontaneity in communication.

Many, perhaps most, interviews fall somewhere between the extremes of highly formal and highly informal. Through their communication participants establish the level of formality that will characterize their interaction. While respondents' behaviors contribute to the overall communication climate of interviews, the interviewer has primary control in setting tone. If your preferred interaction style differs from an interviewer's preference, you may need to adapt rather quickly.

Power Balance

A second dimension of interview style is the balance of power between interviewer and respondent. In the interview setting, power is control over content and pace of communication. Power may be evenly balanced between participants or commanded primarily by one person. Between interviewer and respondent there are four possible balances of power.

Greatest Respondent Power	m i r r o r	d i s t r i b u t e d	a u t h o r i t a r i a n	s t r e s s	Greatest Interviewer Power

Mirror (reflective) interviews. In reflective interviews the respondent has primary control over communication. Although reflective interviews are generally associated with counseling, they may be used for a range of purposes. The distinctive feature of this style is the interviewer's focus on reflecting or mirroring what the respondent says. Through communication that consistently reflects the respondent's ideas, the respondent is defined as the person in control of interaction. In a reflective interview an interviewer is confined to paraphrasing or repeating the respondent's words, a technique which encourages the respondent to elaborate.

I: Tell me about your sales experience.
R: I've worked two summers with Southwestern Books and I earned the outstanding sales representative award last year.
I: It sounds like you've done well with Southwestern.
R: Yes. In fact, last summer I improved my sales by 50 percent over my first year. I was really proud of that.
I: So you take pride in your record as a salesperson.
R: Oh, definitely. I like to see what I can do, how much I can go beyond my own past achievements. I did the same thing earlier when I worked on commission sales for a furniture company.
I: So you have experience in furniture sales too.
R: Yes . . . .

Because the interviewer draws only from the respondent's comments, the respondent has great control over communication content. It is possible for the respondent to direct content to areas of personal strength. People who do not understand reflective interviewing are likely to fumble and to sacrifice the advantage of controlling content. However, those respondents who know how to manage reflective techniques can use this style to promote themselves and to initiate topics they consider important. The reflective style awards maximum potential control to respondents.

Distributive interviews.   Distributive interviews get their name from the fact that participants' communication establishes control as shared or distributed. Both persons ask and answer questions, both initiate topics and suggest directions for conversation. Typically, distributive interviews reflect roughly balanced amounts of communication, with each person engaging in listening as much as talking. This style of interaction tends to define an informal, relaxed atmosphere, making distributive interviews satisfying to both participants.

Authoritarian (directive) interviews.   As the name implies, authoritarian interviews are ones in which communication defines one person—the interviewer—as having primary control over interaction. The interviewer directs interaction, guiding both content and pace. The respondent, by contrast, is defined as having limited control over the directions of talk. A noteworthy advantage of this style is efficiency. In directive fashion an interviewer covers quickly a range of topics and avoids conversation not directly pertinent to the purpose of the interview. On the other hand, authoritarian interviews often frustrate respondents and reduce the amount of information gained. An interviewer may miss important topics by sticking to questions prepared in advance. Formality, a degree of tension, and a quick pace generally accompany this style, making authoritarian interviews somewhat less pleasant, particularly for respondents.

Stress interviews.   Stress interviews—sometimes called "pressure cooker" interviews—are designed to put pressure on respondents, usually to see how well they cope. Control belongs to interviewers. Respondents have even less control than in authoritarian interviews, because they do not know what to expect from moment to moment. Unpredictability is at a maximum and surprises are standard. The atmosphere may be formal or informal; it may even vary during a single interview. Uncertainty is high, so security is low. To create pressure, interviewers deliberately put respondents on the spot with intense questions, planned disruptions, negative responses, apparent lack of attention, trick questions, and other tactics designed to make respondents unsure of themselves.

Stress interviews can be useful. Sometimes they are appropriate, despite the fact that they unnerve respondents. A police officer may resort to stress interrogation to get honest answers from a reluctant suspect; a counselor may use pressure to cut through a client's defensive in order to help the client deal with problems. If you find yourself in a stress interview, try to stay calm. That is the one form of control you have in pressure cooker interviews. Recognize the stress as a test of your ability to cope, and meet the test with alertness and flexibility.

Interview style results from the formality of interaction and the balance of power between interviewer and respondent. Both formality and power relationships are established through communication and both are reflected in communication. To participate effectively, you need to understand these different interview styles and what each implies for your communication.

THE QUESTION-AND-ANSWER PROCESS

The most unique feature of interviewing communication is its question-and-answer format. Unlike other kinds of communication, interviewing proceeds predominantly by questioning. Consequently, the success of an interview depends largely on an interviewer's questioning skills and a respondent's answering skills. There are many types of questions, and each distinctively influences interaction. The form of a question shapes participants' perceptions of a topic and thus the kind of response given. Skilled interviewers appreciate the impact of question form on response, so they select forms appropriate to their communicative goals and contexts. Likewise, respondents increase their effectiveness if they understand the connection between form and content of interaction. We'll examine six common forms of questions to see how each influences content.

Open Questions

Open questions are broad and general. They allow a range of appropriate responses, giving respondents lots of room to choose how to answer. Opening questions are used to start gathering information or to initiate a funnel technique. An interviewer might begin questions about a job candidate's experience with an open question such as "Would you explain your background in this area?" or "Can you tell me about your experiences?" Open questions such as these allow respondents to go in a number of directions and to propose a range of topics for subsequent communication.

Closed Questions

In contrast to open questions, closed questions call for concise responses on specified topics. Frequently, closed questions are used to follow up open questions or to direct respondents' communication. After asking about coursework in general (an open question), an interviewer could follow up with closed questions such as "Are those courses recommended by your department?" or "Do you have any required courses left to take in your major?" Closed questions may further restrict answers by offering limited alternatives. For instance, an interviewer could ask "Do you prefer large or small companies?" "Are you willing to relocate?" or "Do you intend to return to school?" In each case only two answers are possible. The respondent faces closed options when answering.

Mirror (Reflective) Questions

Mirror questions, like mirror style, reflect the respondent's communication. They are used to encourage elaboration of responses, to indicate the interviewer's interest in a response, or to ensure accuracy of understanding. If a respondent indicates no intent to pursue graduate study, an interviewer might say, "So you feel graduate work is not necessary for your career goals?" Mirror questions keep the lines of communication open; they invite further development of ideas. An important use of mirror questions is in counseling interviews, where the therapist may reflect communication to get a client more in touch with her or his own feelings.

Hypothetical Questions

Hypothetical questions describe a hypothetical situation to which the respondent is asked to respond. An interviewer recently presented a woman in one of my classes with this scenario: "Assume we hire you and, after completing your training, we place you in an assistant manager position in one of our branch offices. Now let's say there are two women and six men directly under your supervision and three of those men resent a female manager. How will you handle that so that you can be effective with these male employees?" Hypothetical questions allow an interviewer to test a respondent's ability to respond quickly and insightfully to specific situations.

Probing Questions

Probing questions dig beneath the surface. They probe for additional information on a topic already introduced. After preliminary questions, an interviewer might use probes such as "Why have you not stayed with any previous job for more than a year?" "Why did your grades slip so far last spring?" "Are there any personal problems that are interfering with your work?" Probing questions generally come late in interviews, because they assume a degree of trust between participants. The exception to this rule is stress interviews, which may include intensive probing very early in interaction—a pressure tactic. Probing questions allow interviewer and respondent to explore ideas and to analyze information in depth.

Leading (Loaded) Questions

Leading questions encourage (lead) a respondent to answer in particular ways. The question itself is loaded in such a way that it implies what the answer should be. "You do believe in unions, don't you?" calls for a response of "Yes." "I assume you support the proposal I submitted, right?" suggests the appropriate answer is "Of course." "You've never used drugs have you?" calls for "No" as an answer. Leading questions do not generally encourage honest responses. However, there is one way in which they can be most useful. They can test a respondent's understanding or commitment. An interviewer may deliberately lead a respondent toward an "incorrect" response to see whether the respondent will avoid the trap. One interviewer who screens applicants for positions that involve constant travel likes to ask this question: "After a couple years of travel you'd expect to locate in a permanent spot, wouldn't you?" Unless the respondent clearly wants travel and understands this is part of the ongoing job, he or she will be led to an inappropriate response.

These six forms of questions represent a range of communicative strategies available to interviewers. Choices of when to use each form should be based on communicative purpose as well as adaptation to individual situations and respondents. Particularly in using potentially threatening strategies such as probes or leading questions, interviewers should be sensitive to defensive responses and should be ready to reframe questions in less threatening forms. It takes time and practice to develop skill in the art of questioning. The investment is worthwhile, however, since the content and quality of interviews derive from strategic use of question-and-answer techniques.

PREPARING FOR INTERVIEWS

We've seen that interviews are organized, purposive communication that involve a lot of strategy and perceptiveness. Few people have the native instincts or the experience necessary for effective, spontaneous interviewing. Most of us are effective only if we prepare thoroughly. To do this, participants need to conduct research and engage in mental review prior to participation in interviews.

Research

Participants should research each other and their topics prior to an interview. The purpose of research is to gain an understanding of the other's perspective so that you may take it into account as you prepare for and participate in an interview. As with any kind of communication, dual perspective is essential to effectiveness. The more you learn about the other participant's expectations, values, and priorities, the more effectively you can guide your own communication. It's nearly impossible to develop dual perspective during an interview, because interviews often take place between people without prior acquaintance and because they are so brief. Thus, it's advisable to conduct research before interaction in order to learn as much as possible about the other person's perspective.

Research varies according to interview purposes. For an employment interview, for instance, a respondent would focus on the hiring organization. What is its history? How long has it existed? Where are its plants, departments, or offices? Does it plan expansion of services or size? What is its financial record? What is the organizational philosophy? What benefits other than salary does it offer employees? There are several ways to find answers to these questions. Ideally, you should talk to someone in the organization. Conversation with a personal contact provides maximum information, more than you will ever find in written documents. A second method is to read reports and pamphlets distributed by the hiring organization. Placement offices and libraries often have these on hand. If not, you can write the organization to request informational materials. Naturally, you should realize any information put out by an organization contains bias in favor of the organization, so be appropriately skeptical. A third way to find out about organizations is through library research. References such as *Moody's Manuals* and *Standard and Poor's Index* furnish a wealth of information on major organizations.

Someone preparing for interviews with graduate or professional programs should read school catalogues, available in most university libraries and placement offices. Catalogues provide useful information on school size, requirements, faculty, and financial aid. Another good source is faculty, who can often tell you about the general reputation of various graduate and professional programs. Again, if you can find such a person, consult someone who is in a program or has been in it.

The need for research is obvious with employment and admissions interviews, but it is also important for other kinds of interviews. Before your performance is reviewed, you should find out the norms in your organization and, specifically, those for your position. What is generally expected of new employees? How does your performance to date compare with those of your peers? By checking with a variety of colleagues you learn the views of the generalized other in your organization and can use this perspective to guide your self-assessment. Prior to counseling, you'd want to investigate several counselors' credentials and, if possible, talk to their clients. If you agree to let someone interview you for information, you will want to review your knowledge of the topic to be discussed and make sure you have extra copies of any important materials to give your interviewer. To prepare well, respondents should get whatever background is relevant to the topic and interviewer.

Research is just as necessary for interviewers as for respondents. Preparation is required if the interviewer hopes to structure interaction productively. To prepare for a hiring interview, an interviewer should read carefully the applicant's vita, letters of recommendation, and any other provided documents, such as transcripts. Prior to performance appraisals an interviewer should review employees' records, making notes of special achievements as well as any problems. Before conducting an information interview it's important to complete research on the topic and the respondent's background so that the interview will be focused and efficient. On the basis of research, interviewers often construct initial questions to guide interaction. These may be written down or may be mental notes, whichever is more comfortable for the interviewer.

Mental Review

A second step in preparation is mental review. Interviewers and respondents need to think through the purpose of their interaction and to review pertinent information about themselves.

Respondents should make sure they know why they are being interviewed: What exactly is the position? What is the purpose of an appraisal? Respondents should also make sure they command any personal information they may want to present during an interview: Exactly why do you think you are qualified for a particular job? What specific things have you accomplished since your last appraisal? A useful preparation strategy is to anticipate questions that will be asked and develop answers for them. To do this you adopt dual perspective and ask what kinds of issues and questions are likely to be salient from the perspective of a particular interviewer as well as the overall perspective of the organization (generalized other). For starters, consider those questions that are frequently asked in employment interviews. Many will apply to your situation. For each question, come up with an answer. Try saying it out loud to see how it sounds, then revise it and rehearse it again. Don't worry about "canning" answers, since there's little chance you'll be asked the precise questions you anticipate. The chief value of rehearsal is that it hones your skills in thinking on your feet and clearly expressing your ideas. Mental review should precede any kind of interview. Prior to performance appraisal you should review your own record honestly. Make sure you can cite the responsibilities of your position and how you have met them. Determine whether you have weaknesses or areas of poor performance. What are the reasons for any deficiencies in your work? Can you set up a plan for your own improvement? With this kind of forethought it's unlikely you will be caught off-guard by complaints or difficult topics.

FREQUENTLY ASKED QUESTIONS IN EMPLOYMENT INTERVIEWING

1. Why did you decide to attend (your school)?
2. How do you spend your spare time? What are your hobbies?
3. What attracted you to your major?
4. What type of position with our company are you interested in?
5. Why do you think you would like to work with our company?
6. Do you think your present training fully qualifies you for this position?
7. Are you planning to seek graduate degrees? Why or why not? When?
8. What does success in (marketing, management, sales, teaching, etc.) mean to you?
9. What do you know about our firm? How did you find out about us?
10. What are your special qualifications in this field?
11. If you had your education to do over again, what would you do differently?
12. What do you think determines a person's progress in a good company (school system, etc.)?
13. How do you feel about traveling?
14. What kind of boss do you prefer to work with? Why?
15. Have you had any leadership positions? Tell me about them.
16. What kind of people do you enjoy spending time with socially?
17. How have your previous employers treated you?
18. How important to you is your family life?
19. How old were you before you became self-supporting.?
20. What causes you to lose your temper?
21. What are your major strengths personally and professionally?
22. What are your major weaknesses?
23. What kind of books do you read? Why?
24. Who has been the most influential person in your life? How?
25. Would you eventually like to work for a small or large company? Why?
26. What are your ideas on salary?
27. Where do you intend to be in your field in 10 years?
28. Tell us a story! (This measures an interviewee's quickness of thought as well as facility at social conversation)
29. What have you learned from some of the jobs you've held?
30. What experiences do you have that are relevant to the position you're seeking with us?

31. Define cooperation.
32. What do you consider the disadvantages of your chosen field?
33. Which of your college years was (were) the most difficult?
34. What do you expect this company to do for you?
35. Tell me about yourself.

Interviewers also benefit from mental review prior to conferences. They need to sketch out questions and decide what issues are most important for discussion. Interviewers should also try to anticipate potential problems that may occur in interaction. For instance, many people feel threatened by appraisals, so respondents may be somewhat defensive from the outset. The interviewer who anticipates this possibility can take steps to reassure the respondent and to create a supportive communication climate that reduces anxiety. The interviewer might open with compliments about what the respondent has done well. Tough questions or complaint should come later and should be phrased carefully. Experienced counselors who expect a strained session take special care to offer personal support to respondents.

Surely research and mental review will not prepare you for everything that can happen in interviews. However, these two preparation techniques go a long way in getting you ready for productive, focused interaction. Perhaps their greatest value is that they increase your control over interviews, because they provide you with opportunities to plan and rehearse your communication.

THE INTERVIEW PROCESS AND THE LAW

Laws

Title VII of the Civil Rights Act prohibits discrimination in employment on the basis of sex, race, color, religion, or national origin. The Age Discrimination Act forbids discrimination in employment for those between the ages of 40 and 65. The Rehabilitation Act outlaws discrimination on account of mental or physical handicaps. It applies only to those employers with government contracts.

The Equal Pay Act forbids wage discrimination on the basis of sex where jobs require equal skills, effort, and responsibility, and are performed under similar working conditions.

The EEOC Guidelines

The Equal Employment Opportunity Commission (EEOC) was created to monitor Title VII and to prosecute those employers not complying with it. In 1970, the EEOC issued guidelines on "Pre-Employment Selection Procedures." This category covers formal tests, interviews, application blanks, and other devices used to predict success on the job.

Under the guidelines, an employer must be able to prove that these devices are job-related, accurate predictors of job success, and nondiscriminatory in nature.

Court Cases Involving the Interview

Although psychological tests have so far been the major issue in the courts, one or two cases have involved the interview. In Hector v. Southern Railing, for example, the court decided that "a personal interview that was conducted without the benefit of written or formal guidelines for screening applicants for the position of data typist amounted to unlawful discrimination on account of race." The court specifically objected to the nature of the interview.

Legal experts feel that interviews will be the subject of more court cases in the future.

What Cannot Be Asked in an Employment Interview

Generally, a question is illegal if it seeks to draw out information from the applicant about race, religion, ancestry, age, or sex for discriminatory reasons. For example, questions cannot be asked about the following:

1. Marital status
2. Family
3. Physical requirements, e.g., height, weight
4. Age, date of birth
5. Availability for Saturday or Sunday work
6. Friends or relatives working for the company
7. Experience
8. Education
9. Housing, ownership of car
10. Arrests and convictions
11. Social Security status

In addition, remarks with respect to appearance may not be made. Any of the above questions can be asked if the characteristic is a bona fide occupational qualification (BFOQ), reasonably necessary for the normal operation of a particular organization. However, it is up to the employer to prove this fact.

SUMMARY

The interview is a unique kind of communication that is increasing in importance and frequency. This chapter defined interviews as purposive communication between at least two people, each of whom participates actively through a predominantly question-and-answer format. Interviews serve diverse purposes, 11 of which we considered. Regardless of the specific purpose, interviews tend to follow a three-part sequence of opening, substantive, and closing phases. In each stage participants' communication constitutes the interaction climate and molds the content of interviews. Communication further establishes an overall tone or style by defining the level of formality and the balance of power between participants, both of which influence participants' interpretations of interaction. Interviews proceed primarily through a question-and-answer process in which the kind of question posed shapes participants' perceptions of content and each other. Effective, productive communication in interviews requires preparation, specifically research and mental review. Both interviewer and respondent should prepare thoroughly, and thoughtfully prior to their interaction. During interaction they should rely on communication skills discussed in this chapter and throughout the book to create the kind of climate and relationship that is mutually satisfying and rewarding.

REFERENCES

[1]R. S. Goyer, W. C. Redding, and J. T. Rickey, *Interviewing Princtiples and Techniques.* Dubuque, Iowa: Wm. C. Brown, 1964, pp. 7-8.

[2]K. Metzler, *Creative Interviewing.* Englewood Cliffs, NJ: Prentice-Hall, 1977, p. 4.

[3]R.L. Kahn and C. F. Cannell, *The Dynamics of Interviewing.* New York: John Wiley, 1957.

[4]C.F. Cannell and R.L. Kahn, "Interviewing." In G. Lindzey and E. Aronson (Eds.), *The Handbook of Social Psychology*, 2nd ed., vol. II, *Research Methods.* Reading, MA: Addison-Wesley, 1968, p. 578.

[5]M.L. Knapp, *Social Intercourse: From Greeting to Goodbye.* Boston: Allyn and Bacon, 1978, pp. 15-17.

POSTSCRIPT

The fact that you have read this book and taken a communication course indicates that you care about communicating effectively in a variety of contexts. The results of your choice to study communication are greater understanding of symbols and appreciation of their vital role in human affairs. In turn, this awareness will inevitably enrich your personal, social, and professional life as well as the quality of our overall society through your participation in it. Understanding of communication will serve you well throughout your life.

To conclude this introduction to human communication, let's take a moment to review and integrate key ideas presented in this book. From your reading you should have gained theoretical and practical knowledge about communication and its relationship to human thought and action. This information provides a framework for understanding yourself and the human community of which you are a part.

Throughout this book a major theme has been that we are symbol users, a fact that dominates our lives. To be a symbol user is to be proactive, conscious, and self-reflective, a being who exercises choice in attitude and action. Our ability to think in symbolically sophisticated ways elevates us to a unique position in the universe. It enables us to refashion constantly our world and our own place within it. With appropriate understanding of symbols and respect for their impact on our lives, we can make informed, careful choices about the values and attitudes we embrace and, thus, the kind of communities we contribute to creating. A second, complementary theme of the book centers on our responsibility for the kind of communities we participate in building. We are morally constrained to think about the consequences of our communication, about our impact on situations and other people with whom we interact. Each of us influences those around us. Through our communication we directly affect how others see us, themselves, and their situations. Given this, we should be cautious and always mindful of the impact we have through our communication and the actions, attitudes, and values it promotes. As you communicate in diverse situations, aim for the high road. Use your actions to influence constructively the professional, social, interpersonal, and intimate systems of which you are a part.

In addition to the broad themes of choice and responsibility, this book presented theoretical and pragmatic material that provides a foundation for your choices as a communicator. In interpersonal encounters, strive for communication that shows you respect and accept yourself and others as well as the integrity of the communication process. Let your communication with friends and intimates foster mutual growth and enrich the depth of your relationships. When you work on task groups and committees, be mindful of how your communication will influence the overall climate, focus, and substance of deliberations. In public speaking situations, remember that whatever you seek to achieve must be identified with those to whom you speak. Adapt your communication to listeners' beliefs, attitudes, values, and self-conceptions. Moreover, demonstrate your respect for their rights by presenting ideas and evidence fully and fairly, by relying on persuasion in preference to coercion, by offering reasons for what you advocate, and by tying your advocacy and the reasons underlying it to the welfare and concerns of those who listen. In so doing, your communication will enhance the lives of others. In interview situations where interaction time is limited, make your communicative choices carefully, realizing they will shape perceptions of issues under discussion, your identity, and the regard in which you hold the other person.

Throughout your life you will participate in a range of communicative interactions—interpersonal, social, intimate, and group interactions, public speaking, and interviews. Whenever you communicate, be aware of the power inherent in symbols. The verbal and nonverbal symbols we use shape in large measure the reality in which we live. Thus it is imperative that we use them carefully and knowledgeably, with full recognition of their impact on human perception and conduct. This implies tremendous responsibilities for thoughtful, ethical use of symbols. If this book has heightened your awareness of those responsibilities and the ways in which you may meet them, it has been a worthwhile venture for both of us.

Author Index

Subject Index